Music and Musical Composition at the American Academy in Rome

Eastman Studies in Music

Ralph P. Locke, Senior Editor
Eastman School of Music

Additional Titles of Interest

Analyzing Atonal Music: Pitch-Class Set Theory and Its Contexts
Michiel Schuijer

Concert Music, Rock, and Jazz since 1945: Essays and Analytical Studies
Edited by Elizabeth West Marvin and Richard Hermann

A Dance of Polar Opposites: The Continuing Transformation of Our Musical Language
George Rochberg
Edited by Jeremy Gill

Elliott Carter: Collected Essays and Lectures, 1937–1995
Edited by Jonathan W. Bernard

Elliott Carter's "What Next?" Communication, Cooperation, and Separation
Guy Capuzzo

Intimate Voices: The Twentieth-Century String Quartet, Volumes 1 and 2
Edited by Evan Jones

John Kirkpatrick, American Music, and the Printed Page
Drew Massey

Leon Kirchner: Composer, Performer, and Teacher
Robert Riggs

Three Questions for Sixty-Five Composers
Bálint András Varga

The Whistling Blackbird: Essays and Talks on New Music
Robert Morris

A complete list of titles in the Eastman Studies in Music series may be found on our website, www.urpress.com.

Music and Musical Composition at the American Academy in Rome

Edited by Martin Brody

University of Rochester Press

The University of Rochester Press gratefully acknowledges the following for generous support of this publication: The Howard Hanson Institute for American Music at the Eastman School of Music, University of Rochester; and the American Academy in Rome.

First published 2014

University of Rochester Press
668 Mt. Hope Avenue, Rochester, NY 14620, USA
www.urpress.com
and Boydell & Brewer Limited
PO Box 9, Woodbridge, Suffolk IP12 3DF, UK
www.boydellandbrewer.com

ISBN-13: 978-1-58046-245-7
ISSN: 1071-9989

Library of Congress Cataloging-in-Publication Data

Music and musical composition at the American Academy in Rome / edited by Martin Brody.
pages cm — (Eastman studies in music, ISSN 1071-9989 ; v. 121)
Includes bibliographical references and index.
ISBN 978-1-58046-245-7 (hardcover : alkaline paper) — ISBN 1-58046-245-6 (hardcover : alkaline paper) 1. American Academy in Rome—History. 2. American Academy in Rome—Awards—History. 3. Composition (Music)—Awards—Italy—Rome. 4. Composers—United States—Biography. I. Brody, Martin, 1949– editor. II. Series: Eastman studies in music ; v. 121.
ML33.R66A444 2014
780.71'145632—dc23

2014034314

A catalogue record for this title is available from the British Library.

This publication is printed on acid-free paper.
Printed and bound by CPI Group (UK) Ltd, Croydon, CR0 4YY

Contents

Illustrations

Figures

Introduction

Martin Brody

The United States came late to the game. The French founded a national academy in Rome 110 years before the American Revolution; it took as many years again for the United States to produce a counterpart. Long thereafter, the Americans tended to look over their shoulders at the Académie de France à Rome, if from the high ground of the Janiculum. The French Académie set the stage and established a formidable paradigm for all the ensuing foreign academies that would appear in the Eternal City. The elements were clear: aspiring artists, strong patrons, consecrated antiquities, breathtaking real estate, national glory, cultural hegemony. The composition of the brain trust charged with launching the French enterprise was in itself imposing: Louis XIV's invincible minister of finance, Jean-Baptiste Colbert, joined by the *premier peintre du roi*, Charles Le Brun, and the celebrated Roman sculptor and architect Gian Lorenzo Bernini.

The institution that they established provided a daunting prehistory for the national academy of a self-conscious and still youthful democratic republic an ocean away. Jacques-Louis David, one of the Académie's most illustrious *pensionnaires*, offered an especially inspiring model for generations of Americans aiming to solve the equation of high art, patrician patronage, and democratic society. As a Prix de Rome winner in 1774, David had communed with Johann Joachim Winckelmann and demonstrated the virtually mystical benefits of sketching in Rome. In the ensuing years, he steered deftly through the liminal space between empire and republic; and he conducted a lifelong demonstration of the efficacy of neoclassicism as a premise for nationalist art—both as a hero of the first Republic and then in 1804 as court painter to a newly anointed French emperor. This emperor, the first Napoleon, had overseen the Academy's move to the Villa Medici in 1803, a grand building adjacent to the Spanish Steps, located on the magnificent site of the ancient Horti Lucullani.

It would be yet again seventy years before a cadre of elite Beaux-Arts artists and architects would hatch their plan for a corresponding American organization. The American Academy in Rome's founding fathers included the architects Charles F. McKim, Daniel Burnham, and Richard Howland Hunt, the painters John La Farge and Frank Millet, and the sculptors Augustus Saint-Gaudens and Daniel Chester French, collaborators on the 1893 World's Columbian Exposition in Chicago—an illustrious group that included no composers.[1] Their Chicago collaboration inspired a scheme to establish a national academy for the plastic arts, one that would be set in the Old World and premised on collaboration between select groups of "picked young men."[2]

The grand scheme was at first modestly implemented. "In October, 1894, the American School of Architecture in Rome opened temporary quarters in the Palazzo Torlonia. The school consisted of its Director, Austin Lord, three fellows, and a visiting student; its 'library' contained but one volume."[3] By the summer of 1897, McKim, prime mover in promoting the initiative, began to transform this diminutive training camp for a single discipline into a far more ambitious institution on the French model. By 1905 the renamed and reconstituted American Academy in Rome merited an act of Congress, which declared it a "national institution." Unlike the succession of French regimes, imperial and republican, that had sponsored the Académie de France à Rome, the US government offered no cash. Federal support came exclusively in the form of lip service; ever since, the American Academy in Rome has remained privately funded. The founders list, however, comprised a virtual royal family of American industrialist elites: The Carnegie Foundation, Henry C. Frick, J. P. Morgan Sr., J. P. Morgan Jr., the Rockefeller Foundation, John D. Rockefeller Jr., William K. Vanderbilt, and Henry Walters.

Among the new Academy's illustrious patrons, J. P. Morgan Sr. was the first among equals—a Colbert to Charles McKim's *architect du roi*. By the end of the first decade of the twentieth century, Morgan had patiently acquired more than twenty acres of prime real estate at the top of Rome's highest hill. He gave the land to the young Rome Academy shortly before his death. Thus, in seeking a belated national artistic apotheosis in the ruins of a foreign city, the Americans had found a propitious site. McKim, Mead and White would build a new and permanent home for the Academy on the highest point of Rome's highest hill—as lore would have it, so that the Americans could look down on the French across the city. A sea of ancient temples, medieval churches, Renaissance palaces, and baroque domes lies between the French Academy's Villa Medici and the American Academy's Villa Aurelia.[4] Marian MacDowell, wife of Edward MacDowell, the first composer to argue for music fellowships at AAR, offered a lyrical account of the setting:

> In Rome the Villa Aurelia, headquarters of the Academy, stands upon the summit of the Janiculum, the highest point within the walls of the city. Surrounding it is the terrain over which Garibaldi fought in 1849; it was in this very house that he made his last headquarters and the terrific battle left it in ruins. From the windows of the restored building, the dome of St. Peter's rises level with the garden walls; all of Rome lies below—from Monte Mario

> past the pyramid of Cestus to the tombs of the Appian Way, the Abruzzi, the Sabine and Alban hills, the Campagna, the lighthouse at distant Ostia. Those who are in residence there look down daily from a place of greatest beauty upon "the heart of Europe and the living chronicle of man's long march to civilization."[5]

By the end of the second decade of the twentieth century, the American Academy's location in Rome signaled a culturally youthful nation's belated participation in European civilization's long trek—as well as its arrival on the international stage and the blooming of its artistic potential.[6] Looking back on the early history of AAR, Gorham Phillips Stevens, an architect at McKim, Mead and White who served as the Academy's director from 1917 to 1932, summarized its ongoing raison d'être:

> The object of the American Academy in Rome is not to afford opportunities for a few individuals to perfect themselves for the practice of their chosen professions. The ideal is to create an atmosphere in which a limited number of carefully selected artists and scholars may develop that synthesis of intellectual culture which will make them worthy to preserve and continue the great traditions of the past in order that the standard of art and literature may be handed on from year to year, constantly strengthened and improved.[7]

In this heady atmosphere of hope and anxiety, a Rome Prize in musical composition came to fruition. The terms of the prize were lavish: up to three years of support to live in the "heart of Europe," with generous stipends for travel, copying and publication of fellows' music, and a wide range of opportunities for performances of their work in Rome and beyond. Nonetheless, in the early years of the prize, applications were relatively few; and the appearance of the new Rome Prize in music was hardly met with universal joy. In his *Essays before a Sonata*, Charles Ives threw down the gauntlet, touching on questions of nativism, elitism, and national identity that would haunt the Rome Prize in music for years to come:

> We hear that Mr. Smith [dean of the Yale School of Music] or Mr. [J. P.] Morgan, etc., *et al.*, design to establish a "course at Rome," to raise the standard of American music, (or the standard of American composers—which is it?); but possibly the more our composer accepts from his patrons "*et al.*," the less he will accept *from* himself. It may be possible that a day in a "Kansas wheat field" will do more for him than three years in Rome.[8]

This volume considers the range of voices that attended the founding of an American Rome Prize in musical composition and the complex cultural environment in which the music program emerged. It also includes an account of music activity at the Academy over the last century and several analytical essays that address perennial themes: ideology, patronage, music and national identity, and internationalism.

In most cases, the essays and documentary materials presented here began as contributions to the conference "'To Meet This Urgent Need': Musical Composition at the American Academy in Rome," presented at AAR in January 2005.[9] The conference took its title from a 1920 announcement of the Academy's new composition fellowship written for the Academy's twenty-fifth anniversary book by the Harvard music professor Walter Spalding. "Our Democracy has taken up music more vigorously and sympathetically than any of the other Fine Arts," Spalding declared. "But although there are many schools and academies which turn out performers of the first rank, they never have, and in the very nature of things they cannot produce composers. It is to meet this urgent need for bringing to its full fruition the wonderful musical talent of America that the Academy in Rome proposes to found its musical establishment."[10] Spalding's statement offered a counterargument to Ives by offering the Roman sojourn as an indispensible component of an American composer's development. We may hear the debate between the antipodal positions of Ives and Spalding as a ground bass running throughout the essays in this volume.[11]

Despite Ives's vehement denunciation, the established wealth and ancien régime fantasies of the Morgan-McKim generation fit snugly with the conservatism of the Academy's music program in its early phases. Although Charles McKim and Edward MacDowell, leaders of the first wave of advocacy for a music program, had died before World War I began, the cause was taken up after the Great War by the second generation of Academy leaders, in particular Felix Lamond, the organist at Trinity Church in New York City. Lamond became an effective spokesman for the new prize in music and, after it was funded, the Academy's first and only professor in charge of music. His annual reports to the trustees of the Academy survive as our most detailed primary source on the early years of the music program.[12]

Regardless of Lamond's traditionalism and his strong influence on the selection process of the early fellows in musical composition, the personalities and aspirations of the twenty-two composers who won the prize in the interwar period were hardly uniform. Andrea Olmstead outlines their stories in the opening essay of this volume, "The Rome Prize from Leo Sowerby to David Diamond." Olmstead unveils a world of varied accomplishments and now remote, sometimes astonishing, events that portend largely untold chapters in the history of twentieth-century American music and cultural exchange. Consider, for example, the case of Werner Janssen, whose major work as a fellow, the opera *Manhattan Transfer*, met a curious fate. The year is 1933:

> Productions were waiting in Budapest and Dresden. The manuscripts of *Manhattan Transfer*, along with his rewritten orchestral work *The Eternal Column*, were either stolen from the Academy or possibly mistaken for wastepaper by a servant and thrown out. The subsequent hue and cry—not mentioned in Lamond's reports—stirred Italy. Mussolini . . . had become

> enamored with Janssen's music and enjoyed his conducting. At news of the scores' disappearance he sent his secret service into action: a reward of 5,000 lire was offered.

Although he came to Rome at the beginning of the second decade of the Rome Prize in music, Janssen might be considered a younger sibling of what Carol Oja has called the "forgotten vanguard": a cohort of conservative composers active in a period dominated in the historical record by modernists. Felix Lamond had proudly claimed Janssen as a recruit and, as Olmstead suggests, also a convert to the professor in charge's conservative agenda. She elucidates Felix Lamond's role as one of the "forgotten vanguard's" key mentors and impresarios. Olmstead's essay also touches on the relations between American composers in Rome and their Italian colleagues, especially established figures such as Respighi and Malipiero, Casella, and Pizzetti, and, more broadly, with the Italian musical and political culture. In the interwar period, the relationships with the host country would change rapidly, not only for the American Academy but also for all the foreign academies in Rome. The American Academy closed altogether when Italy declared war on the United States in 1941.

AAR was able to resume full operations in 1947, under the leadership of a dynamic new director, Laurance Roberts. Among his many accomplishments, as Richard Trythall points out in "A History of the Rome Prize in Music Composition, 1947–2006," Roberts instituted a residents' program in the arts and humanities, bringing eminent scholars and artists to Rome as advisors to AAR's residential community. A long line of composers-in-residence, living from a few months to a year at the Academy, came to replace the previously ubiquitous figure of the prewar professor in charge, Felix Lamond. In the first decade of the residents' program alone, this distinguished group included Aaron Copland, Samuel Barber, Randall Thompson, Douglas Moore, Otto Luening, Alexei Haieff, Bohuslav Martinu, and Goffredo Petrassi.

Beginning in 1974, another significant position would have a strong impact on music at AAR. Richard Trythall, who had come to Rome as a fellow of the Academy, formally assumed the new post of music liaison, which was established to support the work of the fellows and residents. Trythall has remained on the staff of the Academy ever since, and for more than four decades has been, de facto, a latter-day Felix Lamond. His impact on the musical life of the Academy has been great; his review of the postwar period in this volume, "A History of the Rome Prize in Music Composition: 1947–2006," draws on his extensive personal archive of music at the Academy over the last half century. Like Olmstead's essay, it touches on numerous crucial episodes in twentieth-century musical exchange between Italy and the United States.

For example, Trythall documents a set of events that changed the dynamic between Roman and American composers during the 1960s: Otto Luening's persistent efforts to create an electronic music studio at AAR.

> During his first residency in the spring and summer of 1958, Luening tapped Columbia's Alice M. Ditson fund to purchase a library of contemporary music recordings for the composers' use. When he returned for a six-week summer visit in 1961, he converted the composers' "listening room" (located in the basement of the Academy) into a rudimentary "electronic music studio." This studio contained three sine wave generators, a spring reverberation unit, a microphone and a mixing console. Added to the listening room's two mono Ampex tape recorders (a studio console on loan from the American Embassy and a portable version) and a radio/record player, this equipment became a laboratory for sound research. In 1964–65, when Luening returned for a second year-long stay as composer-in-residence, he arranged for the Ditson fund to purchase one of the first electronic music synthesizers in existence, the Synket, invented and constructed by Paul Ketoff, a brilliant Roman engineer.

The makeshift electronic music lab that Trythall describes became a magnet for Roman and American composers alike—a shared resource for the vibrant community of international experimental and avant-garde musicians that blossomed in the city.[13] The institution of AAR's electronic music laboratory provided at least a modest bit of competition to the Studio di Fonologia in Milan, and thus helped to bolster an emerging Roman compositional avant-garde. AAR, an institution that had been founded on conservative artistic principles, thus became a touchstone for a vibrant urban experimental music scene.

The second and third parts of this volume include interpretive essays that expand on issues raised by Olmstead's and Trythall's narratives. In "The Classicist Origins of the Rome Prize in Musical Composition, 1890–1920," Judith Tick reviews the principles in play and debates at work in the early formation of the AAR music program. As Tick argues, the Academy scrambled a number of its own founding principles by initiating a fellowship in music in the wake of World War I. Tick delineates the volatile meanings and changing status of classicism during the decades spanning the beginning of the twentieth century. She relates ideological debates about classicism and music to the story of J. P. Morgan's (and, by extension, Charles McKim's and Edward MacDowell's) connection to the first Roosevelt administration, the federal government's shifting ideology of internationalism, and the journalistic din that attended the birth of the new scheme for music in Rome. The success of French Prix de Rome composers would be a touchstone for the first wave of American advocates of a composers' program in Rome, as she notes, but conjuring the French model would hardly solve the problems of American music's elite culture.

In her essay "'Picked Young Men,' Facilitating Women, and Emerging Composers: Establishing an American Prix de Rome," Carol Oja also locates the early phases of the Academy's music program in the context of a complex set of ideological force fields. As Oja observes, the devastation of World War I rationalized the ongoing cultural conservatism of the Academy's founders, which continued to surface in the guise of a broad goal: to save "civilization" *tout court*, if not artistic neoclassicism in all of its particulars. Lamond was particularly stalwart both in his defense of tradition and his diatribes against modernism. At the same time, however, the field of musical composition in the United States had become too unruly—both in the aims of its practitioners and the interests of the broadening circle of its supporters—for the Academy to maintain a pristine ideology of gentlemanly good taste. To support its new program in musical composition, as Oja notes, the Academy turned to a resourceful and astute coterie of wealthy women with strong connections to Italy. This development changed the dynamics of patronage for the institution, even if its crucial relationships with powerful industrialists and bankers would endure. Oja thus narrates a previously occluded story about the cultural and artistic interests within AAR's women supporters and the highly conservative and exclusively male network of experts who adjudicated the Rome Prize composition competition. Her study of the early phases of the Academy's music program provides a foundation for further study of gender dynamics and the Rome Prize in music. Astonishingly, the first woman composer to receive the Rome Prize, Barbara Kolb, was designated a Fellow of the American Academy in Rome (FAAR) in 1971, a half century after the prize in music had been initiated. Even in recent years, women have been relatively few among recipients of the Rome Prize in music.

A second essay by Oja, "Forging an International Alliance: Leo Sowerby, Elizabeth Sprague Coolidge, and the Impact of a Rome Prize," begins a section on internationalism and patronage. Oja's essay on Sowerby focuses on the support systems that bolstered his early career, especially in Chicago and especially constituted by women supporters of concert music. Oja also examines the crucial importance of Elizabeth Sprague Coolidge to Sowerby's prospects both at home and abroad, when he was a Fellow of the American Academy in Rome. As Oja suggests, Coolidge's support was key to the development of the institution's musical identity, both through her involvement in concert programming and her close relationship to Italian composers, particularly Gian Francesco Malipiero. "Forging an International Alliance" is paired here with another study in internationalism, patronage, and the fortunes of an Academy composer, the postwar fellow Elliott Carter. As I argue in the essay "Class of '54: Friendship and Ideology at the American Academy in Rome," AAR was transformed by the dynamics of postwar American cultural diplomacy on the European front. US diplomatic agendas in the era of the Marshall Plan encouraged a new network of actors on the international scene and a new paradigm for arts patronage and international alliances at the Academy. Nicolas Nabokov, the Academy's resident in musical composition during Carter's fellowship year, 1953–54, became a liaison between the Academy and the Congress for Cultural Freedom. His presence had significant ramifications for the Rome Prize composers of the 1950s, none more than Carter.

In addition to the extended essays in its first three parts, this book includes several shorter essays and recollections by conference participants. In "What They Said: American Composers on Rome," Vivian Perlis offers a précis of a small bit of the material from her interviews with Rome Prize recipients and Academy residents, with special emphasis on Aaron Copland's time at AAR in the early 1950s. Elliott Carter and John Harbison prepared brief memoirs of their experiences at the Academy. They are presented in part 4, along with excerpts from a panel of Italian composers and long-term American residents of Rome. Although only a few Italian composers are represented, all of the panel participants spoke eloquently about the role that AAR played in the Roman scene over the last half century. Finally, Christina Huemer, the Drue Heinz Librarian at AAR for fifteen years, provides an account of the Academy's holdings in music and primary source materials.

★ ★ ★

There are many people to thank for bringing this book to realization. I am deeply grateful to all of the authors represented here, both for their sustained interest in and work on the history of music at AAR, and for their forbearance and patience during the long process of moving this project from conference to book. Thanks go also to our colleagues at the University of Rochester Press, Ralph Locke, Julia Cook, Sonia Kane, and Suzanne Guiod, for their guidance and patience in bringing this book to fruition. Several anonymous readers for University of Rochester Press gave us excellent suggestions and helped us give shape to the heterogeneous contributions in this volume. Rachel Vandagriff brought a fine critical eye to the task of preparing all of the materials herein for publication and assembling a bibliography. I am deeply grateful for her support and assistance. Deep thanks go also to the pianist Donald Berman and the soprano Susan Narucki for participating in the 2005 conference and presenting a brilliant recital of music by Academy fellows from 1921 to the present. The series of recordings by AAR fellows that Donald Berman has curated, *Americans in Rome* (Bridge Records), is an essential companion piece to this volume. Don's generosity in sharing manuscript and historical research on the history of music at AAR contributed immeasurably to the development of this project.

Images are provided courtesy of the American Academy in Rome, which holds the rights to the materials and allows fair use access for publications. The staff and trustees of the American Academy in Rome, past and current, have also contributed greatly to this project. Thanks to Adele Chatfield-Taylor, president of the American Academy in Rome, and Elizabeth Gray Kogen, vice president for development, for their generous and enthusiastic support over the years. Academy trustee Jessie Price and her husband Charles Price provided indispensible advice and support at every phase. Music liaison Richard Trythall made this project his own and collaborated crucially in developing the AAR conference program. The Academy's Heiskell Arts Director, Dana Prescott, and her colleagues in the AAR programs office provided friendship and support at every turn. The staff of the Arthur and Janet C. Ross Library of the American Academy in Rome has been extraordinarily helpful and responsive to every inquiry: Sebastian Hierl, Drue Heinz librarian; Denise Gavio, assistant librarian; Antonio Palladino, preservation assistant; and Lavinia Ciuffa and Alessandra Capodifero of the Photo Archive have all helped bring this project to fruition. Sylvia Kollar, AAR archivist in New York, and Shawn Miller, AAR program director, also assisted greatly. Ilaria della Monaca, archivist of the Laurance P. and Isabelle M. Roberts Archive in the Biblioteca Berenson at the Villa I Tatti, and Felix Meyer and Heidi Zimmerman of the Paul Sacher Stiftung have also been enormously generous with their assistance and support. Fellows and residents at the Academy and various other musicians in Rome during the 2005 conference participated with great interest and enriched the proceedings. These included the composers Larry Bell, Steven Burke, Alvin Curran, James Dashow, Arthur Levering, Paul Moravec, and Harold Meltzer and the musicologist Michael Cuthbert. Robert Beaser and Steven Stucky (composers on the American Academy in Rome Board of Trustees), John Harbison (trustee emeritus, who first connected me with AAR), and Thomas Forrest Kelly (musicologist and trustee) also provided their encouragement and aid. As always, my deepest thanks go to Katharine Park, whose critical intelligence and support improve all of my work.

This volume is dedicated to the memory of Christina Huemer, Drue Heinz Librarian of the American Academy in Rome, 1993–2008. A great friend to many in the AAR community, Chris had an ecumenical appreciation of the various disciplines at the Academy and a deep understanding of their interwoven histories. She was an enthusiastic supporter of the work presented here from the inception of the 2005 conference until the end of her life. Her efforts on behalf of music at the Academy and its history affected all of the writing in this volume and immeasurably enriched the lives of many in the AAR extended family.

Notes

1. Judith Tick's essay, "The Classicist Origins of the Rome Prize in Musical Composition, 1890–1920," discusses the origins of the Academy and its ideological foundations in detail.

2. As Carol Oja notes elsewhere in this volume, the phrase "picked young men" occurs repeatedly in the Academy's early phase literature. See, for example, "Rome Fellowships in Music Announced," *New York Times*, July 9, 1921, cited by Oja and others in this volume.

3. "Historical Information," Finding Aid, American Academy in Rome records, 1855–[ca. 1981], bulk dates 1894–1946, Smithsonian Archives of American Art, accessed February

13, 2013, http://www.aaa.si.edu/collections/american-academy-rome-records-6320/more.

4. The Villa Aurelia, originally the Villa Farnese, a seventeenth-century property acquired and developed by Giralomo Farnese, was eventually bought (and renamed by) the Philadelphia heiress, Clara Jessup Heyland. Heyland, a friend of J. P. Morgan Sr., bequeathed it to AAR in 1909.

5. Marian MacDowell, "MacDowell's 'Peterborough Idea,'" *Musical Quarterly* 18, no. 1 (1932): 34. See Judith Tick's essay in this volume for a discussion of Edward and Marian MacDowell's ideas about the relationship of AAR and the MacDowell Colony.

6. At the end of 1912, AAR merged with another fledgling operation, the Classical School in Rome. Henceforth, the Academy included both a School of Fine Arts and a School of Classical Studies.

7. Gorham Phillips Stevens, cited in "Historical Information."

8. Charles Ives, "Essays before a Sonata," 92–93, cited in Howard Boatwright, "Ives' Quarter-Tone Impressions," *Perspectives of New Music* 3, no. 2 (1965): 31.

9. Several companion essays in this volume overlap in their topics. Oja's discussion of the ideology and patronage networks of the music program in its early phase interlocks with Olmstead's account of the first group of music fellows, those dating from 1921 until World War II. My essay on the Academy's Cold War cultural diplomacy networks relates similarly to Trythall's narrative of the fellowship program after World War II. The topics of these essays overlap in some respects, though points of commonality are considered from very different perspectives.

10. W. R. Spalding, "Music Composition," in *American Academy in Rome: Twenty-Fifth Anniversary*, ed. Christopher Grant LaFarge (New York: American Academy in Rome, 1920), 26.

11. The argument between the aesthetically conservative cosmopolitanism and various forms of cultural nativism that was played out in the founding of the Rome Prize in musical composition is considered in detail in Judith Tick's essay in this volume. Both Judith Tick and I discuss Spalding's announcement in our essays.

12. Lamond's annual reports are contained in the American Academy in Rome Annual Reports, which are held in a complete set at the library of the Academy. As Christina Huemer notes in her contribution to this volume, the papers of Felix Lamond, which are also held in the Academy's library, still await systematic study.

13. The brief comments in "The New Music Scene in Rome and the American Presence since World War II: Excerpts from a Roundtable, Moderated by Richard Trythall" offer a sense of this period in the history of new music in Rome.

Part One

A History of the Rome Prize

Chapter One

The Rome Prize from Leo Sowerby to David Diamond

Andrea Olmstead

Fascination with Americans living in post–World War I Europe remains tremendous. Much has been written about American expatriate musicians in Paris: Aaron Copland, Virgil Thomson, Roy Harris, and others studied privately with Nadia Boulanger. Less appears in print about the European experience of equally important composers, such as Howard Hanson, Randall Thompson, Roger Sessions, and Samuel Barber, who won the Rome Prize during the interwar period.[1] There, too, an important composition teacher, Ottorino Respighi, influenced Americans. These composers were being assimilated into the European experience while paradoxically creating an American musical identity.

Rome Prize winners have been competitively selected every year from 1921 through the present, except between 1942 and 1949, the period during and after America's participation in World War II. This study will therefore close in 1942. Rome Prize winners, or Fellows of the American Academy in Rome (FAAR) in Academy jargon, do not include Residents of the American Academy in Rome (RAAR), who began to be asked to stay at the Academy in the late forties. This article discusses the twenty-two Rome Prize fellows during the period 1921 to 1942 and their professor in charge, Felix Lamond.[2]

The American Academy in Rome was founded in 1894 for architects and classicists, and not until 1920, after the Great War, was funding found to include composers. The Academy founder, the architect Charles Follen McKim, had died in 1909 and did not live to see the music fellowships he had endorsed. McKim designed the main Academy building. Henry Higginson, who established the Boston Symphony Orchestra, whose hall McKim had also designed, was a trustee from 1905 to 1909. The composer Edward MacDowell, a trustee of the Academy in 1905, left the board shortly afterward because of his health. He had urged the establishment of a music program: "For years it has been my dream that the Arts of Architecture, Painting, Sculpture and Music should come into such close contact that each and all should gain from this mutual companionship. That students in all these arts should come together under the same roof, and amid such marvelous surroundings, seems almost too good to be true."[3] There was, however, no money to pursue this ideal in 1905. His wife Marian founded the MacDowell Colony in New Hampshire, based on similar principles, after MacDowell's death in 1908.[4]

The next, and by far most important, figure in this history was the organist Felix Lamond (1863–1940). Born in London, he became a US citizen in 1892 by marrying an American, Margaret Draycourt. Lamond lectured at Columbia University, where he might have met MacDowell, and he served as a music critic for the *New York Herald* from 1909 to 1915. In 1913 he suggested to Daniel Chester French, an Academy trustee, that a fellowship in music composition be established. Sixteen trustees met to discuss it, but felt they must repay their debt to J. P. Morgan before undertaking a new endeavor. Lamond nevertheless collected $2,000 for the project.

Charles Dyer Norton (1871–1922), assistant secretary of the treasury and private secretary to President Taft from 1908 to 1911, vice president of the First National Bank in New York, and a trustee of the Metropolitan Museum of Art, became an AAR trustee succeeding Morgan. In 1920, when Norton approached the Carnegie Corporation about money for a music program, they reacted positively. Harry Harkness Flagler offered $25,000 toward a fellowship in the name of the conductor Walter Damrosch (1862–1950), providing the Academy would match that amount.[5]

Although Norton was not a musician, his plan was excellent. Quoting from the Valentine history of the Academy (Lucia Valentine was Norton's daughter), "[The plan] provided for a professor, as well as three fellows in musical composition ('these to be unmarried men') who were to live at the Academy for not less than six months in each academic year of the three-year fellowship. They were required to visit other music centers in Europe, with a generous travel allowance. . . . 'No instruction in music shall be provided for or allowed at the Academy.' They were to be given liberal stipends, studios, and complete freedom. . . . The trustees were to elect to their membership at least one recognized authority in music, to organize open competitions for the music fellowships, and to appoint juries to award them."[6] Damrosch and the composer and music critic Deems Taylor (1885–1966) became trustees, and Damrosch was made chair of the music juries.

The trustees approved the plan and borrowed $36,000 from the Academy's general endowment. Lamond and William A. Boring (1859–1937) traveled to Rome to set up the program with Gorham Phillips Stevens (1876–1963), an MIT architect associated with McKim, Mead and White and the Academy director from 1917 to 1932. Boring had been a trustee of the American School in Rome and an incorporator of the Academy in 1905. Professor and dean of the Columbia University School of Architecture he was treasurer of the Academy from 1908 until his death.

Frederick Juilliard (1867–1937) contributed inherited money for a fellowship in his own name—not Augustus's, his uncle who had been an Academy patron and whose money it had been.[7] The third fellowship was named for the distinguished Yale composer Horatio Parker, who, like Augustus Juilliard, had died in 1919.

A benefit concert at Carnegie Hall, arranged by Mrs. Henry F. Osborn (Lamond's daughter), raised over $10,000; at a second benefit performance she raised another $8,000. In 1925 George Eastman, founder of the Eastman School of Music and close to the Rome Prize fellow Howard Hanson, would give $15,000 to finance part copying or printing of fellows' music. In 1929 Myron Taylor, CEO of US Steel and an Academy trustee, gave $25,000. He later became Roosevelt and Truman's ambassador to the Vatican. In 1931 Elizabeth Sprague Coolidge financed concerts at the Villa Aurelia.

Lamond arranged suitable quarters outside the 1913 McKim, Mead and White main building. The Villa Chiaraviglio (across via Angelo Masina from the McKim Academy building) contained a music hall, the music library, three music studios for the fellows, and four grand pianos purchased for them. Lamond became the first—and only—professor in charge of musical composition from 1921 until his death in 1940. He and his wife moved into the Villa Chiaraviglio. By 1934 Lamond, who did not serve on the selection jury and did not always agree with their choices (with the exception of Randall Thompson), had personally recruited several Rome Prize winners: Sowerby, Hanson, Giannini, Janssen, and (to his later dismay) Sessions.

The numerical odds of winning a Rome Prize then were not overwhelming. Fourteen composers applied the first year—1921—and applicants numbered between eight to ten for the next thirteen years. Lamond had been told that the also newly established Guggenheim prizes had averaged sixty-five applicants. Compare these figures with the seventy-three candidates for the 2005 competition for two music fellowships.

Once chosen, the composers initially stayed for three years (each year needed to be renewed) and overlapped with two others. (See appendix A for a list of pre–World War II fellows, the years of their residencies, and related information about their selection and careers.) Resident quartets played fellows' music, a Chiaraviglio concert series was presented that included both traditional music and new music on each concert, monthly musical receptions were held with music fellows from the other academies in Rome, and a part copying or publication subvention was provided and a travel stipend awarded. Initially, fellows received a $1,000 stipend a year for three years as well as a traveling allowance of $1,000 per year.[8] By far the most important opportunity for music fellows, however, was having their works played by—and they themselves conduct—the principal Rome orchestra at the Augusteo, a concert hall (later torn down) above the Emperor Augustus's tomb.

This article discusses all twenty-two Rome Prize fellows from 1921 to the last composers chosen after the Academy closed and the United States entered World War II. I shall list the jurors who chose fellows each year, as well as the music that fellows submitted, wrote, and had performed in Rome. Their previous training, travel, and subsequent careers shall also be briefly discussed.

The first year produced three fellows: Leo Sowerby, Howard Hanson, and Randall Thompson. The jury consisted of Damrosch, the critics Richard Aldrich and W. J. Henderson, the composer John Alden Carpenter, the teacher Walter Spalding, and the author Owen Wister. After extending the deadline by a month, they met on October 31, 1921, and appointed "red-headed and spunky," but nevertheless shy, Leo Sowerby (1895–1968; at the Academy 1921–24). Lamond was to assert, "I personally appointed Sowerby in 1921."[9] Indeed, Sowerby was not among the fourteen applicants, which had included George Antheil, Wintter Watts, Howard Hanson, and Quincy Porter (who won honorable mention). The Chicago composer Clarence Loomis was "married and not considered." Having moved before the end of 1921, Sowerby became the first composer to take up residence in Rome.

Carpenter, the Chicago composer and juror, probably knew Sowerby, who won on the strength of several chamber works and his 1913 Violin Concerto played by the Chicago Symphony Orchestra. The first piece completed at the Academy by a music fellow was Sowerby's Violin Sonata, performed at his February 1922 concert at the Chiaraviglio along with his piano pieces and a woodwind quintet. A large number of Italian composers were present, and Italian musicians later performed the quintet at the Sala Sgambati. In 1923 Sowerby also wrote a suite (*From the Northland*), a String Quartet in D Minor, and—note the self-conscious title—*Two American Pieces* for violin and piano. In 1924 Sowerby composed a five-hundred-page oratorio, *The Psalms in Human Life*, for three soloists, chorus, and orchestra. He also wrote two pieces for Paul Whiteman: *Synconata* in 1924 and *Monotony* the next year. By 1925 Whiteman's orchestra had played *Synconata* about ninety times. Sowerby's music "drew on a wide range of sources, including American folk music, blues and jazz besides the Western traditions of concert and sacred music."[10] Many of his organ pieces were based on the passacaglia, chaconne, canon, and fugue, but, although an organist, he wrote nothing for the organ at the Academy. At his request, Sowerby's residence was extended nine months—to expire November 1, 1923—by the generosity of Carpenter, Mrs. Coolidge, and Mrs. Edward B. Hill. On April 8, 1923, an audience of 3,500 people attended Sowerby's *Ballata* for two pianos and orchestra, the composer and Carlo Zecchi at the piano with Albert Coates conducting. This marked the first time an American Academy fellow was included on an Augusteo program. After his fellowship Sowerby became a composition teacher at the American Conservatory in Chicago from 1925 to 1962, and he won a Pulitzer Prize in 1946 for *Canticle of the Sun.*

At Lamond's insistence, a second consideration of the applicant pool was held the day after Sowerby was picked, November 1, 1921. The same jury now chose from the fourteen applicants. They selected Howard Hanson (1895–1968; at the Academy 1922–24) as the first Frederick Juilliard Fellow. Because he was serving as dean of the Conservatory of Music, College of the Pacific, in San Jose, California, he could not come to Rome until January 1922. Hanson won with a Grieg-influenced piece called *California Forest Play of 1920* for solo voices, chorus, dancers, and orchestra, and a programmatic piece entitled *Before the Dawn.* Hanson had received a diploma from the Institute of Musical Art—the first incarnation of the Juilliard School—in 1915, where he studied piano with James Friskin and composition with Percy Goetschius. The IMA was founded and run by Frank Damrosch, Walter's older brother.

Although the Academy was not supposed to be a school, Hanson was the first of five fellows to study privately with the non-English-speaking Ottorino Respighi (1879–1936), who taught at the Conservatorio di Musica Santa Cecilia and directed it from 1924 through 1926. Academy lore relates that the nightingales heard in Respighi's *Pines of Rome* (1923–24) were recorded in the yard behind the McKim building. Later fellows such as Elliott Carter remembered the nightingales, but they are no longer there. In addition to Respighi, Gian Francesco Malipiero, Alfredo Casella, and Ildebrando Pizzetti were known collectively as the *generazione dell'ottanta,* influential Italian composers born in the 1880s. All had contact with the music fellows.

Hanson experienced a quintessential Academy encounter with the Renaissance when he and architecture fellow Victor Hafner measured the top of St. Peter's dome, designed by Michelangelo. Although Hanson suffered from vertigo, the two succeeded in discovering a crack in the dome. The Vatican engineers who strengthened the dome made use of Hafner's drawings.

Not to be outdone by Sowerby's February one-man concert, Hanson produced an entire concert of his own music in March 1922 that included Signora Respighi, the Quartetto Romano, and Hanson himself.[11] Hanson conducted the premiere of his *Nordic* Symphony with the Augusteo Orchestra on May 30, 1923. First entitled the *Scandinavian* Symphony, the *Nordic* Symphony, written perhaps incongruously in Rome, was the first of Hanson's seven symphonies. During his first Rome Prize year, he had traveled to Sweden. By 1923 Hanson had written a symphonic poem entitled *Lux Aeterna,* a string quartet commissioned by Mrs. Elizabeth S. Coolidge, and had begun a choral work on a libretto by Mrs. Albert Coates to be performed at the Leeds Festival in 1925, the first time an American work was commissioned for that English festival.

The Eastman School's musical director, Albert Coates, along with the conductor Eugene Goossens, had met the twenty-seven-year-old Hanson during his fellowship in Rome in 1924. Having conducted the *Nordic* Symphony in

Figure 1.1. Howard Hanson in Rome, ca. 1921. Courtesy of the American Academy in Rome.

Rochester and New York, Hanson discovered on his return to Rome a cable asking him to leave his Rome Prize fellowship and become director of the Eastman School; Coates had recommended him. Hanson was to hold this position for forty years and remained active as a conductor for five decades. His students included Jack Beeson, William Bergsma, and Peter and Louis Mennini. Hanson's impact on American music included founding the Institute of American Music at the Eastman School in 1964, which published and disseminated American music and provided for research in the history of twentieth-century styles. Hanson also won a Pulitzer Prize for his Symphony no. 4. He wrote Lamond in 1924 that he felt "that his three years in Rome have been the most fruitful and inspired of his life."[12]

Lamond, Sowerby, Hanson, and the next fellow, Randall Thompson, traveled to Paris in the summer of 1923 to examine the work of the American School at Fontainebleau, where Nadia Boulanger taught composition. "Here we found about 150 of our countrymen and women studying every branch of music under the best French teachers," Lamond wrote. "Much enthusiasm was apparent. We were somewhat depressed, however, to find that few of the students took up composition as their chief study; even those who had entered the composition classes were in the elementary stages."[13] This conclusion was perhaps not surprising since, unlike the Academy, Fontainebleau was a summer school that accepted tuition-paying students; it could not compete with the opportunities the Academy in Rome offered composers.

Randall Thompson (1899–1981), the Damrosch Fellow (1922–25), was "elected" in the second competition five months later on May 1, 1922. Fifteen contestants applied, although five did not submit scores and "all scores were signed with a pseudonym only." Wintter Watts was given second place (honorable mention) and Quincy Porter placed third. Thompson was graduated from Harvard in 1920, where he had studied with Edward B. Hill. In 1922 he earned an MA in music at Harvard while also studying with Ernest Bloch in New York. In Rome he played the prelude to *Pierrot and Cothurnus* on May 17, 1923, and the orchestral prelude to *The Piper at the Gates of Dawn* on May 27, 1924. That year he wrote three short string quartets and worked on a choral setting of eight of the Odes of Horace, sung at the 1925 annual concert of the Academy. At a March 15 event Thompson's string quartet illustrating scenes in Kenneth Graham's *Wind in the Willows* was played by the Quartetto Veneziano and proved a success. Thompson later won two Guggenheims: one of them, in 1930, he spent in Rome. Thompson was to recall fondly the Academy from a distance of a couple of months. After the later sojourn in Rome, he wrote Lamond, "I look back on Rome and my life at the Academy and my friendship with you as one of the most beautiful things in my life."[14] From 1939 to 1941 he was director of the Curtis Institute in Philadelphia, where he was Leonard Bernstein's orchestration teacher.

As did the much older French Academy's Prix de Rome, the American Academy also required their fellows to write a specified amount of original work each year. During the 1922–23 year the Academy gave concerts in the dining room, as well as in the cortile, which was covered and had a temporary stage built for seventy musicians. Works of all three composers were played here for an audience of seven hundred on the first annual concert in May 1923 (see fig. 3.2). (Nostalgically, Hanson repeated this entire concert in Rochester in May 1935.) In 1923 Lamond's daughter, Mrs. Osborn, gave the Music Department a bronze head of Paderewski by Malvina Hoffman.[15] Visitors in the 1923–24 year included Malipiero, the Flonzaley Quartet, and Edward J. Dent. For six days in June 1923 Damrosch himself came to the Academy and thoroughly examined the music done so far. The 1923–24 year was the four hundredth anniversary of the birth of Palestrina, "celebrated with great splendor," Lamond wrote. The composer Gustav Holst and the bass Herbert Witherspoon (who had studied with Parker and MacDowell) were guests at the Chiaraviglio.

On his third attempt Wintter Watts (1884–1962; fellow 1923–25) finally won the Rome Prize, along with a Pulitzer travel scholarship, in 1923 from a field of five entrants. An alumnus of the Institute of Musical Art, like Hanson, Watts had studied with Percy Goetschius and won the Institute's prestigious Loeb Prize for European travel. He then studied voice in Florence and wrote a number of orchestral works, including *Young Blood* and *Two Etchings.* At the Academy he wrote mostly songs, including the cycle *Vignettes of Italy* on poems by Sara Teasdale and two Hawaiian songs sung by Luigi Nardi. Marya Freund, accompanied by Casella, played three of Watts's songs on concerts at the Chiaraviglio during the 1924–25 year. G. Schirmer published at least one of his songs, "Wings of Night." He worked on an opera, *The Piper,* on a libretto by Josephine Preston Peabody. For his required travel period he made a journey through Algeria, Sicily, throughout Italy, and to Munich to study opera. He was let go of his fellowship by Lamond, however, after two years; no reason was reported, although the small output was likely the cause, and Watts's involvment in "trouble"—not paying a local bar bill—is twice mentioned in the director Stevens's diary.[16] Watts returned to the United States in 1931 and fell into obscurity. Robert Sanders, *proxime accessit* in the 1925 competition, was elected to fill the one-year vacancy thanks to Sowerby lobbying on his behalf. (No music fellow was dismissed again until 1986, when Michael Torke's fellowship was revoked because he left the Academy shortly after arriving.)

Ten composers had applied in 1924. Herbert Elwell (1898–1974; 1924–27), who had studied with Bloch (1919–21) and with Boulanger (1921–24), won. During his fellowship he returned to Paris to study for two months with Boulanger. The Juilliard Fellowship–winner Elwell composed a three-movement piano sonata and a string quartet while at the Academy, and he directed his Piano Quartet in Paris on February 27, 1926. Beveridge Webster played a set of his piano pieces in Paris in 1925. Elwell married an Italian he met while on the fellowship. Sowerby felt, however, that Elwell had come under what he considered Watts's negative influence.[17]

Elwell's best-known work is a ballet from 1925—written at the Academy—*The Happy Hypocrite*, after Max Beerbohm; in 1927 he made it into a suite. Elwell conducted *The Happy Hypocrite* for eight hundred Academy guests in 1927. He was made head of composition at the Cleveland Institute of Music, a position he held until 1945. Elwell wrote program notes for the Cleveland Orchestra and music criticism, noted for its wit, for the *Cleveland Plain Dealer* from 1932 to 1964.

Walter Helfer (1896–1959; 1925–28), the Damrosch Fellow, won by beating out nine other contestants, including Normand Lockwood, Virgil Thomson, Otto Luening, Robert Delaney (who won a Guggenheim in 1929 and in 1933 a Pulitzer), and Adolph Weiss (who in 1926 became the first American to study with Schoenberg in Berlin). Sanders placed second and took over Watts's fellowship, while Lockwood placed third. Helfer had been educated at Harvard and studied with Daniel Gregory Mason in Boston. In 1925 he was teaching in Santa Barbara at the Deane School.

Helfer also studied with Respighi during his three-year fellowship. In the 1925–26 year he wrote a piano quintet in three movements and a quartet (both performed at the Chiaraviglio), as well as a setting of "Wynken, Blynken and Nod" for voice and piano, a nocturne for piano, and a suite of five pieces for orchestra. The next year he composed a D-Minor overture, a string trio, the song "The Sparrow," and a violin sonata. His third year produced a cello and piano sonatina, a scherzino and sonatina for piano, a serenade for tenor and voice, and an *a cappella* five-voice setting of Psalm 13. Some of Helfer's work was published: five SSA pieces as well as the cello and piano sonatina were put out by Carl Fischer, and vocal pieces were published by Witmak and H. W. Gray. Universal Edition published his Sonatina for Piano, as well as a barcarolle by a subsequent fellow, Alexander Steinert. Another feather in Helfer's cap was a performance by the Musical Art Quartet, the leading American string quartet of the day, who played his quartet at the American Embassy in Rome. His overture to *A Midsummer Night's Dream* won the prestigious Paderewski Prize in 1939. He toured England and Ireland to collect folk music. Helfer taught at Hunter College in New York from 1938 to 1950.

Robert Sanders (1906–74), the Parker Fellow (1925–29), both studied and taught at the Bush Conservatory in Chicago. He stayed at the Academy for four years, filling in the vacancy created by Wintter Watts and winning his own fellowship in 1926 over a field of nine including Virgil Thomson and Weiss. At nineteen, Sanders is still the youngest composer to win the Rome Prize. Alexander Lang Steinert received honorable mention. Sanders, too, studied with Respighi, from 1925 to 1929, and the Augusteo Orchestra performed his pieces. Lamond recommended that Sanders, only twenty in 1926, spend part of his year at the Schola Cantorum in Paris to study counterpoint. He also studied with Vincent d'Indy in the summer of 1928. At the Academy Sanders wrote a string trio, two songs with orchestral accompaniment, four songs for unaccompanied three-part women's voices, the orchestra suite *American*, and a violin sonata. In the 1926–27 season Sanders and Leopold Mannes (Damrosch's nephew) gave his suite for two pianos for an audience of around eight hundred. During the 1927–28 year Sanders wrote choral music: the Lord's Prayer and "Benedictus es, Domine." Other works included a suite in four movements for orchestra and a piano piece, *Promenade*.

Sanders's best-known piece is the 1933 orchestra work *Saturday Night*. During his career he conducted the Chicago Civic Orchestra (1933–36) and guest conducted the Chicago Symphony Orchestra. He also conducted the New York Philharmonic, playing his own work, Little Symphony in G, which had won an award. The Chicago Symphony and the Minneapolis Symphony performed his compositions. An organist, Sanders's lecture fields were hymnology and liturgical music. From 1938 (at the age of thirty-two) to 1947 he was dean of the Indiana University School of Music; he occupies an entire chapter in a history of the school.[18] He served as chairman of the Music Department of Brooklyn College from 1947 to 1972. Sanders's music is neoclassical and dissonant, and he was particularly known for music for brass. He wrote a Violin Concerto in Rome in 1928, not mentioned in Lamond's annual reports, but found in Sanders's *Grove* works list.

During the 1925–26 year a new musician's studio was arranged at the Villa Aurelia, as its two studios proved too small. The same year, J. A. Fuller-Maitland, the editor of *Grove's Dictionary of Music*, spent the winter in Rome, and Lamond consulted him. None of the *Grove* dictionaries, however, has an entry for Helfer, who was at the Academy during Fuller-Maitland's stay. When Lamond traveled to Brussels in May at the invitation of Mrs. Coolidge to participate in her series of concerts of modern music, he spoke so highly of the Rome Prize that the Belgians began efforts to establish a similar prize for their countrymen.

The tall and handsome Alexander Steinert (1900–1982; 1927–30) attended Harvard, from which he graduated magna cum laude in 1922. He had studied composition with Charles Martin Loeffler in Boston and came from a musical family: his grandfather founded both the New Haven Symphony and M. Steinert & Sons, a piano manufacturing and sales company in Providence and Boston. After Harvard, Steinert's father sent him to Paris; he attended the Conservatoire and studied privately with d'Indy and Charles Koechlin and also worked under Maurice Ravel. In March 1925 he performed as piano soloist with the Boston Symphony Orchestra in Scriabin's *Prometheus*. In October 1926 Serge Koussevitzky and the Boston Symphony had premiered Steinert's *Southern Night* poem (a piece about southern France). Steinert met Sylvia Curtis in Rome and the two married and had a son in 1927: he was the first married music fellow. Only six had applied for the Rome Prize that year, including Ernst Bacon (who later won a Pulitzer Award and two Guggenheims).

During Steinert's first year (1927–28) he wrote a three-movement trio and a choral work on a text of Ben Jonson, "Hymn to Diana." On February

25 Maestro and Signora Respighi performed six songs by Steinert, as well as pieces by Respighi. When Mischa Elman came to the Academy, a concert was given in his honor, which included Steinert's Violin Sonata, Helfer's Allegro Appassionato (the piano work published by Universal), and Sanders's trio. On March 9 Steinert accompanied Hildegarde Donaldson, playing his Violin Sonata, and later Steinert and Casella gave a concert of their own works for the piano. In 1928–29 Steinert wrote a piano sonata and two songs for piano and orchestra. Lamond and Steinert twice visited Monte Carlo. From 1929 to 1930 Steinert composed his *Leggenda,* to be performed December 14, 1930, at the Augusteo under Howard Hanson and by the Boston Symphony under Koussevitzky in March 1931.

The wealthy Steinert had lived lavishly in Paris, entertaining Toscanini, Paderewski, Piatagorsky, Koussevitzky and other Russians, and his teacher Maurice Ravel. Steinert also worked with his close friends George Gershwin and Cole Porter. His orchestral piece with narrator, *The Nightingale and the Rose* (on Oscar Wilde), was performed by the Philadelphia Orchestra with Eugene Ormandy conducting and Basil Rathbone narrating. The orchestral work *Concerto Sinfonica* was played in 1935 by Koussevitzky and the Boston Symphony with Steinert as piano soloist. In the late 1930s he conducted the first performances of *Porgy and Bess* in Los Angeles and San Francisco, lived in Beverly Hills, and wrote for radio, television, and Hollywood movies in the 1940s; he then moved back to New York City. He conducted the memorial concert for George Gerswhin at the Hollywood Bowl.

Roger Sessions (1896–1985) was the Damrosch Fellow (1928–31) at the Academy starting in 1928.[19] He had earned music degrees from Harvard and Yale, where he studied with Hill and Parker, respectively, and later studied and worked with Ernest Bloch while teaching at the Cleveland Institute. Lamond had suggested he apply for the Rome Prize, and letters of recommendation came from Serge Koussevitzky and Nadia Boulanger. That year Sanders was reappointed and honorable mention was given to both Herbert Inch and Normand Lockwood. The jury that picked Sessions over nine others included Carpenter, Hill, and Sowerby, but, atypically, not Damrosch.

Prior to his coming to Rome, Sessions had lived in Paris in the summer of 1926 and worked with Nadia Boulanger, who he later denied having been his teacher.[20] He had received two Guggenheims that supported him in part at Bernard Berenson's Villa I Tatti in Florence from 1926 to 1927. His language ability in Italian was by now on the level of his French and German (and his Latin and Greek), so that he was fluent. After his Rome Prize years he won a year-long Carnegie grant to Berlin, and stayed a year and a half.

Sessions was an atypical choice. He was almost two years older than the stated age limit of thirty. In contradiction to the previous terms of the fellowship, he was not "unmarried"; he had married Barbara Foster in 1920. The French Academy, however, had ceased in 1927 to require celibacy of its fellows. In fact, all three music AAR fellows in 1929—Sessions, Lockwood, and Steinert—were married. The age limit was lifted after the war. The attitude toward married fellows may be seen in Sowerby's 1930 letter to Lamond: "Are all three of the men there now married? (I can imagine the squabbles the respective wives get into—and I can say that I'm glad I was there before they lifted the ban.)"[21]

Before winning the Rome Prize in May 1928, Sessions had just begun, with Aaron Copland, a series of concerts in New York called the Copland-Sessions concerts. The first Copland-Sessions concert was April 22, 1928. Sessions was unable to finish his first Piano Sonata in time for that concert, two movements of which were performed on May 6 by John Duke. Even before Sessions and his wife, Barbara, reached Rome in October 1928, they had begun their campaign to persuade Copland to apply for the Rome Prize so that Copland would be in Rome during some of their stay. Koussevitzky and Boulanger would certainly have written letters of recommendation for him. Copland, however, wished to stay in New York and the United States.

Sessions initially liked Rome enormously; he wrote to Copland how much superior it was to France, which he thought "fundamentally alien to me."[22] In this he was not alone: Randall Thompson had written to Lamond that he had "given up on Paris. . . . If I remember you are not more enthusiastic about it than I am."[23] In November 1928 Sessions wrote Copland, "The shades of Hanson and Sowerby still hang over the [Academy] to a certain extent; but this has not seemed to affect either my status or my peace of mind!" He thought Lamond "more than kind" and "a man of the world, which means a great deal."[24]

Because of his marriage, Sessions could not live at the Academy's McKim building. He and Barbara lived at the Villa Sforza, via Garibaldi 31, a building no longer standing, but near the top of the hill across from both the Villa Aurelia and the Academy. Rather than write much music, Sessions took the opportunity to learn Russian, since the two ladies who ran the Villa Sforza lodging were Russian. He bought a first edition of *War and Peace* to read in the original language. He wrote in Russian to Koussevitzky, whose Boston Symphony Orchestra had played Sessions's Symphony no. 1 in 1927. Sessions brought with him a quartet written and performed in Cleveland, which was played on a concert of fellows' quartets by the Delle Fornaci Quartet on an unspecified date. Sessions gave a talk, "Some Aspects of Contemporary Music," before the fellows from other academies. Not all was well in the city, however: the director Stevens reported in his diary an "unusual amount" of typhoid in Rome.[25]

In Rome Sessions eventually completed his Piano Sonata. Another pianist, Frank Mannheimer, gave the premiere of the Sonata on March 3, 1930, at the Villa Chiaraviglio. (Mannheimer had played the two finished movements in Florence in 1929.) Mannheimer played the Sonata on the radio in London on February 24, 1931, in Rome on March 12, in Germany on July 7, and in Oxford on July 23 for the ISCM Festival. There Copland first heard the finished version and wrote of it, "To know the work well is to have the firm conviction that Sessions has presented us with a cornerstone upon which to base an American music."[26] The Sonata was published by the German firm of Schott's Söhne, which, like being published by Universal, was an unusual sign of acceptance of an American in Europe.

Although fellows signed an agreement to remain in residence eight months of each year, Sessions's 1929–30 year was seven and a half months, and the 1930–31 year only four. Because of intense self-criticism and neuroses, Sessions started and finished only one work, a song, "On the Beach at Fontana" (Joyce), during his entire three-year period at the Academy. No new piece of his was played on any of the three annual concerts. Because Sessions did not meet these expectations of the Academy and did not submit the score to his Violin Concerto before the fall of 1931 (it was finished in 1935), he was not awarded the degree of FAAR in 1931. Irritated, Lamond wrote in 1938 that Sessions "was in Rome for three years, principally owing to my efforts, and in spite of many 'urgings' did very little work."[27] Sessions won the Pulitzer Prize in 1982 for his Concerto for Orchestra.

The next fellow, Normand Lockwood (1906–2002; 1929–32), remembered Sessions in Rome as "a prodigious brain," but one "for whom composition was a long and agonizing process."[28] Lockwood himself was picked in an unusual manner over the other nine contestants. The tall twenty-three-year-old, sporting round rimmed glasses and a thick mustache, had not attended college, but had already studied with Respighi from 1924 to 1925—the two communicated in German—and with Boulanger (1925–27). The jury, consisting of Damrosch, Deems Taylor, Carpenter, Sowerby, and Hill, chose him, but met again a month later at the Institute of Musical Art to hear Lockwood's music—the records do not say which piece—played by the Institute orchestra, to determine whether he would receive the award.

He completed only a few compositions in his three years at the Academy. Lockwood and Steinert performed the two-piano version of his Symphony in E, his earliest ensemble work, one never played by an orchestra. He also wrote *Brass Music for Their Majesties' Entry: At the Opening of the May Exhibition of the American Academy in Rome.* The royal couple traditionally appeared at the annual art exhibition.

Lockwood then taught at Oberlin from 1932 to 1943 (where Peter and Louis Mennini were his students), Union Theological Seminary (1945–53), Columbia University, Trinity, and lastly as composer-in-residence at the University of Denver. He won two Guggenheims in 1943 and 1945 and the Ernest Bloch award. A composer of five hundred works, Lockwood's compositional priority was timbre; his music is bitonal, quartal, and twelve-tone. Kay Norton wrote a book about him.[29]

The next successful candidate in musical composition was Werner Janssen (1899–1990; 1930–33) on the Juilliard Fellowship. Lamond stated, "I found

Figure 1.2. Normand Lockwood in his Academy studio, 1932. Courtesy of the American Academy in Rome.

Janssen in New York in 1930, and had to persuade him to enter the competition."[30] Janssen had studied with Philip G. Clapp at Dartmouth, then, at the New England Conservatory, piano with Arthur Friedheim and composition with Frederick Converse and George W. Chadwick. Eight candidates applied; Vittorio Giannini was awarded honorable mention.

Like Steinert's, Janssen's family was wealthy, but unlike Steinert, Janssen and his father, August, parted ways over his pursuing music. By 1923 Janssen had been entrenched in Tin Pan Alley, writing tunes for Oliver Morosco for five dollars a week. He wrote music for Ziegfeld's *Follies* in 1925 and 1926 and conducted theater orchestras. Janssen could be described as a "symphonic journalist," a writer of philharmonic newspaper articles. He began in Cleveland, depicting in *Jail Wail* the clang of iron doors, the yells of drug addicts, and the general uproar of prison. Another piece was about an ice-breaking trip on the river. The newspapers played up these works, and he became a celebrity for pieces drawn from sounds at the Cleveland airport terminal and an *Airplane* Suite.

After four months in Cleveland, Janssen won the Rome Prize in 1930, awarded for his symphonic work *New Year's Eve in New York*. In places the pandemonium of Times Square "is reproduced dictaphonically, with a cork-popping sequence." Stokowski and "practically every important orchestra in the world" played *New Year's Eve in New York.*[31] The work was dedicated to Carl Engel, who published some of his music at Schirmer.

During his Rome Prize years Janssen studied orchestration with Respighi (1930–33) at the Conservatorio di Musica Santa Cecilia. While at the Academy he wrote *The Eternal Column*, a forty-minute orchestral scenario; the string quartets entitled *American Kaleidoscope* (1930) and *Fantasie Miniature* (1934), the last on American themes; a symphony in one movement entitled *Louisiana*; a Cello Sonata (1930–31); *News Reel* for string quartet; and an opera, *Manhattan Transfer*. After studying conducting in Basel with Felix Weingartner and Hermann Scherchen, he made his debut as a conductor in Rome. According to a two-part 1938 *New Yorker* profile on him, he was the first American conductor taken seriously abroad, conducting in Rome, Berlin, Riga, Budapest, and Moscow. In Finland he conducted all of Sibelius's symphonies. Sibelius himself was overcome by Janssen's work as a conductor and said so: "The Finnish people have tonight discovered Sibelius."[32] On June 7, 1930, Janssen conducted *New Year's Eve in New York* on the Rome Radio.

Lamond concluded his 1933–34 report: "The score of Janssen's Fugue for full orchestra on the theme *Dixie* was published by Eulenberg, of Leipzig. An examination of this score will show what three years in Rome will accomplish in turning the thoughts of a creative mind to classical forms. Previous to obtaining the Rome Prize Janssen was entirely concerned with 'Jazz' music and Broadway shows. . . . His case is a veritable transformation, and I believe that it will help to confirm the Trustees of the Academy in their opinion, oft expressed, that Rome is the ideal place for the development of artists."[33]

While the Academy gave Janssen the opportunities that inaugurated his career as a conductor, it was also the scene of his biggest compositional disaster. During the last few months of his three-year fellowship, he completed the manuscript for *Manhattan Transfer* on a libretto by the novelist John Dos Passos. Productions were waiting in Budapest and Dresden. The manuscripts of *Manhattan Transfer*, along with his rewritten orchestral work *The Eternal Column*, were either stolen from the Academy or possibly mistaken for wastepaper by a servant and thrown out. The subsequent hue and cry—not mentioned in Lamond's reports—stirred Italy. Mussolini had been to the Academy and met all the fellows on February 22, 1933 (Washington's birthday). In his honor the Rome Quartet had played Janssen's *Fantasie Miniature* and a work by Vittorio Giannini. Il Duce met all of the fellows; he had become enamored with Janssen's music and enjoyed his conducting. At news of the scores' disappearance he sent his secret service into action: a reward of 5,000 lire was offered. Janssen, who conducted entire programs of Wagner from memory, had not memorized his own opera and its expensive Dos Passos libretto. The works were never recovered. During Janssen's last year, 1933, he also wrote and had performed two string quartets and two pieces of American folk music, performed by an orchestra in Turin. His last work at the Academy was a Suite for

Orchestra. In 1938 the *New Yorker* remarked, "Whether he will return to composing again is uncertain. . . . Janssen is now Janssen the conductor."[34]

Having twice conducted the Berlin Philharmonic, Janssen canceled his engagement for December 1933. Josef Hofmann, Jacques Thibaut, Alfred Cortot, Bronislaw Huberman, and others had already declined to perform with the Philharmonic because of their cancellation of pieces by Jewish composers. In order to obtain Janssen, the management had even sanctioned his performing Rubin Goldmark's *Gettysburg Tone Poem.* Janssen's late October decision not to conduct was embarrassing to the management, "which gave him to understand he might expect the orchestra 'to make trouble' for him."[35] He returned from Rome to the United States to conduct the New York Philharmonic and later the Baltimore Symphony. About half his programs in New York consisted of American music, including the first orchestral performance of Samuel Barber's *Music for a Scene from Shelly* (1935). Janssen also made the first recording of Barber's overture to *The School for Scandal* (1944). In Hollywood he organized the Janssen Symphony (1940–52) and commissioned American works. Contrary to Lamond's predictions, Janssen returned to his theatrical roots and wrote forty-five film scores, including *The General Died at Dawn* (1936), in a style that incorporated jazz. He married Ann Harding, an actress who starred in forty films, including *The Man in the Gray Flannel Suit,* and made numerous television appearances.

In 1929 Lamond developed a plan for a center of composition at the Villa Roquebrune, at Cape Martin on the French Riviera between Mentone and Monte Carlo. Its managing committee would consist of Lamond, Sowerby, Hanson, an unnamed French musician, and the Academy director. In 1930 Myron Taylor provided funds to acquire the villa for musicians. Roquebrune was independent of the Academy but open to its music fellows; by 1931 it was known as the Anabel Taylor Foundation. A studio was erected and the main building was being remodeled. "The Foundation will be open to composers who have graduated with distinction from the Academie de France (Villa Medici), from the Regia Accademia di Santa Cecilia, Rome, as well as from the American Academy in Rome. . . . The Foundation has no official connection with the Academy."[36] By 1932 Lamond himself had moved there, returning to Rome at intervals to direct the music program at the Academy. He lived at the villa until his death on March 16, 1940.

At least six composers went to the Taylor Foundation, the Fitzgeraldesque villa straight out of *Tender is the Night*: Inch (December 1932–January 1933); Johnson (June–September 1934); Giannini (in 1935); Barber visited Lamond there in 1936; and Woltmann, Kennan, and Naginski lived there. In 1938 and 1939 the entire Music Department stayed at Rocquebrune.

Herbert Reynolds Inch (1904–88; 1931–34), who won the $6,000 Damrosch Fellowship for three years, had already spent 1928–29 at the Academy. Twelve composers vied for the 1931 Rome Prize, including Marc Blitzstein. The jury—Damrosch, Sowerby, Hanson, Hill, and Chalmers Clifton—chose Inch, who had a bachelor's and master's of music from Eastman, where he studied with Hanson. Honorable mention went to Vittorio Giannini, who was to be considered for a fellowship if the money could be raised.

While at the Academy, Inch helped catalogue the music collection at the main library, begun as a music library in 1928–29 at the Chiaraviglio. The two catalogues are still separate. He used this experience when working as a reference assistant at the New York Public Library Music Division from 1935 to 1938. In 1937 he joined the faculty of Hunter College, in New York, and remained there until his retirement in 1965. He was married to Miriam Hirchenbaum. In 1946 he won the Ernest Bloch Award. In the first year alone at the Academy, he composed a suite of thirteen pieces called *December Moods*, a series of twenty-four pieces titled *Mediterranean Sketches* for string quartet, an overture, a Divertimento for brass, a Fantasia for organ, and a Serenade for small orchestra. The next year he wrote a symphonic piece called *To Silvanus*, among other works.

In 1932 Gorham Stevens retired as director of the Academy. His successor, James Hewlett, remained only two years and was replaced in 1935 by Chester Aldrich, the brother of the music critic Richard Aldrich. Their sister Amey helped administer the Academy. In 1932 eight composers competed, again including Blitzstein and Hunter Johnson. The jury consisted of Damrosch, Sowerby, Hanson, Carl Engel, and Deems Taylor. Although Giannini (1903–66) did not apply then, he was awarded the Horatio Parker Fellowship (1932–36). Lamond wrote, "Giannini, undoubtedly the most gifted of our prizemen, was turned down twice in spite of my strong recommendation, and accepted the prize only after I implored him to do so."[37] Giannini was later granted a fourth year, finishing in July 1936. Because of the Depression, the fellowships were reduced from $1,500 a year to $1,250 and travel stipends from $500 to $300. The Academy closed for the summers of 1934 and 1935.

Giannini had an enviable background. Born in Philadelphia, he came from an extremely musical family. His father was the Italian tenor Ferruccio Giannini, his mother a violinist, and two older sisters, Euphemia (1896–1979) and Dusolina (1902–82), were opera singers. Euphemia, known as Madame Gregory, taught on the Curtis Institute voice faculty from 1927 until her death. Dusolina, a student of Marcella Sembrich and internationally known as a singer, lived mostly in Europe. At ten Giannini attended the Milan Conservatory as a violinist. He entered the Juilliard Graduate School in 1925 as, unusually, both a composition student of Rubin Goldmark and a violin student of Hans Letz (a former member of the Kneisel Quartet and Dorothy DeLay's teacher). The leading figure in American opera in the late 1930s, Giannini wrote eleven operas: six were for radio and television, of which the Columbia Broadcasting System commissioned three.

Giannini has been described as extremely extroverted and well liked, and as a heavy cigar smoker who loved good food. He played the violin in Academy concerts, fancied expensive sports cars, played bridge, and was attractive to women. He was married and divorced twice in his sixty-three years and had no children. Giannini came to Rome with his first wife, the pianist Lucia Avella, whom he had married in 1931; she performed in his works at the Academy. During the 1932–33 year he wrote a four-movement symphony, a piano trio, and a work for soprano and tenor soli and small orchestra entitled *Primavera* (Spring).

Dusolina introduced Giannini to the conductor Wilhelm Furtwängler. Her influence got his first opera *Lucedia* scheduled in Frankfurt in 1933, which was later canceled. It was premiered at the Munich National Opera on October 20, 1934, and thus she created the title role of the first opera by an American performed in Germany since Hitler had come to power. *Lucedia* had been translated into German by Hans Redlich and was an enormous success. There is no hope for a revival, however, since the orchestral score and parts were lost in the World War II bombing that destroyed the Munich National Theater.

Giannini and his librettist Karl Flaster collaborated on another opera, *The Scarlet Letter*, which was finished at the Academy by November 1935. Giannini translated it into Italian, and it opened in June 1938 at the Hamburg State Opera, sung in German, and featured Dusolina as Hester Prynne; Hans Hotter sang the role of Roger Chillingworth. The work got twenty-two curtain calls and raves in the press, which called Giannini a "young Puccini." Ironically, his opera on an American subject was more popular in Europe than in the United States. Lamond and Giannini traveled to Vienna to try to secure a performance of the operas and succeeded in getting the composer's Requiem published by Universal. Giannini's and Flaster's later collaboration on *The Harvest*, a *verismo* opera, at the Chicago Lyric Opera was panned by American critics despite the presence of Marilyn Horne as the female lead. His most popular work was the 1950 *The Taming of the Shrew.* Giannini taught at Juilliard from 1939 to 1964, at the Manhattan School of Music, and at the Curtis Institute. He founded the North Carolina School of the Arts and was its first president from 1964 to 1966, during the last fourteen months of his life.[38]

The North Carolinian Hunter Johnson (1906–98; 1933–35) had studied at the University of North Carolina and at Eastman with Bernard Rogers. He taught at the University of Michigan from 1929 until his Rome Prize began in 1933. Johnson competed for the prize against seven others, including Hugo Weisgall. He was awarded the first two-year prize on the Juilliard Fellowship and later won two Guggenheim Fellowships. In Rome he studied with Alfredo Casella. During his first year he wrote a Piano Sonata and a Lento and Fugue for piano and orchestra.

Johnson's music was akin to Ives's and Copland's and contained elements of jazz. Martha Graham commissioned two works, the ballets *Letter to the World* and *Death and Entrances*, which have had hundreds of performances around the world. He wrote another work for Graham, *The Scarlet Letter*, in 1975. His Piano Sonata, written in Rome in 1933–34 (and revised in 1936 and 1947–48), has found a place in the repertoire. Pietro Scarpini premiered it at the Villa Aurelia on December 3, 1934. Johnson taught at Cornell University, as well as at the universities of Michigan, Manitoba, Illinois, and Texas.

The 1934 competition had fourteen applicants, a significant increase over the typical eight or ten. Despite the applications of Robert Whitney (a Sowerby student, later founder of the Louisville Orchestra), Israel Citkowitz (a Boulanger pupil and friend of Copland's), the violinist Robert Gross, and the composers Hugo Norden and Samuel Barber, the jury (Damrosch, Sowerby, Engel, and Deems Taylor) decided for the first and only time that *no one* deserved the award. On learning this, Lamond asked for a three-month stipend for Janssen to study scores in Roquebrune for his New York Philharmonic engagements; that request was denied.

In her definitive book on Samuel Barber (1910–80; 1935–37), Barbara Heyman writes,

> Only a year earlier Barber had submitted the Cello Sonata and *Music for a Scene from Shelley* for the same prize and was turned down. During the summer of 1934, while working at the Bok colony in Maine, he was invited by the American Academy to apply again, and on 31 January 1935, under the pseudonym "John Brandywine," he submitted the same works as he had before. [There were now more contestants than ever: nineteen including Bernard Herrmann and Robert Whitney.] This time Barber was granted the [two-year Damrosch] award, ironically by the same jury that had previously rejected his application. . . . Barber attributed this reversal of fortune in part to the successful premiere of *Shelly* by the New York Philharmonic [conducted by the Rome Prize fellow Werner Janssen].[39]

The public announcement of this two-year award was made over WJZ and NBC radio on May 9.[40]

Barber had attended the new Curtis Institute of Music in its first class in 1924 (when he was fourteen) and studied composition there with the Italian pedagogue Rosario Scalero. He also excelled at piano and voice. Barber's Italian, like Sessions's and Giannini's, was already excellent from trips to Italy to visit both his teacher's family and that of his life partner Giancarlo Menotti. Barber wrote Menotti of his reaction to "the somewhat expatriated Harvard Club atmosphere" at the Academy. "I feel somewhat settled here, that is, as settled as I let myself be. (Do you know that I have not yet unpacked my trunk, out of sheer perversity, because I do not wish to feel at home in this room? My

Figure 1.3. Portrait of Samuel Barber by Robert B. Green (FAAR 1938). Courtesy of the American Academy in Rome.

half-full trunk stands open, in complete disorder, the scandal of the Academy. And I *shall* not unpack it. I will never call this room mine!)"[41]

Barber did not, in fact, unpack for the two years of his stay, but he felt quite differently about his studio. "It was situated apart from the academy, a little yellow house approached from the garden by a winding stair—a renovation of the stables of the old Villa Aurelia and 'full of charm.'"[42] Barber studied Dante, taking lessons twice a week, and, in a classic Academy experience, visited the Sistine Chapel with the painters at the AAR and climbed the scaffolding to view Michelangelo's ceiling. He wrote, "It was as if someone discovered some beautiful new work of Beethoven, after knowing every note of his for a lifetime, and seeing all of a sudden some of his most intimate secrets . . . I cannot tell the impression it made on me, for these sensations are like secrets to be guarded jealously all one's life-time, great and magnificent secrets."[43]

An all-Barber concert at the Aurelia on April 22, 1936, included "Beggar's Song" and four others, all sung by the composer: "With Rue My Heart Is Laden," "The Daisies," "Rain Has Fallen," and "Sleep Now." Barber returned to Rome on November 1, 1936, for rehearsals for his symphony played on December 13 by the Adriano Theatre (formerly the Augusteo) Orchestra. The Curtis Quartet played his Serenade for String Quartet, op. 1, at the Aurelia on November 16, 1936. Barber arranged that the Curtis Quartet not receive a fee from the Academy, as a contribution to the music program.

On Lamond's recommendation, Barber's new String Quartet in B Minor, most of which was written near Salzburg, was given its premiere by the Brussels Pro Arte Quartet the next month on December 14, 1936, at the Villa Aurelia.[44] Barber withdrew it after the concert for a revision of the last movement. Of course, it is the interior slow movement of the quartet, arranged in 1938 for string orchestra as the Adagio for Strings, that is Barber's most enduring masterpiece—one given its world premiere at the Academy.

Barber worked on his first symphony in Rome, but was more prolific composing songs. He set four poems from James Joyce's *Chamber Music*: "Of That So Sweet Imprisonment," "Rain Has Fallen," "Sleep Now," and "Strings in the Ear and Air" were completed in late November and December and several were published by G. Schirmer in 1939 as Opus 10. Barber's 1935 Pulitzer traveling prize of $1,500, in the face of reduced Academy travel stipends, meant he could travel to the Washington, DC, for a performance of the quartet. On June 20, 1937, Barber accompanied Felix Salmond playing his cello sonata in London. Barber won two Pulitzer Prizes, in 1958 and 1963.

In 1936 the idea of a musicology fellowship was already being floated, as was the notion of residents, who did not appear until after the war. Lamond described Ottorino Respighi's death that April as "a severe loss . . . of a faithful friend and counselor of both Professor in Charge and Fellows for fifteen years."[45] The director, Chester Aldrich, was unable to attend the spring fellows' exhibition on June 3 because his brother, the music critic and early Academy music juror Richard Aldrich, had died at the Villa Aurelia on June 1. Richard Aldrich had been music editor of the *New York Times* from 1902 to 1923 and a member of the National Institute of Arts and Letters. The Parker Fellowship almost entirely evaporated (it was twice resurrected in the 1950s, including for the first African American music fellow, Ulysses Kay, FAAR 1952). Fellows were now invited for two years rather than three, indicating an era ending. War was on the way, and in 1939 the State Department declined to issue passports to Italy for new fellows. Paradoxically, in 1939 stipends were raised to $2,000.

Kent F. Kennan (1913–2003; 1936–39), the half brother of the diplomat George W. Kennan, held the Juilliard Fellowship beginning in the fall of 1936. Kennan was chosen from a field of eleven applicants by a jury consisting of Damrosch, Engel, Sowerby, Hanson, and Deems Taylor. He had studied with fellow Hunter Johnson at the University of Michigan from 1930 to

1932. Kennan had graduated with a bachelor's and a master's in music from Eastman, where he studied with Rogers and Hanson. In Rome he composed two movements of a symphony, a Fantasia for flute and piano, a violin sonata, a *Promenade* for small orchestra, a Nocturne for violin and small orchestra, three soprano songs, a piano prelude, and the final movement of *Sea Sonata* for violin and piano. Kennan spent Christmas 1936, and July through September 1937, at Rocquebrune. On June 8, 1938, Kennan's *Promenade* for orchestra and Frederick Woltmann's Variations for piano and orchestra were presented at the Santa Cecilia. In 1938 he and Woltmann attended the master classes in composition at Santa Cecilia with the conservative Ildebrando Pizzetti (1880–1968), a member of the *generazione dell'ottanta.*

Kennan's works list begins with his Rome Prize year: he wrote a Nocturne and *Il Campo dei Fiori* for orchestra in 1937, revised as *From a Rome Diary.* Kennan's works included "Lament" and "Air de Ballet" as movements of Divertimento for Orchestra, four preludes for piano, and "Blessed Are They That Mourn" for chorus and orchestra. On February 29, 1942, Kennan's Andante for solo oboe and orchestra was played by Mitch Miller, with Leon Barzin conducting the National Orchestral Association in New York. Lamond stressed that "in the case of young composers . . . a practical acquaintance with the technique of orchestra instruments is necessary. Arrangements have been made with various artists to help in this direction."[46] We can assume that these arrangements were invaluable to Kennan—and to many other musicians—since Kennan became well known for his books on compositional technique: *The Technique of Orchestration* is now in its sixth edition (2002), and *Counterpoint* reached its fourth edition in 1998. The orchestration book in particular has become a staple in music schools. Kennan served in the military from 1942 to 1946 and spent most of his teaching career at the University of Texas in Austin, from which he retired in 1983.

Frederick Woltmann (1908–65), the Damrosch Fellow (1937–39), had received his bachelor's degree in music from Eastman. Eleven composers applied and the jury consisted of Damrosch (chair as usual, but for the last time), Engel, Sowerby, Hanson, and Deems Taylor. From 1938 to 1939 the whole music department—Kennan, Woltmann, and Charles Naginski—had stayed at Rocquebrune, where Lamond lived. The previous year Woltmann wrote numerous works including *Variations on an old English Folk Song* for piano and orchestra, *The Pool of Pegasus* for orchestra, *Incantation* for orchestra, "Dover Beach" for voice and orchestra, and an introduction and two scenes from *Ethan Frome.*

Woltmann had long wanted to write an opera on the Edith Wharton novel. He had set sail in 1937 for France to speak with the authoress, but while on board was informed of her death. Asked for assistance, the Academy directors sent him to the literary executor, who said it was fine with him (and would have been with Wharton), but Woltmann first had to obtain dramatic rights from

Owen Davis and his son Donald, who had gotten these rights from Wharton. The composer had some difficulty with Davis; finally, by late December 1939, he obtained them.[47] In 1938–39 Woltmann arranged the libretto and designed the scenery, but the opera never came to fruition.

Woltmann's *Two Impressions of Rome* included *The Coliseum at Night* (1939). *The Coliseum*, based on verses from Byron's *Manfred*, was played by Dimitri Mitropoulos and the New York Philharmonic on December 22, 1940, in Carnegie Hall. Mitropoulos had supported Woltmann financially, but because of the war the expected check from the Minneapolis conductor did not appear in Woltmann's bank account. That situation left him somewhat stranded in Europe. Woltmann did not write much music after 1946; by 1950 he was living in Hollywood.

An alumnus of the Juilliard Graduate School, Charles Naginski (1909–40), the Parker Fellow (1938–40), was chosen from a field of eleven contestants. Deems Taylor was the chair of the jury, which consisted of Copland, Sessions, and the composers and organists Eric De Lamarter (1880–1953) and Philip James (1890–1975). The talented and prolific Naginski had studied with Rubin Goldmark from 1928 to 1933 and with Sessions. William Denny won honorable mention. Naginski spent one year in Rome and Rocquebrune, 1938–39. In Rome the composer Jacques Ibert, the director of the French Academy (1937–60), had encouraged him as a composer. He returned to the United States in October 1939 and spent a second year subsidized by the Academy at a studio in Garrison, New York.

During his 1938–39 year Naginski wrote a Piano Sonata; a Divertimento for flute, oboe, clarinet, and bassoon; the first two movements of a Concerto for harpsichord or piano with orchestra; a Sinfonietta for chamber orchestra; sixteen songs; sketches for a symphony; a Divertimento for trumpet, two horns, and trombone; and three poems for chorus and orchestra. A considerable amount of his music was performed and Schirmer published some of it. In the summer of 1940 he drowned in a lake in the Berkshires, possibly a suicide.[48]

In 1939 the jury—Sowerby (chair), Sessions, De Lamarter, Philip James, and the conductor Albert Stoessel—met and heard the finalists' music played at the Juilliard Graduate School, where Stoessel conducted. They chose William Douglas Denny (1910–80) from seven applicants for a two-year, $4,000 Parker Fellowship (1939–41). Denny had attended the University of California at Berkeley, where he had studied with Randall Thompson and Albert Elkus, and he knew Sessions. He also studied fugue with Paul Dukas at the École normale de musique in Paris. He may have won for his Concertino for Orchestra, written in 1937. Denny spent most of the 1939–40 year in Cambridge, Massachusetts, choosing the newly instituted war option of remaining in the United States. Denny taught at Harvard from 1941 to 1942, at Vassar from 1942 to 1944, and at University of California at Berkeley from 1945 to 1978. He stopped writing music around 1965.

The Rome Prizes were again announced over the radio, and Denny's Symphony in A was heard on the CBS broadcast. Well known in the San Francisco Bay area in the 1940s and 1950s, Denny's music is described in the 2001 edition of the *New Grove Dictionary* as "thoroughly personal and abstract, characterized by intense lyricism, with rhythmic elements predominating."[49] The music's symmetry, balance, and rhythmic elements sound similar to Walter Piston's.

The year 1940 was a pivotal year at the Academy, especially in music. The professor in charge of music, Felix Lamond, died and was never replaced, the fellow Charles Naginski died, and the Academy closed for four years and did not award a prize for a music fellow to live there until 1947. On June 10, 1940, Italy entered the war on the side of Germany. The next week Chester and Amey Aldrich shut the Academy, which housed only a handful of fellows. The Janiculum was quiet, except for the guns of ten Italian soldiers manning the nearby Porta San Pancrazio.

In 1940 a jury—Sowerby (chair), Copland, Sessions, Stoessel, and Thompson—met and evaluated thirteen applicants. On December 18, 1940, the Academy announced that no fellowships would be awarded; rather, cash prizes would be made.[50] The Juilliard Fellow Arthur Kreutz (1906–91; 1940–42) was from La Crosse, Wisconsin, where he earned a BS in chemical engineering, a bachelor's in music from the University of Wisconsin, and an MA from Teacher's College of Columbia University. Because the Academy had closed, Kreutz spent his entire fellowship in New York. His *Music for Symphony Orchestra* was broadcast on NBC as part of the public announcement of the Rome Prize winners. Kreutz wrote music for Martha Graham, taught at the University of Texas (1942–44), and won a Guggenheim Fellowship (1944). He taught from 1952 to 1964 at the University of Mississippi.

In 1941 twenty contestants applied and the jury led by Sowerby consisted of Hanson, Copland, Piston, and the pianist Rudolf Ganz. The pianist Harold Shapero (1920–2013; 1941–42) had studied with Ernst Krenek in 1937, with Walter Piston at Harvard (1938–41), and from 1936 to 1938 at the short-lived Malkin Conservatory in Boston. He also studied with Paul Hindemith in Tanglewood in 1940 and 1941 and with Nadia Boulanger from 1942 to 1943 at the Longy School in Cambridge, Massachusetts. Nevertheless, he was only a senior at Harvard when he won the Rome Prize.[51] David Diamond won honorable mention for his Concerto for Chamber Orchestra. Howard Barlow conducted Shapero's prizewinning *Nine-Minute Overture* on the radio. The other winning work by Shapero was his string quartet.

Shapero won the Naumberg Fellowship in 1942 and was asked to head the music department at the new Brandeis University in 1951; he taught there until 1988. He composed little music in the last three decades at Brandeis, but during his fellowship years he wrote *Four Baritone Songs* (texts by e. e. cummings, 1942), a String Quartet (1941, dedicated to Piston), a violin and piano sonata (1942), and three piano sonatas (1944). Considered by Arthur Berger to belong with Berger himself and Irving Fine in the American "Stravinsky school," Shapero, who won the Gerwshin Prize in 1946 and two Guggenheim Fellowships in 1947 and 1948, was considered a neoclassicist. He was close to Leonard Bernstein, who conducted the premiere of Shapero's Symphony in 1948.[52]

A jury under Sowerby—including Copland, Rudolph Ganz, Piston, and Thompson—met in 1942 to choose a winner from twenty applicants. In May David Diamond (1915–2005; fellow 1942) won the Rome Prize as an award of $1,000 on the strength of his String Quartet and his Symphony no. 1, played the previous season by the New York Philharmonic under Dimitri Mitropoulos. In addition, the jury awarded $25 prizes for compositions by Alexei Haieff, Daikeong Lee, Leonard B. Meyer, and Robert Ward. Diamond was a friend of Charles Naginski—both were Sessions students—when Naginski died. Diamond wrote to the Academy on February 4, 1969 (twenty-seven years after the event), "In 1942 I received the Prix de Rome, which was a cash award of $1,000 with a provision that once the Second World War was over, my regular residence as a Fellow of the Academy would be fulfilled. This has never happened."[53] In the margin next to this statement a handwritten note remarks only: "not promised." Indeed, no fellows who received cash awards were able to live at the Academy as fellows after the war. Diamond's much-belated application was, however, successful: he was made a resident for 1971–72.

Diamond lived in Italy from 1951 through 1965 and returned to the United States on one notable occasion, when he was subpoenaed to testify in 1956 for the McCarthy Un-American Activities Committee. Diamond had studied with Bernard Rogers and Nadia Boulanger, as well as with Sessions, and won three Guggenheims (1938, 1942, and 1958), the MacDowell Association Gold Medal, and the American Academy and National Institute of Arts and Letters Lifetime Achievement Award in 1991, among many other prestigious honors. He taught at the Juilliard School from 1973 to 1997.

Due in part to their experience at the Academy, some Rome Prize composers became internationalists, others more American sounding. All were changed profoundly. Although the Academy was not a school, at least five composers studied with Respighi: Hanson, Helfer, Sanders, Lockwood, and Janssen. Kennan and Woltmann also studied at Santa Cecilia. Each composer responded differently to his experience in Italy and Europe. Hanson in 1922 was trying to assimilate into the European aesthetic. Sessions became the epitome of European classicism. Barber, who had never unpacked his trunk, was completely and unselfconsciously American. Janssen and Giannini had successful European careers, grounded in conducting and opera. Both Steinert and Janssen cashed in, as it were, in Hollywood, where Woltmann also moved. An overwhelming number of the remaining fellows became teachers at, or heads of, music schools in the United States (Hanson, Thompson, Sanders, and

Giannini were heads of schools). Elwell became known as a critic, Inch a music librarian, whereas Kennan wrote classic textbooks. Their European credentials and cachet helped make them leaders in the American musical world.

The American Academy in Rome, where fellows were chosen competitively by distinguished juries and provided all the necessary surroundings and opportunities for composers, proved ultimately to have produced many more important composers and more music between the wars than did the open-admission, tuition-driven school at Fontainebleau. In addition to the music produced by Sowerby, Hanson, Thompson, Sessions, Giannini, Barber, Shapero, Diamond, and others, the Academy contributed to Kennan's understanding of the orchestra, the conducting careers of Hanson and Janssen, and the administration of music schools at Indiana University, North Carolina School of the Arts, Eastman, Brandeis, and Curtis. Works premiered at the Academy include, among many others, Hanson's *Nordic* Symphony, Thomson's Piano Sonata, Sessions's First Piano Sonata, and Barber's Adagio for Strings.

Fontainebleau provided one great composition teacher, Boulanger; however, the Academy had the services of Respighi, Malipiero, Casella, Pizzetti, and the faculty of Santa Cecilia. The important advantage it provided was access to a major orchestra, the Augusteo, to perform fellows' works. In addition, a string quartet was on hand to read fellows' music. The Academy could also provide room and board, a studio in which to work, a stipend, travel and part-copying expenses, a professor in charge to look after fellows' interests, a funded concert series, as well as living quarters and performance halls atop the highest hill in Rome. The Academy gave fellows daily social intercourse with architects, classicists, painters, and sculptors. It could grant the status of having won a major prize, as well as the financial support such a prize entailed. And, most important, it consciously exposed American composers to the cultures of ancient, Renaissance, baroque, and contemporary Rome.

As an opportunity for American composers, the American Academy in Rome outweighed Boulanger and the school at Fontainebleau, despite the latter's greater "press" in the scholarly world. By every measure it could give—and continues to provide—select American composers all the advantages of a career in Europe as well as a nigh-perfect environment to compose music.

Notes

1. One example of the disparity between Paris and Rome is the lack of an entry for the American Academy in *The New Grove Dictionary of Music and Musicians*, ed. Stanley Sadie and John Tyrrell, 29 vols., 2nd ed. (London: Macmillan, 2001). The *Grove Dictionary of American Music*, ed Charles Hiroshi Garrett, 8 vols. (Oxford University Press, 2013), has a short entry on the Academy by this author.

2. As the spouse of the music fellow Larry Bell, FAAR 1983, I have been fortunate to live and work at the Academy as a visiting scholar for a full year and five other summers,

as well as shorter visits. When *The Centennial Directory of the American Academy in Rome* was published for the Academy centennial in 1994, I had a chance to repay the Academy's generosity by contributing articles on thirty of the deceased fellows in music, including Leo Sowerby, Vittorio Giannini, Howard Hanson, Roger Sessions, Samuel Barber, and Aaron Copland (a resident). Benjamin G. Kohl, Wayne A. Linker, and Buff Suzanne Kavelman, eds., *The Centennial Directory of the American Academy in Rome* (New York and Rome: American Academy in Rome, 1995).

3. Quoted in Lucia Valentine and Alan Valentine, *The American Academy in Rome: 1894–1969* (Charlottesville: University Press of Virginia, 1973), 82.

4. MacDowell's advocacy for a Rome Prize in musical composition and the founding of the MacDowell Colony are discussed in Judith Tick's essay in this volume.

5. In 1922 Gertrude Vanderbilt (Mrs. Harry Whitney) made a bronze plaque to celebrate the Damrosch Fellowship, which was placed in the cortile above the entrance to the gallery. Damrosch's connection with the American Academy is not mentioned in George Martin's otherwise authoritative book, *The Damrosch Dynasty: America's First Family of Music* (Boston: Houghton Mifflin, 1983). He was, however, a major figure in the music program, chairing the selection committee for many years, despite efforts to unseat him.

6. Valentine and Valentine, *American Academy in Rome,* 86–87.

7. See this author's history of the Juilliard School for more about Frederick's use of Augustus Juilliard's money. Andrea Olmstead, *Juilliard: A History* (Urbana: University of Illinois Press, 1999), chapter 3.

8. The rate of the dollar to the lire was 1 to 19.5.

9. Felix Lamond to John Russell Pope, November 23, 1934, RomeRareB, AAR Archives, Rome, according to Martin Brody's research.

10. Ronald Stalford and Michael Meckna, "Leo Sowerby," in *The New Grove Dictionary of Music and Musicians,* 14: 110.

11. Signora Respighi was Elsa Olivieri-Sangiacomo (1894–1996), herself a composer and the author of her husband's biography, *Ottorino Respighi: Dati biografici ordinati da Elsa Respighi* (Milan: Ricordi, 1954); Gwyn Morris, trans., *Ottorino Respighi: His Life-Story* (London: Ricordi, 1962).

12. In Felix Lamond, Report of the Professor in Charge of the Department of Music, Annual Report—1924, New York, Offices of the American Academy in Rome, 54.

13. Lamond, Annual Report—1923, AAR, 50.

14. Randall Thompson to Felix Lamond, November 11, 1926, folder ML95 T37, AAR archives, Rome.

15. Hoffman also sculpted a bust of Frank Damrosch that sits in the Juilliard School library.

16. Gorham Stevens diary entries for February 11 and June 6, 1925, RomeRareB 176.9.Stev.Dia, AAR archives, Rome, according to Christina Huemer's research. Sowerby wrote Lamond on June 20, 1925: "I am thoroughly mad about Watts, and personally shall be glad for the day when I hear he has been kicked out. Two songs for a year's work is really ridiculous. . . ." Sowerby also wrote that Watts "loaf[ed] and live[d] comfortably on other people's money for nearly two years" (October 19, 1925, ML95 So9, AAR archives, Rome). Randall Thompson also weighed in: "And how did Watts finish out the year? I trust you were not put to any greater or even prolonged agonies" (Fragment, no date, folder ML95 T37, AAR archives, Rome.

17. Letter from Sowerby to Lamond, February 9, 1925, folder ML95 So9, AAR archives, Rome.

18. George Logan, *The Indiana University School of Music: A History* (Bloomington: Indiana University Press, 2000), chapter 3.

19. See Andrea Olmstead, *Roger Sessions and His Music* (Ann Arbor, MI: UMI Research Press, 1985); *Conversations with Roger Sessions* (Boston: Northeastern University Press, 1987; ebook, 2013); *The Correspondence of Roger Sessions* (Boston: Northeastern University Press, 1992); and *Roger Sessions: A Biography* (New York: Routledge, 2008).

20. See Olmstead, *Roger Sessions: A Biography*, 215–26.

21. Letter from Sowerby to Lamond, April 6, 1930, folder ML95 So9, AAR archives, Rome.

22. Roger Sessions to Aaron Copland, October 7, 1928, in Olmstead, *Correspondence*, 126.

23. Thompson to Lamond, 1930, folder ML95 T37, AAR archives, Rome.

24. Sessions to Copland, November 8–9, 1928, in Olmstead, *Correspondence*, 128–29.

25. Gorham Stevens diary entry, June 12, 1929, RomeRareB 176.9.Stev.Dia, AAR archives, Rome.

26. Aaron Copland, "Contemporaries at Oxford, 1931," *Modern Music* 9 (November 1931): 23.

27. Lamond to Roscoe Guernsey, executive secretary of the Academy, February 5, 1938, AAR archives, New York.

28. Kay Norton, *Normand Lockwood: His Life and Music* (Metuchen, NJ: Scarecrow Press, 1993), 29.

29. Ibid.

30. Felix Lamond to John Russell Pope, November 23, 1934, RomeRareB., AAR archives, Rome, according to Martin Brody's research.

31. Alva Johnson, "American Maestro," pt. 1, *New Yorker*, October 20, 1938, 24.

32. Quoted in Lamond, Annual Report—1933, AAR, Rome 30.

33. Lamond, Annual Report—1934, AAR, Rome, 31.

34. Johnson, "American Maestro," pt. 2, *New Yorker*, October 27, 1938, 26.

35. "Janssen Refuses to Conduct in Germany: Displeased Management Warns American," *New York Times*, October 31, 1933, 11.

36. Lamond, Annual Report—1931, AAR, Rome, 24.

37. Felix Lamond to John Russell Pope, November 23, 1934, AAR archives, Rome, according to Martin Brody's research.

38. See Leslie Banner, *A Passionate Preference: The Story of the North Carolina School of the Arts—A History* (Winston-Salem: North Carolina School of the Arts Foundation, 1987).

39. Barbara Heyman, *Samuel Barber: The Composer and His Music* (New York: Oxford University Press, 1992), 134.

40. The portrait of Samuel Barber shown here was made by Robert B. Green, FAAR, 1938. A portrait of Leo Sowerby, made by Frank P. Fairbanks (1875–1939; FAAR 1912), professor in charge of art, appears in chapter 5 of this volume. Fairbanks made a number of portraits of AAR fellows. More recent members of the Academy's artistic and scholarly community view the portraits of the early fellows on its coffee bar wall and remark that, of those represented, only a few are recognizable today: Hanson, Roger Sessions, and Samuel Barber. Fifty years after the Fairbanks portraits were painted, in 1983, the tradition of painting and hanging portraits of Academy arts fellows was resurrected, and portraits of some recent fellows now adorn the adjoining bar wall.

41. Heyman, *Samuel Barber*, 134.

42. Ibid., 134.

43. Ibid., 135.

44. Lamond gives two different dates—December 14 and 17—for the concert; Heyman gives the fourteenth.

45. Lamond, Annual Report—1936, AAR, Rome, 35.

46. Lamond, Annual Report—1938, AAR, Rome, 35.

47. "Opera and Concert Asides: Young Composer Obtains Operatic Rights to *Ethan Frome*," *New York Times*, December 17, 1939, 129.

48. David Diamond told the author about Naginski's suicide. Michael H. Kater, *Composers of the Nazi Era: Egk, Hindemith, Weill, Hartmann, Orff, Pfitzner, Schoenberg, Strauss* (New York: Oxford University Press, 2000), 47. As opposed to Copland, when he headed Tanglewood's summer program, guest composer Hindemith did not think Tanglewood student composers' music ought to be performed. "After one of the Tanglewood courses in 1940 Charles Naginski, a young Jew originally from Egypt, drowned himself in the Housatonic River, apparently because Hindemith had found him wanting in contrapuntal technique."

49. John A. Emerson, "William D. Denny," *The New Grove Dictionary of Music and Musicians*, 7: 217.

50. "War Halts Fellowships at Academy in Rome," *New York Times*, December 18, 1940, 27.

51. "Harvard Senior Wins Rome Music Award," *New York Times*, June 9, 1941, 28.

52. Howard Pollack, "Harold Shapero," *The New Grove Dictionary of Music and Musicians*, 23: 212–13. See also Howard Pollack, *Harvard Composers* (Metuchen, NJ: Scarecrow Press, 1992).

53. David Diamond to the AAR, February 4, 1969, AAR archives, New York.

Chapter Two

A History of the Rome Prize in Music Composition, 1947–2006

Richard Trythall

Preface

I have been closely associated with the American Academy in Rome since I arrived there in September 1964 as that year's Rome Prize Fellow in Music Composition. Following a three-year fellowship, I remained in Rome as a recipient of a Guggenheim Fellowship and, after winning the 1969 *Kranichsteiner Musikpreis* in piano, I settled in Rome as a freelance composer-pianist. In the fall of 1970 I was composer-in-residence at the Academy and began assisting with the Academy's music program on a regular basis. I have continued to do so—first as an adviser to the composers-in-residence and subsequently as the music liaison.

The following history is the culmination of several projects that I have undertaken, in my capacity as music liaison, with the purpose of historicizing the American Academy's music program. It builds on the reports I regularly wrote for Academy publications describing the Academy's musical activities (1974–2006); on the brochure "American Academy in Rome: Music Composition and Performance Activity," which I compiled in 1976 and updated in 1994; on the documentation I gathered while overseeing the digitalization of the Academy's Concert Recordings Archive in 2003; and on my personal knowledge of the Academy's music program throughout the period in which I have been assisting or actively overseeing the program in Rome (1970–present).

Direct contributions by the composers themselves have been crucial throughout these projects. In preparing the "Music Composition and Performance Activity" brochure in 1976 and its update in 1994, I requested fellows and composers-in-residence to fill out questionnaires regarding their creative work while at the Academy. Their written responses provided the corresponding information listed in that brochure. Similarly, in preparation for the present history, I circulated a more detailed questionnaire in 2006—this time by e-mail as well as by mail, fax, and phone contact. My colleagues were, once again, forthcoming and informative, and their responses have been incorporated in the present text.

With regard to the Academy's development as an institution (i.e., the context within which the music program functioned), I have consulted the Academy's *Annual Reports* (1946 to the present) and Academy newsletter publications. Other sources of information have been personal interviews, correspondence, and materials that I have gathered from 1964 to the present.

In writing this history, I have adopted the following convention: Where the text concerns my organization of the Academy's music program in Rome and discusses matters for which I was personally responsible, I write in the first person. Where the text concerns my work as a fellow, composer, or pianist, it is dealt with in the third person.

Introduction

The following account details the creative work accomplished by the ninety-nine Rome Prize winners in music composition and the fifty-two composers-in-residence who took part in the music program of the American Academy in Rome from 1947 to 2006. It also traces the Academy's significant development during the same period. This institutional transformation, in fact, is inextricably connected with the music program and is a remarkable success story in its own right. For purposes of this narrative, the two histories are braided together, alternating discussions of general Academy policy and music program matters with detailed summaries of each year's creative activity in music composition. The former discusses the challenges and institutional responses from 1947 to 2006, explains how these conditioned the music program, and outlines the development of that program. The latter supplies each composer fellow's biographical details and lists their compositions, performances, commissions, awards, and collaborations during the fellowship. The biographical material should help place each fellow in perspective while the work list, in addition to documenting the intense creative activity carried out at the Academy, should explain a good deal about the fellows' varied musical interests. Information is also given about the work of each composer-in-residence and the programs they organized while at the Academy. Rounding out these brief summaries are listings of the visiting artists (composers and performers) who lived in the Academy community for some part of that year—independently or as the "significant others" of fellows or residents—and their contributions to the year's musical offerings. Taken together, this information intends to offer a thumbnail view of each year's varied musical community and the activity carried out by that community. The narrative is subdivided temporally according to the tenures of the Academy's directors.[1]

There is little attempt in these summaries to outline fellows' careers following their fellowship. Although a comprehensive account would demonstrate that fellows and residents had served and frequently led American musical life on multiple levels throughout the United States (approximately 50 percent of the Pulitzer Prizes in Music Composition, for example, have been awarded to fellows or residents of the American Academy in Rome), such documentation lies beyond the scope of a history that is as much a portrait of the institution as it is a portrait of the artists. Nor does this history attempt to analyze or characterize the personal creative styles of fellows.[2]

For those readers interested in forming their own opinion about the music and the composers, the Academy's Recording Archives are available for consultation at the Library of the American Academy in Rome. This collection of eighty-six CDs contains the original Academy concert recordings from 1955 to 2002 of approximately three hundred chamber music and orchestral compositions and provides a wide view of contemporary American musical thought in the last half of the twentieth century. Performances of a large number of the compositions cited in the following account—often the first performance—will be found here. Less comprehensive, but more readily accessible, is the set of four CDs entitled *Americans in Rome: Music by Fellows of the American Academy in Rome* issued on Bridge Records (9271). This set contains the music of thirty-seven composers who were fellows at the American Academy in Rome, twenty-seven of whom are discussed as fellows or composers-in-residence in the following history.

1947–59, Director: Laurance P. Roberts

The Music Program: 1947–59

The American Academy in Rome reopened officially in the fall of 1947—three years and three months after the American army had triumphantly entered Rome. The Marshall Plan for "restoring the confidence of the European people"[3] had just been announced and the Fulbright-Hays program for educational exchange had been initiated the year before. It was a time for new beginnings, fresh approaches, and a new look at the United States' vital relationship with Europe. The Academy, too, was making a fresh beginning under the leadership of its forty-year-old director, Laurance Page Roberts. Roberts, whose upbringing, education, and temperament were tailor-made for this demanding job, had a guiding vision for the new Academy: "to make of the Academy a forum of artists and scholars where the students could share their Academy experiences with men and women who had already made a mark in their profession."[4]

In the field of music composition, this vision meant introducing a program of residencies by older composers—not as teachers, but as guiding spirits who lived at the Academy working on their own, yet associating on a daily basis with the fellows—at meals, Academy functions, and during informal get-togethers organized by the residents themselves. These senior composers also organized the musical events for each year—most particularly the concerts that featured the fellows' music (an annual "Spring Concert" and later the orchestral concerts offered to the Academy by RAI Radiotelevisione Italiana, the Italian national public broadcasting company). They also had the important function of maintaining contact with the surrounding Italian musical world. Their recognized professional standing underscored the quality of the Rome Prize program and was of particular service in securing Italian consent and cooperation in a number of vital Academy musical projects.

During Roberts's remarkable fourteen-year tenure (this figure includes the initial year he spent preparing for the reopening), his program of residencies was to bring many of America's leading composers to live and work at the Academy: Aaron Copland, Samuel Barber, Randall Thompson, Douglas Moore, and Otto Luening, as well as the Russian American composers Nicolas Nabokov and Alexei Haieff, the Czech American Bohuslav Martinů, and the Italian composer Goffredo Petrassi. Some of these composers spent three months or so at the Academy, others remained for the entire year. Certainly all "had already made a mark in their profession" and all brought companionship and counsel of a high level to the fellows. Often they brought additional financial and logistical support as well, thereby considerably expanding the offerings of the music program.

Nicolas Nabokov (RAAR 1953–55)[5] provides a good example of such a contribution. Nabokov, cousin to the novelist Vladimir Nabokov and Secretary General of the Congress for Cultural Freedom headquartered in Paris, served as Composer-in-Residence for an exceptional two-year period. In that time he organized two important events. First, thanks to his executive position with the financially well-heeled Congress, he was able to organize and finance a truly international festival of contemporary music, "Music in Our Time" (April 4–14, 1954). This festival took place at the Academy's elegant Villa Aurelia and composers from throughout Europe and North and South America were brought to Rome to attend the event. American participants, housed at the Academy, included Virgil Thomson, Ben Weber, Lou Harrison, and Elliott Carter. (Carter was currently a fellow at the Academy.) The festival included concerts, roundtable discussions, and an impressive buffet reception offered by the Academy on opening night. In his report as director, Roberts noted that this festival "brought together for the first time many of the world's greatest musical figures" and singled out Elliott Carter's String Quartet no. 1 as "one of the most acclaimed pieces to be played at the Festival."[6] This international occasion was unique in the Roman contemporary musical life of that decade and would be remembered long after by the participants.

Figure 2.1. Goffredo Petrassi and Isabel and Laurance Roberts at AAR Spring Concert reception, 1955. Courtesy of the American Academy in Rome.

Nabokov's second contribution to the Academy's music program was of even more lasting importance. In the following year, he arranged a collaboration between the Academy and the Rome Radio Orchestra—one of four orchestras maintained by RAI Radiotelevisione Italiana. This orchestra was generally acknowledged to be one of the best orchestras in Europe for the performance of contemporary music. (The first flutist Severino Gazzelloni was only the best known among its many fine instrumentalists.) By the mid-1950s, in fact, the Italian musical world had made a brilliant new beginning, producing a set of avant-garde composers of international stature—Bruno Maderna, Luigi Nono, and Luciano Berio—and establishing an infrastructure that included the RAI's four symphonic orchestras (located in Rome, Naples, Milan, and Turin), its electronic music studio in Milan, the Venice Biennale's Contemporary Music Festival, and forward-looking music publishers such as Casa Ricordi and Edizioni Suvini Zerboni. The commissions and performance offered by these institutions supported Italian contemporary musicians in a manner that often left American musicians envious. The collaboration set up by Nabokov consisted of an orchestra concert performed by the Rome Radio Orchestra, recorded and broadcast by the RAI, and devoted to music composed by the recipients of the Rome Prize in Music Composition. This RAI/AAR collaboration was to become an annual event, lasting until 1984. It supplied an additional motivation to the fellows who, in many cases, dedicated much of their fellowship year to composing music for this summer orchestra concert.

Another composer-in-residence who contributed to the Academy's music program throughout this period was Alexei Haieff (FAAR 1947–49,[7] RAAR 1952–53, 1958–59). Among other accomplishments, Haieff arranged for the jury of the prestigious International Society of Contemporary Music (ISCM) composition competition to meet at the American Academy in late January and early February 1959 (Haieff was also part of the jury). The jury's deliberations assigned George Rochberg (FAAR 1951) first prize for his *Cheltenham Concerto* for chamber orchestra (1958) and George Balch Wilson (a fellow at the time) an honorable mention. Later that year, also thanks to Haieff's efforts, the Academy joined with the Italian branch of the ISCM, the Società Italiana per Musica Contemporanea (SIMC), to sponsor a joint concert of contemporary Italian and American music. These collaborative concerts were to continue intermittently for the next eight years and were particularly successful in creating a sense of community between Academy fellows and their Italian colleagues. Additionally, they provided fellows with more performance opportunities and direct exposure within the Roman community.

Still another composer-in-residence, Otto Luening, brought electronic music to the Academy. A pioneer in the tape music developments of the 1950s, cofounder of the Columbia-Princeton Electronic Music Studio in 1959, and a trustee of the Academy from 1950 to 1964, Luening's experience, enthusiasm, and encouragement galvanized the interest of many of the fellows—George Balch Wilson, William O. Smith, John Eaton, and Richard Trythall—to name only a few. During his first residency in the spring and summer of 1958, Luening tapped Columbia's Alice M. Ditson fund to purchase a library of contemporary music recordings for the composers' use. When he returned for a six-week summer visit in 1961, he converted the composers' listening room[8] (located in the basement of the Academy) into a rudimentary electronic music studio. This studio eventually contained three sine wave oscillators, a spring reverberation unit, a microphone, an Ampex stereo portable tape recorder and a mixing console. Added to the listening room's professional 350 Series Ampex tape recorder and a radio/record player console, this equipment permitted composers to carry out experiments with sound.[9] In 1964–65 when Luening returned for a year-long stay as composer-in-residence, the Ditson fund covered the purchase of one of the first portable electronic music synthesizers in existence, the Syn-ket, invented and constructed by Paul Ketoff. Ketoff, an audio engineer involved with creating sound effects for Rome's Cinecittà, had designed the original studio for the Academy and his guidance and unflagging enthusiasm about the electronic production of sound played a key role in making the fledgling studio operable. With the Syn-ket installed, the listening room became a fairly advanced electronic studio for the time and it served as such for many of the fellows. The studio was also used by composers who were not associated with the Academy, both American (Larry Austin, Alvin Curran) and Italian (Aldo Clementi, Mauro Bortolotti).

Throughout the coming years, the presence of the composers-in-residence, as originally envisioned by Roberts, would significantly enrich the Academy's music program. Their knowledge and counsel were invaluable to the fellows and they contributed to the entire community by giving lectures and—for those composers who were also performers—by performing concerts at the Academy. They frequently brought other musicians to visit and perform at the Academy and organized lecture series or developed other initiatives that brought more music to the community. As a group, particularly those who remained throughout the entire academic year, the composers-in-residence were generous with their time and in their efforts on behalf of the fellows and the community-at-large.

The composer-in-residence position also enriched the music program in other ways. It offered the opportunity for senior composers who had not previously had the Rome Prize to come to the Academy—to enjoy the tranquility that the Academy offers for serious creative work, the stimulation provided by the resident community, and the inspiration afforded by Rome itself. For composers who were past fellows, it offered an opportunity to renew their acquaintance with the ongoing mission of the Academy. The residency position, however, was only one of several means that permitted composers to continue their relationship with the American Academy. They could also spend time at the Academy as a visiting artist, work on various Academy committees, take part in the Rome Prize jury, participate in panels, concerts, and fund-raising events designed to publicize the Rome Prize in Music Composition, become active in the Academy's Society of Fellows with its many regional branches, etc. All were means of reaffirming interest and concern for the "fellowship" and of remaining in active contact with the institution. The fact that so many composers chose to continue their involvement in these different ways is perhaps the surest sign of their appreciation of the Academy and the impact their experience in Rome—personally and professionally—had on their lives.

As director, Roberts also recognized the social role the Academy was called on to play in postwar Italy. During the fourteen years of his tenure, Italy would make a slow but steady recovery from its devastated economic and cultural life to arrive at the economic "boom" of the 1960s. The Academy, as the chief representative of American culture and scholarship in Italy, had an important role to play in this transitional period. In addition to opening a window on the best in contemporary American culture, it could, and did, provide a common ground for reaffirming mutual respect. Both Italians and Americans recall Roberts's leadership with genuine gratitude. He and his equally charming wife, Isabel, entertained in the old sense of the word and their warmth and hospitality became proverbial. This gracious social presence—the luncheons, dinners, receptions, and parties—was vital in stimulating interaction among the fellows as well as between fellows and Italian artists and scholars. At the same time, it came to symbolize the genuine American interest in the rejuvenation of the Italian cultural scene and provided the Italian community a tangible point of contact with that interest.[10]

Roberts's active social role translated into a number of advantages for the music program. The ample receptions following the annual RAI/AAR concerts (which were initially held outdoors in front of the Villa Aurelia), for example, served as token repayments for the RAI's immeasurable gift of professional support. The warm reception provided to conductor Serge Koussevitzky when he was hosted at the Villa Aurelia in the spring of 1950 served to generate financial support from the Koussevitzky Foundation for several years thereafter. The reception that Alexei Haieff arranged in honor of his friend Igor Stravinsky was attended not only by the Academy community but by the entire musical elite of Rome as well, thereby underscoring the Academy's cultural presence in the city. Likewise the sumptuous Villa Aurelia reception hosted in honor of Senator and Mrs. Fulbright in December 1956—with 350 guests in attendance—served as a further reminder of the Academy's importance as the United States' prime cultural representative in Italy. It also demonstrated appreciation for a cultural exchange program that had become tightly interconnected with the Academy's own music fellowship program.

Add these festive occasions to the list of Academy concerts showcasing American talent in Rome that included, among many others, John Cage performing a program of his music for prepared piano, Ralph Kirkpatrick performing Scarlatti's harpsichord sonatas, Leo Smit performing Copland's piano work—and to the list of musicians who were privately entertained by the Robertses: Leonard Bernstein, Giancarlo Menotti, Yehudi Menuhin, Paul Hindemith, Lou Harrison, Quincy Porter, Virgil Thomson, Louise Talma, Irving Fine, Ben Weber, Robert Palmer, Noel Lee, Oliver Strunk, Paul Henry Lang—to name only a few—and one has a sense of the intensive efforts Roberts made, both directly and indirectly, in support of the music program—a program that was an important, but by no means the only, jewel in the Academy's brilliant crown of disciplines.[11]

Quite naturally, Roberts also maintained close relations with the United States Information Service (USIS, the cultural and educational division of the American Embassy until 1999), and with its dependent, the Italian Fulbright Commission. In these early years, as Roberts pointed out, Fulbright grantees in music composition were "admitted as Fellows if they have passed the Academy's juries as well as the Fulbright juries."[12] Such interlocking grants were particularly useful since they respected the Academy's jury system and permitted the Academy to maintain a normal quota of three overlapping composer fellowships a year. There were, in fact, three endowed Academy Music Fellowships available at the time: the Frederick A. Juilliard Fellowship, the Walter Damrosch Fellowship, and the Horatio Parker Fellowship, but the funds that supported these fellowships did not necessarily generate sufficient revenue to cover the entire cost of each fellowship.

For that matter, the composer-in-residence position also depended on outside support since no stipend was attached to this position. Composers-in-residence arrived on Guggenheim Fellowships, Senior Fulbright grants, or found other financial support for their stay at the Academy. A telling case in this regard occurred in the 1950–51 academic year. In that year the Academy hosted five composer fellows simultaneously: Ulysses Kay, Harold Shapero, Lukas Foss, Gail Kubik, and George Rochberg—three of whom were on Fulbright grants. In the same year, the Academy also hosted Leo Smit, a Fulbright grantee in piano but also a composer, and Aaron Copland, a Senior Fulbright grantee, as composer-in-residence. This exceptional concentration of musical talent amply illustrates the benefits of interlocking grants.[13]

The Composers: 1947–59

1947–48: For the first fellowship year under Roberts's direction, Samuel Barber (FAAR 1937) was appointed as the composer-in-residence. Barber, who had previously spent two years at the Academy as a fellow (1935–37), was closely involved with Italy, and would, in fact, return to the Academy as a resident in the fall of 1949. (He was on a Guggenheim Fellowship in both years). The new fellows were Alexei Haieff (Biagoveshchensk, Siberia, 1914–94) and Andrew Imbrie (New York, NY, 1921–2007). The jury's choice of these two composers was a sign of things to come. Haieff had studied at the Juilliard School of Music with Rubin Goldmark and Frederick Jacobi and with Nadia Boulanger in both Cambridge and Paris. Personally and aesthetically he was closely linked with Stravinsky and with Stravinsky's music. Imbrie, on the other hand, had been a student of Roger Sessions (FAAR 1931)—first as an undergraduate at Princeton University, then as a graduate at the University of California, Berkeley. Haieff and Imbrie's musical styles differed significantly and the jury would seem to have struck a balance between two competing musical camps. This stylistic breadth was to be a constant throughout the following years, testimony to the width of vision represented on the constantly changing panel of composers and music professionals who comprised the annual Rome Prize juries. During his two fellowship years (1947–49), Haieff would complete several orchestral works: Concerto in One Movement for violin and orchestra, Ballet in B-flat ("Beauty and the Beast"), and much of his Piano Concerto no. 1. Imbrie, who was an instructor at the University of California, Berkeley, when he received the Rome Prize, would also remain at the Academy for two years (1947–49). He composed his Piano Sonata, a *Divertimento* for flute, bassoon, trumpet, violin, cello, and piano, *Three Songs* for soprano with piano or orchestral accompaniment (1949) and began *On the Beach at Night* for mixed chorus and string orchestra (premiered at UC Berkeley in 1950). The year concluded with a chamber music concert devoted to the fellows' work. This concert, the Spring Concert, was to be held during each fellowship year (usually in the late spring) and served (and continues to serve) both as a showcase for fellows' earlier work and as a stimulus for writing new works to be premiered during this concert. In addition to paying all costs of the concert, the Academy provided a copying fund to help cover the expenses of preparing scores and parts. The first Spring Concert presented Haieff's Ballet Suite *The Princess Zondilda and Her Entourage* (written for Merce Cunningham, 1946) for flute, bassoon, trumpet, violin, cello, and piano, his *Five Pieces for Piano* (1947), and the first performances of Imbrie's Piano Sonata and *Divertimento.*

1948–49: Both Haieff and Imbrie remained at the Academy through the following year (the fellowship's term of residence was for two years with the occasional possibility of a third-year extension) and, with the arrival of the new fellow, Jack Beeson (Muncie, IN, 1921–2010), the 1948–49 year completed the Academy's design to have three overlapping fellowships in music composition. Such overlapping fellowships had numerous advantages, not the least being that the second-year fellows could help the first year fellows by, in Roberts's words, "passing on some of their experience to the new comers."[14] Fellows Beeson, Imbrie, and Haieff were joined in March by Douglas Stuart Moore: composer-in-residence, Academy trustee (1945–67), McDowell Professor at Columbia University, and longtime chair of Columbia University's music department. In residence from March through June 1949, it is possible that Moore was working on his opera, *Giants in the Earth* (premiere: Columbia Opera Workshop, March 1951; Pulitzer Prize 1951). Beeson had already worked as Moore's assistant at the Columbia Opera Workshop. Pursuing his operatic interest, Beeson would take full advantage of his two-year fellowship (1948–50) by composing and writing the libretto for a three-act opera, *Jonah* (play by Paul Goodman). The Spring Concert contained performances of Beeson's Fifth Sonata for Piano (1946), Haieff's Sonata for Two Pianos (1945), and Imbrie's *Three Songs* for soprano and piano (premiere) and String Quartet (1942; New York Music Critics' Award, 1944). The orchestral version of Imbrie's *Three Songs* was premiered in Lucca, Italy, in 1949 and his *Ballad* for orchestra (1947, composed for his master's thesis at UC Berkeley) was premiered by the Rome Radio Orchestra in 1949. Shortly after the Spring Concert, Moore arranged for two further concerts: John Cage performed his works for prepared piano and Andor Foldes played a piano recital of contemporary American music. With the completion of their fellowship years, Andrew Imbrie returned to the University of California, Berkeley, as an assistant professor. He would return to the Academy as a visiting artist (1953–54) and as composer-in-residence for the 1967–68 fellowship year. Alexei Haieff remained in Rome on a Guggenheim Fellowship, completing his Piano Concerto (premiered by the Boston Symphony Orchestra, October 1952; New York Music Critics' Circle Award in 1952). Haieff, in fact, maintained his home in Rome, with occasional absences while filling lecture positions in the United States, until his death in 1994. He served as the Academy's composer-in-residence in 1952–53 and in 1958–59, lived there as visiting artist in 1956–57, and appears to have given assistance on other occasions throughout the 1950s as well. Very likely his elegant manner, wry humor, and aristocratic charm would have endeared him to the Robertses. Certainly Haieff remembered them warmly, and for him the Academy was never quite the same once they had left.[15]

1949–50: This fellowship year brought Ulysses Kay (Tucson, AZ, 1917–95) and Harold S. Shapero (Lynn, MA, 1920–2013) as fellows. Kay, the first African American composer to receive the Rome Prize in Music Composition, had studied at the University of Arizona, at the Eastman School with Howard Hanson, at Yale University with Paul Hindemith, and at Columbia University with Otto Luening immediately prior to the fellowship. He remained for three years (1949–52) and completed four chamber works: String Quartet in F (premiered by the American University Quartet, National Gallery of Art, Washington, DC, 1953), Brass Quartet (premiered by the Third Street Music School Quartet, Brooklyn Museum, New York, 1952), Partita in A for violin and piano (premiered on the Spring Concert, 1952), *Fugitive Songs* for mezzo-soprano and piano (premiered at Town Hall, NY, 1957), and several larger works: *Pietà* for English horn and string orchestra (premiered by the Knickerbocker Chamber Orchestra, Town Hall, NY, 1958), *Sinfonia in E* for orchestra (premiered by Eastman-Rochester Symphony Orchestra, 1951), a *Short Suite for Concert Band* (commissioned and premiered by Baylor University Golden Wave Band, TX, 1951), and a good part of his *Three Pieces after Blake* for soprano and orchestra (premiered at Cooper Union, NY, 1955). His *Suite for Orchestra* (1945) was performed by the Turin Radio Orchestra in 1952. Shapero, who had worked with Walter Piston and Paul Hindemith at Harvard and studied with Nadia Boulanger while she was living in the United States, had been awarded the AAR World War II Prize in 1941.[16] He was a Fellow of the Academy from 1949–50 under a Fulbright Fellowship and was awarded the Academy's Walter Damrosch Fellowship as a second-year fellow (1950–51). During his time at the Academy, Shapero composed *Credo for Orchestra* (premiered by the Louisville Orchestra, 1957). Samuel Barber returned as composer-in-residence for three months in the fall. This period, which included his two residencies at the American Academy, saw the completion of *Knoxville Summer of 1915*, the *Medea: Ballet Suite* (in 1947), and his Piano Sonata (in 1949). The Spring Concert, which was moved forward to November in order to coincide with Barber's residency, contained Beeson's *Fourth Sonata* for piano, Haieff's *Three Pieces* for violin and piano, Kay's *Suite* for oboe and piano (1943), Kay's *Quintet* for piano and strings (premiere), and Shapero's *Second* and *Third Sonata* for piano (performed by the composer). At the conclusion of this year, Jack Beeson returned to his position at Columbia University. He took an active role in the Academy's Society of Fellows, returned to Rome as composer-in-residence in 1965–66, and served as a trustee of the Academy from 1975–87.

1950–51: This fellowship year was a particularly intense year for the music program. In addition to Kay and Shapero, new fellows Lukas Foss (Berlin, Germany, 1922–2009), Gail T. Kubik (South Coffeyville, OK, 1914–84), and George Rochberg (Paterson, NJ, 1918–2005) arrived. Foss, who had studied in Berlin, in Paris, at the Curtis Institute, and at Yale University with Paul Hindemith, had been the pianist for the Boston Symphony Orchestra for several years preceding his fellowship. He would remain at the Academy from 1950 through part of the 1952–53 year. Kubik, who had studied at the Eastman School of Music, the American Conservatory of Music, and with Walter Piston at Harvard and Nadia Boulanger in Paris, remained for two years (1950–52), while Rochberg, who had studied at the Mannes School and at the Curtis Institute (where he was teaching when he received the Rome Prize), would remain for one year (1950–51). Here again is a particularly telling example of the wide stylistic variety nurtured by the Academy. During his residency as a fellow, Foss worked on his Piano Concerto no. 2. Premiered in the fall of 1951 at the Venice Biennale Festival and then in Boston (with Foss as pianist on both occasions), the Concerto received the Boston Symphony's award for the best contemporary work of that year, and in 1954 it received the New York Music Critics' Award as well. Foss also completed an oratorio on Rilke poetry, *Parable of Death.* Kubik, who had composed numerous film scores during the 1940s, had just completed his score for the cartoon *Gerald McBoing-Boing* when he arrived at the Academy (Academy Award: Best Animated Short Film, 1950). During his time on the fellowship he completed both his score for the film *Two Gals and a Guy* and his *Symphony Concertante* for trumpet, viola, piano, and orchestra (drawn from his 1949 score for the film *C-Man*; commissioned and premiered by the Little Orchestra Society of New York, January 1952; Pulitzer Prize 1952). Rochberg composed his *Concert Piece* for 2 pianos and orchestra and began his String Quartet no. 1—a work he completed in 1952 (premiere: Galimir String Quartet, NY, 1953). During this year Rochberg developed his friendship with Luigi Dallapiccola, Italy's leading twelve-tone composer. Aaron Copland, who arrived on January 1, 1951, as composer-in-residence, was busy not only with his own composing, but also with conducting and lecturing engagements. He conducted the Rome Radio Orchestra in a concert of his own works, lectured in Florence, Naples, and Rome, and organized two concerts of American music at the Academy. These functioned as the fellows' Spring Concert and were funded by a grant from the Koussevitzky Music Foundation. In addition to music by Piston, Diamond, Rorem, Thomson, and Sessions, the programs presented music by fellows Lukas Foss (*Oboe Concerto*),

Gail Kubik (two movements from his Symphony in E-flat), composer-in-residence Aaron Copland (Quartet for Piano and Strings), and visiting artist Leo Smit (*Variations in G*). Smit was at the Academy on a Fulbright grant in piano (1950–52). A composer as well as a pianist, he contributed in both capacities. He returned as composer-in-residence for the 1972–73 year. Harold Shapero returned to Boston midway through his second fellowship year owing to a death in the family. Subsequently he became a founding member of Brandeis University's music department. He would return as composer-in-residence in 1971. At the end of his fellowship year, George Rochberg returned to his position on the faculty of the Curtis Institute in Philadelphia.

1951–52: Kubik, Foss, and Kay were joined by Frank Wigglesworth Jr. (Boston, MA, 1918–96). Wigglesworth, educated at Bard College and Converse College, had studied composition with Otto Luening, Henry Cowell, and Edgard Varèse, and, immediately prior to the Rome Prize, had been teaching at Columbia University. Like Kay, he was to hold the fellowship for three years (1951–54). He completed his Symphony no. 1 (premiere, Vienna Orchestra, 1956), two Masses, a String Trio, Sonata for Harp, began his Symphony no. 2 for strings, and, in an affectionate gesture toward the Academy community, he dedicated *A Book of 9 Easy Pieces* for violin, cello, and piano to cofellows who were also amateur musicians. Randall Thompson (FAAR 1922–25), on sabbatical from his teaching position at Harvard University, was composer-in-residence.[17] He served as an Academy trustee from 1954 to 1969. The Spring Concert presented the premiere of Kay's *Partita* for violin and piano, Wigglesworth's *Serenade* for flute, viola, and guitar, the premiere of Leo Smit's *Fantasy* in F Minor for piano and Thompson's Trio for Oboe, Clarinet, and Viola. With the completion of their fellowships, Ulysses Kay took a job as editorial advisor for Broadcast Music Inc. (BMI) and Gail Kubik remained in Rome to fashion a concert version of *Gerald McBoing-Boing* and compose music for another experimental cartoon, *Transatlantic: A Short Cut through History*. He subsequently returned to America to write the score for William Wyler's film *The Desperate Hours* (1955).

1952–53: New fellow Robert Moevs (La Crosse, WI, 1920–2007) joined Wigglesworth and Foss for the academic year 1952–53. Moevs had studied with Walter Piston at Harvard University, with Nadia Boulanger in Paris (Écoles d'Art, Fontainebleau, and Conservatoire National de Musique), and had just completed his master's degree at Harvard when he received the Rome Prize. He would remain at the Academy for three years (1952–55), in which time he completed his *14 Variations for Orchestra* (commissioned by the Koussevitzky Foundation for the Boston Orchestra), *Three Symphonic Pieces* (premiered by the Cleveland Orchestra, George Szell conducting, 1958), *Cantata Sacra* for baritone, flute, chorus, and instrumental ensemble (premiered on the first RAI/AAR concert, 1955), his *Duo* for oboe and English horn (premiered on the Spring Concert, 1953), and began his Sonata for solo violin. During the course of this year, Foss resigned his third-year fellowship in order to replace Arnold Schönberg as professor of composition at the University of California, Los Angeles. Alexei Haieff (FAAR 1949) served as composer-in-residence. He worked on his *Theme and Variations*, a recasting of material taken from his earlier *Ballet* in B Flat, and organized two concerts, again with the support of the Koussevitzky Music Foundation. Each fellow's work appeared on both concerts: Moevs's Sonata for piano and *Duo* for oboe and English horn (premiere), Wigglesworth's *Four Summer Scenes* for flute, oboe, and string quartet, and *Lake Music* for flute (1946). Haieff's work was represented by *Three Bagatelles* and String Quartet and the programs were completed by Gail Kubik's Second Piano Sonata and Irving Fine's *Partita* for wind quintet.

1953–54: Continuing fellows Moevs and Wigglesworth were joined in 1953–54 by two new fellows: Yehudi Wyner (Calgary, Canada, b. 1929) and Elliott Carter (New York, NY, 1908–2012). Wyner, fresh from his studies at Harvard and Yale University, where he had worked with Paul Hindemith, remained for three years (1953–56), in which time he wrote his Sonata for Piano (premiered on the Spring Concert, 1955, by the composer), *Concert Duo* for violin and piano (commissioned by the sculptor Dimitri Hadzi; premiered on the Spring Concert, 1956, also with Wyner at the piano), as well as *Medieval Latin Lyrics* for voice and piano (1955) and an incomplete String Quartet (1954–55). His *Psalm 143* for chorus, written earlier, was performed on the RAI/AAR concert, 1955. Carter, educated at Harvard University and the École Normale de Musique, Paris, where he had studied privately with Nadia Boulanger, was by this time a well-established composer. His String Quartet no. 1 had been completed in 1951 and his Sonata for Flute, Oboe, Cello, and Harpsichord had been completed in 1953. He would remain at the Academy for one year working on his *Variations for Orchestra* (commissioned by the Louisville Orchestra). Nicolas Nabokov was the composer-in-residence. Possibly he was working on his opera, *Rasputin's End* (completed in 1958) while preparing the international music festival "Music in Our Time," which, as secretary general of the "Congress for Cultural Freedom," he organized for April of this year. The Spring Concert included Wigglesworth's *Concertino* for piano and string orchestra, Carter's *Woodwind Quintet,* Robert Moevs's *Fantasia sopra un motivo* for piano (performed by the composer), Andrew Imbrie's *Serenade* for flute, viola, and piano, and Nicolas Nabokov's *Concerto Chorale* for flute, strings, and piano. Imbrie, on a Guggenheim Fellowship, was a visiting artist for the year. With the conclusion of the fellowship year, Frank Wigglesworth returned to New York to teach at Queens College and The New School for Social Research. He would return as composer-in-residence in 1969–70. Carter returned to the United States, where he completed his *Variations for Orchestra* in 1955 (premiered by the Louisville Orchestra in 1956). This, however, would be the first of numerous residencies that intertwined Carter's creative life with the American Academy in Rome. He would return as composer-in-residence in 1962–63, 1968–69, and 1979–80, and frequently as a visiting artist. He was a trustee of the Academy from 1968 to 1984, serving the music program in a number of vitally important capacities. As he commented later, "The Academy has always been a good place for me to work, and over the years I have usually sought to go there when I had a very large piece to write. . . . The prospect of being in Rome, living there, and carrying on my life in a way I love to do has been very valuable to me."[18]

1954–55: Wyner and Moevs were joined by new fellow Billy Jim Layton (Corsicana, TX, 1924–2004). Layton, educated at the New England Conservatory, Yale, and Harvard, would remain for three years (1954–57), during which time he wrote *Twenty-Four Years* (premiered on the first RAI/AAR concert, July 1955) and *In My Craft or Sullen Art*—both settings of texts by Dylan Thomas for mixed chorus and brass sextet, String Quartet in Two Movements (premiered on the Spring Concert, 1956), and *Three Studies* for piano. The RAI/AAR orchestra concert of 1955 also included his *O Make Me a Mask* for chorus and brass sextet, and his Overture ("An American Portrait") was performed on the RAI/AAR concert, July 1957. As described earlier, thanks to the efforts of Nicolas Nabokov, now in his second year as composer-in-residence, this was the first year of the Academy's collaboration with the Rome Radio Orchestra. The program of the first RAI/AAR concert included, in addition to the premiere of Layton's *Twenty-Four Years* and *O Make Me a Mask,* Wyner's *Psalm 143,* Moevs's *Cantata Sacra* (premiere), as well as Goffredo Petrassi's *Nonsense, "Five Limericks for Four-Part Chorus."* The concert was performed at Villa Aurelia on July 4, 1955, and, symbolically, for the next eleven years the Academy fellows' concert would be scheduled by the RAI to take place on the Saturday evening that fell within the week of July 4. Roberts immediately recognized the importance of this collaboration with the Rome Radio Orchestra and, in his director's report for that year, expressed his hope that the occasion "will set a pattern for similarly sponsored concerts in the future."[19] The Spring Concert featured Wyner's Sonata for piano (premiere), Moevs's *Youthful Songs* for soprano and piano and *Pan* for solo flute, Layton's *Five Studies* for violin and piano, Nabokov's *Silent Songs,* and Vittorio Rieti's *Old English Songs* for soprano and piano. The composer Louise Talma was at the Academy as a visiting artist. At the conclusion of this year, Robert Moevs took a position on the faculty of Harvard University. He would return to the Academy as composer-in-residence in 1960–61.

1955–56: Stanley Walker Hollingsworth (Berkeley, CA, 1924–2003) joined Layton and Wyner as the new composition fellow. Hollingsworth had studied with Darius Milhaud at Mills College, with Giancarlo Menotti at the Curtis Institute, and had taught at Curtis as Menotti's assistant prior to his fellowship.

He was to remain three years (1955–58), in which time he completed a television opera commissioned by NBC, *La Grande Bretèche* (performed in New York by NBC in January 1956), a *Stabat Mater* for mixed chorus and orchestra (premiered by the Turin Radio Orchestra in 1958), a ballet for the first year of Menotti's Festival of Two Worlds, *The Unquiet Graves* (premiered by the John Butler Dance Theatre, Spoleto, summer 1958), and *Dances for Summer* for orchestra (dedicated in part to the Robertses and premiered on the RAI/AAR concert, July 1958). Along with Lee Hoiby, he also helped orchestrate much of Giancarlo Menotti's opera *Maria Golovin* (completed in 1958). Goffredo Petrassi, who was teaching at Rome's St. Cecilia Conservatory and serving as president of the International Society of Contemporary Music (ISCM), acted as composer-in-residence for most of the year. Nabokov, however, returned to oversee the RAI/AAR concert when Petrassi left in order to teach a summer course at the Tanglewood Music Center in Massachusetts. The Spring Concert featured Hollingsworth's Sonata for Oboe and Piano, Wyner's *Four Songs* for tenor and piano, and the premiere of his *Duo* for violin and piano (both with Wyner as pianist) as well as Layton's String Quartet in Two Movements (premiere). The RAI/AAR orchestra concert, July 1956, featured Barber's *Capricorn Concerto* and, in the second half, a concert performance of Hollingsworth's earlier opera, *The Mother*, based on a tale by Hans Christian Andersen. Upon completing his fellowship, Wyner returned to New York as a freelance musician. He would return to the Academy as composer-in-residence in the spring of 1991 and on several other occasions as a visiting artist. He was awarded the Pulitzer Prize in 2006 for his Piano Concerto ("Chiavi in Mano").

1956–57: Two new fellows joined Layton and Hollingsworth: Richard M. Willis Jr. (Mobile, AL, 1929–97) and Salvatore Martirano (Yonkers, NY, 1927–95). Willis, who had studied at the University of Alabama and the Eastman School and had been teaching at Georgia's Shorter College, would remain for one year. He completed *The Playground* (a suite for orchestra) and his *Sonatina* for violin and piano. His Symphony no. 1, written earlier, was performed on the RAI/AAR orchestra concert, July 1957. Martirano, who had studied at Oberlin College and the Eastman School, studied with Luigi Dallapiccola in Florence under a Fulbright grant from 1952 to 1954. He would remain at the Academy for three years (1956–59), during which time he composed *Chansons Innocentes* (three poems by e. e. cummings) and *Ninna Nanna* for soprano and piano (both premiered on the Spring Concert, 1957) and *O,O,O,O, That Shakespeherian Rag* for chorus and instrumental ensemble (1958, commissioned by the League of Composers/International Society for Contemporary Music). His *Contrasto* for orchestra, completed prior to his fellowship (winner of the Sagalyn Prize), was performed on the RAI/AAR orchestra concert, July 1957 (conducted by Bruno Maderna). The composer-in-residence was Bohuslav Martinů, who was working on his opera, *Greek Passion* (based on Nikos Kazantzakis's book *Christ*

Recrucified). Martinů was assisted in his duties by Alexei Haieff, who was living at the Academy as a visiting artist. Haieff arranged the Spring Concert, which presented Willis's *Sonatina* for violin and piano, Martirano's *Chansons Innocentes* and *Ninna Nanna* (premieres), and Martinů's *Three Madrigals* for violin and viola (1947). Upon conclusion of the year, Billy Jim Layton returned to study for his PhD at Harvard University and Richard Willis returned to his teaching post at Shorter College, Rome, Georgia.

1957–58: This fellowship year brought two new fellows to join Martirano and Hollingsworth: Higo H. Harada (Hanford, CA, b. 1927) and William Overton Smith (Sacramento, CA, b. 1926). Harada had studied with Marcel Dick at the Cleveland Institute of Music and was studying in Paris on a Harriet Hale Woolley Scholarship when he received the Rome Prize. He remained at the Academy for three years (1957–60), completing, among others: *Sinfonietta* (premiered on the RAI/AAR concert, July 1958), *Double Concerto* for violin and piano (premiered on the RAI/AAR concert, July 1960), and String Quartet (premiered on the Spring Concert, 1960). He was also active in conducting contemporary music concerts in Rome. Smith, who had studied at the Juilliard School, Mills College, and the University of California, Berkeley, had been teaching at the University of Southern California in Los Angeles when he received the Rome Prize. He remained in Rome for one year, writing a commissioned work to celebrate the opening of the new music building at the University of California, Berkeley, *A Song for Santa Cecilia's Day* for symphonic band and chorus, as well as *Four Pieces* for clarinet, violin, and piano and *Quartet* for clarinet, violin, cello, and piano. Otto Luening arrived for the spring and summer as composer-in-residence. The Spring Concert featured the premieres of Smith's *Four Pieces* for clarinet, violin, and piano, of Hollingsworth's Andante for String Quartet and Agnus Dei for String Quartet, Flute, and Voices, as well as a performance of Luening's *Song, Poem, and Dance for Flute and String Quartet* (with flutist Severino Gazzelloni). At the conclusion of the year, Stanley Hollingsworth, completing his three-year fellowship, continued his compositional work in Vienna on a Guggenheim grant, while William O. Smith returned to take up his teaching post at the University of Southern California. Smith would return to the Academy on a Guggenheim Fellowship two years later.

1958–59: The fellows Harada and Martirano were joined by George Balch Wilson (Grand Island, NE, b. 1927). Wilson had studied at the University of Michigan and at the Conservatoire Royale de Musique in Brussels under a Fulbright grant. His teachers were Ross Lee Finney, Nadia Boulanger, and Roger Sessions. Prior to winning the Rome Prize, he had been working on his doctorate at the University of Michigan. He remained at the Academy for three years (1958–61), in which time he composed *Six Pieces for Orchestra* (premiered

Figure 2.2. AAR Director Laurance Roberts and Alexei Haieff, 1955. Courtesy of the American Academy in Rome.

on the RAI/AAR concert, 1960) and *Six Pieces for Piano* (premiered at the Spring Concert, 1960). During this period he became well acquainted with the contemporary music scene in Italy, with the music of Maderna, Berio, and Nono, and with Karlheinz Stockhausen's electronic works through performances sponsored by the German Academy in Rome.[20] Alexei Haieff (FAAR 1949), once again the composer-in-residence, was working on his Symphony no. 3 in this period. He inaugurated a Tuesday evening series of recorded music for interested fellows, brought the ISCM jury to meet at the Villa Aurelia, and set up a collaborative concert that included music by Higo Harada and the Italian composers of SIMC. The Spring Concert included Haieff's *Five Piano Pieces*, Wilson's *Fantasy* for violin and piano, Beeson's *Six Lyrics* for soprano and piano, and Harada's *Adagio and Allegro* for String Trio. Haieff also arranged for a closing concert, held in the gardens of the Villa Aurelia in July, that featured music by Haydn, Tomasi, Varèse, Mozart, and Barber. Jack Beeson, on a Guggenheim Fellowship, was a visiting artist during the year. At the year's conclusion, Salvatore Martirano returned to New York to compose. He received a Guggenheim Fellowship in the following year and joined the faculty of the University of Illinois in 1963.

1959–69, Directors: Richard Arthur Kimball, Frank E. Brown

The Music Program: 1959–69

The fellowship year starting in 1959 coincided with the arrival of the sixties and with a "change of the guard" for the American Academy. The architect Richard Arthur Kimball replaced Laurance P. Roberts as director in December 1959. Kimball would remain in charge for six years; he was then succeeded by Professor Frank E. Brown, who was director until the fall of 1969. Although not as socially spectacular as the preceding decade, the Academy under these directors was just as comfortable and conducive to serious work. Continuity for the fellows was assured by the interlocking fellowships, by the length of the fellowship itself, by the composer-in-residence program, and also by the Academy's Italian office staff, Bianca Passeri and Maria Verzotto, who proved to be a constant source of information regarding Rome. Of particular importance to the music program was Principessa Margherita Rospigliosi, who was on the staff of the Academy for almost two decades—from 1951 through 1969. She was the daughter of Principe Don Giambattista Rospigliosi and Ethel Bronson from Boston and, consequently, understood both the Italian and the American mentality. She also knew Rome and Roman society extremely well and was particularly partial to music and musicians. She kept a piano in her home on the Academy's grounds (Villino Bellacci), often housed visiting musicians who might need a room, and facilitated connections with the Roman musical scene—assisting fellows and residents alike in entering that world. Through the years her advice was of great assistance to the music program, while her mix of aristocratic grace and down-to-earth humor made for many a lively evening and cheered many a fellow in time of need.

Throughout this period, the music program continued in the same way as it had been developed during the fifties. Three-year fellowships would be discontinued after 1967, but the pattern of three, occasionally four, overlapping two-year fellowships was to continue until 1975. As had become the custom by the late fifties, the composers' fellowship year was defined by the annual chamber music concert (the Spring Concert) and the summer RAI/AAR orchestra concert; these two occasions provided ample stimulus for compositional projects.

For much of this period and beyond (until 1975), most of the composers-in-residence lived at the Academy for the entire year. Many had previously been fellows and, therefore, were familiar both with the Academy and with Rome. This continuity and experience contributed stability and a sense of perspective to the fellows' year and also allowed the residents time to establish the contacts necessary to generate projects that might be useful to the fellows. Although the concert budget administered by the composer-in-residence was limited, it did permit some extra initiatives. Additional support might be obtained from

USIS and further performance opportunities were made available through collaborations with various Italian institutions: the Società Italiana per Musica Contemporanea (1958–66), the Accademia Filarmonica (1964–66), and the Amici della Musica di Perugia (1961–63). Jack Beeson joined Otto Luening in supporting the electronic studio and the Academy's concerts of contemporary Italian and American music through Columbia's Alice M. Ditson Fund. On occasions, composers-in-residence also contributed personally to cover extra expenses. These additional concerts were primarily arranged by the composer-in-residence, but concerts were occasionally generated through the fellows' contacts as well.

In and around Rome, the sixties were quite congenial to *stranieri*. The exchange rate was favorable to the dollar and Americans could live nicely on relatively little. There was, in fact, a steady flow of American artists and musicians passing through Rome in the sixties (usually on study grants of some sort) and many decided to stay for a while, some for a good while. Some of these were also past fellows of the Academy—particularly in the visual arts, but a few were composers as well. On the musical side this scene included (for varying lengths and at different periods) performers such as the flutist Fritz Kraber, the clarinettist Jerry Kirkbride, the sopranos Joan Logue and Carol Plantamura, the violist Joan Kalisch, the pianists Joe Rollino and Paul Sheftel, and composers such as William O. Smith, John Eaton, Richard Trythall, John Heineman, Alvin Curran, James Dashow, Frederic Rzewski, Richard Teitelbaum, Allan Bryant, Jeffrey Levine, Joel Chadabe, Jerome Rosen, Lawrence Moss, and Larry Austin (whose experience with group improvisation at the University of California, Davis, stimulated similar experiments in Rome)—to name just a few. This group, particularly those living and working independently in Rome for a length of time, formed an extremely useful network of contacts and reference points. Their knowledge of the Roman music scene and their direct acquaintance with Italians was a further resource in facilitating the newly arrived fellows' entrance into that milieu. And, of course, the Academy was useful in turn: first, by its very presence in Rome, the role it played and the number of American musicians it annually attracted to Rome as fellows, residents, visiting artists, significant others; second, by the breadth and quality of its scholarly and artistic activities; and third, by the direct support it gave to American performers and composers in Rome. Many of the performers mentioned above performed regularly on Academy programs and works by nonfellow composers were frequently included in concerts sponsored by the Academy. It was, in effect, a mutually beneficial situation and made the sixties in Rome a particularly stimulating period.[21]

The Italian musical world of the sixties was also in ferment. In addition to the Rome Radio Orchestra's remarkable support for contemporary orchestra music, a new organization, Nuova Consonanza, was founded in 1959. This association of Rome-based composers and performers was to become the primary contemporary music organization in Rome. From 1963 onward, it sponsored an annual festival that presented both European and American contemporary music to Rome. For a while Nuova Consonanza had its own chamber orchestra and even a pioneering improvisation group organized by the composer Franco Evangelisti. The American Academy's collaboration with Nuova Consonanza began immediately—both privately through composer-performer fellows such as the clarinetist William O. Smith, the pianists John Eaton and Richard Trythall, the trombonist John Heineman, who played in many of the earliest performances, as well as institutionally—by cosponsoring or hosting concerts, housing guests, facilitating contacts with American artists, providing rehearsal space, and so on.[22] Through the years the Academy has collaborated with a number of Roman new music organizations, but Nuova Consonanza has remained the principal contact organization to the present day.

The Composers: 1959–69

1959–60: New fellow John C. Eaton (Bryn Mawr, PA, b. 1935) joined Wilson and Harada at the Academy. Eaton, a student of Roger Sessions, Milton Babbitt, and Edward Cone at Princeton University, was in graduate school there when he received the Rome Prize. He would remain at the Academy for three years (1959–62), working principally on an opera, *Heracles* (parts of which were premiered on the RAI/AAR concerts of 1962 and 1965 and all of which was performed and broadcast by RAI's Turin orchestra, chorus, and soloists in 1968.) He also composed a number of chamber music pieces including *Concert Music for Solo Clarinet, Three Epigrams for Clarinet and Piano, Concert Piece for Clarinet and Piano, Adagio and Allegro for Flute, Oboe, and Strings,* and *Encore Piece for Flute and Piano.* His *Overture,* written previously and subsequently entitled *Tertullian Overture,* was premiered on the RAI/AAR orchestra concert, July 1960. Alexei Haieff remained as acting composer-in-residence for a month in the fall to assist the incoming fellows while the composer-in-residence, Ross Lee Finney of the University of Michigan, arrived in March. Finney organized the Spring Concert, which contained his String Quartet no. 7, Harada's String Quartet (premiere), Eaton's *Song Cycle on Holy Sonnets of John Donne,* and Wilson's *Six Pieces for Piano* (premiere). In addition to the premieres of Wilson's *Six Pieces for Orchestra,* Harada's *Double Concerto for Violin and Piano,* and Eaton's *Overture,* the RAI/AAR orchestra concert, July 1960, contained Finney's *Variations for Orchestra.* Later in the year, following his State Department sponsored tour through Greece, Finney entertained the Academy community by accompanying himself on the guitar in a program of American folk songs. The composer Robert Palmer, on sabbatical leave from Cornell University, was at the Academy through the year as a visiting artist. At the conclusion of the year, Higo Harada returned to the United States, where he would eventually join the faculty of San Jose State College in California.

1960–61: The new fellow Paul E. Nelson (Phoenix, AZ, 1929–2008) joined fellows Eaton and Wilson. Nelson, educated at Columbia Teachers College and at Harvard University, had been at the University of Vienna prior to his fellowship. He was to remain at the Academy for three years (1960–63). In that time he completed *Sinfonietta* for orchestra (premiered on the RAI/AAR orchestra concert, July 1962), composed *Songs of Life* for mixed chorus, strings, and harp (premiered on the RAI/AAR concert, July 1963), *Idyll for Horn and Strings*, and a number of chamber works including *Psalm auf die Ehe mit ihm* for mezzo-soprano and piano (premiered on the Spring Concert, 1962), *How Happy the Lover*, for mixed chorus, and *Two Madrigals on Old English Airs* and *Cantata da Camera* for soprano, baritone, and small ensemble (premiered on the Spring Concert, 1963). Robert Moevs (FAAR 1955) was the composer-in-residence for the entire year. He was writing his *Concerto for Piano, Percussion, and Orchestra* for the Connecticut Symphony—a later version of which won the 1978 Stockhausen International Prize in Composition. With the financial assistance of USIS, Moevs organized a particularly rich concert schedule that included a collaboration with SIMC and a joint German and American Academy concert presenting the work of Eaton, Wilson, Moevs, and the German composers Hans Ulrich Engelmann and Bernd Alois Zimmermann.[23] Also present at the Academy was William O. Smith (FAAR 1958), who had returned to Rome on a Guggenheim Fellowship. In the meantime he had been invited by Otto Luening to work in the Columbia-Princeton electronic studio and had been entrusted with representing the United States at the Venice Biennale's Festival of Electronic Music. Upon arriving in Rome, he was given a studio at the Academy and was active, along with George Balch Wilson and John Eaton, in bringing about the Academy's "electronic studio" under the guidance of Otto Luening. Smith remained in Rome until 1966, composing, performing with John Eaton, and pursuing his pioneering work on multiphonics for the clarinet.[24] The Spring Concert contained Nelson's *String Trio*, Eaton's String Quartet no. 1, and Smith's *Five Pieces for Flute and Clarinet* (premiere). There was no RAI/AAR orchestra concert in 1961. Otto Luening arrived in the summer, both to conduct diplomatic discussions to restore the momentarily interrupted RAI/AAR concerts and to set up the electronic music studio. At the conclusion of his third year, George Balch Wilson returned to the University of Michigan, where he, along with Ross Lee Finney, created an electronic music studio patterned after the Columbia-Princeton studio. He directed that studio for the next thirty years.

1961–62: Composer Leslie Bassett (Hanford, CA, b. 1923) joined Fellows Eaton and Nelson in 1961–62. Bassett, who had studied at the University of California, Fresno, at the University of Michigan with Ross Lee Finney, and worked with Nadia Boulanger in Paris, had been teaching at the University of Michigan since 1952. He was to remain at the Academy for two years (1961–63), in which time he wrote *Variations for Orchestra* (premiered on the RAI/AAR orchestra concert, July 1963, and awarded the Pulitzer Prize in 1966 following its American premiere by the Philadelphia Orchestra under the direction of Eugene Ormandy). He also composed *Quintet* for piano and strings (premiered on the Spring Concert, 1962), *To Music* for soprano and piano (premiered at the Santa Cecilia Auditorium in 1962, USIS/Santa Cecilia collaboration), *Third String Quartet* (premiered on the Spring Concert, 1963), and *Eclogue, Encomium, and Evocation* for women's chorus with instruments. He also had performances of *Mobile* for piano, *Sonata* for cello and piano, and *Sonata* for viola and piano while at the Academy. John LaMontaine (Pulitzer Prize 1959) arrived in midwinter to be the composer-in-residence. He was working on *A Summer's Day,* a sonnet for chamber orchestra. Another series of concerts were organized in collaboration with the Academy of Santa Cecilia, with SIMC and with the Amici della Musica di Perugia.[25] The Spring Concert featured the premieres of Leslie Bassett's *Quintet* for piano and strings, Eaton's *Concert Music for Solo Clarinet,* the Finale from Nelson's *String Trio* and his *Psalm* for mezzo-soprano and piano, as well as LaMontaine's String Quartet no. 1. The RAI/AAR orchestra concert featured Nelson's *Sinfonietta* (premiere), Bassett's *Five Movements for Orchestra,* and Eaton's *Three Arias from Heracles* (premiere). The RAI/AAR concert was permanently moved from the Villa Aurelia to the RAI Auditorium, *Foro Italico,* to permit proper recording conditions. At the conclusion of the year, John Eaton remained in Rome to tour in a duo and in a jazz ensemble with William O. Smith. He would stay on in Rome, composing and pursuing his interest in microtonal music and live synthesizer performance on the Syn-ket,[26] until 1970 when he left to join the faculty of Indiana University.

1962–63: This fellowship year brought the composer Marvin David Levy (Passaic, NJ, b. 1932) to join fellows Bassett and Nelson. Levy studied with Philip James at New York University and Otto Luening at Columbia University. Levy dedicated his two years (1962–64) to working on his opera, *Mourning Becomes Elektra* (commissioned to celebrate the opening of the Metropolitan Opera at Lincoln Center, premiered by the Metropolitan Opera, 1967). The composer-in-residence was Elliott Carter (FAAR 1954), who began work on his *Piano Concerto* (commissioned by the pianist Jacob Lateiner through the Ford Foundation, premiered in 1967 by the Boston Symphony Orchestra with Lateiner as soloist). Carter's String Quartet no. 2 (Pulitzer Prize 1960) was performed at the Villa Farnese on a joint concert featuring music of the French, German, and American Academies and his *Double Concerto* was performed at the Eliseo Theatre. In the latter concert, Aaron Copland conducted his own *Music for the Theater* and *Nonet.* The Spring Concert included Bassett's *Third String Quartet* (premiere), Carter's *Sonata for Violoncello and Piano,* Nelson's *Cantata da Camera,* and Levy's music for a film based on poems by Walt Whitman. The concert was held in the American Embassy's theater to accommodate screening of the 35mm film using Levy's music. The RAI/AAR orchestra concert, July 1963, featured Bassett's *Variations for Orchestra* (premiere), Nelson's *Songs of Life* (premiere), Levy's *Kyros Poem for Orchestra*, and Petrassi's Concerto no. 4 for strings. Concluding the year, Paul Nelson joined the faculty of Brown University while Leslie Bassett returned to his position on the faculty of the University of Michigan.

1963–64: Two new fellows joined Levy: Ezra Laderman (New York, NY, b. 1924) and Vincent Frohne (La Porte, IN, b. 1936). Laderman, who studied with Miriam Gideon at Brooklyn College and Otto Luening at Columbia University, spent one year at the Academy, in which time he composed his Symphony no. 1 (premiered on the RAI/AAR orchestra concert, July 1964). His earlier work, String Quartet no. 2, was performed on the Spring Concert. Frohne, who had studied at DePauw University and the Eastman School, had been studying with Boris Blacher in Berlin prior to his fellowship. He was to remain at the Academy for three years (1963–66), composing three orchestral works: *Adam's Chains* for soprano and orchestra (1964), *Ordine II* (1965), and *Counterpoise* (1966) (premiered on successive RAI/AAR concerts, 1964–66), as well as *Sonata for Cello Solo* and the completion of *Quartet for Horn and String Trio*. He also wrote a flute work (premiered by James Galway, Berlin, 1967) and began work on his *String Quartet* (commissioned by the Koussevitsky Foundation, 1966). There was no composer-in-residence, but both Robert Moevs (Rutgers University) and Stefan Wolpe (Long Island University) were visiting artists living at the Academy under Guggenheim grants. The Spring Concert featured two movements of Frohne's *Quartet for Horn and String Trio*, his *Sonata* for piano, and Laderman's String Quartet no. 4. The RAI/AAR concert contained the premieres of Laderman's Symphony no. 1 and Frohne's *Adam's Chains* for soprano and orchestra. The visiting artist Richard Wilson, a pianist and composer, performed a recital including Robert Moevs's work. Concluding the year, Ezra Laderman returned to New York and, after completing the score for the film *The Eleanor Roosevelt Story* (1965), became director of the Bennington Composers Conference. Marvin David Levy remained in Rome working on his opera under a Guggenheim Fellowship.

1964–65: Richard Trythall (Knoxville, TN, b. 1939) arrived as fellow to join Frohne. Trythall had studied with David Van Vactor at the University of Tennessee, Leon Kirchner at Tanglewood, and Roger Sessions at Princeton University, and had spent the previous year on a Fulbright grant studying with Boris Blacher at the *Hochschule für Musik*, Berlin. He remained at the Academy for three years (1964–67). This was the last three-year fellowship awarded in music composition. During these years he composed three orchestral works: *Composition for Piano and Orchestra* (1965), *Penelope's Monologue* for soprano and orchestra (1966, text from Joyce's *Ulysses*), and *Costruzione* (1967) (premiered on successive RAI/AAR concerts, 1965–67), and worked in the Academy's electronic studio (Study no. 1 for electronic sounds). The composer-in-residence, Otto Luening, organized a series of "Thursday Evenings" devoted to concerts and music lectures. On one of these, Luening presented an "Electronic Music Evening." The program included William O. Smith's work for clarinet and tape recorder (played by the composer), an excerpt from a work by John Eaton, and pieces composed by Luening, Vladimir Ussachevsky, and others who worked in the Columbia-Princeton Electronic Music Studio. The occasion also served to introduce the recently acquired portable synthesizer created by Paul Ketoff, the Syn-ket. The Spring Concert featured Frohne's *Quartet for Horn and String Trio,* Trythall's *Trio* for violin, cello, and piano, Gail Kubik's *Sonatina* for clarinet and piano, and Alexei Haieff's *Saint's Wheel* for piano. At the end of this concert a surprise addition to the program honored Otto Luening on his sixty-fifth birthday. The composers Alexei Haieff, Gail Kubik, John Eaton, William O. Smith, Vincent Frohne, Richard Trythall, and Everett Helm (all present at the concert) had each written a variation on Luening's "Song," a brief lyrical movement (35 measures in length) from his *Second Suite* for solo flute. Director Richard Kimball introduced the surprise performance and the flutist Severino Gazzelloni played Luening's *Second Suite* followed by the *Birthday Variations.* Later in June, Luening oversaw two concerts in collaboration with the Accademia Filarmonica that featured music by Italian and American composers. The American contingent included Lawrence Moss, Richard Teitelbaum, Joel Chadabe, and Alvin Curran, all living in Rome at that time, as well as John Eaton, who presented the premiere of his *Songs for RPB* for soprano, piano, and Syn-ket.[27] The RAI/AAR concert, July 1965, concluded the year and featured Frohne's *Ordine II* (commissioned by DePauw University), Eaton's "Three Arias" from *Heracles,* William O. Smith's *Tangents for Clarinet and Orchestra* (with the composer as soloist), and Trythall's *Composition for Piano and Orchestra* (with the composer as soloist). All were premieres.

1965–66: Stephen Albert (New York, NY, 1941–92) and Charles Whittenberg (St Louis, MO, 1927–84) joined Frohne and Trythall as fellows in the 1965–66 fellowship year. Albert, educated at the Eastman School of Music, the Philadelphia Musical Academy, and the University of Pennsylvania, remained for two years (1965–67). In this time he orchestrated his *Winter Songs* for tenor and orchestra (premiered on the RAI/AAR orchestra concert, July 1966), orchestrated his *Supernatural Songs* for soprano and chamber orchestra, and composed *Prologue to the Bacchae* for orchestra (the latter two works were premiered on the RAI/AAR concert, July 1967, under the title of *Departure*), as well as composed *Imitations* for string quartet (premiered on the Spring Concert, 1967). Whittenberg, educated at the Eastman School, had been composing under two Guggenheim fellowships (1963 and 1964) immediately prior to receiving the Rome Prize. He remained at the Academy for one year (1965–66), in which time he wrote String Quartet in One Movement (premiered on the Spring Concert, 1966) as well as a harpsichord work, *Four Forms and an Epilogue*, written for the harpsichordist-musicologist Frederick Hammond (FAAR 1966). Hammond performed the work at the Academy in April during an all-baroque program and at Rome's Accademia Filarmonica later in the spring. The composer-in-residence was Jack Beeson (FAAR 1950), who, in addition to writing several small instrumental works, began work on the libretto and the music for *My Heart's in the Highlands* (after the play of William Saroyan, commissioned and premiered by National Educational Television Opera Theatre, March 1970). His orchestral work, *Transformations*, was performed by the RAI Orchestra in Turin, December 1966. Beeson, with the help of the Alice M. Ditson Fund, organized two additional concerts, again in collaboration with the Accademia Filarmonica, featuring music by fellows and Italian and American composers living in Rome: Edward T. Cone, Jerome Rosen, Alvin Curran, and William O. Smith. The Spring Concert featured Albert's *Five Songs*, the first movement of Frohne's *Sonata for Cello Solo*, Trythall's *Four Songs on Poems by Rainer Maria Rilke*, and Whittenberg's String Quartet in One Movement (premiere). The RAI/AAR orchestra concert included Trythall's *Penelope's Monologue* for soprano and orchestra, Albert's *Winter Songs* for tenor and orchestra, and Vincent Frohne's *Counterpoise*—all premieres. Rounding out the year were concerts by Steve Lacy's jazz combo, the pianist Daniel Kunin, and the piano duo of Rollino and Sheftel. Visiting artists included Ross Lee Finney, Gail Kubik, John Eaton, and Daniel Kunin. At the conclusion of the year, Vincent Frohne returned to Berlin to continue his work on a Guggenheim Fellowship and Charles Whittenberg returned to the United States to join the faculty of the University of Connecticut.

1966–67: Morris Moshe Cotel (Baltimore, MD, 1943–2008) and Philip G. Winsor (Morris, IL, 1938–2012) joined Trythall and Albert as fellows. Cotel, who had completed his studies with Vincent Persichetti and Roger Sessions at the Juilliard School of Music, was teaching at Juilliard when he received the Rome Prize. He remained in Rome for two years (1966–68), working on his *Concerto for Piano and Orchestra* (premiered on the RAI/AAR orchestra concert, September 1968). His *Symphonic Pentad* for mezzo-soprano and orchestra, written previously, was premiered during the RAI/AAR concert, July 1967. Winsor, who had studied at Illinois Wesleyan University, San Francisco State University, and the Music Conservatory of Milan, was studying at the University of Illinois when he received the Rome Prize. He remained for one year. During this time he wrote his *Concerto for Chamber Orchestra* (premiered on the RAI/AAR concert, July 1967) and *Melted Ears* for two pianos (written for Loren Rush and R. Moran). Hugo Weisgall, the composer-in-residence, worked on a new opera, *Nine Rivers from Jordan* (commissioned by the New York City Opera, premiered in 1968), and, in addition to his normal duties, organized a concert to raise funds for the city of Florence following the disastrous flood of that year. The Spring Concert featured the premieres of Albert's *Imitations* for string quartet and Trythall's *Study no. 1* for electronic sounds, as well as performances of Cotel's *A Study in Pitch* for piano and string quartet, Winsor's *Sound Study III,* Weisgall's Four Songs op. 1, and songs by Barber and Ives. The RAI/AAR orchestra concert presented Cotel's *Symphonic Pentad* and the premieres of Albert's *Departure,* Winsor's *Concerto for Chamber Orchestra,* and Trythall's *Costruzione.* Visiting artists included Louise Talma and Ward Davenny, who gave a piano recital at the Academy. At year's end, Richard Trythall remained in Rome on a Guggenheim Fellowship composing *Continuums,* an orchestral work commissioned by the Fromm Foundation/Berkshire Music Center at Tanglewood. Philip Winsor returned to the United States and joined the faculty of Minnesota State University, Moorhead, as assistant professor and director of the electronic music studio. Stephen Albert received a Ford Foundation CMP (Contemporary Music Project) grant to be a composer-in-residence in the public school system. In 1985 he received the Pulitzer Prize for his Symphony no. 1, "RiverRun."

1967–68: Two new fellows arrived to join Cotel, John Heineman (Queens, NY, b. 1939) and Jack Fortner (Grand Rapids, MI, b. 1935). Heineman, educated at the Mannes College of Music and Columbia University, had been living in Italy since 1963, studying privately with the composer Boris Porena and subsequently with Goffredo Petrassi at Rome's Santa Cecilia Academy. During his two fellowship years (1967–69), Heineman brought a new thread to the already complex weave of musical styles nurtured by the Academy. He completed two music-theater pieces, *You Are in Danger* (premiere, Spring Concert, 1968) and *The Melting Pot* (premiere, Spring Concert 1969), a four-channel tape composition, *Air Piece* (premiere, February 1970, under the title "I've Flown Every Goddamn Thing in Christ's Cockeyed World"), and worked on *Carsonoma II* for orchestra and tape. He was a founding member of the composers-only Nuova Consonanza Improvisation Group alongside, among others, the Italian composers Franco Evangelisti and Ennio Morricone. Jack Fortner was educated at Aquinas College, studied with Hall Overton in New York, and did graduate work at the University of Michigan. He was teaching and conducting the "Contemporary Directions Ensemble" (founded by George Balch Wilson) at the University of Michigan when he received the Rome Prize. He remained at the Academy for one year, in which time he wrote *Quartet (4 Pieces for String Quartet)* and *S pr ING* for voice and piano. The composer-in-residence was Andrew Imbrie (FAAR 1949), who was working on his *Chamber Symphony* (commissioned by Dartmouth College; premiered Hanover, NH, 1968) and *Dandelion Wine* for oboe, clarinet, piano, and string quartet (commissioned by University of Wisconsin, Milwaukee; premiered there by the Fine Arts Quartet, 1968). The Spring Concert included Cotel's *Suite Nonsense* for narrator and nine instruments, Fortner's *Quartet* (premiere), and John Heineman's *Sospesi* for flute, clarinet, cello, piano, and actors. The RAI/AAR's slightly delayed orchestra concert, September 1968, included Fortner's *Quadri*, Cotel's *Concerto for Piano and Orchestra* (premiere, with the composer as soloist), Heineman's *Consequents* (written previously but receiving its premiere), and Imbrie's *Legend* (originally commissioned by the Ford Foundation in 1959). With the conclusion of their fellowship years, Jack Fortner returned to his position at the University of Michigan and two years later joined the faculty of California State University, Fresno. Morris Moshe Cotel went to Israel for four years, where he pursued his career as a composer and pianist while teaching at the Rubin Academy of Music. He then returned to the United States to join the faculty of the Peabody Conservatory of Music.

1968–69: Two new fellows joined Heineman: Henry Weinberg (Philadelphia, PA, b. 1931) and Louis Weingarden (Detroit, MI, 1943–89). Weinberg, who had studied at the University of Pennsylvania, at Princeton University with Roger Sessions and Milton Babbitt, and with Luigi Dallapiccola while on a Fulbright grant in Florence, had been on the faculty at Queens College, CUNY, when he received the Rome Prize. He would remain at the Academy for two years (1968–70), completing, among other works, *Double Solo* for violin and solo voice. His *Cantus Commemorabilis 1* for chamber orchestra was performed on the RAI/AAR orchestra concert, October 1969, his Quartet no. 2 was performed on the Spring Concert of 1969, and his *Song Cycle* was performed in January 1970. Weingarden attended the Jewish Theological Seminary, Columbia University, and studied composition privately with Miriam Gideon and subsequently with Elliott Carter at the Juilliard School. He also remained at the Academy for two years (1968–70), composing *Ghirlande* for soprano and chamber orchestra (text by Michelangelo, premiered on the RAI/AAR concert, October 1969), *Triptych* for piano (premiered on the Spring Concert, 1969), and *The Orphic Hymns: To the Moon, Prologue* for two sopranos, alto, and two pianos (premiered at the Academy, March 1970). The composer-in-residence was Elliott Carter (FAAR 1954), who was composing his *Concerto for Orchestra* (commissioned by the New York Philharmonic for its 125th anniversary in 1969, dedicated to Leonard Bernstein). The Spring Concert was expanded to two concerts with the assistance of USIS and of Carter himself. In addition to the premieres of Weingarden's *Triptych* for piano, Heineman's *The Melting Pot* for four amplified voices and tape, and a performance of Weinberg's String Quartet no. 2, the programs included compositions by American composers living in Rome at the time: Alvin Curran, Richard Teitelbaum, Richard Trythall, and Jeffrey Levine, as well as music by the Italian composers Mario Bertoncini and Giacinto Scelsi. The RAI/AAR orchestral concert, delayed to October 1969,[28] presented the premiere of Weingarden's *Ghirlande* and performances of Henry Weinberg's *Cantus Commemorabilis I*, Carter's *The Minotaur Suite*, and Carl Ruggles's *Men and Mountains.* At the conclusion of his fellowship years, John Heineman remained in Rome composing and performing with the Nuova Consonanza improvisation group until 1970. After a number of years in Canada and New York, he would return to live in Rome and pursue his work as a composer, filmmaker, and conceptual artist.

1969–74, Directors: Bartlett Hayes Jr., Frank E. Brown (Acting)

The Music Program: 1969–74

1969–70 once again ushered in a new decade with a significant change of the Academy's leadership. The trustees of the Academy, in an unusual move, created a paid position in the New York office:[29] executive vice president. Fund-raising was to be a major part of this job. Reginald Allen, who had managed both the Metropolitan Opera and the Philadelphia Orchestra and had been executive director for operations at Lincoln Center, was employed in this capacity. He would also serve as acting director in Rome until the new director, Bartlett Hayes, director emeritus of the Addison Gallery in Andover, Massachusetts, would arrive in March 1970. Both men would be called on to deal with several challenges.

The first and greatest challenge was the economic situation—the Academy was, essentially, living beyond its means. Although this problem had already been diagnosed in 1963, it had been significantly aggravated by the Italian inflation that followed—at times more than 20 percent per year. This in turn caused a steep rise in the cost of the staff's wages and building maintenance, and, of course, necessitated a commensurate increase in fellows' stipends. At home little attention had been given to increasing the Academy's endowment and, consequently, operating budgets were now cutting into the capital investment. Inevitably this situation, which could not be resolved in a short time, would face successive directors and presidents and condition all programs through the seventies onward. In fact, it would become even more severe in the mid-seventies because of the worldwide energy crisis. Not surprisingly, this steep rise in the cost of living, when coupled with the growth of political terrorism (the Red Brigade) and organized crime (the mafia) that characterized Italy during that decade, was to take its toll on the number of Americans living independently in Rome. This group would dwindle considerably in the seventies, effectively eliminating what had been the sixties scene.

A second challenge for Allen and Hayes was presented by the Italian anti-American sentiment, which would occasionally focus on the Academy as a convenient, though mistaken, symbol of United States' involvement in the Vietnam War. The Academy was firebombed on two occasions. The Visual Arts

Fellows themselves protested the war by shrouding their works in black for the spring exhibition of 1970. The music program also suffered when members of the Rome Radio Orchestra, incensed by the American bombings in Cambodia, voted to boycott the RAI/AAR orchestra concert that had been scheduled for December 1972.

A third challenge was that the entire community of fellows, as they indicated to the acting director Allen in a meeting held in the fall of 1969, felt isolated from the Roman world, not sufficiently in contact with their Italian colleagues. Fortunately their feelings dovetailed with the new director's intention to "bring the Academy closer to the Roman community and the Italian environment."[30] Of the many ideas that Allen and Hayes considered to address this issue, one, suggested by the composer-in-residence Frank Wigglesworth (FAAR 1954) and the sculptor-in-residence Sidney Simon, seemed both attractive and within the Academy's means. The idea was to develop a series of miniconcerts/exhibitions to take place on a regular basis throughout the year. This would create multiple occasions to serve as "mixers" to bring Roman audiences to the Academy. The fellows' final Art Exhibition and the Spring Concert, which occurred independently in late May or early June, were occasions that attracted large publics, but they occurred at the conclusion of the academic year and were not conducive to mingling. The miniconcert/exhibition formula, instead, was intended to mix the art and music audience, wed it to the Roman scene, and spread the occasions for meeting throughout the entire year. Both the concert (of a half-hour duration) and the exhibition would draw from the works of fellows, Italians, and fellows from other Academies. This proposal was accepted and a series of these events took place throughout the 1969–71 years, achieving considerable public success.

A further problem also needed to be addressed—one particularly vital to the music program. In both 1968 and 1969 the fellows' RAI/AAR orchestral concerts had been shifted away from the traditional summer date and scheduled later in the fall. This raised a number of practical problems both for the composer fellows who might already have left Rome and would need to return for the fall concert and for the Academy's long-term organization of the concerts themselves. The problem was further exacerbated in the fall of 1970, however, when word arrived in early September that the concert, scheduled for September 26, would have to be cancelled since the RAI auditorium was not available for use. It was at this point that the author was requested to intercede with the RAI, as composer-in-residence, in an attempt to salvage the concert.[31] The problem was to find an adequate auditorium for the concert and to convince the RAI that "the show must go on." Fortunately a substitute hall was kindly offered by the Pontifical North American College (with whom the Academy shares the Janiculum Hill), and, though it was hardly an ideal recording situation—as the RAI technician pointed out during our inspection of the hall—the RAI changed their plans and the concert took place as scheduled in the new venue. Director

Hayes subsequently asked me to "help with the concerts at the Academy this year,"[32] and so began my official organizational role at the Academy.[33]

The Composers: 1969–74

1969–70: This fellowship year brought the composers Barbara Kolb (Hartford, CT, b. 1939) and Loren Rush (Fullerton, CA, b. 1935) to join Weinberg and Weingarden at the Academy. Kolb, the first woman to receive the Rome Prize in Music Composition, had studied at the Hartt College of Music and, as a Fulbright grantee, at the Vienna Academy of Music. She was a freelance composer in New York when she received the Rome Prize. Kolb remained at the Academy for two years (1969–71), where she composed *Trobar Clus* for chamber ensemble (commissioned by the Fromm Foundation in cooperation with the Berkshire Music Center)[34] and *Solitaire* for piano and tape (1971; premiered at Carnegie Recital Hall, fall 1972). Kolb's *Crosswinds* for twenty-one winds and percussion, composed previously, was premiered on the RAI/AAR concert, 1970. Loren Rush, educated at San Francisco State University, the University of California, Berkeley, and Stanford University, had been working at Stanford's Computer Music Center prior to receiving the Rome Prize. He also remained at the Academy for two years (1969–71), in which time he composed *Oh, Susanna* for piano, *soft music, HARD MUSIC* for three amplified pianos (both premiered at the Academy), completed two orchestral works, *Dans le Sable* (orchestral version) and *Cloud Messenger* (premiered on successive RAI/AAR orchestra concerts, September 1970 and July 1971), and sketched *A Little Traveling Music* for enhanced piano with computer-generated four-channel audio playback. Subsequent works based on material created at the Academy include *Dreaming Susanna* for electronically enhanced orchestra and six-channel audio playback (based on *Oh, Susanna*) and *Song and Dance* for amplified orchestra with computer-generated four-channel audio playback (first movement based on *soft music* and the second on the sketches for *A Little Traveling Music*). The latter two works were commissioned by the San Francisco Symphony Orchestra. Composer-in-Residence Frank Wigglesworth (FAAR 1954) composed *Three Portraits* for orchestra (premiered on the RAI/AAR concert, 1970). He also proposed and developed the idea of the miniconcerts, as described earlier. The Spring Concert contained Kolb's earlier work, *Chanson bas* for soprano, harp, and percussion, Rush's *soft music, HARD MUSIC* for three amplified pianos (premiere), and a performance of Wigglesworth's *Duo* for oboe and clarinet. The four miniconcerts for this year included, among others, Rush's *Hexahedron* for piano (performed by the composer), Kolb's *Figments* for flute and piano, Heineman's *I've Flown Every Goddamn Thing in Christ's Cockeyed World* for tape (premiere), Weingarden's *The Orphic Hymns: To the Moon, Prologue* (premiere), and Henry Weinberg's *Song Cycle (1960)* for soprano and piano (texts by Hopkins, Valéry, and Stevens). The RAI/AAR orchestra concert, delayed to September 1970 and performed at the Pontifical North American College, featured Rush's *Dans le Sable*, Kolb's *Crosswinds* for winds and percussion, and Wigglesworth's *Three Portraits*—all were premieres. Stefan Wolpe was a visiting artist during the year. At the conclusion of the year, Louis Weingarden returned to New York to complete his studies at the Juilliard School and Henry Weinberg returned to his position at Queens College.

1970–71: Two new fellows, Daniel Perlongo (Gaastra, MI, b. 1942) and James Heinke (Cedar Rapids, IA, b. 1945) arrived to join Rush and Kolb for the 1970–71 fellowship year. Perlongo had studied at the University of Michigan and completed his diploma at the Accademia di Santa Cecilia in Rome while under a Fulbright grant. Immediately preceding the Rome Prize, he was teaching at the Indiana University of Pennsylvania. He spent two years at the Academy (1970–72), during which he composed *Changes* for wind ensemble (premiered at the Indiana University of Pennsylvania, fall 1972) and *Ephemeron* for orchestra (premiered by the University of Michigan summer orchestra at Interlochen, 1975), as well as *Fragments* for flute and cello (premiered on a joint concert with the French Academy, spring 1972), *Solo* for violin (premiered on a miniconcert, spring 1971), and *Tre Tempi* for flute, oboe, horn, viola, and violoncello (premiered on the second 1972 Spring Concert). His *Myriad* for orchestra, written previously, was performed on the RAI/AAR concert, July 1971, but unfortunately his *Ephemeron* only reached the dress rehearsal stage of the RAI/AAR concert, December 1972, owing to the orchestra's decision to boycott the concert. His *Movement for Eight Players* was performed at the Academy on a concert featuring musicians of the North Carolina School of the Arts Summer Program in Italy, July 1971. James Heinke, educated at Oberlin College and Brandeis University, also remained for two years (1970–72). In that time he composed his *Quartet* (for string quartet, premiered on the Spring Concert, 1971), *Eden Road* for flute, cello, and piano (premiered on a joint concert with the French Academy, Spring 1972), *Tigellinus Fragment*, and began an orchestral work, *Canto*. His *Music for Orchestra* was premiered on the RAI/AAR concert, July 1971. The composer-in-residence for the fall was Richard Trythall (FAAR 1967), who was also employed to oversee the concert program throughout the year. At this time, Trythall was working on a multimedia work in collaboration with the visual artist-filmmaker Milton Cohen, *Doors* (later entitled *Verse*).[35] Harold Shapero (FAAR 1951), composer-in-residence for the winter and spring, worked on his *America Variations* for piano and his work-in-progress *Concerto for Orchestra*. The Spring Concert contained the premieres of Rush's *Oh, Susanna* for piano, Perlongo's *Semblance* for string quartet, Heinke's *Quartet*, and Trythall's *Overplay* for piano and tape, as well as Shapero's *Sonata for Piano Four Hands* performed by Shapero and Leo Smit. Miniconcerts included, among others, performances of Kolb's *Figments* for flute and piano, Shapero's

3 Pieces in C# for piano and synthesizer, and the premiere of Perlongo's *Solo* for violin. Another concert, held in collaboration with the USIS library, featured performances of Heinke's *Second Skandha* for cello and piano, Rush's *soft music, HARD MUSIC*, and Shapero's *Sonata for Violin and Piano*. The RAI/AAR orchestra concert (which momentarily returned to its traditional summer position in July) contained Perlongo's *Myriad*, Heinke's *Music for Orchestra*, the premiere of Rush's *The Cloud Messenger*, and Trythall's *Continuums* for orchestra. Visiting artists included the pianist-composer Leo Smit, the soprano Suzanne Thorin, the violinists Roman Totenberg and Sydney Harth, and the composers Stefan Wolpe and George Balch Wilson. Smit, Thorin, and Harth performed on Academy concerts and a concert in honor of Stefan Wolpe was given in December. At the conclusion of the year, Barbara Kolb returned to the United States on a Guggenheim Fellowship and subsequently took a position on the faculty of Brooklyn College. She returned to the Academy as composer-in-residence in 1976 and served as a trustee from 1975 to 1977. Loren Rush, also a recipient of a Guggenheim Fellowship, returned to cofound and codirect the Stanford Center for Computer Research in Music and Acoustics (CCRMA) and to create the computer-generated four-channel audio for *Song and Dance*.

1971–72: The composer Eugene J. O'Brien (Paterson, NJ, b. 1945) joined Perlongo and Heinke as the new fellow for the 1971–72 year. O'Brien had studied at the University of Nebraska and the Staatliche Hochschule für Musik in Cologne on a Fulbright Fellowship. Prior to receiving the Rome Prize, he was a doctoral student at Indiana University. He remained at the Academy for two years (1971–73), during which time he completed his *Concertino* for violoncello and orchestra (also scheduled for performance on the ill-fated RAI/AAR orchestra concert, December 1972) and most of *Dédales* for soprano and chamber orchestra (commissioned by the Koussevitzky Foundation, premiered by the Cleveland Orchestra, May 1976, and performed on the RAI/AAR concert, December 1976), as well as *Lingual* for flute, violoncello, and soprano (premiered at the French Academy on a mixed French-American concert in the spring of 1972), *Ambages* for piano, four-hands, and *Intessitura* for cello solo. David Diamond, who had received the AAR World War II Prize in 1942, was composer-in-residence. He spent his residency working on *The Noblest Game*—a "political opera" with an original libretto by Katie Loucheim (a leader in the Democratic Party and the first woman to be appointed deputy assistant secretary of state). Commissioned by the National Opera Institute in 1971 for performance by the New York City Opera, the opera was completed in 1975 but remained unperformed. Diamond, who had lived in Florence for many years, also arranged a number of concerts at the Villa Aurelia including an ambitious three-concert series held on Sunday afternoons in May. This series included the traditional Spring Concert within a larger context. The concerts presented music by Dallapiccola, Malipiero, Casella, Louvier, Murail, Copland, Rochberg, and Sessions, as well as O'Brien's *Elegy for Bernd Alois Zimmermann*, Diamond's String Quartet no. 9, Heinke's *Eden Road*, and the premiere of Perlongo's *Tre Tempi*. The composer Luigi Dallapiccola was present at the first concert to conduct his *Parole di San Paolo* for mezzo-soprano and eleven instruments. At the request of the fellows, the miniconcert/exhibition series that had begun two years earlier, though admittedly popular, was abandoned since it was felt that they "did not reflect the musical stature of the Academy in a dignified way."[36] The traditional summer RAI/AAR concert was once more delayed until December 1972 and subsequently cancelled following the final rehearsal by the orchestra as a protest gesture against the Vietnam War.[37] Visiting artists at the Academy included Gail Kubik and Luigi Dallapiccola. At the conclusion of the year, Daniel Perlongo returned to his teaching post at the Indiana University of Pennsylvania and James Heinke joined Stanford University's Computer Music Project on a research grant and undertook doctoral studies.

1972–73: The composers Jeffrey Jones (Santa Ana, CA, b. 1944) and William Hellerman (Milwaukee, WI, b. 1939) arrived to join O'Brien for the 1972–73 fellowship year. Jones, educated at the Immaculate Heart College, Los Angeles, Rome's Santa Cecilia Conservatory (on a Fulbright grant), and, immediately preceding the Rome Prize, at Brandeis University, remained at the Academy for two years (1972–74). He wrote *Archaica* for orchestra (premiered on the RAI/AAR concert, December 1974), and *Heterefonis* and *Pièce Mouvant* for piano (both premiered on Spring Concerts). Hellerman was educated at the University of Wisconsin, Columbia University, and studied privately with Stefan Wolpe. Prior to receiving the Rome Prize, he was on the faculty of Columbia University. He also remained at the Academy for two years (1972–74), in which time he composed *Row Music (tip of the iceberg)* for piano, *Distances/Embraces* for guitar, and *On the edge of a node* for prepared guitar, violin, and cello (all premiered at the Academy), as well as *behind bars* for "seven performers and runner," *to the last drop* for six mallet instruments, *in the mind's ear* for two instruments and tape delay, *on another level* for twenty-one vibraphones, *on the vanishing point* for variable ensemble, *Long Island Sound* for any four instruments (SATB), *For Otto: A line in return for solo piano*, and *Stop/Start* for chamber orchestra. He also had performances of his music at the Istituto Italo-Latino Americano and Beat 72. His orchestral work, *Time and Again*, was premiered on the RAI/AAR concert of December 1973. The composer-in-residence was Leo Smit, who worked on *Copernicus: Narrative and Credo* for four-part chorus, narrator, and instrumental ensemble, text by Sir Fred Hoyle. Written in commemoration of the five-hundredth anniversary of the birth of Copernicus, the work was premiered with Hoyle as the narrator at the National Academy of Sciences, Washington, DC, in 1973. The Spring Concert featured Hellerman's *Distances/Embraces* (premiere with the composer performing), Jones's *Heterefonis* (premiere), O'Brien's *Lingual*, Smit's *Academic Graffiti* (quatrains by W. H. Auden for histrionic voice and four instruments, 1962), and Nils Vigeland's *All in Due*

Time for piano (the composer at the piano). The RAI/AAR concert for this academic year was once more delayed to December 1973. At the conclusion of the year, Eugene O'Brien joined the faculty of the Cleveland Institute of Music.

1973–74: Hellerman and Jones were joined by two Massachusetts-born fellows: C. Tison Street (Cambridge, MA, b. 1943) and George Edwards (Boston, MA, 1943–2011). Street, who studied at Harvard University, had been an instructor at Harvard prior to arriving at the Academy. He would remain at the Academy for one year, during which he completed a *String Quintet* (commissioned by the Fromm Foundation/Berkshire Music Center at Tanglewood, premiere, summer 1974) and *Three Sacred Anthems* for *a cappella* chorus. George Edwards, who had studied at Oberlin College and Princeton University, had been teaching at the New England Conservatory prior to receiving the Rome Prize. He stayed in Rome for two years (1973–75), in which time he composed *Exchange-Misère* for flute, clarinet, violin, cello, and piano (premiered on the Spring Concert, 1975), *Wild Air, Sonda* (commissioned by the New York New Music Ensemble), and *Giro* for orchestra. His *Kreuz und Quer* for flute, clarinet, violin, viola, and cello was performed on the Spring Concert, 1974, and his *Three Hopkins Songs* were performed on a joint Academy-USIS concert in the spring of 1975. The composer-in-residence was Leon Kirchner (Pulitzer Prize 1967), who was working on his forthcoming opera, *Lily*, based on Saul Bellow's novel *Henderson the Rain King* (premiered by the New York City Opera, 1970). He shared his knowledge with the community both in lectures, "The Irreducible, the Immeasurable: A Shop Talk with Examples from the Viennese Classicists," and, on several occasions, as a pianist, performing, among other works, Mozart four-hand sonatas with Lorin Hollander and Mozart piano quartets with Bruno Giurana and friends. The Spring Concert presented the premieres of Jones's *Pièce mouvant* for piano and Hellerman's *On the edge of a node*, as well as performances of Street's *String Quartet*, Edwards's *Kreuz und Quer*, and Kirchner's *Piano Trio*. The RAI/AAR orchestra concert of December 1973 presented Hellerman's *Time and Again*, Leo Smit's *Four Kookaburra Marches*, and Kirchner's *Music for Orchestra*. Barbara Kolb was a visiting artist during the summer. At the conclusion of the year, Tison Street returned to Cambridge to continue his performing and composition. Jeffrey Jones elected to remain in Rome and William Hellerman returned to complete his doctoral studies at Columbia University.

1974–80, Directors: Henry A. Millon, John D'Arms

The Music Program: 1974–80

In January 1974, Henry A. Millon, RAAR 1965 (professor, history of art, Massachusetts Institute of Technology), took up his duties as the new director.

Shortly thereafter Harold Martin (president, Union College, 1965–74) was installed as president of the Academy. Both were faced with the Academy's ongoing economic problems. In his well-argued first report to the Board of Trustees, Martin suggested, "if instead we think of the continuing financial crisis not as a disaster but as an opportunity to examine purpose and program in the light of greatly changed circumstance, I believe we can make something useful of it."[38] This mix of bad news and hopeful intentions characterized the period. The bad news was that drastic changes were indeed necessary. In the fall of 1976, the Academy's most glamorous property, Villa Aurelia, was rented to the Indian Ambassador to Rome for five years (1976–81) in order to generate revenue. Among other inconveniences, this deprived the music program of the use of the villa's acoustically and visually satisfying Sala Musica. On the other hand, it was far better than the alternative solution—to sell the Villa Aurelia outright. At the same time (1975–76) the Board of Trustees voted to eliminate two-year fellowships because of the continuing financial difficulties. Henceforth fellowships would last for one year only. This meant there would no longer be overlapping fellowships. Additionally, given the chronic inadequacy of the music fellowship endowment, only one fellowship in music composition could be guaranteed by the Academy. In the following year the board also severely reduced the support given to the residency program, effectively curtailing year-long residencies for composers-in-residence.

The good news was that both Millon and Martin were determined to change this situation and, while making difficult decisions to retrench, were also planning for growth. Much of this growth was predicated on making the Academy better known and thereby "developing a base for giving."[39] It was felt that the Academy, which had made such a unique contribution to American culture and scholarship throughout the century, was, in effect, little known in the United States and even less well understood. This needed to be addressed in order to seriously solicit support.

For the music program the positive intentions and fence-building measures resulted in several new initiatives during the following three and a half years of Millon's tenure. In the spring of 1974 Millon proposed that the author should become the music liaison: a new position charged with handling the RAI concerts, carrying out special projects, promoting the fellows' music in Rome, overseeing the electronic studio, providing advice on musical equipment and music-related budget matters, and assisting the composers-in-residence with their projects and in their contact with Rome.[40] Traditionally, of course, most of these duties had been carried out by the composers-in-residence, but with the Academy's changing financial circumstances year-long residences gradually disappeared and short-term residents simply could no longer be expected to fulfill these responsibilities.[41] The music liaison position, therefore, insured continuity at a time when continuity was, of necessity, systematically being removed from the fellowship program.

In line with the intent to call attention to the Academy music program's particularly distinguished lineage, it was decided to produce a record of recent fellows' work. One of my first duties as music liaison was to oversee the production of this LP. Recorded in Rome over three successive summers, it was subsequently produced and distributed by CRI Records under grants from the Academy and the Alice M. Ditson Fund of Columbia University. The record, *Music from the American Academy in Rome*, included the music of fellows William Hellerman, Jeffrey Jones, George Edwards, and Martin Bresnick. Originally this recording project was to have become a biannual event, but it remained an isolated initiative.

Other activities taken to strengthen the music program included refurbishing the electronic studio. In 1974 two new loudspeakers and an amplifier were bought and the two portable Revox A-77 tape recorders (acquired previously) were serviced. The Roman engineer Paul Ketoff restructured the mixing board. The following year two quality AKG microphones were purchased in order to permit internal recording of the Academy's concerts, a necessity in order to assure a minimum of quality control. Systematic preservation of copies of all concert recordings was also begun at this time.[42] Since I was an advocate of electronic music, I also submitted a cost estimate for creating a more sophisticated studio, but under the financial circumstances this was impossible. In the long run, a true state-of-the-art electronic studio proved to be an impractical goal and, with the arrival of computer technology, ultimately unnecessary. Beginning with the composer James Mobberley in 1989–90, the fellows simply brought their personal studios with them—in their computers.

Improvements were also made in the Academy's vital collection of seven grand pianos (located in composers' studios or used as concert instruments in the Villa Aurelia and the McKim building).[43] In 1974 the Academy purchased a new Steinway C grand piano to serve as its principal concert instrument[44] (replacing an aging Steinway B) and, in the same year, the Academy received a donation of a Steinway L piano from Ambassador and Mrs. James Dunn (December 1974). A further windfall, although of a completely different nature, was provided by the musicologist Oliver Strunk's decision to donate his extensive personal library and archives to the American Academy's Library.

Continuing with the idea of publicizing the music program at the Academy, I launched the idea in 1976 of producing a brochure that would document both the compositional output of fellows while at the Academy and the performance activity that occurred each year. This brochure "Music Composition and Performance Activity, 1948–1977" was published in 1977 and later updated for the Academy's centennial celebration in 1994. It served to make a permanent, visible record of the considerable musical activity carried out at the Academy annually.

As music liaison I was also asked to develop a systematic concert season at the Academy—a concert series that would serve the purposes of the music program, the Academy community (concerts traditionally played a vital socializing role for the community), and the general interest of the Academy in connecting with Roman audiences and institutions. Unfortunately there were no additional funds available to support this idea, but there were several factors that made such a concert season plausible: the Academy was a prestigious venue, it offered an elegant performing space, a fine piano and an informed audience; it also offered flexible scheduling and it was interested principally (though not exclusively) in presenting contemporary American and Italian music. This made it appetizing for traveling American musicians who wished to play in Rome and for Italian performers and contemporary music organizations in search of an attractive performance situation.[45]

The concert series was subdivided into formal concerts (held in the Villa Aurelia) and informal concerts (held in the *Salone* of the McKim building). In the course of the six remaining years of the seventies, concerts would be given by the SUNY Buffalo "Evenings for New Music" Ensemble, Dorian Woodwind Quintet, Pentagon Brass Quintet, Five Centuries Ensemble, Ciompi String Quartet, American String Quartet, Composers String Quartet, Nuove Forme Sonore, Suonosfera, Musica d'Oggi, Percussione Ricerca di Venezia, and the Blackearth Percussion Group; the pianists Bella Davidovich, Lorin Hollander, James Avery, Yvar Mikhashoff, Frederic Rzewski, Barbara Shearer, Ena Bronstein, Mona Golabek, Carla Hübner, Max Lifchitz, Matthias Kriesberg, Mark Seltzer, Virginia Eskin; the harpsichordists Ralph Kirkpatrick, Frederick Hammond, Thomas Culley, Victor Hill; the sopranos Joan Logue, Carol Plantamura, Nelda Nelson, Michiko Hirayama, Delia Serrat, Martha Herr; the cellists Frances-Marie Uitti, Richard Boch; the violinist Anna Pelech; the double bassist Eugene Levinson; the clarinetist F. Gerald Errante; and the guitarist David Starobin.

These concerts presented, above all, contemporary American music, but there were also performances devoted to Italian contemporary music. In this regard, a concert performed by *Nuove Forme Sonore* (Michiko Hirayama, voice, Frances-Marie Uitti, cello, and Giancarlo Schiaffini, trombone) bears special mention. Held in Villa Aurelia's Sala Musica, December 1975, in honor of the seventieth birthday of the Italian composer Giacinto Scelsi, this all-Scelsi concert symbolized the privileged relationship that bound the Academy's community of composers with Scelsi.[46] Through the years, many of the fellows had come to know Scelsi personally and to appreciate his extremely original work. In fact, the Academy had been the scene of numerous performances of Scelsi's music during a time when his music was essentially ignored elsewhere in Rome. As Robert Mann, an American composer who had lived in Rome since 1948 (he was, for several years, the secretary general of the ISCM under President Goffredo Petrassi) confirmed, "through the 60s and 70s, the American Academy was practically the only place in Rome where Scelsi's work was performed."[47] This special relationship was recognized by the Scelsi

Foundation when, following Scelsi's death, they placed his family's Steinway piano at the Academy's disposal.[48]

This intense musical activity would continue uninterruptedly with the arrival of the Academy's new leadership at the beginning of the 1977–78 fellowship year. Bill Lacy (director of the Architecture and Environmental Arts Program of the National Endowment for the Arts, 1971–77) was the new president and John D'Arms, RAAR 1972 (chair, Department of Classical Studies, University of Michigan) was the new director. Like their predecessors, both were extremely supportive of the music program. D'Arms, who had been the Academy's Resident in Classical Studies and Archaeology in 1972, was even something of a ragtime musician himself, quite capable of strutting his stuff at the keyboard. Lacy, a strong advocate of the virtues of communication, created a new publication, *Amacadmy*, the second issue of which was devoted to the Academy's music program and, with its interview of Elliott Carter and its overview of the music program by the music critic George Gelles, remains to this day an articulate testimony to the program.[49]

The Composers, 1974–80

1974–75: This fellowship year brought new fellows Gerald H. Plain (Sacramento, KY, b. 1940) and David S. Bates (Massillon, OH, 1936–74) to join Edwards. Plain, who had studied at Murray State University and Butler University as well as at the University of Michigan, was teaching at DePaul University when he received the Rome Prize. He was to remain at the Academy for two years (1974–76). (This was the last two-year fellowship to be granted in music composition). While at the Academy, Plain revised his work for cello solo, *Raccoon Song* (premiered by Frances-Marie Uitti, Spring Concert, 1975), and completed his orchestral work *and left ol' Joe a bone, AMAZING!* (premiered on the RAI/AAR concert, December 1975; US premiere by the Brooklyn Philharmonic in 1984; American Academy of Arts and Letters Award, 2001). He also began composition on a work that became his *Violin Concerto* (Prince Pierre of Monaco Musical Composition Prize, 1980; premiere by the *Orchestre Philharmonique de Monte-Carlo*, 1982). His *Arrows* for orchestra, written previously, received its premiere on the RAI/AAR concert, December 1974. His *Golden Wedding* for stereo tape was performed at the *Teatro Satiri* in the spring of 1975 and his *Showers of Blessings* for clarinet, ring modulator, and tape was played on the Spring Concert, 1976. With his references to Appalachian folk music and culture, Plain brought another unique color to the Academy's palette. David Bates received his bachelor's, master's, and doctorate in music from the University of Michigan. Tragically, shortly after his arrival in Rome, he fell ill and returned to California, where he died of cancer. The composer-in-residence was John Eaton (FAAR 1962), who was composing his opera, *Danton and*

Robespierre (premiere, Indiana University Opera Theater, Bloomington, April 1978), and developing the idea of another opera, ". . . *inasmuch*," with the poet, exquisite host, and longtime Roman resident Eugene Walter. During his stay, Eaton's *Guillen Songs, Blind Man's Cry,* and *Land of Lampedusa* for two sopranos and piano (text by Marilyn Perry) were performed. He also gave lectures on two of his operas, *Myshkin* and *The Lion and Androcles.* The Spring Concert contained Edwards's *Exchange-Misère* (premiere), Bates's *Sueña* for viola and piano (the viola part was performed by his wife, Susan), Plain's *Racoon Song* (premiere), and Eaton's *Trio* for violin, cello, and piano. The RAI/AAR orchestra concert, December 1974, featured Plain's *Arrows* (premiere), Bates's *Fantasy in Two Parts* for piano and orchestra, and Jones's *Archaica* (premiere). Visiting artists included Lukas Foss, Gail Kubik, and the mezzo-soprano Nelda Nelson, who contributed her talents to several performances of both the contemporary and traditional repertoire. At the conclusion of the year, George Edwards returned to his teaching post at the New England Conservatory.

1975–76: Composer Martin Ira Bresnick (New York, NY, b. 1946) joined Gerald Plain as a fellow. Bresnick, educated at the University of Hartford and Stanford University, had also studied in Vienna on a Fulbright grant. Previous to winning the Rome Prize, he had been a lecturer at Stanford University. Like all fellows thereafter, he would remain for only one year at the Academy. During that time he wrote *Ants,* a music-theater work for chamber ensemble, soprano, mezzo-soprano, tenor, bass, narrator, and four actors (premiered by the San Francisco Conservatory New Music Ensemble, March 1977). His *Ocean of Storms,* composed previously, was performed on the RAI/AAR orchestra concert, December 1975, and his *Three Intermezzi* for solo cello were performed at the Academy in the following spring. The composer-in-residence for the fall was Barbara Kolb (FAAR 1971). Kolb was revising the orchestral version of her 1972 chamber orchestra work, *Soundings* (premiered by the New York Philharmonic, Pierre Boulez conductor, December 1975), and working on *Appello* for piano (written for the pianist Diane Walsh, premiered Kennedy Center, fall 1976). Her *Solitaire* for piano and tape was performed in the season's inaugural concert with Richard Trythall's *Omaggio a Jerry Lee Lewis* for stereo tape and music by Brahms and Chopin as performed by pianist Thomas Culley, S.J., FAAR 1967. Claus Adam was composer-in-residence for the spring. He was working on his *Concerto Variations* for orchestra (premiered by the National Orchestral Association Orchestra, 1977; finalist, Pulitzer Prize 1978). In May he gave a cello recital accompanied by Thomas Culley at the keyboard. The Spring Concert contained Adam's *Sonata for Piano,* Plain's *Showers of Blessings* for clarinet, ring modulator, and tape, as well as Bresnick's *Garlands* for eight cellos. The RAI/AAR orchestra concert, December 1975, featured Bresnick's *Ocean of Storms,* Kolb's *Soundings,* and the premiere of Plain's *and left ol' Joe a bone, AMAZING!.* Upon completion of the year, Gerald Plain returned to freelance composing and subsequently took

teaching jobs at the University of Wisconsin, Stevens Point, and at the Eastman School of Music. Martin Bresnick assumed a position on the faculty of the Yale Department of Music and joined the faculty of the Yale School of Music in 1981.
1976–77: Only one fellowship in music composition could be offered for the 1976–77 fellowship year. This was awarded to Chester Biscardi (Kenosha, WI, b. 1948). Biscardi had studied at the University of Wisconsin and the Yale School of Music, where he was teaching when he received the Rome Prize. While at the Academy, he composed a *Trio* for violin, cello, and piano (commissioned by the Cambium Trio under a grant from the National Endowment for the Arts/University of Wisconsin, premiered on the Spring Concert), and *At the Still Point* (premiered on the RAI/AAR orchestra concert given a year later in December 1977).[50] He also completed an analytical article: "Pitch Relations in Stockhausen: *Stop.*" There was no composer-in-residence this year. For the next five years the Academy's concerts took place without the Villa Aurelia's gilt frame. Given the rental of the villa, they were transferred to the dining room of the McKim building. In the fall Biscardi gave a concert as pianist along with the violinist Clara Zahler, performing works by Dallapiccola, Webern, and his own *Tartini* (1972). He and Zahler presented a similar program at the American Consulate in Florence under the auspices of USIS (spring 1977). The Spring Concert featured Biscardi's *Tenzone* for two flutes and piano, *They Had Ceased to Talk* for violin, viola, French horn, and piano, and *Trio* for violin, cello, and piano (premiere). The RAI/AAR orchestra concert, December 1976, presented Edward MacDowell's *Indian Suite* and the Italian premieres of Roger Sessions's Symphony no. 7 and Eugene O'Brien's *Dédales* for soprano and chamber orchestra. At the completion of the year, Chester Biscardi returned to join the faculty of Sarah Lawrence College. He also received a National Endowment for the Arts Composer/Librettist Fellowship Grant, 1977–78.

1977–78: Thanks to a grant from the National Endowment for the Arts, the Academy was able to offer two one-year fellowships for this fellowship year. The recipients were Robert H. Beaser (Boston, MA, b. 1954) and John Holland Thow (Los Angeles, CA, 1949–2007). Beaser, who completed his studies at the Yale School of Music, was serving as the assistant conductor of the Norwalk Symphony Orchestra and as assistant conductor to Yale University's Contemporary Ensemble prior to his fellowship. While at the Academy, he composed a woodwind quintet, *Shadow and Light* (premiered on the Spring Concert), and completed his *Symphony* for soprano and orchestra (premiered on the RAI/AAR orchestra concert, December 1977). During the year he also collaborated with the poet fellow Daniel Mark Epstein (FAAR 1978) on a group of songs that included "Quicksilver"—a work that became the final movement of his *Mountain Songs* some five years later. Thow, who had studied at the University of Southern California, in Italy on a Fulbright grant, and, prior to the fellowship, was completing his doctoral studies at Harvard University, where he studied with Leon Kirchner and Earl Kim, composed a *Wind Quintet* (premiered on the Spring Concert), *A Noiseless Patient Spider* for soprano and piano (premiered at the Villa Aurelia along with a performance of Thow's *Two Songs to Poems by Robert Bly* on a concert celebrating the thirtieth anniversary of the Fulbright-Hays Program), and *Siempre* for soprano and orchestra (text by Pablo Neruda, premiered on the RAI/AAR orchestra concert, February 1979). Lukas Foss (FAAR 1952) arrived in February as the composer-in-residence. He worked on his orchestral composition *Quintets* (premiered by the Cleveland Orchestra, 1979; finalist, Pulitzer Prize 1980) and in March, along with a select group of Roman musicians, performed Bach's Concerto in F Minor, Brandenburg Concerto no. 5, and Concerto in D Minor as the piano soloist. President Bill Lacy aptly described how Foss transformed the Academy's dining room "into a gilt candlelit baroque drawing room. . . . Foss didn't play and conduct music—he was music and the audience responded."[51] Also living at the Academy as a visiting artist from January through the summer was the composer Olly Wilson, on a sabbatical leave from the University of California, Berkeley. The Spring Concert presented Beaser's *Shadow and Light*, Thow's *Wind Quintet*, Foss's *Ni Bruit Ni Vitesse* for two pianos and percussion, Wilson's *Echoes* for clarinet and tape, and Trythall's *Variations on a Theme by Haydn* for woodwind quintet and tape. The evening following the Spring Concert, Foss led a spirited panel discussion involving all the composers of the previous evening's concert. The RAI/AAR concert, held earlier in December of 1977, featured premieres of both Beaser's *Symphony* for soprano and orchestra and Chester Biscardi's *At the Still Point* as well as performances of Charles Ives's *Decoration Day* and *Central Park in the Dark*. At the conclusion of the year, Robert Beaser returned to New York as conductor and co–music director of Musical Elements. He became an Academy trustee in 1993. John Thow returned to join the faculty of Boston University.

1978–79: The composers Sheila Jane Silver (Seattle, WA, b. 1946) and Dennis Eberhard (Cleveland, OH, 1943–2005) were the fellows for the 1978–79 year. Silver, educated at the University of California, Berkeley, at Brandeis University, and at Stuttgart's Hochschule für Musik, was a Radcliffe Institute Fellow when she received the Rome Prize. She spent the year composing *Dynamis* for French horn (premiered on the Spring Concert) and *Canto, A Setting of Ezra Pound's "Canto XXXIX"* for baritone and chamber ensemble (commissioned and premiered by the Berkshire Music Center at Tanglewood, 1979). Her work *Chariessa* for soprano and orchestra (texts from fragments by Sappho, a transcription of the original version for soprano and piano written in 1978) was premiered on the RAI/AAR concert, June 1981 (ISCM Award, 1981). The original soprano and piano version was performed at the Academy in the fall. Eberhard, who had studied at Kent State University, with Salvatore Martirano at the University of Illinois, and with Wlodzimierz Kotonski at the

Warsaw Music Conservatory, Poland, composed *Visions of the Moon* for soprano, percussion, and instrumental quartet (text by e. e. cummings, commissioned by the National Endowment for the Arts, premiered on the Spring Concert) and *Janus Music* (premiered on the RAI/AAR orchestral concert, June 1981). In the spring, William Albright, on sabbatical leave from the University of Michigan, was composer-in-residence. He composed *Four Fancies* for harpsichord, *The Birth of Jesus* for choir and organ, *A Full Moon in March* (incidental music to the W. B. Yeats's play of the same name), and completed his *Organbook III* for organ. He also gave a lecture-concert on ragtime that, in addition to classic rags, featured his own original rags. The Spring Concert featured Silver's *Dynamis* for horn and Eberhard's *Visions of the Moon* (both premieres) as well as Albright's *Five Chromatic Dances* for piano. The RAI/AAR delayed concert, February 1979, included the premiere of John Thow's *Siempre* for soprano and orchestra, Lukas Foss's *Orpheus* for cello and orchestra, Charles Ives's *From the Steeples and the Mountains*, and Copland's Concerto for piano and orchestra. Lukas Foss conducted. James Avery, pianist, on leave from the faculty of the University of Iowa and a visiting artist during the fall, shared his considerable talents on many occasions. At the end of the year, Sheila Silver joined the faculty of the State University of New York at Stony Brook while Dennis Eberhard, following a residence at the MacDowell Colony, taught at the University of Nebraska and then joined the faculty of Cleveland State University.

1979–80: The new fellows were Allen Raymond Shearer (Seattle, WA, b. 1943) and Arthur V. Kreiger (New Haven, CT, b. 1945). Shearer, educated at the University of California, Berkeley, and at the Akademie Mozarteum, Salzburg, composed a madrigal setting of *Nude Descending a Staircase* (poem by X. J. Kennedy, premiered by Chanticleer in 1982), *Four Poems of Wallace Stevens* (premiered on the Spring Concert, later became *Five Poems of Wallace Stevens*), and *Fantasy* for piano and orchestra (premiered on the RAI/AAR orchestra concert, July 1982, and winner of the Cabrillo Composers Project for performance at the 1991 Cabrillo Festival). A trained singer (baritone) as well as a composer, he and his wife, the pianist and visiting artist Barbara Shearer, made many additional musical contributions during the year. Kreiger, a graduate of the University of Connecticut and of Columbia University, had been teaching at Rutgers University and working in the Columbia-Princeton Electronic Music Center prior to receiving the Rome Prize. While at the Academy, he composed *Complaint* for chorus and electronic tape (premiered by The New Calliope Singers, Alice Tully Hall, February 1980) and *Remnants* for orchestra (premiered on the RAI/AAR orchestra concert, October 1983). His work *Four Settings of William Carlos Williams* for mezzo-soprano, viola, and piano was performed on the Nuova Consonanza Festival. Also performed during his stay were *Fantasy* for piano and electronic tape and *Short Piece in Memory of My Father* for electronic tape. The composer-in-residence for the fall was Elliott Carter (FAAR 1954); he was completing his *Night Fantasies* for piano (dedicated to the pianists Ursula Oppens, Charles Rosen, Paul Jacobs, and Gilbert Kalish, premiere 1980). On December 11, 1979, Nuova Consonanza sponsored an evening at the Foro Italico Auditorium with Carter, Kreiger, Shearer, and Trythall, in which they discussed American music and celebrated Carter's seventy-first birthday with the audience. In February, the Composers String Quartet performed Carter's *Second String Quartet* at the Academy. The composer-in-residence during the spring was William O. Smith (FAAR 1958), who wrote a *Suite for Jazz Orchestra* (premiered by the Milan Radio Jazz Orchestra), *Ritual* for soprano, and a *Clarinet Quartet*. Along with the soprano Michiko Hirayama and the pianist Enrico Pieranunzi, he also performed an evening of his "Compositions and Improvisations" for the Academy community. The Spring Concert included Kreiger's *Tapestry* for four percussion (premiere), Shearer's *Four Poems of Wallace Stevens* (premiere by Allen and Barbara Shearer), Trythall's *Bolero* for four percussion, and Smith's *Duo* for clarinet and cello. There was no RAI/AAR orchestra concert. At the conclusion of the year, Allen Shearer returned to his teaching post at the University of California, Berkeley, and Arthur Kreiger returned to the United States to continue his composition under a Guggenheim Fellowship.

1980–88, Directors: Sophie Consagra, James Melchert

The Music Program: 1980–88

The 1980–81 fellowship year opened with a new administrative slate and a number of significant changes. Calvin Rand (formerly president of the Niagara Institute) was the Academy's new president and Sophie Consagra (director of visual arts and architecture, New York State Council on the Arts, 1977–80) was the new director. The first woman to serve in that function, Consagra was an administrator who was equally at home in the artistic and social scenes of Italy and the United States. She was director from 1980 to 1984 and president from 1984 to 1988, and the sculptor James Melchert (chair, art department at University of California, Berkeley) was director from 1984 to 1988. Melchert was also a first: the first—and only—practicing artist to occupy the post of director during the 1947–2006 period covered by this history.

This period saw a number of fresh, interrelated initiatives aimed at reorganizing the Academy, solving the Academy's economic problems, and gaining increased visibility. First, a fundamental change was made in the Academy's board of trustees: it was reproportioned to include "a core of corporate leaders," according to Rand, who would "bring a new depth to the Academy's financial resources."[52] John W. Hyland Jr., an investment banker, became chairman of the board of trustees. Rand also proposed that one of the trustees' meetings should be held in Rome rather than New York, and, in June 1982, the spring trustees' meeting was indeed held in Rome at the Academy—a tradition that has continued. This meeting was arranged to coincide with the Academy's closing activities (among others, the fellows' Spring Art Exhibition and the Spring Concert) and proved to be of fundamental importance as an occasion where all the members of the rapidly expanding Academy community could become better acquainted. Later in February 1983, the Academy's New York office held its first fund-raiser since 1927. This successful event paved the way for subsequent events, and in April 1987, *Notte Musicale*, an evening honoring Aaron Copland, Elliott Carter, and Lukas Foss (who conducted a concert of the Brooklyn Philharmonic Orchestra prior to the dinner),[53] would raise a record $175,000 toward the endowment of an additional fellowship in music composition.

Positive signs were soon seen in Rome as well. The fellowship year 1981–82 began with a collective sigh of relief as the Academy moved back into the Villa Aurelia after five years of exile. The Villa's Sala Musica was reopened the following spring with a gala concert in the presence of the American ambassador to Italy, Maxwell Rabb, and his wife. This was to be the first in a series of Academy-embassy concerts that took place alternately at Villa Aurelia and at Villa Taverna (the American ambassador's residence in Rome), and which were designed to bring attention to contemporary American music and to the Academy's role in Rome.

Another initiative intended to bring attention to the music program was begun in the same year. Director Consagra and Raymond Green, president of WFLN, Philadelphia, discussed the possibility of broadcasting recordings made in Rome of fellows' music. The Spring Concerts from 1974 to 1982 and the RAI/AAR orchestral concerts from 1973 to 1982 provided material for two series of broadcasts, moderated by George Diehl and aired in Philadelphia. The first series of seven programs (1983) presented the RAI/AAR orchestra concerts and the second series of nine programs (1984) offered selections from the fellows' chamber music. These two series, entitled "Music from the American Academy in Rome," were subsequently broadcast by WFLN's associated stations throughout the United States. This was the first time that the recording archives of the Academy had received such national attention. In addition, through his connection with Philadelphia's Musical Fund Society, Raymond Green was able to secure funding to cover the cost of a second Fellowship in Music Composition. This crucial and generous support would remain intact for several years.

In the spring of 1983, RAI's third program "Pomeriggio Musicale" also devoted a series of radio transmissions to the musical activity of the American Academy in Rome. In the course of five broadcasts, nine composers associated with the Academy were profiled and their works subsequently broadcast. This series was researched, prepared, and delivered by the American pianist and longtime Rome resident Joseph Rollino.[54]

A number of further collaborations in Rome benefited the music program throughout the eighties. Two of these were particularly useful in exposing the fellows' music locally. In the summer of 1983, the composer fellows had their works performed at the Pontino Contemporary Music Festival (organized by the Campus Internazionale di Musica), which is held each summer near Rome in Latina. The theme of that year's festival was "Contemporary American and Italian Music," and, in addition to the American Academy fellows, Elliott Carter (as guest of honor), Charles Wuorinen, Donald Martino, and Christian Wolff were present for performances of their works. In June 1984 three concerts were held at Rome's Centre d'Etudes Saint-Louis de France featuring the work of composers from the French, German, and American academies and the Swiss Institute. This inter-Academy concert series, Festival International de Musique, included performances of two to three works by each composer. It was organized by the Swiss composer Serge Arnauld, and the American participation was supported by a generous contribution from USIS. The concerts provided fellows exposure and a forum for meeting colleagues and sharing work. It was such a popular idea among the respective academies that it continued through four successive editions.

The collaboration with USIS during this period also included hosting performances by many of the artists selected to participate in their "Artistic Ambassadors" program. These gifted American musicians performed the traditional concert repertoire along with American contemporary music, and their concerts further enriched the Academy's musical offerings. The cooperation with USIS, which had begun with the reopening of the Academy, was kept alive over this entire period by a series of interested and supportive cultural attachés including, among others, Richard Arndt, Alan Dodds, Gilbert Callaway, Warren Obluck, Carol Ludwig, Anne Callaghan, and Mark Smith.

Throughout the eighties and early nineties, the American Academy's concert series continued to present a panorama of American contemporary music and to bring a rich array of American and European performers before the Roman public: Kronos Quartet, Audubon Quartet, Lydian Quartet, Composers String Quartet, David Short Brass Ensemble, American New Music Consortium, New York Contemporary Music Band, Five Centuries Ensemble, I Solisti di Roma, Musica d'Oggi, and Musicisti Americani; the piano duos Gold and Fizdale and Double Edge; the violin and piano duos Ellen Zaehringer and Eric Moe, and Violaine Melancon and Seth Knopp; the cello and piano duos Leopold Teraspulsky and Estella Olevsky, Eric Bartlett and Larry Bell, Geoffrey Rutkowski and Wendell Nelson, and Antonio Lysy and Andrew Tunis; the clarinet and piano duo Raffaello Orlando and Ghit Moy Lee; the tenor and guitar duo Robert Harrison and Charles Wolzien; the pianists Ursula Oppens, Kazimierz Morski, Yehudi Wyner, Judy Carmichael, Mary Humm, Bruce Brubaker, Eric Moe, John Kamitsuka, Richard Trythall, Richard Cass, Patricia Tao, Elizabeth DiFelice, Eugenio Russo, Alexis Smith, Philip Hosford, John Kamitsuka, Sally Pinkas, Barbara Shearer, Anthony de Mare, Werner Bärtschi, Robert Shannon, and Cynthia Peterson; the sopranos Neva Pilgrim,

Joan Logue, Patricia Griffin, and Lisa Stidham; the flutists Megan Meisenbach and Carin Levine; the clarinetists Robert Spring, William O. Smith, and David Keberle; the violinists Gregory Fulkerson and Rose Mary Harbison; the guitarists Lily Afshar, Michele Greci, and William Mathews; the saxophonist Tim Berne; the contrabassist Stefano Scodanibbio; the harpist Claudia Antonelli; and the harpsichordist Sylvia Kind.

The eighties, unfortunately, also brought sad news to the music program. The RAI/AAR collaboration that, from its inception in 1955 under Nicolas Nabokov, had played such an important role in the fellows' life, ended with the December 1, 1984, concert. The demise of this series was essentially part of a larger shift in the RAI's attitude, one with which the Academy had already been dealing for several years. Increased attention was given to ratings and market shares and less interest was shown in pursuing purely cultural ends. On a larger institutional level, there was talk about the excessive cost of the four orchestras maintained by the RAI. The times were changing, and the loss of the Academy's annual concert was an early sign of the course that, only a few years later, led to the total dismantling of three of the four RAI symphonic orchestras (Rome, Milan, and Naples)—a substantial blow to the cultural life of Italy. Certainly the Academy's music program owes an enormous debt of gratitude to the RAI and to the Rome Radio Orchestra for this series of concerts, born as a symbol of gratitude, which spanned twenty-nine years and served the composer fellows so well. It offered, as it were, a prize within a prize, and a number of the works composed and premiered in Rome would serve as impressive visiting cards for many Rome Prize winners when they returned to participate in the musical life of the United States. As Jack Beeson observed in 1966, "the availability of the RAI orchestra performance is one of the strongest attractions of the Rome Prize, at a time when young composers find it almost impossible to obtain orchestral performances in the United States."[55]

The Composers: 1980–88

1980–81: This fellowship year brought Stephen Jaffe (Washington, DC, b. 1954) and John Anthony Lennon (Greensboro, NC, b. 1950) to the Academy. Jaffe, educated at the University of Pennsylvania and in Switzerland at the Geneva Conservatory, had been an instructor at Swarthmore College and director of the "Soloists and Composers" series, Painted Bride Art Center, Philadelphia, when he received the Rome Prize. While on the fellowship, he composed *Partita* for cello, piano, and percussion (commissioned by the National Endowment of the Arts for the Da Capo Chamber Players, premiere 1981), *Arch* for chamber ensemble (premiered on the Spring Concert), and *Intrada* for orchestra (premiered on the RAI/AAR orchestra concert, July 1982). *Intrada* became the first movement of Jaffe's *Four Images for Orchestra* completed later (premiered by the New Jersey Symphony Orchestra, 1988). Lennon, educated at the University of San Francisco and the University of Michigan, was on the faculty of the University of Tennessee, Knoxville, prior to receiving the Rome Prize. At the Academy he composed *Death Angel* for piano (premiered on the Spring Concert), part of his String Quartet, *Voices*, and *Metapictures* for small orchestra (premiered on the RAI/AAR orchestra concert, July 1982). Two earlier guitar pieces, *Evening Color Wind* and *Morning Wings*, were performed in February 1981. The composer-in-residence during the fall was Robert Hall Lewis, who composed String Quartet no. 3, *A Due I* for flutes and harp, *A Due II* for oboe/English horn and percussion, as well as *Atto* for string orchestra (premiered by the Baltimore Symphony Orchestra, October 1983) and *Moto* for orchestra (premiered by the Baltimore Symphony Orchestra, September 1981). His *Nuances* for violin and piano was performed in February. John Harbison (Pulitzer Prize 1987) was the composer-in-residence in the spring; he composed *Piano Quintet* (commissioned by the Santa Fe Festival, premiered in 1981) and Symphony no. 1 (commissioned for the centennial of the Boston Symphony Orchestra, premiered in 1984). He was an Academy trustee from 1991 to 1993. The Spring Concert presented the premieres of Jaffe's *Arch* (conducted by Harbison), Lennon's *Death Angel*, and a performance of Lewis's *Monophony I* for flute. The RAI/AAR orchestra concert (which was out of synch with the music program by approximately two years) took place in June 1981 with performances of previous fellows' music: Dennis Eberhard's *Janus Music*, Sheila Silver's *Chariessa* for soprano and orchestra (both premieres), and Samuel Barber's *Medea* ballet suite. With the completion of the fellowship, Stephen Jaffe joined the faculty of Duke University and John Anthony Lennon continued his compositional work in Paris on a Guggenheim Fellowship before returning to his faculty position at the University of Tennessee, Knoxville. Later he would join the faculty of Emory University.

1981–82: The new fellows were Todd Brief (New York, NY, b. 1953) and Nicholas C. K. Thorne (Copenhagen, DK, b. 1953). Brief was educated at the New England Conservatory of Music and Harvard University, where he was a teaching fellow pursuing his doctorate when he received the Rome Prize. While on the fellowship, he composed *Cantares* for soprano and large orchestra (performed on the RAI/AAR orchestra concert, October 1983). Thorne studied at the Berklee College of Music and the New England Conservatory, where his principal teachers were John Heiss and William Thomas McKinley. He was an instructor at Vermont's Johnson State College when he received the Rome Prize. While in Rome, he wrote an orchestral work, *Symphony from Silence* (premiered by the New York Philharmonic, 1983). The composer-in-residence for the spring was Jacob Druckman (Pulitzer Prize 1972), who worked on the early sketches of an opera. The Spring Concert contained Thorne's *Piano Sonata*, Brief's *Fantasy* for violin and piano, Druckman's *Valentine* for contrabass, and

Daniel Brewbaker's Piano Sonata no. 2 (Brewbaker, who was working with composer Hans Werner Henze, was a visiting artist at the Academy). The RAI/AAR orchestra concert in July featured Lennon's *Metapictures,* Shearer's *Fantasy* for piano and orchestra, Jaffe's *Intrada* (all premieres), and Druckman's *Aureole* (commissioned and premiered by the New York Philharmonic, 1979). With the completion of the fellowship, Todd Brief returned to Harvard to complete his doctoral studies and Nicholas Thorne returned to Vermont to continue composing on a Guggenheim Fellowship.

1982–83: The new fellowship year brought the fellows Larry Bell (Wilson, NC, b. 1952) and William Neil (Pontiac, MI, b. 1954) to the Academy. Bell, educated at the Appalachian State University and the Juilliard School, was on the faculties of the Boston Conservatory and the Juilliard School and the recipient of a Guggenheim Fellowship when he received the Rome Prize. While at the Academy he completed his String Quartet no. 2, *Miniature Diversions* for piano (which he premiered at the Academy), *Revivals* for piano, and *Fantasia on an Imaginary Hymn* for cello and viola (commissioned by Joel Krosnick, premiered in New York, 1985). Along with Eric Bartlett, cellist, he gave a program as pianist that featured his *Variations* and *Miniature Diversions* for piano and *Caprice* for solo cello. His *Continuum* for orchestra was performed on the RAI/AAR orchestra concert, December 1984. Neil, educated at the Cleveland Institute of Music, the University of Michigan, and in Cologne on a Fulbright grant, was teaching and directing the new music festival at DePauw University School of Music when he received the Rome Prize. While at the Academy he composed *Harlem Dances* for guitar, *Deserted Places* for soprano and string quartet (premiered on the Spring Concert), and *A Play of Poems* for soprano, baritone, and orchestra (premiered by the Lyric Opera of Chicago Orchestra, First Chicago Center, 1984). Ezra Laderman (FAAR 1964) was composer-in-residence and worked on the completion of a choral work, *A Man for Cain.* The Spring Concert included Bell's String Quartet no. 1, Neil's *Deserted Places* for soprano and string quartet, *Fantasia* for flute, guitar, and cello, and Laderman's String Quartet no. 6. Both Bell's String Quartet no. 1 and Neil's *Deserted Places* were also performed during the Pontino Contemporary Music Festival in Latina. There was no RAI/AAR orchestra concert. At the conclusion of the year, Larry Bell returned to the faculties of the Boston Conservatory and the Juilliard School. He would return to the Academy frequently as a visiting artist. William Neil remained in Rome for another year composing under a grant from the National Endowment of the Arts before returning to the United States as composer-in-residence for the Lyric Opera of Chicago.

1983–84: Tamar Diesendruck (Tel Aviv, Israel, b. 1946) and Jay Anthony Gach (New York, NY, b. 1955) were the new fellows. Diesendruck had studied at Brandeis University and was completing her doctoral dissertation at the

University of California, Berkeley, when she was awarded the Rome Prize. While at the Academy she wrote *The Palm at the End of the Mind* for contralto and eight instruments (premiered at the San Francisco Conservatory, 1985) and *Quartet* for violin, cello, clarinet, and piano (premiered on the Spring Concert). Gach received his PhD from the State University of New York at Stony Brook shortly before receiving the Rome Prize. At the Academy, he composed *Scenic Chamber Music: Clarinet Quintet* (premiered on the Spring Concert), *Leib Variations* for violin (premiered on the Festival International de Musique concert series), *I Venti d'Estate* for chamber orchestra (winner, 1985, St. Paul Chamber Orchestra American Composers Competition), various pieces for two violins, and *Anthem for Doomed Youth* for large orchestra (renamed *Front Lines,* selected for the Whitaker Readings by the American Composers Orchestra, 1988). The slow movement of his *Scenic Chamber Music: Clarinet Quintet* was later rescored and premiered by the London-based Haydn Chamber Orchestra with support from the Fromm Music Foundation. The composer-in-residence for the winter and spring was Hugo Weisgall, who worked on a large song cycle, *Lyrical Interval* for low voice and piano (poetry by John Hollander, commissioned by the Serge Koussevitzky Music Foundation in the Library of Congress, premiere 1988). Weisgall also lectured on his work and conducted Gach's *Clarinet Quintet* on the Spring Concert. Also present for the entire year as visiting artists were the composer-pianist Eric Moe and the violinist Ellen Zaehringer, both of whom contributed their talents graciously to several musical events. The Spring Concert contained Gach's *Scenic Chamber Music: Clarinet Quintet* (premiere), Diesendruck's *Mana* for clarinet, and *Quartet* for violin, cello, clarinet, bass clarinet, and piano (premiere), Eric Moe's *Fantasy* for piano (premiere performed by the composer), and Weisgall's *Liebeslieder* for soprano and piano. Three weeks later, Diesendruck's *Mana* and *Quartet* were also performed on the Festival International de Musique concert series along with her *Tangents* for piano, while Gach was represented by his *Scenic Chamber Music: Clarinet Quintet,* his previously written *Sonatina* for piano, and the premiere of his *Leib Variations* for violin. Earlier in the year, Diesendruck's *Context* (1978) for prepared piano was performed by Eric Moe. The RAI/AAR concert, which occurred in October, featured Arthur Kreiger's *Remnants* (premiere), Todd Brief's *Cantares* for soprano and orchestra, Richard Trythall's *Ballad* for piano and orchestra (premiere of revised version with the composer as pianist), and Aaron Copland's *Quiet City.* At the end of the year, Tamar Diesendruck returned to teach and compose in San Francisco and Jay Anthony Gach remained in Europe, eventually returning to New York in 2000.

1984–85: The new fellows were Paul Moravec (Buffalo, NY, b. 1957) and Aaron Jay Kernis (Philadelphia, PA, b. 1960). Moravec, educated at Harvard University and Columbia University, where he was pursuing his doctorate when he received the Rome Prize, wrote *Music Remembers* for piano, *The Open*

Secret for violin, cello, and piano, and *Innocent Dreamers* for soprano and piano (premiered on the Spring Concert). Kernis, educated at the San Francisco Conservatory of Music, Manhattan School, and Yale School of Music, was freelancing in various music-related jobs in New York City when he received the Rome Prize. He spent his year working on a large orchestra work, *Mirror of Heat and Light (Cycle V-Part 2)* (commissioned and premiered by the New York Youth Symphony, February 1985). David Del Tredici (Pulitzer Prize 1980) arrived in March as composer-in-residence. He was working on *Haddock's Eyes* for soprano and ten instruments (premiered by the Chamber Music Society of Lincoln Center, 1986). The Spring Concert contained Moravec's *Innocent Dreamers* (premiere) and *Wings* for soprano, flute, clarinet, cello, and piano, Kernis's *Music for Trio (Cycle IV)*, and Del Tredici's *Fantasy Pieces* for piano (performed by the composer). The Festival International de Musique concert series featured Kernis's *Music for Trio* and *Meditation* and Moravec's *Timepiece* and *Songs* for violin and piano. The final RAI/AAR orchestra concert was held in December of 1984 and featured Larry Bell's *Continuum*, Roger Sessions's *The Black Maskers Suite*, Charles Ives's *The Unanswered Question*, and George Gershwin's *An American in Paris*. A special concert in honor of the visiting artist Elliott Carter's eightieth birthday was performed in February by the Musica d'Oggi Ensemble conducted by Richard Dufallo. This concert, given in collaboration with the Aspen Institute, contained Carter's *A Mirror on Which to Dwell* for soprano and chamber orchestra and *Riconoscenza per Goffredo Petrassi* for solo violin. This was preceded a few days earlier by a roundtable discussion at the Villa Aurelia with Roman Vlad, Goffredo Petrassi, and Carter, who discussed the American and Italian musical scene over the past forty years.[56] Other visiting artists who spent varying periods of the year at the Academy included Lukas Foss, Hugo Weisgall, Larry Bell, Ezra Laderman, Stephen Jaffe, and Jacob Druckman. Upon completion of their fellowships, Aaron Jay Kernis returned to New York as a freelance composer and Paul Moravec returned to finish his doctorate at Columbia University. Kernis would win the Pulitzer Prize in 1998 and Moravec would win it in 2004.

1985–86: Composers Scott A. Lindroth (Cincinnati, OH, b. 1958) and Rand Steiger (New York, NY, b. 1957) were the new fellows. Lindroth, educated at the Eastman School and Yale University, was freelancing in New York when he received the Rome Prize. While at the Academy, he composed two orchestral pieces: *Two-Part Invention* (commissioned and premiered by the New York Youth Symphony, May 1986) and *Relations to Rigor* for fifteen-piece chamber ensemble (later also written for six instruments and tape). His *Chasing the Trane Out of Darmstadt* for tenor sax and piano and *Pieces of Piano* were performed on both the Spring Concert and the Festival International de Musique concert series. Steiger, educated at the Manhattan School of Music, the California Institute of the Arts, and with studies in computer music at IRCAM (Institut de recherche et coordination acoustique/musique) in Paris, was on the composition faculty of the California Institute of the Arts when he received the Rome Prize. While at the Academy, he completed *ReSonata* for cello and piano (commissioned by the National Association of Professional Music Teachers for Erika Duke), the third movement of *Tributaries* for orchestra (premiered by the St. Paul Chamber Orchestra), and his *Double Concerto* for piano, percussion, and double chamber orchestra (premiered by the Los Angeles Philharmonic, John Harbison conductor, 1987). There was no composer-in-residence. The Spring Concert included Steiger's *ReSonata* and *Quintessence* for clarinet, percussion, piano, electric piano, and cello, Lindroth's *Pieces of Piano* and *Chasing the Trane Out of Darmstadt,* and *Arabesque 2* for piano by Trythall (composer at the piano). Visiting artists included Elliott Carter, Jerome Rosen, Susan Blaustein, and Larry Bell. At the conclusion of the year, Rand Steiger returned to his position at the California Institute of the Arts and subsequently joined the faculty of the University of California, San Diego. Scott Lindroth returned to New York and, following residencies at the MacDowell Colony and at CalArts, received a Guggenheim Fellowship, completed his doctorate at the Yale School of Music, and joined the faculty of Duke University in 1990.

1986–87: The new fellow was Thomas Oboe Lee (Beijing, China, b. 1945). Lee, who had studied at the University of Pittsburgh, the New England Conservatory, and Harvard University, was on the faculty of New England Conservatory when he was awarded the Rome Prize. While at the Academy, he wrote a number of chamber works: *Harp Trio* for flute, harp, and cello (premiered at the Spring Concert), *29 Fireflies, Book II, v–xi* for solo piano (premiered on the Festival International de Musique concert series and performed on the Spring Concert), String Quartet no. 5, *Chôrinhos* for flute, clarinet, oboe, violin, cello, piano, and percussion, *Apples* for mezzo-soprano and piano (text by poet Richard Kenney, FAAR 1987), as well as a *Concertino* for trumpet, timpani, and string orchestra. His *String Trio* for violin, viola, and cello was performed on both the Festival International de Musique concert series and the Spring Concert. The composer-in-residence from February through May was Earle Brown. While in residence, Brown composed *Three Graphic Works for Orchestra* and worked on his *Double Quartet* for saxophones and strings. The RAI, in collaboration with Nuova Consonanza, USIS, and the Academy, devoted a concert at their Foro Italico Auditorium to Brown's chamber orchestra music. The program included his *Windsor Jambs* for voice and chamber orchestra, *Corroboree* for three pianos, *New Piece* for approximately twenty musicians, and *Centering* for violin solo and ten instruments. The Spring Concert contained Lee's *String Trio, 29 Fireflies* for piano, and *Harp Trio* (premiere), and Alexei Haieff's (FAAR 1949) *Three Pieces for Violin and Piano* and *Duo for Flutes* (premiere). Also present at differing periods in the year as visiting artists were the composers Robert Ashley, Matthias Kriesberg, Martin Mailman, and Chester Biscardi. At the conclusion of his fellowship, Thomas Oboe Lee joined the faculty of the Massachusetts Institute of Technology.

1987–88: This fellowship year brought Kamran Ince (Glendire, MO, b. 1960) and Steve Rouse (Moss Point, MS, b. 1953) to the Academy. Ince, educated at Oberlin College and the Eastman School of Music, was completing his doctorate at Eastman when he received the Rome Prize. He composed two piano works, *An Unavoidable Obsession* (commissioned by the Brooklyn Conservatory of Music) and *My Friend Mozart,* as well as *Deep Flight* for chamber orchestra (commissioned by ASCAP and Meet the Composer, premiered by the Brooklyn Philharmonic, New York, 1988) and *Waves of Talya* for flute, clarinet, percussion, piano, violin, and cello (commissioned by the Koussevitzky Foundation, premiered by *Terra Australis,* New York, 1989). Rouse, who had studied at the University of Southern Mississippi and the University of Michigan, wrote *Ribbons* for string orchestra (premiered by the Louisville Strings in June 1991). The composer-in-residence for the fall, Fred Lerdahl (finalist, Pulitzer Prize 2001), was composing *Waves* (commissioned and performed by the Orpheus, St. Paul, and Los Angeles chamber orchestras, 1988), and John Adams (Pulitzer Prize 2003), the composer-in-residence for the spring, was working on *Fearful Symmetries* (commissioned and premiered by the Orchestra of St. Luke's, Avery Fisher Hall, October 1988). Both composers gave lectures on their recent work, and Adams went into detail about his recent opera *Nixon in China.* The Spring Concert contained three works by Ince: *Cross Scintillations* for two pianos, *Unavoidable Obsession* for piano (premiere by the composer), *Kac* for sax, piano, and percussion, Rouse's *Piano Sonata,* and Alexei Haieff's *Quintet for Winds* (premiere). Also present at different times through the year as visiting artists were the composers John Eaton, Ingram Marshall, Larry Bell, Lukas Foss, Hugo Weisgall, Louise Lerdahl (both Weisgall and Lerdahl also gave lectures), and the conductor Harold Farberman. At the conclusion of the year, Kamran Ince moved to Ann Arbor to compose his Symphony no. 1 ("Castles in the Air") under a Guggenheim Fellowship and Steve Rouse joined the faculty of the University of Louisville.

1988–94, Director: Joseph Connors

The Music Program: 1988–94

The 1988–89 fellowship year once more brought a change of leadership to the Academy. The new director was Joseph Connors, RAAR 1987 (professor, history of art, Columbia University), and the new president was Adele Chatfield-Taylor, FAAR 1984 (director of the NEA Design Arts program, 1984–88). Sophie Consagra remained with the Academy as vice chair of special projects for the next two years, overseeing several ongoing development projects. Connors had been the art historian-in-residence at the Academy during the previous year and moved seamlessly into the responsibilities of director. He would remain director for four years before returning to his post at Columbia University. Adele Chatfield-Taylor also knew the Academy well since, five years earlier, she had been a fellow in design arts—the same year that Sophie Consagra finished her term as director and simultaneously signed on as president. During her remarkably long and successful tenure, Chatfield-Taylor would preside over a number of extremely significant changes at all levels of Academy life.

Together Connors and Chatfield-Taylor inherited an institution that, though still faced by financial problems (the stock market crash and fall of the dollar in 1987, for example), was nevertheless moving forward energetically thanks to the combined efforts of many and to the leadership that Sophie Consagra had provided over the past eight years. The substantial remodeling that had gone on metaphorically within the Academy community would now find its concrete equivalent in the renewal of the Academy properties. The Villa Aurelia was remodeled in 1988–89 and, shortly afterward, a long-term program for the restoration of the Academy's eleven acres of gardens was begun. The Academy's library (located within the McKim building) was renovated and expanded in 1991 and subsequently the remainder of that magnificent building (which also contains the Academy's administrative offices, dining facilities, and the living quarters and studios for the majority of the fellows) was totally renovated (October 1992–April 1994). The completion of this latter renovation was timed to coincide with the Academy's centennial celebration in June 1994—a commemoration of one hundred years of nurturing American scholarly and artistic development. The restoration of this monumental building was, indeed, both a celebration of past accomplishments and an unmistakable sign that this mission would continue. As Joseph Connors wrote in the fall of 1989, these were decisions "which will affect life at the Academy for several generations."[57]

Inevitably such far-reaching structural changes would interrupt life at the Academy. There were no fellows during the 1992–93 year, nor was there a director. The Academy's main building, with the sole exception of the library, which continued to operate, was closed for renovation and the staff was relocated to Villa Bellacci, the small building next to the Academy that now hosts the director. The concert series at the Villa Aurelia continued throughout the year with the intent of maintaining a tangible presence in the cultural life of Rome while the Academy was closed.[58]

When the Academy resumed operation for the 1993–94 fellowship year, it began with a reduced contingent of ten fellows living and working in the Villa Aurelia and in various subsidiary buildings on the grounds of the Academy. In January the new director, Caroline A. Bruzelius, FAAR 1986, RAAR 1989 (professor, history of art, Duke University), arrived. She had been a fellow in 1985–86 and art historian-in-residence in 1988–89 and, consequently, knew the

Academy well. This preparation stood her in good stead in resolving the manifold problems involved with "getting the show back on the road."

In April, with the renovation completed, everyone, director, staff, and fellows, returned to occupy the refurbished McKim building. In June 1994, the centennial celebration featured the Spring Concert, a jazz concert by William O. Smith (FAAR 1958), a retrospective concert by the composer-pianist Yehudi Wyner (FAAR 1956), a visit from First Lady Hillary Rodham Clinton and US Ambassador Reginald Bartholomew, and a celebration at Rome's Campidoglio under the auspices of Mayor Francesco Rutelli.

The Composers: 1988–94

1988–89: The composers Kathryn Alexander (Waco, TX, b. 1955) and Michelle Ekizian (Bronxville, NY, b. 1956) were the new fellows. Alexander, educated at Baylor University, the Cleveland Institute of Music, and the Eastman School, was teaching at the Oberlin Conservatory of Music when she received the Rome Prize. She completed three works during her stay: *You Will Be We* for chorus and organ (commissioned and premiered by the Old Stone Singers, June 1989), *Song of Songs* for soprano and chamber ensemble (commissioned by the National Endowment for the Arts, premiered by Boston Musica Viva, February 1990) and . . . *APPEARS!* for orchestra (premiered by The Women's Philharmonic, November 1997). In addition to the works performed on the Spring Concert, her earlier work for flute and electronic tape, *And the Whole Air Is Tremulous,* was performed in May. Ekizian, who had studied at the Manhattan School of Music and had just completed her doctorate at Columbia University when she received the Rome Prize, composed *Beyond the Reach of Wind and Fire: For Orchestra with Mezzo Soprano at Epilogue* (commissioned and premiered by the American Composers Orchestra with support from the Jerome Foundation, Carnegie Hall, December 1989). There was no composer-in-residence this year. The Spring Concert featured Alexander's *Rainbows Stretched Like Endless Reins* for solo violin, *One Haze, One Incandescence* for electronic tape, *Dance the Orange!* for trombone, and Ekizian's *Swan Song* for soprano and *Octoéchos* for double string quartet and soprano. Given the theatrical nature of part of their program, the composers elected to use the Academy's Atrium as the location for their Spring Concert. A number of composers resided at the Academy as visiting artists for various periods during the year: Hugo Weisgall, Tamar Diesendruck, Eric Moe, and John Harbison. Weisgall gave a lecture on "Opera's Latest Crises." At the conclusion of the year, Kathryn Alexander returned to the United States, where she received a Composer's Fellowship from the National Endowment for the Arts, 1989–90. In the fall of 2002, she cocurated a concert series held at Carnegie Recital Hall, *Americans in Rome: Music by Fellows of the American Academy in Rome.* Upon returning to the United

States, Ekizian was awarded the Indiana State University/Louisville Orchestral Composition Prize 1989 for her orchestral work *Morning of Light*, which was subsequently premiered by the Louisville Orchestra in the spring of 1990. She also completed two earlier National Endowment of the Arts commissions: *The Crane: Double Concerto for Clarinet and Conga Drums* (premiered by the Contemporary Chamber Players of the University of Chicago, 1991) and *David of Sassoon* (premiered by the San Francisco Contemporary Chamber Music Players, 1993). Ekizian served as a vice president, music, in the AAR Society of Fellows from 1990 to 2001.

1989–90: In this year, Walter Winslow (Salem, OR, 1947–97) and James C. Mobberley (Des Moines, IA, b. 1954) were the fellows. Winslow, educated at Oberlin College, Oberlin Conservatory, and the University of California, Berkeley, had been teaching at Columbia University when he was awarded the Rome Prize. While at the Academy, he composed *Sette Bagattelle di Primavera* for flute (premiered on the Spring Concert), *Trio Rustico* for flute, clarinet, and cello (commissioned and premiered by the Earplay ensemble, 1989), and an orchestral work, *The Piper of the Sacred Grove*. Mobberley had studied with Roger Hannay at the University of North Carolina and with Donald Erb at the Cleveland Institute of Music. He was teaching at the University of Missouri, Kansas City, when he received the Rome Prize. He composed *Soggiorno* for violin and tape (premiered on the Spring Concert), *On Thin Ice* for tuba/euphonium ensemble (premiered at the Sapporo International Festival, Japan, 1990), and *In Bocca del Lupo* for violin and tape (winner, Kazimierz Serocki International Composers' Competition, Polish Section, ISCM) while at the Academy. The composer-in-residence for the fall, Harvey Sollberger, composed *Aurelian Echoes* for flute and alto flute and a *Trio (. . . from winter's frozen stillness)* for violin, cello, and piano. Also well-known as a performer, he gave a flute recital that included his *Aurelian Echoes* (premiere), *Riding the Wind IV (1974)*, and *Quodlibetudes (1988)*, as well as Mobberley's *Going with the Fire* (for flute and tape) and music by Roger Reynolds and Sandra Sprecher. Ellen Taaffe Zwilich (Pulitzer Prize 1983), composer-in-residence during the spring, worked on a *Quintet* for clarinet and string quartet. Zwilich gave an illustrated lecture during the spring concentrating on her recently premiered *Flute Concerto* (commissioned and premiered by the Boston Symphony Orchestra, 1989). During the spring the Italian translation of David Schiff's book *The Music of Elliott Carter* was presented at the Villa Aurelia. In addition to a roundtable discussion with Elliott Carter, Goffredo Petrassi, and the Italian musicologist Franco Carlo Ricci, there was a performance of Carter's *Night Fantasies* by the Italian pianist Giuseppe Scotese followed by a dinner in Carter's honor. The fellows' Spring Concert contained Winslow's *Four Kauai Studies* for piano, *A Modern Evangelist* for trombone, *Six Songs on Poems of William Stafford* for soprano and piano (first complete performance), and Mobberley's *Soggiorno* for violin and tape (premiere), *A Plurality of One* for clarinet and tape, and *Beams!* for trombone and tape. Mobberley also had a performance of *Caution to the Winds* for piano and tape earlier in the year. Composers who spent time at the Academy as visiting artists included Wayne Peterson, Sandra Sprecher, Elliott Carter, and Todd Brief. At the conclusion of the fellowship year, Walter Winslow returned to teach at the Lawrenceville School while James Mobberley returned to his position on the faculty of the University of Missouri, Kansas City.

1990–91: Lee Hyla (Niagara Falls, NY, 1952–2014) and David Lang (Los Angeles, CA, b. 1957) were the new fellows. Hyla, who studied with Malcolm Peyton at the New England Conservatory and David Lewin at SUNY, Stony Brook, was a freelance composer living in New York when he received the Rome Prize. While at the Academy, he completed *Ciao Manhattan* for viola, alto flute, cello, and piano (written for the Dinosaur Annex Ensemble of Boston) and began his Concerto for Piano and Chamber Orchestra no. 2 (commissioned by the Shifting Foundation for *Speculum Musicae* and Aleck Karis, premiered at the Miller Theater, NY, 1991). David Lang, educated at Stanford University, the University of Iowa, and the Yale School of Music, was codirecting the "Bang on a Can" concert series in New York when he received the Rome Prize. While at the Academy, he wrote *The Anvil Chorus* for solo percussionist (commissioned by the Fromm Foundation, premiered on the "Bang on a Can" Festival, 1991), *Incidental Music and Songs for The Resistible Rise of Arturo Ui by Berthold Brecht* (CSC Repertory Theatre, NY, 1991), *Hunk of Burnin' Love* for thirteen players (premiere, Munich New Music Ensemble, 1991), and *Bonehead* for orchestra (premiered by the American Composers Orchestra, NY, 1990). The composer-in-residence for the fall was Charles Wuorinen (Pulitzer Prize 1970) and for the spring Yehudi Wyner (Pulitzer Prize 2006). During their residencies, Wuorinen delivered a lecture on his music and Wyner performed a piano concert that included his music from 1952 to the present: *Partita, Sonata for Piano, Three Short Fantasies,* and *Toward the Center.* He also composed a new work for piano, *New Fantasies,* during his residency. The Spring Concert featured Hyla's *Mythic Birds of Saugerties* for bass clarinet, *Pre-amnesia* for alto saxophone, *The Dream of Innocent III* for amplified cello, percussion, and piano (with the composer at the piano), and Lang's *Drop* for bass clarinet, cello, percussion, piano, and synthesizer, and *Orpheus Over and Under* for two pianos. Visiting artists included Elliott Carter, Paul Moravec, Larry Bell, Richard Danielpour, Harvey Sollberger, and Richard Willis. Following the fellowship year, Lee Hyla returned to New York, where he completed his Concerto for Piano and Chamber Orchestra no. 2 and wrote *We Speak Etruscan* for saxophone and bass clarinet. David Lang retuned to New York to continue his direction of the "Bang on a Can" Festival.

1991–92: The fellows this year were Bun-Ching Lam (Macau, b. 1954) and Stephen Hartke (Orange, NJ, b. 1952). Bun-Ching Lam, who studied at Chung

Chi College, Hong Kong, and the University of California, San Diego, was living in New York City when she received the Rome Prize. While at the Academy she composed *Last Spring* for piano and string quartet (premiered at Merkin Hall, New York, by Ursula Oppens and the Arditti Quartet, and performed on the Spring Concert) and began *Circle* for orchestra. Hartke, educated at Yale University, the University of Pennsylvania, and the University of California, Santa Barbara, was teaching at the University of Southern California when he received the Rome Prize. He wrote *Un tout petit trompe l'oreille* for guitar and composed much of his Concerto for violin and orchestra ("Auld Swaara") (commissioned by the Koussevitzky Music Foundation for Michelle Makarski and the Albany Symphony Orchestra) while at the Academy. The composer-in-residence during the fall was Donald Erb, who was completing his *Ritual Observances* for orchestra (commissioned and premiered by the St. Louis Symphony Orchestra, spring 1992). There were two monographic Spring Concerts. The first concert featured Lam's compositions: *Bittersweet Music 1* for piccolo, *After Spring* for two pianos, *L'Air du Temps* for string quartet, *Another Spring* for flute, cello, and piano, and *Last Spring* for string quartet and piano. The second concert featured Hartke's compositions: *Oh Them Rats Is Mean in My Kitchen* for violin duo, *Iglesia Abandonada* for soprano and violin, *Sonata-Variations* for violin and piano, *Night Rubrics* for cello, and *The King of the Sun* for violin, viola, cello, and piano. The visiting artist, soprano Lisa Stidham, performed a concert during the year. Upon completion of the year, Bun-Ching Lam returned to New York and Hartke returned to his position on the faculty of the University of Southern California.

1993–94: No fellowships were offered during the 1992–93 year because of the renovation work outlined previously. When fellowships resumed for the 1993–94 year, the fellow in music composition was Sebastian Currier (Huntington, PA, b. 1959). Currier, educated at the Manhattan School of Music and the Juilliard School, was teaching at the Juilliard School when he received the Rome Prize. While at the Academy, he completed *Brainstorm* for piano (written for the pianist John Kamitsuka, premiered in a concert honoring the newly arrived American Ambassador Reginald Bartholomew, June 1994) and *Quartetset* for string quartet (written for the Cassatt Quartet). *Brainstorm,* along with another work by Currier, *Scarlatti Cadences,* would later win the First American Composers Invitational awarded by the Van Cliburn International Piano Competition, 2005. His *Theo's Sketchbook* for piano was performed in May. Currier also devoted his time to orchestrating Symphony no. 2 by his close friend, the late Stephen Albert (FAAR 1967). Two fine pianists, Emma Tahmizian and John Kamitsuka, were living at the Academy as visiting artists for most of this period and both shared their considerable talents with the small but sturdy community. There was no composer-in-residence. The year culminated in June with a week of festive centennial ceremonies that included the Spring Concert, featuring Sebastian Currier's *Clockwork* and *Entanglement* (both for violin and piano) as well as music by Brahms and Mozart. With the conclusion of his fellowship, Sebastian Currier returned to his position at the Juilliard School and thereafter joined the faculty of Columbia University.

1994–98, Director: Caroline A. Bruzelius

The Music Program: 1994–98

That fall, the beginning of the Academy's second century of activity, seemed truly auspicious. The sensation of rediscovered splendor, transmitted by every detail of the McKim, Mead and White building, was palpable. In addition to revealing its original beauty, there were numerous improvements that made life in the building easier and more comfortable. Of particular interest to the music program was the discovery that the newly renovated cryptoporticus (the subterranean corridor that runs beneath the Academy's central cortile) had become an acceptable performance space with good acoustics and a large seating capacity. While Villa Aurelia's Sala Musica, the traditional location for most of the Academy's concerts, offered the most elegant performance setting, it could seat no more than 100 people. Overflow audiences congregated in the side and back rooms—a solution that was neither ideal acoustically nor in accordance with recent Italian fire regulations. The white, brick-lined cryptoporticus, on the other hand, though underground and totally lacking in the festive baroque ornamentation of the villa, could seat 150 people easily—often more. For certain events its "underground" character was even preferable to that of the villa.

The cryptoporticus was inaugurated as a concert hall in November 1994 with an Academy "family" concert that united the combined talents of all the musicians associated with the Academy that year: the pianists Francis Thorne, Edmund Campion, John Eaton, Richard Trythall, and John Kamitsuka, and the soprano Tamzen Flanders. From that moment on, the cryptoporticus became an alternative performance location for the music program. Later in the year, in gracious recognition of the music program, Director Caroline Bruzelius hosted a dinner at the Villa Aurelia in honor of my twenty-five years of service as music liaison. The occasion served to recognize and thank a number of Italian musicians and administrators who had collaborated with the Academy's music program through those years. Those attending the dinner included Maestro Massimo Pradella, who had conducted many of the RAI/AAR orchestra concerts; Landa Ketoff, music critic for Rome's prestigious *La Repubblica* and wife of the audio engineer Paul Ketoff; Franco Muzzi and Renata Bertelli, the RAI administrative personnel who had been instrumental in maintaining the Academy's RAI concerts throughout the years; and a number of Roman and American musicians. Also honored were three members of the Academy staff who had been crucially important in supporting the music program: Patricia Weaver, Caroline Howard, and Pina Pasquantonio.

The results of the Academy's ambitious fund-raising program for music, begun in 1990, were also being savored in Rome. The 1990–91 fellowship year, the seventieth anniversary of the Rome Prize in Music Composition, had, in fact, been declared the Academy's "Year of Music." An imposing New York benefit in honor of Elliott Carter, Giancarlo Menotti, William Schuman, and George Weisman got things started (April 1991) and a fund-raising campaign sparked by the forthcoming centennial celebration, the "NOTEworthyFUND," carried it forward. That winter there was a series of three concerts featuring fellows' music given at the Juilliard School as part of a plan to bring more attention to the Academy's music program. Over the next years, the fund-raising activities set in motion at this time would lead to the endowment of the composer-in-residence position (1992, by the Fromm Foundation), the endowment of a new composer's studio, the Copland Studio (1993, the Aaron Copland Foundation), the complete renovation of five of the Academy's grand pianos (1992–93, by The Whitaker Fund),[59] annual gifts in support of the fellows' Spring Concerts (1995–present, by the Aaron Copland Foundation), and the completion of the endowment for the second Fellowship in Music Composition, the "Samuel Barber Fellowship" (1997). Furthermore, in the fall of 1996 the Academy completed the endowment necessary to reinstate the position of artist-in-charge of the School of Fine Arts that had been suspended sixty years earlier. This position, the Andrew Heiskell Arts Director, was the equivalent of the Andrew W. Mellon Professor in Charge of the School of Classical Studies position that had traditionally overlooked the scholarly side of the Academy's activities.[60] In his report of ten years earlier, the artist and Academy director Jim Melchert—a strong advocate for the arts at the Academy—had likened the Academy's arts program to "a car that is running on only half of its cylinders," pointing out that "a strong program in the arts has to restore the position of a person in charge of the School of Fine Arts."[61] Fortunately his advocacy, and that of many others as well, did not go unheeded. For the artist fellows, this new position meant that there was finally a full-time person, living on the Academy grounds, who could attend to their varied professional needs in the fields of architecture, landscape architecture, design, historic preservation and conservation, creative writing, music composition, and the visual arts, as well as give cohesion and resonance to the Academy's artistic presence in Rome. The first Heiskell Arts Director was the art curator Peter Boswell (1996–99), followed by the art curator Linda Blumberg (1999–2002) and the artist Dana Prescott (2002–7). Although their expertise was primarily in the visual arts, they were extremely sensitive to the needs of the individual composers and supportive of the music program, for which they were now administratively responsible.

The arrival of the first arts director in the fall of 1996 coincided with a collaboration between the Academy and Nuova Consonanza that has remained in place since then: the presentation of the six-hour marathon, Festa d'Autunno, that traditionally opens Nuova Consonanza's fall concert season. This event, organized by Nuova Consonanza and hosted by the Academy, includes multiple concerts of all sorts—from the Italian National Carabinieri Band to Italian folk music to the most erudite contemporary music ensemble—as well as, depending on the year, dance productions, art exhibitions and installations, poetry readings, video projections, book displays, roundtable discussions, and more. The McKim building's renovated spaces offered six spacious locations to be utilized during such a happening—the cortile and the park located directly in front of the Academy for outside events and the dining room, the salone, the cryptoporticus and the atrium for inside activities. Events could, and did, take place simultaneously and the audience was provided with a map and timetable to orient itself. Suitably for a festa, food and drink were also available. Such an occasion, of course, placed Rome's contemporary musical life right at the Academy's doorstep and the good will it generated certainly encouraged the ready acceptance of Academy fellows and initiatives within the Roman musical scene. In later seasons, fellows' works were performed within this framework, serving to "jumpstart" their presence in the Roman musical world. Attendance of this event would generally run anywhere from four hundred to five hundred spectators each year and, at this writing, the collaboration is in its eleventh edition.

The Composers: 1994–98

1994–95: Edmund Campion (Dallas, TX, b. 1957) was the 1994–95 Fellow in Music Composition. Campion, educated at the University of Texas, Columbia University, and the Paris Conservatory, where he studied with Gérard Grisey, was working in Paris at IRCAM when he was awarded the Rome Prize. While at the Academy he composed *Quadrivium*, completing the first three of four pieces for instruments or electronics: *Mathematica* for flute with quadraphonic tape (developed with the flutist Lauren Weiss), *Geometria* for solo clarinet (developed with the composer-clarinettist David Keberle), and *Astronomia* for marimba with quadraphonic tape (developed with the mallet player Vincent Limouzin). Campion also collaborated as composer, pianist, and conductor with the design fellows Kristin Jones (FAAR 1994) and Andrew Ginzel (FAAR 1994) to create *Ellipsis*—an evocative three-hour music and art event that took place in the center of Rome at the Acquario Romano (a unique, elliptical building that had originally housed the city's aquarium) on June 21, the night of the summer solstice. This event, which involved covering the floor with piles of "lunar" sand, setting out several thousand wine glasses in random order, creating a shrub-lined space for the concert grand piano that would be played by Campion, mounting the amplification and the suggestive penumbra lighting effects, rehearsing a chamber chorus scattered throughout the upper tiers of the building to surround the audience, and so forth, was a particularly ambitious and successful example of what can be done when the Academy fellows and Rome interact.[62] The Spring Concert presented the premiere of the first three sections of Campion's *Quadrivium* as well as his *Losing Touch* for vibraphone and quadraphonic tape. (This latter work won the *Concours International de Musique Electroacoustique, Bourges* for that year.) During the fall, Francis Thorne was the Paul Fromm Resident in Music Composition. Thorne completed his Symphony no. 7 ("Along the Hudson") for chorus and orchestra (premiered by the Albany Symphony Orchestra, 1996) and, in addition, shared his fine singing voice with a standing-room-only audience at the Villa Aurelia in renditions of classic songs by George Gershwin and Cole Porter. Also present during the fall as visiting artists were John Eaton and Harvey Sollberger. At the end of the year, Edmund Campion returned to Paris for further work at the IRCAM center and subsequently joined the faculty of the University of California, Berkeley.

1995–96: Thanks to the generosity of Lily Auchincloss, the 1995–96 fellowship year once more offered two fellowships in music composition. The fellows were David Rakowski (St. Albans, Vermont, b. 1958) and Nathan Currier (Huntington, PA, b. 1960). Rakowski, educated at the New England Conservatory and Princeton University, was teaching at Columbia University when he received the Rome Prize. While at the Academy, Rakowski wrote *Piano Études #8–11* (#8 was premiered at the Spring Concert), *The Burning Women Revisited* for soprano and clarinet (premiered at the Spring Concert), *Two Can Play That Game* for bass clarinet and marimba, *Weather Jazz* for soprano and Pierrot ensemble, *Tight Fit* for cello and piano, *Last Dance* for soprano, clarinet, and piano, *Nothing But the Wind* for soprano and orchestra, and *Sesso e Violenza* for seven players. He also completed the last half of *No Holds Barred* for cello and fifteen instruments, started a ballet with children's chorus, *Boy in the Dark* (commissioned by Boston Musica Viva), and completed the first movement of *Persistent Memory* for chamber orchestra (commissioned by the Orpheus Chamber Orchestra, finalist for the Pulitzer Prize in 1999). Currier, educated at the Peabody Institute of Johns Hopkins University, the Belgian Royal Conservatory in Liège under a Fulbright grant and the Juilliard School, was on the faculty of the Juilliard Evening Division when he received the Rome Prize. While at the Academy, he put the final touches on two works in progress: *Hildegard's Symphony* for large orchestra with harp solo and *From the Grotto: A Sonata for Mozart's Secret Society* for piano solo (premiered on the Spring Concert), and he composed *In a Burning Forest* for violin, clarinet, and piano (commissioned by the Verdehr Trio, premiered 1996). There was no composer-in-residence. Two Spring Concerts presented a panorama of each fellow's work. Rakowski was represented by *Diverti* and *Mento* for clarinet and piano; *Silently, A Wind Goes Over,* and *Three Songs on Poems of Louise Bogan* for soprano and piano; *Terra Firma* for five instruments; *Close Enough for Jazz* and *Mano à Mano* for piano (premieres); and *The Burning Woman Revisited* for soprano and clarinet (premiere). Currier was represented by his *Kafka Cantata* for tenor and seven instruments, and premieres of his *Hush Cries the Lamb* for violin and piano, *Sonata for Flute and Piano* (written in the year preceding his fellowship), and *From the Grotto: A Sonata for Mozart's Secret Society* (performed by the composer). These were the first Spring Concerts to be funded by a grant from the Aaron Copland Foundation. The composer-performers Francis Thorne and Beth Wiemann were visiting artists and both shared their talents generously with the community. At the conclusion of the year, David Rakowski joined the faculty of Brandeis University while Nathan Currier returned to teach at the Juilliard School.

1996–97: The Fellow in Music Composition this fellowship year was Arthur Levering (Baltimore, MD, b. 1953). Levering was educated at Colby College, Yale University School of Music, and Boston University School for the Arts. He was a freelance composer living in Boston, recently commissioned to write a work for Boston Musica Viva, when he won the Rome Prize. While at the Academy, he composed that work, *Still Raining, Still Dreaming* for six players (commissioned by the Barlow Endowment, premiered by Boston Musica Viva, and performed later on the Spring Concert); *Musica Ambiente* for computer-driven synthesizer (written as background music for the architecture show of Luigi Centola AFAAR 1997);[63] and *Cloches II* for eight players (commissioned and premiered the following year by Rome's Gruppo Strumentale Musica d'Oggi). The Spring Concert also featured his *Clarion* for clarinet, violin, and piano; *Uncle Inferno* for piano, six hands; *School of Velocity* for piano; and *Twenty Ways upon the Bells* for flute, clarinet, piano, percussion, violin, viola, and cello. His trio *Clarion/Shadowing* was also performed at the Nuova Consonanza Festival and at the Acquario Romano by the Gruppo Strumentale Musica d'Oggi. The Paul Fromm Resident in Music Composition during the spring was Mario Davidovsky (Pulitzer Prize 1971), who was working on his Quartet no. 2 for oboe violin, viola, and cello. Ellen Taaffe Zwilich was a visiting artist. At the conclusion of the year, Arthur Levering returned to Boston, where he received the 1997 Heckscher Foundation Composition Prize.

1997–98: The composers P. Q. Phan (Da-nang, Vietnam, b. 1962) and Andrew Rindfleisch (Walnut Grove, MN, b. 1963) were the fellows this year. Phan, who studied architecture in Vietnam and composition at the University of Southern California and the University of Michigan, was teaching at the University of Illinois, Urbana-Champaign, when he received the Rome Prize (the first

Samuel Barber Fellowship following completion of the endowment campaign). While at the Academy he completed a seventy-minute "instrumental opera" for string quartet, *An Duong Vuong: Submersion in Trust and Betrayal* (commissioned by the Kronos Quartet and premiered in the following year). Rindfleisch, educated at the University of Wisconsin, Madison, the New England Conservatory, and Harvard University, was a teaching fellow at Harvard University (where he also conducted the Harvard Group for New Music) and a recipient of a Guggenheim Fellowship in the year prior to receiving the Rome Prize. While in Rome he wrote *Hallucinations* for solo viola (premiered at the Spring Concert), *Psalm* for unaccompanied mixed chorus (commissioned and premiered by Modus Novus, Cologne, June 1998), and he began composing *What Vibes* for flute, clarinet, violin, cello, piano, and percussion (commissioned by the Paul Fromm Foundation, premiered by the Phantom Arts Ensemble, Boston, March 1999). He also gave a concert as pianist along with the violinist Benjamin Kreith, performing works by Feldman, Gershwin, Webern, as well as a free improvisation. The Paul Fromm Resident in Music Composition was Tania León, who arrived in the spring. She composed *entre nos* for clarinet, bassoon, and piano (commissioned by the Trio Neos) and gave a lecture on her music and her recent opera, *Scourge of Hyacinths*. During the winter, Southern Regional Visiting Artist[64] Kenneth Frazelle (AFAAR 1998) performed a concert of his piano music and worked on his composition for chorus and chamber orchestra, *The Motion of Stone* (premiered by the Gardner Chamber Orchestra, Boston, 1999). The two Spring Concerts contained Phan's *Rough Trax* for oboe and saxophone, *Unexpected Desire* for violin, cello, and piano, *Beyond the Mountains* for clarinet, violin, cello, and piano, and *My Language* for piano and clarinet (all written previously), as well as Rindfleisch's *Trio* for violin, cello, and piano, *Birthday Music* for piano, and the premiere of his *Hallucinations* for viola solo. Visiting artists included the composers John Adams, Arthur Levering, and Yehudi Wyner. Upon completion of the year, P. Q. Phan returned to the faculty of the University of Illinois, Urbana-Champaign, and Andrew Rindfleisch joined the faculty of Cleveland State University.

1998–2005, Director: Lester K. Little

The Music Program: 1998–2005

The 1998–99 year opened with a new director, Lester K. Little, RAAR 1996 (professor, history, Smith College). Little, who had been the Academy's resident in postclassical humanistic studies in 1996, would serve as director for the next seven years. In his opening interview he commented, "It's a source of tremendous pleasure to move into such a strong institution. A monumental effort has been made over the last several years to put the Academy on firm financial footing."[65] Things were indeed finally settling onto an even keel, but neither the renovations nor the financial difficulties were over yet. First, a massive historic preservation project was about to begin on the Academy's treasured Villa Aurelia. The project, which included both structural reinforcement of the villa and a painstaking restoration of its elegant interior, began in 2000 and was completed by May 2002. Extensive renovation also needed to be carried out on the large apartment building that stood next to the Academy. This building (via Angelo Masina, 5B) had recently been leased by the Academy with the intention of making apartments available to members of the community who were living in Rome with their families. Prior to this, these fellows were living in apartments off the Academy grounds—an unhappy solution for them and the community as a whole. Finally, in addition to these local concerns, the terrorist attack of September 11, 2001, closely followed by the war in Afghanistan and Iraq and by the political and economic consequences of these epoch-shaping events, would bring very real problems. Of necessity, the new century would once more become a time of "belt tightening" and of increased concern about security issues. Yet, notwithstanding these extremely disturbing events, the Academy continued to be a tranquil and serene haven for scholarship and creativity.

For the music program, the total renovation of the Villa Aurelia provided an unexpected bonus. The auxiliary building, originally the stable for the villa, later transformed into two contiguous apartments for residents, underwent a further transformation during the renovation. It became a large single hall, the Sala Aurelia, that could seat approximately two hundred persons and, as luck would have it, had appropriate acoustics for music. Accordingly, in the fall of 2002, Nuova Consonanza's marathon Festa d'Autunno was moved from the Academy's McKim building to the Villa Aurelia. The villa and its grounds now offered numerous elegant locations suitable for concerts and events: the new Sala Aurelia with its ample seating capacity, and, in the villa itself, the atrium and the salone on the first floor, the Sala Musica and the Sala Conferenza on the second floor. Additionally there were a number of outside locations throughout the grounds. Such facilities were, in fact, tailor-made for the marathon's multilevel happenings, and subsequent *Feste* have continued to exploit the villa's potential to its fullest. For the Academy's music program, the renovated facilities meant that there were now two concert spaces available at the villa: the Sala Musica, the traditional home of the music program concerts, and the Sala Aurelia. The former remained active for smaller concerts whereas the latter became the hall of choice for Spring Concerts and other events that drew larger audiences.

Another Italian collaboration with the Academy's music program was introduced in the fall of 2002. The Academy agreed to host an annual concert organized by Nuovi Spazi Musicali, a Roman new music group interested in cultivating contacts with American composers and performers.[66] As with

Nuova Consonanza, Nuovi Spazi Musicali would take care of organizing and financing the concerts while the Academy offered its performance facilities. This collaboration led to the appearance of several fine American performers at the Academy as well as further performance and networking opportunities for the composer fellows.[67]

In the fall of 2004, the American Academy had the unique opportunity to pay homage to Luciano Berio on his home ground—in Rome's new auditorium complex, Parco della Musica, that Berio had overseen in the last years of his life. Thanks to a generous trustee donor, the Academy organized and financed a concert, *Born in the USA*, that featured compositions by Berio with strong connections to the United States. The concert took place in the Sala Sinopoli of the Parco della Musica and was given in collaboration with Nuova Consonanza, the Fondazione Accademia Nazionale di Santa Cecilia, and under the patronage of the American Embassy. It featured a performance of Berio's *Circles* (originally commissioned by the Fromm Music Foundation in 1960) that had not been performed in Rome for at least twenty-five years. In the following year (2005), another gift that will certainly bear remarkable fruit in the future was announced: the Lotti Foundation agreed to provide funding in support of residencies at the Academy by promising young Italian composers.

In the continuing effort to bring greater attention to the Academy's music program and to historicize its considerable achievement in the support of the American musical community, three particularly pertinent initiatives occurred during this period. A series of four chamber concerts featuring compositions by American Academy fellows was performed in New York's Weill Recital Hall during the fall of 2002. This yielded a set of commercial CDs, *Americans in Rome*,[68] which features the compositions of thirty-seven Fellows in Music Composition, twenty-seven of whom are discussed in this history. In the winter of 2003, the Academy's extensive recordings archive, which included the original tape recordings (open-reel and DAT) of fellows' works performed in Rome from 1955 to 2002, was transferred to digital format. This initiative (supported by the Gladys Krieble Delmas Foundation and with myself as music supervisor) was intended both to preserve the content of the original tapes from deterioration and to make it readily accessible in CD and DVD format.[69] Then, in January 2005, a three-day conference "To Meet This Urgent Need" took place at the Villa Aurelia. Conceived and organized by Martin Brody (RAAR 2002), this conference brought together well-known American musicologists, composers, and a number of important Italian musical figures to discuss the significance of the Rome Prize and the American Academy in both the American and the Italian musical life. At the conclusion of this conference, the Aaron Copland Composer's Studio, located on the villa grounds, was dedicated along with a newly arrived Steinway A grand piano.

I continued to organize the general Academy concert season throughout these years and it remained a center of social and artistic focus for the entire

Academy community. The list of ensemble and musicians who performed at the Academy from 1994 to 2006 includes: Everett Symphony Orchestra, Italian National Air Force Band, Italian National Carabinieri Concert Band, Wellesley College Choir, Ebenezer Baptist Church Choir, University of Michigan School of Music Singers, La Frottola madrigal ensemble, Nuovarmonia Wind Band, Musica d'Oggi Ensemble, Rome Brass Quintet, Musica Elettronica Viva, Atlanta Chamber Players; the string quartets Borodin Quartet, Borciani Quartet, Borromeo Quartet, Ciompi Quartet; the violin and piano duos Gerard Rosa and Linda Laurent, Benjamin Kreith and Andrew Rindfleisch, Joseph Gold and Stefano Fiuzzi, Sunghae Anna Lim and Donald Berman, Silvia Mandolini and Maria Grazia Bellocchio, Cristina Buciu and Lisa Moore, Veronica Kadlubkiewicz and Gregorio Nardi, Robert McDuffie and Charles Abramovic; the voice and piano duos Constance Beavon and Keith Griggs, Annette Meriweather and Richard Trythall, Joan Morris and William Bolcom, Susan Narucki and Donald Berman, Timothy Martin and Richard Trythall; the piano duo Morelli and Simonacci; the chitarrone and baroque violin duo Richard Kolb and Rachel Evans; the accordion duo Acco-Land; the percussion duo Ars Ludi; the pianists Francis Thorne, Joel Hoffman, Sally Pinkas, Donald Berman, Cristiano Grifone, Kenneth Frazelle, Patricia Goodson, Daniele Lombardi, John Davis, Richard Trythall, Lisa Moore, Kim Bum-suk, Andrea Padova, Guy Livingston, Eleanor Perrone, Michael Harrison, Roberto Arosio, Sara Cahill, Lara Downes, Peter Kairoff, Daria Monastyrski, Max Lifchitz, David Northington, Ashlee Mack; the percussionists Amy Knoles and Christopher Froh; the flutists Roberto Fabbriciani, Lauren Weiss, Jayn Rosenfeld, Patti Monson; the accordionists Mikko Luoma, Mario Pietrodarchi, Dario Flammini; the violinists Veronica Kadlubkiewicz, Robert McDuffie, Mark Menzies, Gil Morgenstern; the cellists Frances-Marie Uitti and Madeleine Shapiro; the guitarists Bryce Dessner and Paul Bowman; the five-string banjoist Paul Elwood; the soprano Tony Arnold; the contrabassist Corrado Canonici; the tubist Velvet Brown; the bassoonist John Veloz; the harpsichordist Joyce Lindorff; and the fortepianist Arthur Schoonderwoerd.

Included among these concerts, as befits the Academy's pivotal role as a vital point of exchange between the American and Italian musical worlds, were also a number of events honoring careers in music: A retrospective concert commemorating the Italian American composer Vittorio Rieti (1995); a concert of George Rochberg's piano music with Rochberg and his wife in attendance (1996); a concert by Musica Elettronica Viva celebrating its thirtieth anniversary (1996); a concert commemorating the American virtuoso violinist Albert Spalding and his lifelong connection with Italy (1998); a concert held in honor of the ninetieth birthday of Rodolfo Caporali, the concert pianist and copresident of Rome's foremost musical institution, L'Accademia di Santa Cecilia (2000); a concert featuring the work of the late Walter Winslow, FAAR 1990 (2000); a concert in commemoration of Francesco Pennisi, the Italian composer and friend of the Academy (2001); a concert celebrating the centennial of Aaron Copland's birth (2001); a concert devoted to the musicologist Oliver Strunk's voice and piano music (2002), based on manuscripts found in the Strunk collection when donated to the library (2001); a concert presenting a panoramic survey of songs by past and recent fellows during the conference on "Music at the American Academy in Rome, 1921 to the Present" (2004); a concert dedicated to the music of the American composer and longtime Roman resident Robert W. Mann on the occasion of his eightieth birthday (2005); and a concert featuring the music of Giacinto Scelsi in collaboration with the Scelsi Foundation's celebration of the centennial of the composer's birth (2005).

The Composers: 1998–2006

1998–99: The new fellows were Christopher Theofanidis (Dallas, TX, b. 1967) and Mark Wingate (Ithaca, NY, b. 1954). Theofanidis, educated at the University of Houston, the Eastman School, Yale University, and in France on a Fulbright Fellowship, was teaching as a postdoctoral fellow at the University of Houston when he received the Rome Prize. While at the Academy, he wrote *Rainbow Body* for orchestra (commissioned and premiered by the Houston Symphony Orchestra, winner of the Masterprize International Composition Competition, 2003), *O Vis Aeternitatis* for string quartet and piano (commissioned by the Norfolk Chamber Music Festival for Speculum Musicae), and *Song of Elos* for soprano, string quartet, and piano on a text by the visiting artist poet Judith Freeman (performed on the Spring Concert). Wingate, educated at Berklee College of Music, the University of Tennessee, the University of Texas, and in Stockholm on a Fulbright Fellowship, was finishing his doctorate at the University of Texas when he received the Rome Prize. He wrote *Ruckamuck*, an acoustic/electronic studio work based on the poetry of the visiting artist Danella Carter as delivered by the digitally processed voice of colleague Christopher Theofanidis (commissioned by Rome's Edison Studio). His tape works, *Klang, Kar und Melodie* and *La Nuit Sauvage*, were performed at Nuova Consonanza's "Festa d'Autunno," and *Ruckamuck* was premiered by Edison Studio at Rome's Sala Uno. In January and again in March the Paul Fromm Resident in Music Composition was Betsy Jolas, who discussed her work during a concert lecture. At the Academy she was completing her *Motet III* for five vocal soloists, choir, and orchestra (premiere, Les Arts Florissants, Luxembourg, 1999). During his fall residence, the Southern Regional Visiting Artist Paul Elwood (AFAAR 1999) composed *Le Repos Éclairé* for piano, *Altars Altered* for flute/alto flute and piano, and *Two Extremities* for soprano, piano, bowed five-string banjo, flute, violin, and wine glasses (all of which were premiered at the Academy). The latter two works were premiered on the program organized by Elwood, "Bringin' Music to the Masses," which mercilessly exploited the talents of all of the musicians gathered at the Academy (and then some) in an evening highlighted by Elwood's five-string banjo pickin', his "buck and wing" tap dancing on velcro, and a performance by "The Rome on the Range Gospel Choir." The group chemistry was particularly surreal that fall and it continued to a high point of community participation in the July 4 Grand Prix de Rome soapbox derby organized by the performance artist fellow Pat Oleszko. The Spring Concert featured Theofanidis's *Flow, My Tears* for viola solo, the premiere of *Song of Elos* (performed in its original instrumentation for soprano, clarinet, viola, and piano), *Statues* for piano (with the composer performing), and *Ariel Ascending* for string quartet, as well as Wingate's *Prophecy* for flute and electronics, String Quartet no. 2, and *Sombras* for piano and digital delay. During the summer Theofanidis's *Statues* and *Flow, My Tears* and Wingate's String Quartet no. 2 and *Sombras* were also performed at the "Incontri in Terra di Siena" at La Foce in Tuscany—an annual summer music festival held on the beautiful estate of its founder, Signora Benedetta Origo. Visiting artists at the Academy included Lukas Foss, Andrew Imbrie, Arthur Levering, Paul Moravec, Thomas Oboe Lee, David Rakowski, and the pianist Donald Berman. Berman, who was at the Academy through the fall, shared his talents frequently with the community (also performing a concert of Ives's piano music) and conducted research in the Academy's music archives. With the conclusion of the year, Christopher Theofanidis returned to New York and joined the faculty of the Juilliard School while Mark Wingate joined the faculty of Istanbul Technical University, where he designed and codirected the Electronic Music Studio.

1999–2000: The new fellows were Carolyn Yarnell (Los Angeles, CA, b. 1961) and Shih-hui Chen (Taipei, Taiwan, b. 1962). Yarnell was educated at the San Francisco Conservatory of Music, in Iceland on a Fulbright Fellowship, and at Yale University. She was freelancing in San Francisco when she was awarded the Rome Prize. While at the Academy she wrote *Horizen* for Mozart orchestra (premiered by the Albany Symphony Orchestra, December 1999) and *The Same Sky* for piano, video, and electronics (commissioned by Kathleen Supové/Meet the Composer, premiered on the Spring Concert). Her piano works, *Invention* and *Tenaya,* were performed during Nuova Consonanza's "Festa d'Autunno" along with Martin Bresnick's *The Dream of the Lost Traveler.* Her electronic work, *Love God,* was performed on the Festa Europea della Musica. Chen, who was educated at Northern Illinois University and Boston University, was teaching at the Longy School of Music in Cambridge when she received the Rome Prize. While at the Academy she wrote *Fu II* for pipa and five Western instruments (commissioned by the Paul Fromm Foundation) and *Twice Removed* for saxophone solo (commissioned by the Longy School of Music for Kenneth Radnofsky). Both works were premiered on the Spring Concert. During the fall, the Paul

Fromm Resident in Music Composition was Martin Bresnick (FAAR 1976). He completed *Songs of the Mouse People* for cello and vibraphone (commissioned by Maya Beiser and Steven Schick with the assistance of the Connecticut Commission on the Arts) and began work on *Grace*, a concerto for two marimbas and orchestra. The Spring Concert included Yarnell's *EchoBox/Burning Man* for processed baroque flute and the premieres of her *William Tomorrow* for two pianos, violin, and cello. Chen was represented by *Fu I* for pipa and the premieres of her *Fu II* and *Twice Removed*. Visiting artists during the year included the composers Thomas Oboe Lee, Arthur Levering, Christopher Theofanidis, Robert Xavier Rodriguez, and the pianist Lisa Moore. Moore, the pianist of the "Bang on a Can All-Stars," graciously shared her talents in several concerts for the community. At the conclusion of the year, Carolyn Yarnell returned to freelance work in California and Shih-hui Chen joined the faculty of Rice University. She would return to Rome in 2002 at the invitation of the Roman new music group Freon Ensemble, which performed a concert devoted to her music at Rome's Sala Casella.

2000–2001: The fellows this year were Pierre Jalbert (Manchester, NH, b. 1967) and Michael N. Hersch (Washington, DC, b. 1971). Jalbert, educated at Oberlin Conservatory and the University of Pennsylvania, was teaching at Rice University when he was awarded the Rome Prize. While at the Academy, Jalbert completed *Les espaces infinis* for chamber orchestra (premiered by the Albany Symphony, February 2001) and *Toccata* for piano (premiered by the composer on the Spring Concert). He also composed *Symphonia Sacra* for orchestra (commissioned and premiered by the California Symphony, April 2001) and *Sonata for Marimba* (commissioned and premiered by Makoto Nakura, Kobe, Japan, October 2001) and began composing *Centerpiece* (a commission from the Albany Symphony). While at the Academy he received word that his orchestral work, *In Aeternam*, was a finalist in the Masterprize International Composition Competition. This work won that competition in the fall of 2001. Hersch was educated at the Peabody Conservatory of Music and the Moscow Conservatory. While on the fellowship, he composed an *Octet* for strings (commissioned by the Kronberg Akademie, premiered August 2002); two piano works, *Tramontane* and *Reflections on a Work of Henze*; and Sonata no. 2 for unaccompanied violoncello (premiered at Musica XXI Romaeuropa Festival, October 2003). He performed a concert of his solo piano works at the Academy as well as for the Belgian Academy, the Austrian Institute, and the Goethe Institute. The concert included *Tramontane*, *Mistral*, *Piano Quartet* (second movement), *Night Unending*, and Sonata no. 2. There was no composer-in-residence. The two Spring Concerts included Jalbert's *String Quartet*, *Songs of Gibran* for soprano and chamber ensemble, *Relativity Variations* for piano, and the premiere of *Toccata* (the latter two works performed by the composer), as well as Hersch's *Two Pieces* for cello and piano, *Sonata* for unaccompanied violin,

Sonata no. 1 for unaccompanied cello, and *Tramontane* for piano. Jalbert's *Agnus Dei* for piano trio and Hersch's *Unending Night* for piano were performed in the fall at Nuova Consonanza's "Festa d'Autunno." Visiting Artists included Arthur Levering, Dinu Ghezzo, and Marta Arkossy Ghezzo. Following the completion of the year, Pierre Jalbert returned to his position at Rice University and Michael Hersch took up residence at the American Academy in Berlin as recipient of the 2001 Berlin Prize.

2001–2: The new Fellows were Derek Bermel (New York, NY, b. 1967) and Kevin Puts (St. Louis, MO, b. 1972). Bermel, educated at Yale University, the University of Michigan, and in Amsterdam, worked on a number of orchestral pieces: a narrated fable, *The Sting* (commissioned and premiered by the St. Louis Symphony Orchestra, March 2002); *Thracian Echoes* (commissioned and premiered by the Westchester Philharmonic Orchestra, November 2002); *The Ends* (commissioned and premiered by the National Symphony Orchestra, September, 2002); and *At the End of the World* for voice and large ensemble (commissioned and premiered by the Albany Symphony "Dogs of Desire"). He also collaborated with the poet Mark Halliday (FAAR 2002), who wrote the narration for Bermel's *Animal Jam* (composed for the Albany Symphony Orchestra). Bermel, also a clarinettist, composed and performed the soundtracks for a garden installation by the landscape designer Andrew Thanh-Son Cao (FAAR 2002) and for two films by the filmmaker Kevin Everson (FAAR 2002), *Fumble* and *Special Man.* Puts, educated at the Eastman School of Music and Yale University, was teaching at the University of Texas at Austin when he received the Rome Prize. While at the Academy, he completed three orchestral works: *Inspiring Beethoven* (commissioned and premiered by the Phoenix Symphony Orchestra, 2002), *Falling Dream* (commissioned and premiered by the American Composers Orchestra, 2002), and Symphony no. 2 ("Island of Innocence") (commissioned and premiered by the Cincinnati Symphony Orchestra and the Utah Symphony Orchestra, 2002). He also composed *Einstein on Mercer Street* for bass-baritone and chamber ensemble (commissioned and premiered by the Pittsburgh New Music Ensemble, 2002). Martin Brody was the Paul Fromm Resident in Music Composition for the fall. He wrote *Beasts* for ten instruments (texts by James Merrill, Richard Wilbur, and Walt Whitman; commissioned and premiered by Collage New Music, premiered 2002) and organized a lecture/listening series by composers at the Academy, "How We Listen." In addition to lectures by Puts, Bermel, and Brody, the series included the visiting artist Michael Harrison (a composer-pianist who lectured on his harmonically tuned piano), composer Aaron Jay Kernis (who lectured on his recent orchestral music), and composer-pianist Richard Trythall (who performed and discussed his transcriptions of Jelly Roll Morton's piano music). The two Spring Concerts included Bermel's *Theme and Absurdities* for clarinet and *SchiZm* for clarinet and piano (with the composer as clarinettist); *Turning, Dodecaphunk,* and *Three Funk*

Studies for piano; Quartet no. 1; and *Seven Songs* for baritone and piano. Puts was represented by his *Dark Vigil* for string quartet; *And Legions Will Rise Within* for violin, clarinet, and piano; *Ritual Protocol* for marimba and piano; and *Aria* for violin and piano (premiere, with the composer as pianist). Visiting artists included James Lentini, Larry Bell, and Robert Xavier Rodriguez. At the end of the year, Derek Bermel returned to New York to continue work as a freelance composer and performer. During that year he performed his *Clarinet Concerto* with the BBC Radio and Los Angeles Philharmonic orchestras. Kevin Puts returned to his teaching position at the University of Texas at Austin and composed several orchestral works including his Symphony no. 3 ("Vespertine") and *This Noble Company* (commissioned by the Atlanta Symphony Orchestra).

2002–3: This fellowship year brought new fellows David Sanford (Pittsburgh, PA, b. 1963) and Mark Kilstofte (Winona, MN, b. 1958) to the Academy. Sanford, educated at the University of Northern Colorado, the New England Conservatory, and Princeton University, was teaching at Mount Holyoke College when he received the Rome Prize. While in Rome he wrote four works for jazz ensemble that, along with *Bagatelle* from 1999, formed a suite of works: *Fenwick, Link Chapel, Una Notte all'Opera, Bagatelle,* and *V-Reel* (premiered on the Spring Concert). He also completed *Dogma74* for Pierrot ensemble (commissioned by the Empyrean Ensemble at UC Davis, premiered in San Francisco, 2002), composed *Alchemy* for big band, and finished an article on Miles Davis's Music of 1972–75 for a book to be edited by Michael Veal. Kilstofte, educated at St. Olaf College and the University of Michigan, was on the faculty of Furman University and had just won the Dale Warland Singers "Choral Ventures" competition when he received the Rome Prize. While at the Academy, he completed *Gazing Up at Stars* for mixed chorus (translation of Latin hymn, *Ave, maris stella,* by Michele Mulchahey FAAR 2003, commissioned by the Music Teachers National Association/South Carolina Music Teachers Association, premiered by Furman Chamber Choir, November 2002), *Peace* for mixed chorus (text by Gerard Manley Hopkins, commissioned by June Adell and Norman Wetzel, premiered by Trinity Lutheran Church Choir, Greenville, South Carolina, November 2004), and Symphony no. 1 for large orchestra. He revised *Being* for chorus (commissioned and premiered by the Dale Warland Singers, March 2004) and *Ballistic Etude no. 1* for brass and percussion and began work on *Grandeur* for *a cappella* chorus (commissioned and premiered by the Dale Warland Singers, Minneapolis, MN, March 2004) and *Of Rivers Within* for soprano, chorus, and orchestra (commissioned and premiered by the Greenville Chorale, Greenville, South Carolina, October 2005). For a month in the spring, the Paul Fromm Resident in Music Composition was Ned Rorem (Pulitzer Prize 1976), who gave a lecture on his life and work. A small concert of songs performed in honor of Rorem and the resident poet William Jay Smith was given in May with Kilstofte, a trained singer (baritone), performing with the soprano Amalia Dustin and the pianist Richard Trythall. The Spring Concert featured the premiere of Sanford's suite of jazz works, *Fenwick, Link Chapel, Una Notte all'Opera, Bagatelle,* and *V-Reel* (performed by the Corvini e Iodice Roma Jazz Ensemble with the composer conducting), and Kilstofte's String Quartet no. 1 ("You [unfolding]") for cello solo and *Sonata* for saxophone and piano. Additional performances during the year included Sanford's *Sanctus* for viola and piano and Kilstofte's *You [unfolding]* as part of Nuova Consonanza's "Festa d'Autunno" that inaugurated the new Sala Aurelia as a concert hall, and a performance of Kilstofte's brass quintet, *A Past Persistence,* in the FontanonEstate 2003 summer concert series. Long-term visiting artists included the violinist Robert McDuffie, the cellist Leslie Nash, and the composer Anna Weesner. Each contributed to enriching the year's music program. Robert McDuffie prepared a special evening featuring Robert Beaser's *Violin Sonata,* movements from David Sanford's *Piano Trio,* and Mark Kilstofte's *String Quartet* performed by himself, Nash, and members of the Santa Cecilia orchestra.[70] Leslie Nash also performed Mark Kilstofte's *You [unfolding]* on several occasions. Anna Weesner offered an evening of her compositions for violin, clarinet, and piano, including the premiere of her new *Duo* for violin and piano. Also present briefly as a visiting artist was D. J. Spooky. At the conclusion of the year, David Sanford returned to the faculty of Mount Holyoke and Mark Kilstofte returned to his position at Furman University.

2003–4: Mason Bates (Richmond, VA, b. 1977) and Jefferson Friedman (Swampscott, MA, b. 1974) were the Fellows in Music Composition. Bates, educated in the Columbia-Juilliard Program, received degrees in music composition and English literature. He was studying at the University of California, Berkeley, and working as a DJ in various San Francisco clubs when he received the Rome Prize. While at the Academy, he composed *From Amber Frozen* for string quartet, *Omnivorous Furniture* for sinfonietta and electronica (commissioned and premiered by the Los Angeles Philharmonic's New Music Group, November 2004), and *Music for Underground Spaces* for string bass, electronic drum pad, turntables, and piano (premiered on the Spring Concert). He also began work on a chamber opera with electronics. Active as a DJ and live electronica artist, Bates established himself in Rome's club scene, working regularly at both Testaccio's Metaverso and Trastevere's Scarabocchio. He was also the house DJ for a number of the Academy's art exhibitions. Friedman, educated at Columbia University and the Juilliard School, was living as a freelance composer in New York when he received the Rome Prize. While at the Academy, he composed *eight songs* for amplified baritone saxophone, voice, and drum set that referenced works by Crom-Tech (commissioned and premiered by Yesaroun' Duo on the Spring Concert), and *The Throne of the Third Heaven of the Nations Millennium General Assembly* for large orchestra (commissioned by the National Symphony Orchestra/ASCAP Foundation, premiered by NSO October 2004). During the fall, the Paul Fromm Resident in Music Composition was William Bolcom (Pulitzer Prize 1988). Bolcom completed work on the opera *A Wedding* (based on the Robert Altman movie of the same name; premiered by the Chicago Lyric Opera in the fall of 2004), and accompanied his wife, the visiting artist soprano Joan Morris, in a concert entitled "The Cabaret Songs of William Bolcom and Arnold Weinstein." The Spring Concert was given in the cryptoporticus, which Friedman and Bates had darkened even further in order to accentuate its "underground" character. The concert presented Bates's earlier work *String Band* for piano trio and *Music for Underground Spaces* (premiere), as well as Friedman's *eight songs* (premiere) and String Quartet no. 2. The composers' individual works were integrated into a larger weave of sound supplied by Bates's *Music for Underground Spaces*, which began approximately a half hour before the concert started, with Bates manning the controls. Earlier in the year Bates's *Rodeopteryx* for tape was performed during Nuova Consonanza's "Festa d'Autunno." At the conclusion of the year, Mason Bates went to Berlin's American Academy as the recipient of the 2004 Berlin Prize while Jefferson Friedman returned to the United States to follow, among other things, the National Symphony Orchestra's premiere of *The Throne of the Third Heaven of the Nations Millennium General Assembly*.

2004–5: Composers Harold Meltzer (Brooklyn, NY, b. 1966) and Steven Burke (Brooklyn, NY, b. 1967) were the new fellows. Meltzer, who had studied at Amherst College, King's College, Cambridge, Columbia University School of Law, and the Yale School of Music, had been living in New York on a Guggenheim Fellowship when he received the Rome Prize. While in Rome he composed *Full Faith and Credit*—a double concerto for two bassoons and string orchestra (commissioned by the Brooklyn Friends of Chamber Music, Chamber Orchestra Kremlin, The San Francisco Chamber Orchestra, and the Westchester Philharmonic; premiere, San Francisco Chamber Orchestra, December 2004); *Sindbad* for narrator, cello, violin, and piano (commissioned by Meet the Composer for the Peabody Trio and the Yellow Barn Music Festival, premiere, April 2005); *Toccatas* for harpsichord (for Jory Vinikour, premiere, September 2005); and began *Brion* for six instruments (commissioned by the Barlow Endowment for the Cygnus Ensemble). Burke, educated at Sarah Lawrence College, the University of Wisconsin, Madison, the Yale School of Music, and Cornell University, was teaching at Sarah Lawrence College when he received the Rome Prize. While at the Academy, he collaborated with the poet Lisa Williams (FAAR 2005) and the visual artist Franco Mondini-Ruiz (FAAR 2005) to create *Songs from the Bass Garden* for soprano, violin, cello, piano, and percussion (written for Susan Narucki, soprano, and the Yale Summer School of Music). He also composed *Untitled Universe* for English horn, violin, viola, and cello, and he began a work for bass clarinet and chamber ensemble, *Over a Moving Landscape* (dedicated to Nancy Brown

Negley, commissioned by the Fromm Foundation for Michael Lowenstern and Sequitur, premiere, June 2006), as well as a work for orchestra commissioned by Nancy Negley. In the fall, the Paul Fromm Resident in Music Composition was Lee Hyla (FAAR 1991), who wrote *Amore Scaduto* for violin, cello, and two dancers (commissioned by the Philadelphia Music Project and the National Endowment for the Arts; premiered by Network for New Music and Phrenic New Ballet, Philadelphia, March 2005) and began two works—a saxophone quartet, *Paradigm Lost* (commissioned by Chamber Music America; premiered by the Prism Quartet, NYC, May 2005) and *Polish Folk Songs* for clarinet, violin, viola, cello, piano, and percussion (premiered by Boston Musica Viva, May 2005). The Spring Concert featured Meltzer's *Sindbad* and *Two Songs from Silas Marner* for soprano and cello, as well as Burke's *In Time's Wake* for cello and piano, *Philter* for clarinet, violin, and piano, *Night Fantasy* for piano, and *Spring Fever* for clarinet, violin, cello, and piano. Earlier in the year, the flutist Patti Monson had performed a program including Meltzer's *Rumors* for alto flute, flute, piccolo, and bass flute, and Burke's *Nervosa* for solo flute. Visiting artists included Martin Brody, Paul Moravec, and Larry Bell. At the conclusion of the year, Steven Burke spent time in France composing at the Dora Maar House. Subsequently he returned to the United States to join the faculty of Bronx Community College while Harold Meltzer joined the faculty of Vassar College.

2005–6: The composers this fellowship year were Susan Botti (Wichita Falls, TX, b. 1962) and Charles Norman Mason (Salt Lake City, UT, b. 1955). Botti, educated at the Berklee College of Music and the Manhattan School of Music, was teaching at the University of Michigan when she was awarded the Rome Prize. She composed *Tagore Madrigals* for six voices and *Stelle* for six voices, harp, and piano (both of which use texts by Rabindranath Tagore), as well as *2 Gregerson Songs* for soprano and piano and *Make-Falcon* for six voices, harp, piano, and two percussion (a work in progress), both with texts by Linda Gregerson. All of these compositions were premiered on the Spring Concert. Mason, who studied at the University of Miami and the University of Illinois, was teaching at Birmingham-Southern College when he received the Rome Prize. While at the Academy, he completed seven works: *Entanglements* for violin, cello, and prerecorded sound; *Incantesimi: Omaggio a Scelsi e Berio* for violin and piano (both of which were premiered on the Spring Concert); *Leaden Echo, Golden Echo* for choir and prerecorded sound; *Cor Cordium* for guitar quartet and chamber orchestra; *Ospedaletto* for cello and prerecorded sound (premiered by Madeleine Shapiro, Nuovi Spazi Musicali, fall 2006); *Oh What a Beautiful City* for string quartet; and, in collaboration with photographer Richard Barnes (FAAR 2006) and the architect Alex Schrader (FAAR 2006), *Flow* for electro-acoustic sound (premiered during the Spring Art Exhibition). Performance artist, musician, and composer Laurie Anderson was a resident artist for two weeks during the fall, working on her own projects and sharing her experience with the community. The Paul Fromm Resident in Music Composition during the spring was Steven Stucky (Pulitzer Prize 2005), who was working on *Radical Light* for orchestra (commissioned and premiered by the Los Angeles Philharmonic, October 2007). The Spring Concert included the premieres of Botti's *Tagore Madrigals, Stelle, Make-Falcon,* and *2 Gregerson Songs,* as well as performances of her *Jabberwocky* for voice and percussion and *listen, it's snowing* for voice and piano. Botti herself was the vocal soloist while students from the University of Michigan Chamber Choir performed the vocal ensemble works. Mason was represented by the premieres of his *Entanglements, Incantesimi: Omaggio a scelsi e berio,* and by earlier works: *Il Prigioniero* for piano, *Three-Legged Race* for piano trio, *The Artist and His Model* for cello and prerecorded sound, and *Fast Break!* for flute, clarinet, violin, cello, piano, and prerecorded sound. His *Mirrors, Stones, and Cotton* for guitar and tape was performed at the Academy earlier in the year and other works performed in Rome included his *Senderos que se Bifurcan* for clarinet and piano on the RAI-Quirinale concert/transmissions and *Gems* for electroacoustic playback on the ArteScienza Festival organized by Centro Ricerche Musicali. Visiting artists included Martin Brody and Thomas Oboe Lee. The composer Dorothy Hindman and the composer-percussionist Roland Vazquez, both year-long visiting artists, made significant contributions to the Academy's musical community throughout the year.

2005–6, Director: Carmela Vircillo Franklin

The Music Program: 2005–6 and Conclusion

The 2005–6 fellowship year, which has just been reviewed, is the final year to be discussed in this account. It was another year of change for the leadership of the Academy. Carmela Vircillo Franklin, FAAR 1985 (faculty, classics department, Columbia University) became the first Italian-born director of the American Academy. An Academy fellow in postclassical humanistic studies in 1985 and a resident in 2001, she easily moved into her new position, joining the succession of scholar-administrators who had successfully directed the Academy for the great majority of the fifty-nine years of activity under consideration.

It was also a year of reflection and planning in the Academy's continuing evolution with regard to the arts. A three-day Performing Arts Retreat was held at the Villa Aurelia to "discuss ways in which the performing arts are becoming part of what the Academy has traditionally defined as the fine arts."[71] Attended by the trustees Mary Schmidt Campbell and Robert Beaser, the recent resident Laurie Anderson, Bill T. Jones (dancer and choreographer), Jim Houghton (artistic director, Signature Theatre), Catherine Wichterman Maciariello (Mellon Foundation), and Academy staff and arts fellows, the retreat discussed ways in which the Academy might be supportive of this trend in the future.

Such a forward-looking conference balanced perfectly with the historical music conference held the preceding year. While this earlier conference was convened to analyze and document the role the American Academy had played in the musical life of the United States and Italy since the inception of the Rome Prize in Music Composition in 1921, the Performing Arts Retreat was organized to discuss what the Academy's expanding artistic concerns might and should be in the future. In short, both conferences were business as usual, part of an ongoing process for an institution that, like the Janus head in its logo, has long since learned it must look to the future and to the past with the same intensity in order to stay in touch with the present.

This was another year of action as well. A dinner and concert, hosted at Villa Taverna by the United States Ambassador to Italy Ronald P. Spogli and his wife to acquaint the highest levels of the Italian business community with the Academy, continued the process of acquiring new supporters and expanding contacts. This sort of event would have pleased the former director Laurance Roberts, who, from the earliest days of the reopening of the Academy, had understood the social role the Academy was required to play in support of its primary mission to further the interests of its fellows. Perhaps the documentation included here would also find favor with Roberts. Certainly the amount of music composed, its quality and relevance to the American musical scene as well as the subsequent careers of the fellows and residents, amply confirm the high hopes invested in this program by him and by countless others who have worked toward the same end for more than a century. The uninterrupted time to concentrate and create, accompanied by the added stimulus of a like-minded community and the constant inspiration provided by the beauty of Rome itself, is an inimitable gift, an experience, and often an epiphany, that has touched each and every one of these composers and, through them, enriched the quality of America's cultural life. Edward MacDowell's joy and amazement about the American Academy in Rome still ring clear today, a century later: "For years it has been my dream that the Arts of Architecture, Painting, Sculpture and Music should come into such close contact that each and all should gain from this mutual companionship. That students in all these arts should come together under the same roof, and amid such marvelous surroundings, seems almost too good to be true."[72]

Notes

1. 1947–59, Laurance P. Roberts; 1959–69, Richard Arthur Kimball, Frank E. Brown; 1969–74, Reginald Allen (acting), Bartlett Hayes Jr., Frank E. Brown (acting); 1974–80, Henry A. Millon, John D'Arms; 1980–88, Sophie Consagra, James Melchert; 1988–94, Joseph Connors; 1994–98, Caroline A. Bruzelius; 1998–2005, Lester K. Little; 2005–6, Carmela Vircillo Franklin.

2. Neither does this history discuss the Academy's Rome Prize Fellowships in the area of musicology, nor cite its considerable support to advanced musicological research in

Italy through the years. That falls outside the scope of my topic, but is most certainly another musical area to which the Academy has made a significant contribution.

3. John Gimbel, *The Origins of the Marshall Plan* (Stanford: Stanford University Press, 1976), 6.

4. Lucia Valentine and Alan Valentine. *The American Academy in Rome, 1894–1969* (Charlottesville: University of Virginia Press, 1973), 110.

5. RAAR 1953–55: Resident of the American Academy in Rome for the academic years 1953–54 and 1954–55. The shortened form, RAAR 1955, only specifies the final portion of the academic year in which the residence took place.

6. American Academy in Rome, *Report*, 1951–55, 25.

7. FAAR 1947–49: Fellow of the American Academy in Rome for the academic years 1947–48 and 1948–49.

8. By the mid-sixties, the listening room contained numerous 33 rpm records of contemporary music, a few open-reel tape recordings of previous Academy fellows' concerts, and quite a number of well-marked open-reel tapes that had been recorded by previous fellows from RAI radio broadcasts of contemporary music. These recordings supplied arriving fellows with an invaluable introduction to European contemporary musical life. (The contents of the RAI's music broadcasts were listed in detail in the weekly *Radio Corriere* magazine, which was eagerly consulted at the beginning of each week by composer fellows.)

9. Most certainly such a studio is rudimentary by today's standards, but precisely those limits often proved to be the source of inspiration.

10. The Laurance P. and Isabel S. Roberts Papers, 1910–2005, held at the Biblioteca Berenson, Villa I Tatti, Harvard University Center for Italian Renaissance Studies, contain a wealth of primary source material on the Roberts years at AAR.

11. American Academy in Rome, *Report*, 1943–51, 32–33; 1951–55, 38–39.

12. American Academy in Rome, *Report*, 1943–51, 39–40.

13. Such a number of simultaneous residencies in the same discipline far exceeded the Academy's fellowship possibilities and even violated something of a rule of thumb regarding the Academy community: when there is a large number of fellows in one discipline, there is concern that they may separate from the rest of the community. That, on the contrary, this was a brilliant moment in the Academy's social life is amusingly recalled by Leo Smit in his article "Guess Who Dropped By," published in *AMACADMY* (summer 1991): 8.

14. American Academy in Rome, *Report*, 1943–51, 14.

15. I met Alexei Haieff in Rome during my first year as a fellow (1964–65) and remained friends with him for the rest of his life. For many years we lived on opposite sides of Piazza Venezia in the heart of Rome and I spent numerous evenings with him discussing music, the Academy, and his memories of the Russian musical community. After his death, I contacted the New York Public Library regarding his papers and, along with a mutual friend, the composer Robert Mann, we organized and saw to the transferal of Haieff's material to the archives there.

16. The American Academy in Rome closed following Italy's declaration of war on the United States on December 11, 1941. Cash prizes in the fine arts were offered in lieu of fellowships in 1941 and 1942. The war years and the reopening of the Academy are summarized in the following report: American Academy in Rome, *Report*, 1943–51, 5–9.

17. From the days of his Rome Prize Fellowship (1922–25), Randall Thompson maintained an enduring love of the Italian people, their music, and their language. In 1959 Italy recognized Thompson as a Cavaliere Ufficiale al Merito della Repubblica Italiana.

18. Elliott Carter, "On the American Academy in Rome," *AMACADMY* (summer 1991): 6.

19. American Academy in Rome, *Report*, 1951–55, 54.

20. George Balch Wilson introduced the audio engineer Paul Ketoff to the Academy community.

21. The significant influence that this American presence exerted on the Roman musical scene was documented in the conference "To Meet This Urgent Need" held in January 2005 at the Villa Aurelia, during which a number of Italian composers and musicologists discussed this period and gave their personal impressions.

22. The Academy, for example, hosted the rehearsals of the Nuova Consonanza Improvisation Ensemble in 1969–70.

23. George Balch Wilson, letter to the author, February 23, 2007.

24. In an interview (August 6, 2006) with the author, Smith explained that his work with multiphonics had been inspired by his experience with tape music and by having heard the flutist Severino Gazzelloni "play such high notes, I couldn't believe they existed."

25. This concert series Amici della Musica di Perugia was directed by Signora Alba Buitoni, a gracious and truly enlightened patron of the arts. In addition to offering a classical program of international level, the series was one of the most respected contemporary music venues in Italy.

26. Eaton worked very closely with the inventor Paul Ketoff in the development of the Syn-ket as a live performance instrument.

27. It is quite likely that the performance of Eaton's *Songs for RPB*, Villa Aurelia, June 16, 1965, also marked the first occasion in which a written composition utilized live performance on a modern sound synthesizer. (The Syn-ket was played by Paul Ketoff and Otto Luening.)

28. From this point on, most of the RAI/AAR concerts were held in the fall.

29. The president of the Academy lives in New York and works at the American Academy's New York office, while the director of the Academy lives in Rome on the grounds of the Academy.

30. American Academy in Rome, *Report*, 1968–73, 25.

31. I remained in constant contact with the Academy community following the conclusion of my fellowship in 1967 and I was regularly included in events—as composer and as pianist—by the composers-in-residence (1967–70). After winning the Darmstadt Festival's *Kranichsteiner Musikreis* for pianists in the summer of 1969, I had undertaken a solo career in Italy. I recorded extensively for the RAI and frequently worked with the Rome Radio Orchestra both as orchestral pianist and as soloist. This familiarity with the situation, with Italian institutions and with the people involved, facilitated my future work as liaison between the Academy and the Italian music world.

32. Mary T. Williams (executive secretary, American Academy in Rome). Letter to the author, October 23, 1970.

33. The central challenge at this time was administering the RAI/AAR orchestral concerts—maintaining contact with the RAI and dealing with the scheduling problems created by the shifting concert dates. The changes eventually threw the concerts completely out of synch with the Academy's music program and, consequently, maintaining the order of precedence for fellows' orchestral performances became difficult. Essentially dealing with these problems required an on-the-scene continuity that no composer-in-residence could supply. Over the next three years I handled that aspect for the Academy, notwithstanding that in the winter and spring of 1972 and 1973, I

was at SUNY Buffalo as a member of the Center for the Creative and Performing Arts Ensemble.

34. The formal structure for *Trobar Clus*, a twelfth-century Rondeau form, was developed from suggestions given to Kolb by the art historian Susan Saward (FAAR 1971). This sort of cross-disciplinary collaboration characterizes the Academy experience, as will be shown by the frequency of the instances detailed here.

35. Milton Cohen was a painter, sculptor, filmmaker, and cofounding member of the "Once Festival."

36. American Academy in Rome, *Report*, 1943–51; 1968–73, 81.

37. The RAI's recording of the dress rehearsal performance, however, was made available to the composers.

38. American Academy in Rome, *Report to the Board of Trustees*, October 1974, President Harold C. Martin, 1. Martin's analysis of the Academy's financial situation, in which he compares the Academy with a Victorian household attempting to survive in the twentieth century, is particularly telling.

39. Ibid., 2.

40. Henry A. Millon, letter to the author, November 8, 1974.

41. Beginning with the 1976–77 year, there were several lengthy periods with no composers-in-residence.

42. This was not always the case, unfortunately, and the Academy's archive of earlier recordings was incomplete.

43. The Academy's majestic main building, Via Angelo Massina 5, was designed by the New York–based architectural firm McKim, Mead, and White.

44. John Eaton and I went to the Steinway factory in Hamburg to select the instrument.

45. The American Academy's music season usually contained from nine to twelve events distributed from September to June. Although the main focus was on contemporary American and Italian music, these programs also featured the standard classical music repertoire, and the series broadened in scope throughout its thirty years of existence to encompass jazz and gospel music as well.

46. In my welcoming remarks to Maestro Scelsi, I reminded the audience of the friendship between Scelsi and composer fellows, and concluded: "I am pleased I can express my thanks to Maestro Scelsi in this moment, in this place, and in the name of us all, for his friendship and, above all, for his music." (From the author's notes for the occasion.)

47. Author's interview with Robert W. Mann, August 4, 2006. This statement is confirmed by the 1994 "Music Composition and Performance Activity" brochure, which lists performances of eighteen works by Scelsi performed on twelve concerts given at the Academy during this period.

48. The piano was donated in 1995 by the Isabella Scelsi Foundation thanks to the suggestion of the cellist Frances-Marie Uitti and in recognition of the friendship that had bound Maestro Scelsi with the Academy.

49. George Gelles, "Music at the Academy: An Overview," *AMACADMY* 2, no. 1 (1979): 6–7.

50. Since the RAI/AAR concerts were now frequently performed in December—too early for a one-year fellow who arrived in late September to prepare a new orchestral work—the Academy elected to pay the travel expenses (courtesy of the Society of Fellows) to enable the composer to return for the concert in the following year. The copying funds were also extended to works completed following the fellowship year but

intended for performance in this concert. In this way composers maintained the option to spend the fellowship year writing an orchestral piece if they wished.

51. Bill Lacy, "Rome Journal, March 14–27, 1978," *AMACADMY* 1, no. 1 (1978): 22.

52. Calvin G. Rand, "Report from the President," *AMACADMY* 6, no. 1 (83/84): 2.

53. The concert program included George Gershwin's *Rhapsody in Blue* with myself as piano soloist. The choice of the *Rhapsody* was particularly apropos since the second performance of the *Rhapsody in Blue* had been during a fund-raising event for the American Academy in Rome.

54. The series was entitled *Souvenirs: Compositori all'Accademia Americana a Roma.* It presented works by Ezra Laderman, Harold Shapero, Alexei Haieff, William O. Smith, John Eaton, Leon Kirchner, Lukas Foss, Barbara Kolb, and Richard Trythall. A copy of the text and two cassette tapes containing the broadcasts are in my possession.

55. Jack Beeson, "Music," *American Academy in Rome News* (spring 1966): 3.

56. Elliott Carter, Goffredo Petrassi, and Roman Vlad had been friends since their meeting at the "Music in Our Time" festival organized by Nicolas Nabokov at the Villa Aurelia in 1954. Carter and Petrassi had remained particularly close and Carter had dedicated his solo violin work *Riconoscenza* to Petrassi in 1984.

57. American Academy in Rome, *Annual Report of the Director, 1989–1990,* Joe Connors, 2.

58. There were nine music events, five of which were held in collaboration with Italian music associations.

59. The pianos were restored in Pescara at the workshop of the Ditta Angelo Fabbrini. Angelo Fabbrini was the piano technician of choice for Benedetto Michelangeli and Maurizio Pollini. The extremely high technical standard of his workshop was acknowledged throughout Italy.

60. The Academy comprises both a School of Classical Studies, headed by the professor-in-charge, and a School of Fine Arts, headed by the arts director. While the former position was regularly occupied, the arts director position had been suspended sixty years earlier.

61. American Academy in Rome, *Annual Report of the Director, 1986–1987,* Jim Melchert, 19.

62. It was also an example of the crucial financial assistance that USIS had so frequently provided the Academy music program. Following this event, Director Caroline Bruzelius wrote the cultural attaché Carol Ludwig: "The Academy's continued success in proposing American music and musicians to the Roman community is, of course, USIS's success as well. USIS—through its generous contributions—has made a dramatic difference in past years in terms of the scope and the variety of our music program." Letter Caroline Bruzelius, director, to Carol Ludwig, cultural attaché, cc to the author, USIS, June 25, 1995.

63. AFAAR: Affiliated Fellow of the American Academy in Rome.

64. Over a period of three years (1996–99), the Southern Regional Visiting Artists Program (directly administered by the Southern Arts Federation in Atlanta, Georgia) sent eleven artists in a variety of fields to live and work for three months each at the Academy. Two of these were composers: Kenneth Frazelle and Paul Elwood.

65. Pamela Keech, Peggy Brucia, and Ron Musto, "An Interview with Lester K. Little," *The Society of Fellows News (SOF News)* (1998/99): 10.

66. Nuovi Spazi Musicali was organized by the Italian composer Ada Gentile. Each fall it proposed a program of contemporary music concerts located in various academies and cultural institutes in Rome.

67. Once more the cultural branch of the American Embassy played a significant role in supporting this initiative.

68. *Americans in Rome, Music by the Fellows of the American Academy in Rome,* Bridge Records 9271A/D.

69. The catalogue of these archives can be accessed on the website of the American Academy in Rome (www.aarome.org) and via the Academy library's catalogue (URBS, Unione Romana Biblioteche Scientifiche).

70. In the following year, Robert McDuffie began a two-week summer music festival, "The Rome Chamber Music Festival," which, for the first two years, took place in Villa Aurelia's Sala Musica.

71. Adele Chatfield-Taylor, e-mail message to the author, June 20, 2006.

72. Edward MacDowell, memorandum to Charles McKim, cited in Valentine and Valentine, *American Academy in Rome,* 85. See Judith Tick, "The Classicist Origins of the Rome Prize in Musical Composition, 1890–1920," in this volume for a discussion of this document in context.

Part Two

Origins, Ideology, Patronage

Chapter Three

The Classicist Origins of the Rome Prize in Musical Composition, 1890–1920

Judith Tick

Prelude: Classicism and Classicalism

In 1893 the music critic William Apthorp titled a long essay on "Two Modern Classicists in Music," explicitly inviting readers of the *Atlantic Monthly* to contemplate the challenge in his title—what he wished to mean and not mean by the word "classicist":

> That which we call a word is but the shadow of our thought; it may mean this to us, but that to another . . . how many different meanings in as many minds has not this one word "classicism"! *Classic, classicism, classicist,* have grown to be very vague terms. To those who look for the meaning of a word in its etymology they are impregnated with a flavor of the academy, they reek with associations with the categorical imperative, the "thou shalt" and "thou shalt not" of the schools. To others they convey an idea of authority based on a survival after long sifting and a gradual recognition of what is fine, worthy, and, as the Germans say, *mustergiltig* [model-worthy]. To others, again, they imply merely something old, that was doubtless admirable once, but has had its day like other dogs, and should by rights be obsolete now. And who shall say that any of these interpretations is wholly without warrant? What we call a "classic" has become so in virtue of being recognized as fine and worthy by successive generations, and should be looked upon as a model in its way, as far as it goes; being a model, it naturally has been held up as such by the schools, and departure from its scheme has been deprecated, with more or less reason. . . . All these meanings of "classic" and "classicism" have truth in them; it is only by holding too fast by one, to the exclusion of the others, that we run the risk of error.[1]

This article begins with Apthorp's quotation because of its last sentence. The relationship of "classic" and "classicism" to the Rome Prize in music is not about the history of an idea, but instead about the practices associated with it. (One can argue whether in fact ideas do have a history independent of the practice of them.) In this case, the Rome Prize in music came about precisely because of the "spins of the terms," so to speak, which is to say, the clever and sometimes contradictory ways ideologically driven language was adapted and manipulated to serve the purpose at hand. Multiple meanings of classicism were invoked in developing an American Rome Prize in music composition.

Despite the obvious relationship of the topic to music, "musical classicism" is not a road that leads directly to Rome. The usage of the term in musical scholarship refers to the era from ca. 1770–1830 (Haydn, Mozart, Beethoven, Schubert). It has its own complex history, which is still relatively uncharted in nineteenth-century American music studies. Furthermore, musical classicism leads us to too many cities other than Rome and too many issues that are far beyond the limited purview of this essay. Instead, the term "classicism" here is employed as a general term with three related definitions: first, "an interest in the culture and art of Antiquity," which is its most common usage today;[2] and then two definitions associated with the (now archaic) late ninteenth-century terms—"classicalism," meaning "close adherence to the rules of Greek or Roman art," and "classicalist," meaning "a devoted admirer of classicism."[3] Musical composition as a liberal art depended on the understanding that these definitions of classicism could be expanded to include the "great tradition" of European concert music and opera.

Classicism as a "Central Intellectual Project" and an "Esoteric Byway"

As an art receiving the support of residential fellowships, music entered the American Academy in Rome a little more than twenty-five years after the Academy's founding in 1894. In 1921 the first competition for a Rome Prize in musical composition, open to unmarried male composers under the age of thirty and of American citizenship, was formally announced as part of a new Department of Musical Composition. Music remains the only performing art receiving regular Academy sponsorship to this day and the Rome Prize is so firmly established as one of the most important honors and opportunities available today for American composers that in retrospect we wonder why it took so long. Here we ask the opposite question: how it happened at all.

The idea for a Rome Prize in music emerged in the 1890s, at a time of decline of American engagement with classicism in framing a broad cultural agenda. The cultural historian Caroline Winterer explains how:

> Next to Christianity, the central intellectual project in America before the late nineteenth century was classicism. Given our devotion to more modern

concerns today, it is difficult for us to grasp how dazzled Americans were by the ancient Greeks and Romans, how enthusiastically they quarried the classical past for more than two and a half centuries. . . . Then in the last third of the nineteenth century the classical world quite rapidly receded from its important position in American intellectual and civic life, pooling instead in the esoteric byways of elite, high culture, where it remains today.[4]

Those "esoteric byways" locate the origins of the Rome Prize in music in time, place, and ideology. The rise of the popular music industry, that is to say, Tin Pan Alley, the emergence of African American idioms like ragtime, to take another example, may have caught the oral fancies of some American composers of this era, but the idea of an egalitarian aesthetic that equated democracy with popular expressive culture did not carry any fungible value at this time.

I will discuss three moments along the way as the idea of a Rome Prize in music moved from the private affairs of the Academy's board of trustees into public life. The first concerns the founding father figure of the American Academy in Rome, the architect Charles McKim. Fin de siècle American architectural classicism served as the aesthetic and ethical compass that led to his decision to include music ca. 1896–97. The second leads us to the composer Edward MacDowell. Classicism helps explain his commitment to a liberal arts education for composers and his fervent belief in creative collaboration. The third moment is the public coming-of-age of the Rome Prize for composers between 1919 and 1923. As music critics responded to the news of the prize, they added to and in some cases reshaped the public conversations justifying financial support for American composers. Their nuanced arguments reflect the changing climate for intellectual and cultural values after World War I.

Thus this exploration of the origins of the Rome Prize offers a critical angle from which to consider an influential discourse around creative achievement during formative decades in the history of American classical music. It helps us understand the priorities of the "governing class"—or the urban and educated elite in American society—who supported and funded the Rome Prize in the waning decades of the old political order.[5] Finally, it speaks to familiar debates in American intellectual life over old country versus new, identity, competition, and nationalist pride. From our point of view today, we can see how the Academy's promotion of classicism served as an ideological foundation for its decisions around patronage more or less at the same time as American modernism was on the rise.

Part One: Music at the Margins

Whose "American Renaissance"?

The founding of the American Academy in Rome is well known to architectural historians of the era, particularly through its association with the Chicago

Figure 3.1. Charles Follen McKim. Courtesy of the American Academy in Rome.

World's Fair. We need only recapitulate the outlines of this history as it has been typically told.[6] The idea for the Academy took hold directly after the conclusion of the Columbian World Exposition in Chicago, typically called the Chicago World's Fair, in 1893. So greatly admired were the classical pavilions and monumental buildings of the "White City" of the fair that the artists who had worked together on its construction, among them the administrating architect of the fair, Daniel Burnham, his colleague, Charles McKim, the sculptor Augustus St. Gaudens, and the painter John La Farge, were emboldened to dream of replicating their experience of collaboration. As Academy historians have written, "A Renaissance tour de force was being re-created as architect, painter, sculptor, landscaper, and builder wrought together in the classical manner. It was an experience that bit deeply into the minds of those who shared it; it influenced the course of American art for decades to come."[7]

This great idealistic adventure of establishing an American counterpart to the prestigious Académie française, located in the architectural masterpiece the Villa Medici on the imposing Pincian Hill, began in an iconic American building that could not be more different from the villa. McKim and his colleagues met in a replica of a log cabin that served as a temporary worksite before it turned into an exhibit on the fairgrounds. Initially the group focused on a modest goal of an American "atelier"—a studio/school, limited to architecture. Its ambition to secure a foothold in Rome was so speedily satisfied that the following year they rented some rooms and founded the American School of Architecture in Rome.[8]

The project had several goals. McKim and his colleagues believed without question that American architects had to study abroad. As is well known, they advocated a classicist style based on a modern emulation of models from antiquity and the Renaissance. They planned to establish a program of residential fellowships for already accomplished young architects that that would yield an elite cadre of practitioners who had breathed in the authentic spirit of the past on-site and would return home bearing gifts of renewal for the present. Further, they wanted to raise the standards of architecture and professionalize it by distinguishing it from the building trades.[9] Daniel Burnham wrote that "sending home three men [from their years at the Academy] annually who shall become a true leaven in America seems to me to be our great object."[10]

McKim, and later through his famous firm McKim, Mead, and White, led by example. Suffice it to say here that Boston, New York, and Washington, DC, bear the hallmarks of their enduring achievement, shaping even to this day our experience of these cities.[11] Architectural critics and historians have retained a term from this era and call this period an "American Renaissance" in architecture in the "Gilded Age" or in Beaux-Arts style.[12] The architectural historian Richard Wilson has written how "the belief that the United States had a special relationship with the Renaissance was a product of rediscovery and reinterpretation of the past."[13] McKim reinterpreted the past by developing a hybrid style, part Italian, part French Beaux-Arts, part American, and part McKim himself. The best models from classical antiquity were to be internalized, not slavishly imitated.

Where did American composers stand within this world of a retrofitted American Renaissance? It was not theirs. Composers did not produce a musical counterpart to the White City of the Chicago Worlds' Fair. On the contrary: quarrels about commissions and performances, along with mixed reviews for new works, marred the representation of classical music at the World's Fair, even temporarily sullying the reputation of Chicago's own Theodore Thomas, the legendary conductor who traveled annually across the continent with his own orchestra. While crowds flocked to hear Sousa's band play nightly and strolled the Midway listening to various exotic musics and new popular crazes such as ragtime, sparse audiences attended concerts of oratorios and symphonic music. Contemporary accounts by disappointed critics lamented how "the grandest opportunity this century has yet afforded for evidencing to the world America's present musical status and promise was not fully availed of by the Columbian Exposition powers." As the music historian E. Douglas Bomberger sums it up, "American Art Music [was] Humiliated" at the Fair."[14] Thus within the history of the American Academy of Rome, the origins of the Department of Musical Composition has a very different cultural profile from that of architecture and painting.

In the following decades as well, American classical composers lagged behind their colleagues not only in architecture but also in literature and painting when it came to cultivating an enthusiastic and loyal public. In contrast to American architects engaging a conveniently distant past, American composers measured themselves against German and Italian repertories of great music in the recent past or their own present. Furthermore, they also competed for attention with celebrity conductors and performers who were bringing glorious European music to American cities. An astute observer of this age, Joseph Horowitz writes how the focus on performers, which marked this period, proved prophetic for decades: "America's musical high culture has at all times (alas) been less about music composed by Americans than about American concerts of music composed by Europeans."[15]

Three leading composers of the period, George Chadwick, Edward MacDowell, and Horatio Parker, felt these professional growing pains throughout their careers.[16] The music historian Nicholas E. Tawa reports Chadwick's "bitter remarks": "The composers of America (some of them once referred to by an evening newspaper as 'local and suburban composers') have reason to be grateful that they have not been put into a class by themselves as freaks and curiosities."[17] Another case in point comes from a speech given by Horatio Parker in 1900, at the first open meeting of the National Institute of Arts and Letters, founded in 1898. According to Parker, who spoke for the academic mainstream from his position as the first professor of music appointed at Yale University, American classical music was a baby art as compared with sculpture and painting. . . . We go to Europe and brag splendidly about our mechanical and industrial achievements, but in speaking to foreigners about American music we do so deprecatingly and apologetically. Thank God, it is not necessary to be apologetic about American sculpture and painting. By American music I mean American composers. We have a school of literature, and we have made large strides toward a school of painting. We must have a vigorous school of music. It is impossible that this great country will always remain a parasite on the artistic nations of Europe.[18]

Parker's exhortations make McKim's early commitment to American composers all the more remarkable.

McKim's "Ardent Classical Convictions" Expand to Include Musical Composition

Charles Follen McKim's own appreciation for music supplied the first rung on the ladder leading to the Rome Prize for composers. Although not much is currently known about McKim's musical background, he came from a Quaker family whose abolitionist politics and values produced in his sister an important figure in American music history. Lucy McKim Garrison is remembered today as a coeditor of the famous collection *Slave Songs of the United States* (1867). Beyond that, a few details from the work of Charles McKim's biographers give the impression that he was known in New York as an active amateur music lover and patron. One biographer claims he sang with the Mendelssohn Glee Club, an "up-town organization composed of musical amateurs of high social standing," who gave private concerts in their own clubhouse, and whose members were mostly rich "business men who enjoyed singing good music."[19] A newspaper report in 1897 lists him among a "number of local [New York] music lovers" who started a fund to establish a permanent orchestra for a handsome inspirational conductor, Anton Seidl.[20] In 1892 under a commission from Henry Lee Higginson, the founder of the Boston Symphony Orchestra, McKim began planning Boston Symphony Hall. It was completed in 1900.

McKim was ready to be persuaded that music belonged in his American Academy, and at a right moment he met a right person. During a three-month visit to Rome, which began in December 1895, McKim became friendly with a "Mrs. Winthrop Chanler," a "resident and leader of American society there." McKim called her a "remarkable musician," and according to the Academy historians Lucia and Alan Valentine, she "left him convinced that music must also be represented."[21]

Margaret Terry Chanler (1862–1952), an American born and brought up in Rome, was indeed a serious pianist, having trained with Giovanni Sgambati, a distinguished pupil of Liszt. As Chanler herself later wrote in one of several volumes of memoirs, "we were a musical colony passionately attached to the German classics; we saw no virtue in any other music."[22] Her memoirs offer reliable accounts of how Franz Lizst, then living in Rome, played Chopin at his master classes that she occasionally attended. In short, McKim met an upper-class cosmopolitan "Europeanized American" woman, to use a term from the period.[23] Her musicianship and her own sophisticated taste reassured him that Rome could nurture the artistic development of American composers.[24]

An intriguing account of a visit with McKim some years later widens Margaret Chanler's relevance to this narrative. When McKim met her, Chanler, a member of the New York Social Register, was already ensconced in a privileged life in a milieu that recalls heroines in novels by Edith Wharton (another friend of hers). During the winter of 1896–97, which the Chanlers spent in Manhattan, she received a request that proved immensely important to the future of the Rome Prize. One of her friends was:

> Mr. Charles McKim, the architect, partner of Stanford White. He was a charming man of exquisitely fastidious taste and ardent classical convictions. He had just completed the Boston Public Library and was devoting all his energy to the founding of the American Academy in Rome, collecting funds and framing the plans on which the organization should be run. Mr. Pierpont Morgan had already given a generous endowment and other contributions were coming in. Mr. McKim was so enthusiastic about the scheme that he told me he would rather be known as the founder of the Academy than for his many architectural achievements. He asked me to give a little dinner at which he could talk things over with a group of experienced men, representing different arts—sculpture, painting, music; he would speak for architecture himself. He did not want any ladies invited. It was an interesting evening.
>
> Mr. St. Gaudens was the sculptor and gave his whole-hearted approval to the undertaking. He told us how he owed everything to classic art; how Rome had opened his eyes to beauty and how hard it had been for him to leave it, after spending a few penurious months there as a poor student. He had come back to New York to make his way as a sculptor, had hired a studio in a grim office building, and was so homesick in the unlovely surroundings that his only consolation had been to let the water run in the faucet all night, and go to sleep making believe he was hearing the splash of Roman fountains. What would he not have given for a Roman scholarship!
>
> McKim, himself a great music lover, was not sure whether music should be included with the other arts; not certain that Rome offered enough musical opportunities. Mr. MacDowell had been invited to represent music. He was not enthusiastic; he seemed to think that Germany was the only country where music could be studied with profit. Yet McKim felt very strongly that a few years' stay in Rome would benefit any artist, and his opinion eventually prevailed, for musicians are given scholarships at the Academy along with painters, sculptors, and architects, but are allowed to spend part of their time elsewhere.[25]

Chanler's report exposes a fault line recognized early on and dealt with in different ways by later supporters of the Department of Music. Why Rome? was a recurring question.

The prestige of the French Prix de Rome in music helped resolve the issue in some ways. If France sent architects to Rome, so could the United States. If France sent composers to Rome, then McKim might hope that the United States would follow that lead as well. So widespread among the American urban elite was the glowing reputation of the Prix de Rome in music that in the very first publication of the Academy—the Catalogue for the Annual Exhibition in 1896—the authors quoted the French composer, Charles Gounod, winner of the Prix de Rome in 1839. The catalogue adopted Gounod's words as a banner for the Academy: "[Rome's] past as well as its present, its present as well as its destiny, makes it the capital of not merely a country, but humanity."[26] Gounod's statement carried special weight because of his popularity among American opera lovers.[27] Just as his *Faust* stayed a fixture of the season year in and out in this period at the Metropolitan Opera in New York, so his endorsement of Rome was reiterated in later Academy publications before the Rome Prize in musical composition was established.

The scope of Charles McKim's actions—his certainty that his views could and should override that of a major American composer—came from his belief in "classical education." A phrase taking in its sweep far more than the study of Greek and Latin, it was explained recently by the classics scholar Lee Pearcy as the "grammar of civility," or to put this another way, a hegemonic language for Western culture over a huge swath of time:

> Between the [Italian] Renaissance and the First World War the governing classes in Britain and America came to the richness of Western high culture through an artificial structure whose purposes were to explain that civilization and ease the way to its complexities and hard truths, to encode values and attitudes that tempered and strengthened the collective self-awareness of those classes. That artificial structure or enabling code, that grammar of civility was classical education. . . .
>
> Together, liberal arts education and *Alterumswissenschaft* [the systematic scholarship about anquitity] formed the grammar of classical education. Until early in this century, that grammar reflected a language in which meaningful statements could be made. . . . From, very roughly, the [Italian] Renaissance until the First World War, classical education made sense because of the interaction in it of these two paradigmatic beliefs. During this period, any belief that was paradigmatic for classical education was also paradigmatic for Western high culture.[28]

These views were widely shared among the educated and moneyed elite circles in which McKim moved. His client base included many among the first group of American millionaires (such as Henry Lee Higginson and J. P. Morgan). As is well known, some of these fabled Gilded Age rich co-opted images of the Medici for their homes, built Italianate palazzos in New York and Newport, and furnished them with Renaissance art. They patronized opera and built concert halls. Furthermore, as an extension of their receptiveness to classicism, they were also not averse to supporting an ideology about music that placed it within the context of the "humanities" and "liberal arts" in the culture at large. Thus the connective associations link as follows: classicism as the model leads to the Prix de Rome; the Prix leads to the Eternal City, that is to say, Western High Culture; this in turn leads to the decision to incorporate music, and music, wearing its laurel leaf, leads to advocacy for a Department of Musical Composition within the American Academy in Rome.

No matter that an American counterpart to either Leonardo da Vinci or Ludwig van Beethoven had yet to be born. Only by placing oneself as a link in the chain between past and present could a musical creator absorb the civilizing forces of tradition. Only this produced genuine education and genuine culture, and only if contemporary artists embraced tradition could they empower their own country's patrimonial growth. Therefore, even though musical composition did not fit comfortably into the practice of emulating classical art, it belonged to the "humanities," whose wellspring was the Italian Renaissance and whose spiritual center was Rome. Such ideological expansiveness launched the Rome Prize in musical composition.

Part Two: Alliances between McKim and MacDowell Move from Rhetoric to Policy

MacDowell and the "Closer Cooperation of the Arts"

Thus, through their shared belief in the humanities, McKim and MacDowell came to understand that Rome could serve their mutual interests. In December 1896 MacDowell had already committed himself to this inclusive approach to classical education or "liberal culture," as he called it, or the "liberal arts" as one might still stay today, as a prerequisite for musicians. In the early years heading the Department of Music at Columbia University, he stated that "music, painting, history, and literature, including languages, should be elements of liberal culture, elements that are also indispensable to the specialist in art. . . . I am firmly convinced that one art can learn more from another in a year than in a decade of delving into hidden causes and abstruse technic that belong in the domain of science."[29]

In the early 1900s MacDowell became the standard-bearing composer of the campaign to bring music into the American Academy in Rome. MacDowell was then regarded as America's first indisputable entry into the pantheon of greatness.[30] In 1896 Robert Watson Gilder, the editor of *Century Magazine,* wrote a tribute in his collection *Music* that included, along with poems about Beethoven, another called simply "MacDowell":

> REJOICE! Rejoice!
> the New World hath a voice;
> voice of tragedy and mirth,
> sounding clear through all the earth;
> voice of music, tender and sublime,
> in to the master-music of all time.[31]

The praise flowed from many quarters. "He is the greatest musical genius America has produced," stated the appointments committee from Columbia University, who, after MacDowell's premieres of the *Indian Suite* and two New York premieres of his piano concertos, hired him as its first professor of music in 1896.[32] At that point MacDowell joined the ranks of two other composers credentialed through their employment at the prestigious Ivy League universities Harvard (John Knowles Paine) and Yale (Horatio Parker). When the National Institute of Arts and Letters formed the more selective newly established American Academy of Arts and Letters in 1904, MacDowell was the only musician elected on the first ballot. MacDowell wrote to the poet Robert Underwood Johnson: "I am proud of this great distinction not only for myself, but also for the recognition of the Art of Music in this land."[33]

MacDowell continued to argue for curricular reform at Columbia University, basing his agenda on the ideals of classical education. In 1901 he suggested that architecture be relocated from Columbia's School of Mines and, along with music, join painting, sculpture, and literature to comprise a faculty of fine arts.[34] In effect, MacDowell adopted and expanded the blueprint for the American Academy in Rome to his university. As Jack Beeson, another Columbia composer and winner of the Rome Prize in musical composition, wrote decades later: "Had MacDowell been any better acquainted with the universities of his time, he would not so wholly have committed his boundless energy, imagination, and teaching abilities to such ambitious plans."[35] Seeking too much institutional change from his position within a relatively weak department, MacDowell ran afoul of Columbia's powerful president, Nicholas Murray Butler. Butler had ascended to the presidency from his post at Teachers' College, the last place MacDowell would accept as a home for music. MacDowell resigned his Columbia position in 1904.

This did not derail McKim's support for his friend in the slightest. In 1905 McKim facilitated the appointment of MacDowell to the Board of Trustees of the American Academy, drawing him into the inner circles of power. On January 11, 1905, MacDowell attended the annual dinner of the American Institute of Architects on a special celebratory occasion. The lone composer among the ca. 230 guests in the room, MacDowell sat at the head table along with J. P. Morgan and several speakers at the dinner, among them President

Theodore Roosevelt, his designate secretary of state Elihu Root, the French ambassador Jules Jusserand, and MacDowell's nemesis, Nicholas Murray Butler.[36] Officially intended to honor the recently finished renovations to the capital city and to the White House itself, the dinner also promoted the agenda of the American Academy in Rome. At stake was a bill in Congress to dignify the American Academy with a national charter.

MacDowell heard two speeches that evening that bear on his own role within the history of the Rome Prize. He heard President Theodore Roosevelt temper his usual chauvinist rhetoric about national character and the need for independence from Europe. Just a few years earlier, in a controversial article titled "True Americanism," Roosevelt successfully fanned the flames of anti-intellectualism by demeaning "cosmopolitanism."[37] (According to one of his biographers, Edmond Morris, such articles were "worshipfully pondered" by a gullible American public.[38]) After a sumptuous banquet, standing in front of the wealthy elite known for furnishing their mansions with European art and building facsimiles of European palaces in New York and Newport, Roosevelt did not choose to rail against the "Europeanized American." On the contrary: he changed course and presented himself as a reborn cosmopolitan. Having issued an injunction that the White House should be "restored to what it was planned to be by [George] Washington," he chose McKim to carry out the mission of translating George Washington's classicist ideals to the symbolic homestead of a nation.[39] That is to say, the White House had been renovated in accordance with McKim's "Europeanized American" prescriptions, and with the blessings of Theodore Roosevelt himself. Thus future generations of American architects trained in Rome might also carry on the classical traditions of their forefathers as enlightened bearers of an American aesthetic grounded in historical symbols.

McKim's authoritative presence and the example of his recent renovations and improvements to the White House in 1902 made Roosevelt's embrace of classical values in his speech for the American Institute of Architects seem less opportunistic. Roosevelt even embellished his rhetoric to embrace aesthetic values for their own sake. He acknowledged the civic claims of "beauty" and by extension the mission of the American Academy in Rome.

> We hear a great deal about true Americanism. Now, the real American whom it is worthwhile to call such, is the man whose belief in and work for American are not merely for the America of today, but for the America of the future. . . . There are things in a nation's life more important than beauty; but beauty is very important. And in this nation of ours, while there is very much in which we have succeeded marvelously, I do not think that if we look dispassionately at what we have done, we will say that beauty has not been exactly the strong point of the nation! It rests largely with gatherings such as this, and with the note that is set by men such as those I am addressing tonight, to determine whether or not this shall be true of the future.[40]

In effect, Roosevelt recast cultural ambition in terms of national uplift. This theme was further embellished by his future secretary of state, the Honorable Elihu Root—whom we can truly call a "classicalist." Root made classicism a priority for progressive policy. Recalling again the impact of the White City of the Chicago World's Fair, and comparing Lake Michigan to the Ionian Sea between Italy and Greece, Root said:

> It was reserved for the great city of the middle West, by the example of that fair White City by the Lake, which remains with us as a dream of Ionian seas, to lead our people out of the wilderness of the commonplace to new ideas of architectural beauty and nobility. The lesson of the Chicago Exposition has gone into every city and town and hamlet of America. The architects now for the first time are beginning to have the nation with them.
>
> The people of America are beginning to see that it is not necessary to be commonplace in order to have common sense. The people of America are no longer content that the multi-millionaire in his palace, the great railroad corporation in its monumental station, the great banks, and insurance companies, and trust companies in their massive business buildings, shall be the sole inheritors of the beauty and art which our fathers loved. They wish for themselves in the public buildings of municipalities and of States and Nation to have the best results of time and the best attainments of genius. What the people desire, their representatives in State legislature, in municipal body, and in the Congress of the United States, desire for them. The art of our fathers, the art of our private citizens, is to be the art of our people and of our whole people.[41]

Such a canyon between then and now: What contemporary politician would utter the phrase "the wilderness of the commonplace" in today's political arena?

Root extended the long reach of his remarks about art into the arena of progressive policy. What responsibility do artists have toward their fellow citizens in a democracy? His memorable answer resounded with classicist goals: to reinforce the artistic priorities of the founding fathers, to bring the people into contact with the best ideals of Western culture. Hence a *policy position* for Roosevelt's new administration justified support for the American Academy in Rome. On March 5, 1905, the day after Roosevelt was sworn in for his second term, the House passed the bill to incorporate the American Academy of Rome as a national institution.[42]

MacDowell Persists

A few months later, in May 1905, MacDowell moved forward with his advocacy of music fellowships for the Academy. Even though his illness (syphilis), which would kill him four years later, had already triggered a serious collapse, MacDowell summed up enough intellectual energy to dictate a memo about the fellowships to his wife, Marian, which she sent to Charles McKim. The memo, which, according to Marian, was not "formally submitted to the Board," reiterates MacDowell's favorite themes and inflects them this time with nationalist nuances of public relevance.[43]

MacDowell emphasized more than ever before the potential for creative synergy within an arts community. As is well known in Academy history, the collaborations among American architects, sculptors, and painters, working together on projects for the World's Fair, became the paradigm for the "collaborative projects" among the fellows at the Academy.[44] Even though composers could not and did not fit into this curricular model, MacDowell invigorated the notion of cooperative inspiration so effectively that one sentence from the memo turned into an Academy mission statement of sorts: "For years it has been my dream that the Arts of Architecture, Painting, Sculpture and Music should come into such close contact that each and all should gain from this mutual companionship."

The most provocative section of his memo responded to a common issue of the time. How could one instill nationalist cultural responsibility into the hearts and minds of recipients of the fellowships? MacDowell worried that Rome Prize composers, seduced by the charms of Europe, would be tempted into postures of superiority. The historian Alan Levy has summed up this familiar theme, noting how "in Germany many of the American composers developed a veneer of polish and disdain for their nation as a provincial culture."[45] Even if in his youth MacDowell himself had to be urged by a fellow American musician to come back home from Germany, he had changed enough to recognize the problem, as this excerpt from the memo makes clear:

> It seems quite possible that in the future it may be wise for the student to break the [time] there of a four-year course of study in Europe, returning for a winter's study in his own country, putting himself against American students in his own art, and avoiding, it seems to me, the one danger in connection with foreign study, the inclination to look down upon American art in America, and of sometimes a distinctively original note being stifled by the overwhelming and picturesque surroundings of Europe. A great genius may come out of a small New England town. Transplanted to Europe his youthful mind is naturally dazzled and the dangerous feeling is fostered that little or no art exists on this side of the water. Let him, however, break his four-year scholarship perhaps at the end of his second year, by a return to America to study the artistic life not only in the big Eastern cities but in the far West, and he will return for his final European study sobered and enlightened as to the present condition and the future possibilities of art in his native land.[46]

Thus, American composers whose sensibilities have been honed by Roman vistas will drink in the heroic redemptive landscapes of the West. Theodore Roosevelt would have approved. In the end, however, MacDowell and McKim, while succeeding in raising the profile of American composers within Academy circles during their lifetimes, effected little institutional change regarding music within the Academy itself. A small entry from the minutes of the Executive Committee of the American Academy dated November 5, 1906, conveys a welcoming informal climate for music but not much else.

> The painters and sculptors divide their time, according to the requirements of their scholarships, between travel, study, copying in the galleries, churches etc. and original work done in the studios provided by the Academy. . . . Wishing the student life at the Academy to be well rounded out we have encouraged the social side. Finding some musical talent amongst our men we rented a piano for the common living room, thus attracting the musicians and music lovers from other academies. Sometimes the musicale was made a little more formal by being held in the rooms of the Director, and by the presence of invited friends.[47]

And that was that, or so it seemed. In fact, there was an unintended consequence of MacDowell's activity for the Academy in which American classicism played no small part.

"Classicizing" the MacDowell Colony

At the funeral service for MacDowell on January 26, 1908, the *New York Herald* reported how "among the friends and associates of the composer . . . were members of the MacDowell Association, an organization formed to carry out the composer's ideas of a closer co-operation among the arts." Among them were the Academy stalwarts McKim and Augustus St. Gaudens.[48] The "suitable memorial" mentioned as well took shape in what we know today as the MacDowell Colony. Around this time Marian MacDowell began her long career of fund-raising for this new enterprise. She ran into one unexpected stumbling block from a major benefactor of the American Academy: "Marian MacDowell approached J. P. Morgan for money for the colony but without success. He offered a pension for life but not a cent for a 'damn-fool scheme for indigent Bohemians that would never work.' Marian MacDowell refused the pension and decided to raise the funds herself."[49] Morgan went so far as to withdraw his $500 subscription to the MacDowell Memorial Fund.[50] However, women's amateur arts associations and clubs, which constituted an economic stratum of arts development in this country, responded to her campaign. As the cultural historian Karen Blair notes, they "applauded Marian MacDowell's performances of her husband's compositions and donated steady sums for the building of an artistic haven for the best talent in America. Cabins, library, swimming pool, amphitheatre, and other facilities were built through women's clubs contributions. In turn, Marian MacDowell saw that half the awards made in her lifetime went to women artists."[51]

Given that women were not admitted to the American Academy in Rome for many decades, the colony's de facto "affirmative action" policies helped compensate for the pervasive discrimination against women and the masculinization of cultural authority typical as well of other honorary arts societies.[52] Here the model of the Prix de Rome in France did not seem to set a precedent, for the eligibility of women for that competition began in 1903.[53] In contrast, the American Academy at Rome did not award the title "fellow" to a female composer until 1971.[54]

Classicist rhetoric played an important role in the presentation of the colony to the outside world. In her memoir about the founding of the MacDowell Colony, Marian MacDowell transformed Morgan's "indigent Bohemians" into respectable citizens by "classicizing" the identity of the colony. She honored her husband's relationship to McKim. In 1933 she appropriated the rhetoric of the discourse that had developed about the Academy to ground the colony as an ideological partner in a mutual cultural enterprise planted on *terra alta.* In writing a major statement of purpose for the project she cared most about in the world, the MacDowell Colony, she declared:

> The American Academy at Rome and the MacDowell Colony at Peterborough, New Hampshire—far separated in terms of time and space—have more than a little in common, standing, each of them, a monument to a man whose vision penetrated the future of the country he loved and in whose art he firmly believed, the one to Charles McKim—the other to Edward MacDowell. The idea of the American Academy at Rome belonged to Charles McKim; that of the MacDowell Colony at Peterborough to Edward MacDowell. For twenty years McKim planned and worked to bring about the materialization of the American Academy at Rome. Early in these years MacDowell joined forces with him, eventually becoming the first representative of music on the Academy's Board of Directors.
>
> On first thought it may seem inappropriate to compare the American Academy at Rome and the MacDowell Colony at Peterborough, yet the former had a great deal to do with the making of the latter. MacDowell always felt very strongly the close relation of all the arts, and still more strongly that the artists had much to gain from each other, the painter offering valuable companionship to the composer or poet, the sculptor opening new worlds to those working in the other arts. There gradually evolved in his mind this concrete idea of the great usefulness of the correlation of the arts and, furthermore, of the immense advantage it would be, should there come into existence a place where a man might find not only the ideal conditions for work, but ideal companionship. And this is the thing sought, and it is hoped, accomplished by the MacDowell Association. Had MacDowell lived to see the fulfillment of his idea as it now stands at Peterborough, I think he would have dared to hope that there might be some direct connection between the American Academy at Rome and the MacDowell Colony.[55]

It is a bit of a stretch to compare the pines of Rome with those of the New Hampshire woods, or Peterborough with Rome, or the view from Mount Monadnock with views from the Janiculum Hill. That each is beautiful in its own way is not the point. Rather, Marian MacDowell's appropriation of classicism testifies to the impact of the American Academy in Rome as an ideological wellspring for cultural nationalism. Writing retrospectively but nevertheless reflecting the period in which the ideology of the colony took shape, Marian MacDowell reshaped antiquity into a utopian present so that Edward's MacDowell's version of the dream for the Academy could take root in New England soil.

With the deaths of MacDowell (1908) and McKim (1909), hopes for any immediate action for a Rome Prize in music faded. No musician and no trustee rose from the ranks of the faithful to replace them until—unpredictably—a few years later in 1913 a relative outsider in Academy circles, Felix Lamond, the church organist for Trinity Chapel (a branch of the famous Trinity Church), took up the baton to run the next lap of the long-distance relay race to the finish line. As described by Academy historians, Lamond proposed to his friend and Academy trustee Daniel Chester French that a fellowship in musical composition be established. "Sixteen trustees of the Academy met in New York to discuss it, but although sympathetic to the idea they decided they must reduce their debt before undertaking a new project."[56]

Despite this deferral an important threshold had been crossed: in theory, music now belonged in the Academy, although in practice, funding had to be secured. A letter from a trustee, the architect E. P. Mellon, to Roscoe Guernsey, secretary of the AAR, on July 1, 1921, confirms: "It was agreed during all of at least the last six years that such a Department was to be established as soon as sufficient funds were collected."[57] Thus the prospect of fellowships for musical composition in the Academy was discussed on an annual basis throughout the war years. How the priorities shifted, how the funding was secured—how Lamond gathered support and organized the actual grassroots work of implementation—these aspects of the process belong to another chapter in this book.[58] Suffice to say here that the board of trustees formed a separate endowment committee in November 1919 to endow fellowships in landscape architecture and music. On December 2, 1919, the board approved funds to produce a general pamphlet for the fund-raising drive.

Part Three: The Rome Prize in Music Enters the Public Arena

Classicism and Subsidized "Artistic Nourishment"

The general pamphlet for the endowment campaign, published as a commemorative volume for the twenty-fifth anniversary of the American Academy in Rome, contained the first public endorsement of the Rome Prize in music. In it Walter Spalding, a professor of music at Harvard, wrote a short statement.[59]

For his opening salvo Spalding relied on the old strategy of a familiar comparison to the French Academy. He then substituted generalities about Italy for the specific humanistic symbolism associated with Rome itself:

> As the French Academy, with its "Prix de Rome" has sheltered and developed such illustrious composers as Berlioz, Gounod, Bizet, Massenet, and Debussy, so our Academy will provide for young musicians of marked promise. . . . For more than a hundred years the achievements of French artists who have had the inspiration and artistic nourishment which the first Napoleon believed that they would derive from Italy, have fulfilled his expectation and justified his plan. . . . A long line of German composers from Mozart to Strauss has sought and found the same inspiration in Italy. That our youths of talent should also be matured in this artistic climate is the aim of our Academy.[60]

Spalding also offered a critique of the role of art in a capitalist economy by transforming the old ideal of "closer cooperation among the arts" into a "society of comrades" seeking a respite from the marketplace: "It is more important to American artists than to Frenchmen that in the formative years they should have the companionship and surroundings created by the society of comrades with similar aspirations, rather than to live sporadically in the community chiefly commercial, with the immediate physical and mental burden of self-support."[61] American composers, he implied, could not flourish in the financial milieu that had so abundantly filled the pockets of the Academy's patrons. Already the term "commercial" wedges itself between art and entertainment, separating the business of business from the business of art. Without mentioning the word "money," or worse yet, "poverty," Spalding implies the absent terms by alluding to "sporadic" living, or, as one might say today, living on freelance employment. Words like "nourishment" and "nurturing" soften the notion of subsidy and welfare. Then Spalding took a surprising jab at democracy: "Our Democracy has taken up music more vigorously and sympathetically than any of the other Fine Arts. . . . But although there are many schools and academies which turn out performers of the first rank, they never have, and in the very nature of things they cannot produce composers."[62] What this "very nature of things meant" Spalding never said. That same year he finished the manuscript of what proved to be an extremely successful music appreciation book in which he contradicted himself, or at the least, qualified his prior critique. There he wrote about the generation of American composers just preceding the implementation of the Rome Prize:

> We see this clearly in the rapid growth of music among peoples and nations, which comparatively a short time ago, were thought to be quite outside the pale of modern artistic development. . . . What now can be said of America? This much at least: when we consider that, beyond the most rudimentary attempts, music in our land is not yet a century old, a start has been made which promises great things. Such pioneers as Paine, Chadwick, MacDowell,

> Foote, Parker, Osgood, Whiting and Mrs. H. H. A. Beach have written works, often in the larger forms, showing genuine inspiration and fine workmanship, many of which have won permanent recognition outside of their own country. Of late years, a younger group has arisen. . . . These composers all have strong natural gifts, have been broadly educated, and above all, in their music is reflected a freedom, a humor and an individuality which may fairly be called American; that is, it is not music which slavishly follows the "made-in-Germany" model.[63]

Spalding ignored past idealizations of Rome as the site of humanity or humanism. Nor was reciprocal public service stressed, in the manner of Roosevelt or Root. However atrophied his classicist values seem in comparison with McKim's generation, for Spalding the Prix de Rome established a sufficient precedent justifying aid for the individual classical composer.

The twenty-fifth anniversary pamphlet published by the endowment committee of the American Academy soon had its desired effect. In the space of three months, between April and October 1920, three substantial features by the leading New York music critics Richard Aldrich, Walter J. Henderson, and the now obscure but then widely read Charles Henry Meltzer ushered the possibility of a Rome Prize in music into public cultural conversation. The following year a well-known composer and professor of music at Columbia University, Daniel Gregory Mason, published his views as well, soon followed by the prominent musician Walter Damrosch. Looked at collectively, these writers afford us a final chance to watch the ideology of classicism within the Academy retain its traditions and adapt to a new present, all the while framing the way the Rome Prize prepared for its future.

Richard Aldrich's long feature, published on April 18, 1920, in the *New York Times*, was headlined "Aid for American Composers." Written before the final plans had settled, Aldrich struck a new note in arguing for the Rome Prize from the start.[64] He began with a tribute to Charles Tomlinson Griffes, an American composer whom he deemed a victim of cultural neglect. Paying tribute to Griffes's music in high praise reserved for only a few other Americans of his generation, Aldrich lamented his early demise and his lack of opportunity to grow into his gifts.

All of this served as a prelude to Aldrich's main question: What responsibility do we—meaning the general public as opposed to professionals—have toward the artists in our midst? He pointed his finger at the American public.

> [Griffes's] lot is not one of which the American public can feel very proud. Whether Mr. Griffes would have developed into a commanding genius can naturally not be known. He had shown originality and distinction, the possession of abundant ideas and the ability to use them. These things are rare, and the fact is undoubted that he was not allowed the opportunity to use them to the best advantage. . . . We speak with pity or scorn for a public that could let a Mozart or a Schubert die and like to think that those bad

> old days are gone, but from time to time something uncomfortably like them and of the same sort is revealed in the present. Perhaps one means to help in avoiding this lamentable sort of thing will be the new project of the American Academy in Rome.

"Genius"—the elusive deity of cultural patrimony—was held out as the possible reward in this conflation of patronage with civic duty. Aldrich juggles McKim's sense of priorities. Instead of McKim's aspiration that artists returning from Rome raise the cultural standards of American society, now the sense of responsibility shifted to what American society owed its artists.

Other more familiar themes animate Aldrich's article as well. The French Prix de Rome continued to loom large as the foundational rationale for the American Rome Prize. Following the lead of Walter Spalding, Aldrich duly reflected on the glory France's composers had brought to that nation. Still, not one word about classical models or classical education appeared in Aldrich's feature. He decorated Spalding's phrases with expressive clauses, extolling the benefits to the individual artist. He defended imagination and beauty in the eloquent language of aestheticism. The fellowship was

> a gift of leisure, of tranquility. It is a gift of beautiful surroundings, of companionship and the environment created by the society of comrades with similar aspirations. It involves removal from a more or less "sporadic" life in a community chiefly commercial, with the immediate physical and mental burden of self-support. Most of all, it involves a life in an atmosphere of supreme beauty, a nourishment of the aesthetic sense as nowhere else it can be nourished.

Aldrich tackled the why Rome question head-on, countering the unspoken preference for Germany in a postwar language that signaled the end of an era:

> It is said that Rome is not a notably musical city: that Italy is not the most musical nation at present, in the highest sense of the word musical; that the greatest composers, the most potent musical influences, are now elsewhere; that some of the best French musicians have not been Roman prizemen. Some have said that young American composers sent abroad for their ripening come back dissatisfied with America, out of touch with her artistic movement. Henry F. Gilbert in an article in *The New Music Review* speaks of the "old German tradition for aspiring Americans, now broken up by the war—going to Germany to complete studies, returning home full of counterpoint, beer, and watery semi-German compositions."

After World War I, German music, Aldrich implied, no longer functioned as the singular fount of musical achievement. Moreover, even if Paris had not yet fully emerged as a mecca for a new generation of American composers, the Rome Prize might set the stage for other options, mooting the debate between Germany and France as rival destinations. In Aldrich's vision, the ideology of classicism associated with the Rome Prize could be more fluid and less site specific. After a residency period, fellows could wander at will.

At the end, knowing that such an argument required a rigorous selection process, Aldrich reminded the board of trustees about the administration of the fellowship, how the selection and appointments had to be managed with "wisdom and care." In fact, the Academy took him at his word, appointing Aldrich to the jury for the first fellowships in 1922.

Enter the hard-edged voice of dissent from Charles Henry Meltzer, a now obscure critic writing for a relatively new journal, the *Weekly Review*, with circulation aimed at the upper-class business elite.[65] Repudiating analogies between the American Academy and the Académie française, Meltzer went on the attack:

> Of all the plans proposed for helping musicians in this great but careless land, the most futile and illogical is one much talked in New York just now. It would provide for the endowment of two or perhaps three fat scholarships in Rome for young composers of marked talent. It assumes, heaven knows why, that their brief sojourn among classical surroundings would help the person chosen to write great music. . . .
>
> The devisors of the plan are clearly hypnotized by what they mistake for the example of the French. They must have fancied that, because French Prix-de-Rome men in the past hundred years have done good work, this is due not to their training at the Conservatoire, but to their temporary stay at the Villa Medici. They argue that results of the same kind though they should have genius, to sit down on the Janiculum, when they could find much more to inspire them in Paris, in Munich, or in Russia?
>
> The "Prix-de-Rome" is an exploded fallacy, a worn-out stale tradition. The great need of young composers is not Rome, but training, with the chance of getting what one may compose heard and produced. To send a half-trained student from New York in the wild hope that Rome will change him is an absurdity. If he has genius, what he needs is the best schooling. He needs a mastery of technique, not classic landscapes.
>
> It is many years since Rome produced musicians of world-wide importance. Those who seek music and the companionship of masters of that gracious art, go not to the Seven Hills, but north, to Milan. Americans who may win the Prix de Rome will be more remote, much more remote, from music in their exile than in the avenues of Boston or New York. They will be lulled by the soft, balmy airs that blow about the crest of the Janiculum. They will hear the mandolins. They will be able to look down the steps of St. Peter's and to retrace the steps of many martyred saints. But music?[66]

On one level Meltzer's why Rome arguments appealed to musical common sense. Rome was not a musical center. MacDowell himself initially had been filled with misgivings about the Academy on just these grounds. He had been convinced by McKim at the peak of the architect's reputation. Classicism twenty-five years later appeared ever more fragile and anachronistic, especially after World War I. Prizes like the Prix de Rome evoked an ancien régime. Italy was recovering from a war.

On the other hand, Meltzer took the analogy between the Académie française and the American Academy too literally. He underestimated the selection process, which might bring fully trained rather than "half-trained" composers to Rome. Resistant to the powers of classicist ideology to transcend these problems, he would have obstructed the Rome Prize because Americans lacked a national federally funded conservatory. By that reasoning the Academy itself stood on sterile soil, since the United States lacked a federally funded national school of painting and a federally funded national school of sculpture as well.[67] How surprising that a critic known as a fin de siècle aesthete, who until the end of his life "wore the long hair and cape of the vintage of the eighties and nineties," who translated the librettos of Wagner and advocated opera in English, and who even collaborated with that roughhouse composer Carl Ruggles, should have challenged the credibility of the Academy as a whole in the pages of a conservative magazine.[68]

Meltzer's objections surfaced at least in part because he focused on musical practices rather than on the artistic and social values associated with American classicism. The Rome Prize in music was not about models of apprenticeship and guilds that supported the French Conservatoire. Nor was the Rome Prize actually about craft. It was about the privilege of freedom conferred by an elite class, who acceded to the imperatives of an eroding system of classical education. The very phrase "Prix de Rome" represented the way that grammar of civility functioned to legitimate an American Rome Prize. It was a supremely effective rationalization for a democratic society, whose own history valued antiquity but whose political policies resisted public subsidy of cultural enterprises, particularly for one person at a time. American classicism made it possible for a major form of private subsidy for American composers to come into being. The point was not the "Prix de Rome" as the French practiced it, but rather the Rome Prize as Americans imagined it.

Meltzer caused enough worry to rouse the trustees into defensive action. Recorded in the minutes of the board, November 9, 1920, is their response and strategy:

> The attention of the Board is called to a letter from Major Lamond to Mr. Mead in explanation of the article which appeared in *The Weekly Review* in the early summer. It was considered best that the article should not receive a formal reply, but a reply appeared on October 31st in the *New York Herald*, by Mr. W. J. Henderson, the foremost music critic of this city, which completely refuted the statements in the article of the *Weekly Review*, although it did not mention that article by name. Major Lamond's letter to Mr. Mead gives the favorable opinion of musical men of the highest standing in regard to the advantages of the musical establishment in the Academy. Among these endorsers are the Heads of the Musical Departments of Harvard and Yale

Universities and the two most foremost composers of America—Horatio Parker and John Alden Carpenter.[69]

W. J. Henderson's virtual rebuttal was published in the *New York Herald* in his column "Favors Scheme of American Academy in Rome to Aid the Composer of Music" on October 31, 1920. Henderson counterpunched with a genteel fist:

> Composers have no friends. A reviewer of musical activities may write anything about a composition—excepting always the operas of Mr. Meyerbeer—without evoking a single word of protest. . . . No one will pay the slightest attention to him. But let him declare that a certain inferior opera singer has achieved a flat failure in the field of the song recital . . . or that Mr. Sawyer should let the poor violin rest awhile and then he will discover that his newspaper has a large circulation. Every little petty performer is followed by a small company of adorers. [Any aid to performers attracts attention but] Let someone form a fund for the training of young musicians who show certain gifts in the line of composition and it is difficult to get a quarter of a column printed about it.
>
> If any movement looking to the help of composers carries with it the necessity of a sojourn in Europe the musical journals are likely to take notice of it and bestow upon it their vigorous opposition. It is unnecessary to point out the reasons for this. They should be obvious to the most careless reader.
>
> All of which is prefatory to the assertion that the scheme of the American Academy in Rome to do something for the American composer is one entirely worthy of serious consideration. This plan does not contemplate musical education. The beneficiary will have to be a musician, not merely a student. The best summary of the scheme is that it closely resembles the Prix de Rome of the French Conservatoire, and that it will be an addition to the Academy's present departments of painting, sculpture, architecture, classical studies, and landscape architecture. . . .
>
> It is not contended that these masters [French composers] attained their importance because they had won the Prix de Rome. The point to be observed is that at the period in their career when they most needed to be freed from the problems of money making, when their youthful talents most required opportunity to assume definite shape and direction, when they clamored most loudly for a wholly untrammeled expression of their individuality, the support of the prize foundation furnished the essential security.[70]

Conjuring the rhetoric of American classicism, Henderson reminded readers of French Prix de Rome winners and echoed MacDowell's ideals of a community of artistic mutual friends. His statement that "musicians are prone to narrowness" and that "composers ought to have an outlook as broad as the human mind" sustains the customary practice of linking artistic high culture with classical education.

Then Henderson emphasized ideas about the Rome Prize that were muted in discussions of classicist stylistic protocols. In a section of his feature titled

"Spring from the Liberated Spirit," Henderson described the potential benefits of the Academy's artistic community with the romantic fervor of a Wagnerite describing a total art utopia. Berlioz's achievements, he took as a case in point, were "not the outcome of scholastic application. They spring from the liberated spirit, working out its own mission in accordance with its own laws."

> A young American composer entering into the life of the American Academy in Rome might not perhaps derive from it all that Berlioz got from the French Academy; but it would be impossible for him to escape the operation of beneficial influences. If there were nothing else, the contact of minds as young as his own, eager, searching, fearless intelligences, delving into the secrets of painting, architecture, and other arts, would constitute a splendid stimulus.

How far Henderson roams from the political rhetoric of Elihu Root, whose speech emphasized order and gentlemanly dignity! This eloquent defense of artistic adventure into unpredictable "individuality" via classicism shows the elastic nature of the point of reference. At the end of this evocative article, Henderson leaves the reader with description of a sensuous musical imagination developing like a Renaissance pearl within the shell of the Academy:

> A composer who steeps his soul in the spirit of the Italian *cinque cento* and then bathes it in the foamy waters of the Italian present will gain much, but he will obtain an equal benefit from the continual irritation of his mentality by the restlessness of the other young minds around him. . . . When the necessary sum has been raised there will be a brilliant opportunity for some budding American musical genius.

As these critics respond to the possibility of the Rome Prize, the discourse around the ideas fluctuates in tone, sometimes singing familiar themes of the classical ideals of the Gilded Age, other times demanding closer ties to modernity. Although the arguments remain superficially similar to those mustered in the past, involving standard homage to the model of the Prix de Rome and allusions to the benefits of congenial artistic companionship, the treatment of these themes implicitly challenged the values of musical classicism on which they were premised. No one style prevailed as the paradigm of tradition. No particular European composers were promoted for their "model worthiness."

We see as well fluidity in the way new critical conversations expanded the range of possibilities for thinking about the relationship between Europe and the United States. Both Aldrich and Henderson offered alternatives to false dichotomies between old and new worlds. It *was* possible to reconcile tradition and innovation, or at the least exploit the creative potential of the tensions between them through art. Mobility made a transatlantic bicultural life possible. The old so-called dilemma of the "Europeanized American," which was alive and well in the late nineteenth-century speeches of Theodore Roosevelt, the novels of Henry James, and the music of Charles Ives, no longer commanded center stage. Instead these critics stressed the potential of a new generation to embark upon voyages across an ever-shrinking ocean. By virtue of the life experience Rome offered, American composers had the opportunity to grow in spirit, confidence, and imaginative power, each choosing how to handle their sense of cultural responsibility in his—and eventually her—own way.

Such expressions of confidence were not universally shared. A mean-spirited essay on the "Music Fellowship at Rome," written by the composer Daniel Gregory Mason, appeared several months later in a short-lived bimonthly magazine.[71] A professor of music at Columbia University, Mason began in the routine manner, applauding the Rome Prize in familiar terms of cultural remediation with a touch of envy for "the lucky young Americans to whom for the first time, in an organized, systematic way, is opened up the priceless opportunity to acquire at its source in the great European traditions, the cosmopolitan attitude and point of view."

Then he seized the moment to turn the Rome Prize into a boxing match between two stereotypical rivals. In one corner, cosmopolitans—acting on the courage of American composers to "develop their artistic muscle on a par with their fellow Europeans." In the other corner, the "chauvinists, the boomers, the one-hundred-percenters" who wore the stars and stripes of homegrown art:

> But if those who have planned the fellowships succeed, in spite of the one-hundred percenters, in hurling away this crutch [of patriotism], . . . then we shall be at the beginining of the end of protection (and smotheration) in American music. We shall begin to discern dimly ahead of us a day coming when our composers will be able to write symphonies that can interest us without being named for Washington or Lincoln, symphonic poems that do not have to be called "At Niagara" or "In the Grand Canyon"; a day when commonplaces of melodic thought, crudity of harmony, ineptitude of polyphony and fragmentariness of form no longer have to be given a fictitious interest by the use of Indian or Negro tunes, as an ill-cooked steak must be sprinkled with Worcestershire sauce; a day when the "All-American Concert," that last insult of charity to incompetence, that musical home for decayed gentlewomen. . . . For it cannot be too often repeated, the way to emasculate an art is to over-protect it.

Without the long history of American classicism in mind, it is hard to understand Mason's belligerence. Apparently, Mason believed that Rome would purge the American imagination of parochialism, challenging American composers to write more abstract "universal" music. Even so, Mason set up another illogical opposition between excellence and nationalist subject matter. He himself had already composed a *String Quartet on Negro Themes* (1919) and would later write the *Lincoln Symphony* in 1936.

In contrast to both Aldrich and Henderson, Mason drowned his opponents with contempt. How remote for him was the possibility of an "American

Figure 3.2. Spring Concert in Cortile of the American Academy in Rome, 1923. Courtesy of the American Academy in Rome.

genius." Yet others returned to this ideal within the context of justifying the Academy, among them Walter Damrosch. Damrosch was elected a trustee of the Academy in 1921 and had a fellowship named after him. Recalling a visit to the Academy in the early 1920s, Damrosch wrote: "It is, of course, impossible for any man-made institution to guarantee that every incumbent will develop into a great genius, but it is certain that as only the best are chosen, they will become still better through such happy three years, and if among every two hundred only one real genius is found and thus encouraged the academy will have justified its existence."[72] Ever the promoter of "greatness" and the European canon, Damrosch would also prove to be a loyal friend to American composers. His performances of music by Gershwin and Copland, to take two examples, are well known in American music history.

The diversity of opinions that greeted the establishment of the American Rome Prize in music shows how the meanings of American classicism shifted between 1890 and 1920, reflecting and adapting to changing times. The glories of the American Renaissance in architecture, so fruitful and inspiring in 1900 for McKim and his followers, the doctrine of collaborative creativity, the political reinterpretation of aesthetics as civic virtue—these interpretations of classicism were either outdated or at the least attenuated after World War I. What was progressive could, if embraced too tightly, turn into reaction. In the 1920s, according to some historians and critics, the program in architecture fell victim to this problem. Here the Academy "resisted change," became "conservative," supporting an antimodernist "Establishment."[73] Modernism, with its doctrines of originality, and the rise of popular art, with its emphasis on vernacular expressive culture, increasingly challenged the relevance of classicist values. The notion of nurturing American art through European ideals would provoke charges of paternalism for a new generation of American composers who went to Europe because they wanted to, not because they had to.

The Rome Prize in music arrived at just the very moment when old arguments about classical models and the study of the glorious empires of the past confronted the new realities of postwar Europe. Classical education or liberal arts education had to renew its sense of mission to fit more modern times. We look back on the various permutations it underwent between 1890 and 1920 as the adaptive processes of a hegemonic ideology. It was, and in some vestigial ways still is, as Pearcy writes: "a form of education that encodes the babble of culture into a system that rationalizes and explains the culture's contradictions and makes possible the orderly, sensible, creation of new forms and statements within that culture."[74] The shifting meanings of classicism have continued to be both a challenge and a stimulus for the Rome Prize in musical composition. Since the origins of the prize in the fin de siècle, when musical neoclassicism was still waiting in the wings, the history of the contributions of the Rome Prize winners in musical composition belongs to an ongoing story about the ways in which classical values both enable and constrain. By helping to effect "what is inevitable—the joining of the newest present to the oldest past," and yet resisting the new,[75] the debates about American aesthetic classicism played out in the early years of the American Academy in Rome have affected the history of the achievements associated with the institution for the rest of the twentieth century.

Notes

1. William F. Apthorp, "Two Modern Classicists in Music," *Atlantic Monthly*, October 1893, 488. Apthorp's examples were Robert Franz and Otto Dresel, explained as follows: "But if Mendelssohn was the last universally recognized great musical classicist, there were two men, younger than he and less widely famous, whose lives were intimately associated with musical life in Boston, whose memory is green in the hearts of many of us, and in whom the spirit of the truest classicism still breathed in as perfect purity as in Mendelssohn himself: Robert Franz and Otto Dresel" (490).

2. This is a current definition in the *Oxford English Dictionary*.

3. These definitions are taken from *The Imperial Dictionary of the English Language*, ed. Charles Annandale (London: Blackie, 1883), 1: 483–84.

4. Caroline Winterer, *The Culture of Classicism: Ancient Greece and Rome in American Intellectual Life, 1780–1910* (Baltimore: Johns Hopkins University Press, 2002), 1.

5. The phrase "governing class" comes from Lee T. Pearcy, *The Grammar of Our Civility: Classical Education in America* (Waco, TX: Baylor University Press, 2005). It refers to the intellectual, cultural, and economic elite.

6. The standard history is Lucia Valentine and Alan Valentine, *The American Academy in Rome, 1894–1969* (Charlottesville: University Press of Virginia, 1973). This article is indebted to the solid research and lively narrative in this book.

7. Valentine and Valentine, *American Academy*, 2.

8. The dates in this article follow those given in "A Finding Aid to the American Academy in Rome Records (http://www.aaa.si.edu/findingaids/ameracar.htm).

9. Spiro Kostof and Dan Cuff, *The Architect: Chapters in the History of the Profession*, reprint ed. (Berkeley: University of California Press, 2000), 215–16.

10. Valentine and Valentine, *American Academy*, 9, cite this phrase without attributing it to Burnham. The phrase comes from a letter Burnham sent to Frank Millet on January 10, 1910, and the draft of the letter is reprinted in Charles Moore, *Daniel Burnham, Architect: Planner of Cities* (Boston: Houghton Mifflin, 1921), 2: 95–6.

11. For an introduction, see Wayne Andrews, "McKim, Mead, White: Their Mark Remains," *New York Times*, January 7, 1951.

12. Richard Guy Wilson, "Architecture and the Reinterpretation of the Past in the American Renaissance," in *American Architectural History: A Contemporary Reader*, ed. Keith L. Eggner (New York: Routledge, 2004), 227–46. This essay was originally published in 1983, following the exhibition "American Renaissance: 1876–1917" at the Brooklyn Museum in 1979.

13. Wilson, "Architecture," 227.

14. E. Douglas Bomberger, *A Tidal Wave of Encouragement: American Composers' Concerts in the Gilded Age* (Westport, CT: Praeger, 2002), chap. 10, "The World's Columbian Exposition of 1893: American Art Music Humiliated." See also Kiri Miller, "Americanism Musically: Nation, Evolution, and Public Education at the Columbia Exposition, 1893," *19th-Century Music* 27, no. 2 (2003): 1137–55.

15. Joseph Horowitz, *Classical Music in America: A History of Its Rise and Fall* (New York: W. W. Norton, 2005).

16. Chadwick's opinion is mentioned by R. W. B Lewis, "1898–1907: The Founders' Story," in *A Century of Arts & Letters: The History of the of Arts & Letters and the American Academy of Arts & Letters as Told, Decade by Decade, by Eleven Members* (New York: Columbia University Press, 1998), 10. Lewis writes of the membership in the National Institute of Arts and letters: "The department of music in its first phase showed a mix of the comfortably established and the cautiously innovative similar to that of Literature and Art. It was the smallest department by far—fourteen members in 1898, with one addition in 1905—and it suffered from less vigorous attention. There was, as well, a feeling among the musical participants that music in America was still in an uncertain stage. Writing to Hamlin Garland in March 1907, George Chadwick—composer (overtures, symphonies, choral works), director of the New England Conservatory of Music, and one of the most interesting of the charter members—remarked that 'the musicians in this country who have accomplished enough serious work to be worthy of membership in the Institute are not very plenty.'" Lewis cites a letter from Chadwick to Hamlin Garland, March 20, 1907.

17. Nicolas Tawa, "Chadwick and Parker of New England: Composers, Allies, and Friends," in *Vistas of American Music: Essays and Compositions in Honor of William K. Kearns*, ed. Susan L. Porter and John Graziano (Warren, MI: Harmonie Park Press, 1999), 240. See also Tawa, *The Coming of Age of American Art Music* (Westport, CT: Greenwood Press, 1991).

18. Horatio Parker, as quoted in the article "For Art and Literature; the First Public Meeting of the National Institute. History and Aims Explained. Addresses by Charles Dudley Warner, Horatio William Parker, and the Rev. Dr. Henry Van Dyke," *New York Times*, January 31, 1900. Composers elected to the National Institute of Arts and Letters: Arthur Bird, Dudley Buck, George Chadwick (into Academy 1909); Walter Damrosch (into Academy 1932); Reginald De Koven, Arthur Foote (both into Academy 1913); William Wallace Gilchrist, Edward MacDowell (into Academy 1904); Ethelbert Nevin, John K. Paine, Horatio Parker (into Academy 1905); Harry Rowe Shelley, Edgar Stillman-Kelley (both into Academy 1898).

19. Alfred Hoyt Granger, *Charles Follen McKim: A Study of His Life and Work* (Boston: Houghton Mifflin, 1913), 117, describes McKim as an "enthusiastic member of the Mendelssohn Glee Club." "McKim is not listed in either the List of Members or the Attendance Records from 1880–1900" in the papers of the club located at the New York Public Library, according to Jennifer Jones Wilson, who assisted with archival research to verify this point. The phrase describing the club comes from the article "Mistake of a Word: Mendelssohn Glee Club Angered by Vaudeville Friends," *New York Times*, February 5, 1893.

20. Henry Theophilus Finck, *Anton Seidl: A Memorial by His Friends* (New York: C. Scribner, 1899), 75.

21. Valentine and Valentine, *American Academy*, 24.

22. Margaret Chanler, *Memory Makes Music* (New York: Stephen-Paul, 1948), 77.

23. The term "Europeanized American" is in usage by 1883, as defined in *The Imperial Dictionary of the English Language*, 3:203: "To assimilate to Europeans in manners, characteristics, and usages." Roosevelt famously used this term in his article "True Americanism," published in *The Forum Magazine* in April 1894. The term occurs frequently in literary scholarship about McKim's contemporaries, American authors, Henry James, and Edith Wharton—both of whom knew Margaret Chanler.

24. For some discussion of Chanler in context, see William Vance, *America's Rome* (New Haven: Yale University Press, 1989), 2: 211, 215.

25. Mrs. Winthrop [Margaret] Chanler, *Roman Spring: Memoirs* (Boston: Little, Brown, 1934), 266–67.

26. Gounod as quoted in Fikret K. Yegül, *Gentlemen of Instinct and Breeding: Architecture at the American Academy in Rome, 1894–1940* (New York: Oxford University Press, 1991), 23.

27. John Dizikes, *Opera in America: A Cultural History* (New Haven: Yale University Press, 1993), 288.

28. Pearcy, *Grammar of Our Civility*, 5, 7.

29. Edward MacDowell, "Music at Columbia, Columbia University Bulletin, 1896," as quoted in Bridget Falconer-Salkeld, *The MacDowell Colony: A Musical History of America's Premier Artists' Community* (Lanham, MD: The Scarecrow Press, 2005), 22–23.

30. Richard Crawford, "Edward MacDowell: Musical Nationalism and an American Tone Poet," *Journal of the American Musicological Society* 49, no. 3 (1996): 536.

31. Richard Watson Gilder, *A Book of Music* (New York: The Century Company, 1906), 53. In an obituary for Gilder, he is described as sharing MacDowell's aesthetic outlook: "He [Gilder] had, as a poet, the same sympathies that MacDowell, as a musician, showed—a sense of the unity of art; and as he could not divorce beauty from the other elements of life, he could not separate poetry from the other arts." George Edward Woodberry, "Mr. Gilder's Public Activities," *The Century Magazine*, February 1910, 626.

32. Lawrence Gilman, *Edward MacDowell: A Study* (John Lane Company, 1908), 38.

33. Marjorie Lowens, "The New York Years of Edward MacDowell" (PhD diss., University of Michigan, 1971), 320.

34. Alan Howard Levy, *Edward MacDowell: An American Master* (Lanham, MD: The Scarecrow Press, 1998), 211–12.

35. Jack Beeson, "Da Ponte, MacDowell, Moore, and Lang: Four Biographical Essays by Jack Beeson," *Columbia Alumni Magazine*, accessed December 10, 2013, www.columbia.edu/cu/alumni/Magazine/Legacies/Beeson/Beeson.html.

36. Charles Moore, *The Promise of American Architecture: Addresses at the Annual Dinner of the American Institute of Architects, 1905* (New York: American Institute of Architects, 1905), 77.

37. Theodore Roosevelt, "True Americanism," *The Forum Magazine*, April 1894. "One may fall very far short of treason and yet be an undesirable citizen in the community. The man who becomes Europeanized, who loses his power of doing good work on this side of the water, and who loses his love for his native land, is not a traitor; but he is a silly and undesirable citizen. He is as emphatically a noxious element in our body politic as is the man who comes here from abroad and remains a foreigner. Nothing will more quickly or more surely disqualify a man from doing good work in the world than the acquirement of that flaccid habit of mind which its possessors style cosmopolitanism."

38. Edmond Morris, *The Rise of Theodore Roosevelt*, rev. ed. (New York: Random House, 2000), 480. Morris calls Roosevelt "one of the bores of all ages" on this topic.

39. Edmond Morris, *Theodore Rex* (New York: Random House, 2001), 174.

40. Moore, *Promise of American Architecture*, 16.

41. Ibid., 43.

42. Charles Moore, *The Life and Times of Charles Follen McKim* (Boston: Houghton Mifflin, 1929), 37. See also Valentine and Valentine, *American Academy*, 33–38.

43. Valentine and Valentine, *American Academy*, 85, give this date and write that "Mrs. MacDowell sent to Charles McKim on May 11, 1905, direct quotations from MacDowell's memorandum"; Marian MacDowell, "MacDowell's Peterborough Idea," *Musical Quarterly* 18, no. 1 (1932): 33: "MacDowell did not live to see his ideas carried out. Indeed they were never even formally submitted to the Board, but among his papers still exists the outline he made and dictated, embodying his hopes for the composer who went to Rome and his further hope that his plans might affect the future of those working in other arts"; Papers of Edward MacDowell, box 34C, Special Collections, Music Division, Library of Congress, Washington, DC. MacDowell's final illness is discussed in A. T. Schwab, "Edward MacDowell's Mysterious Malady," *Musical Quarterly* 89, no. 1 (2006): 136–51.

44. Yegül, *Gentlemen of Instinct and Breeding*, 61–62.

45. Alan Howard Levy, "The Search for Identity in American Music, 1890–1920," *American Music* 2, no. 2 (1984): 72.

46. Marian MacDowell, typescript, notebook no. 1, pp. 62–63, Music Division, Library of Congress, as quoted in Lowens, "New York Years of Edward MacDowell," 71–73, 812. The Boston conductor B. J. Lang visited the MacDowell in Wiesbaden in the summer of 1888. "[Lang] rubbed it so hard and so vividly that it was MacDowell's duty to come back to his own country and not become an American foreigner of which there were too many. . . . Reluctantly we refused . . . although we were on the very edge of using up the little we had. Mr. Lang . . . was so insistent as to its being his duty that finally MacDowell yielded. He had had a great success in those early years in Germany; he was finally recognized immediately as a composer, had endless concert engagements for he was a fine pianist, and we could have struggled along there and really made a fairly good place for

ourselves, but he was made by Mr. Lang to feel that he ought to go back home"; "New York Years," 73.

47. From the minutes of the meetings of the executive committee of the American Academy in Rome from April 24, 1905, to and including September 17, 1909. F. D Miller, secretary in 1905.

48. "Pay Tribute to E. A. MacDowell. Friends of Composer Attend Funeral Services Held in St. George Episcopal Church. His Own Music Rendered. Members of Association Bearing His Name Present at Ceremonies—Interment at Summer Home in Peterboro, N.H.," *New York Herald*, January 26, 1908. Incorporated in 1907, the Association united two smaller groups, the Mendelssohn Glee Club and the MacDowell Club, with its membership "composed of men and women who are active in the drama, literature, music, architecture, painting, and sculpture."

49. Falconer-Salkeld, *MacDowell Colony*, 39, quoting Theodore Pratt, "Place of Dreams Untold, The Famed MacDowell Colony Created by One Woman's Devotion Observes Its Fiftieth Anniversary," *New York Times*, March 24, 1957.

50. Falconer-Salkeld, *MacDowell Colony*, 47.

51. Karen J. Blair, *The Torchbearers: Women and Their Amateur Arts Associations in America, 1890–1930* (Bloomington: Indiana University Press, 1994), 38.

52. In 1907 Julia Ward Howe became the first woman to be elected to the National Institute of Arts and Letters. Although the issue of female participation was raised intermittently over the next decade, change was glacial. Edith Wharton not admitted until 1926. Mary Cassatt's name never came up. Amy Cheney Beach was not mentioned.

53. Julia Lu, "The Prix de Rome Competition: Prophetic or Irrelevant?," in *Music Research: New Directions for a New Century*, ed. Michael Ewans, Rosalind Halton, John A. Phillips (Cambridge, MA: Scholars Press, 2004), 277.

54. There was some intention to include women in the transitional period between the public announcement of the Rome Prize and its final implementation. See Carol Oja's essay in this volume.

55. MacDowell, "MacDowell's Peterborough Idea," 33.

56. Valentine and Valentine, *American Academy*, 86. The great benefactor of the Academy, J. P. Morgan, had died in Rome in March of that year.

57. This letter contained his signed approval of the plan for the establishment of a Department of Musical Composition. New York Office Staff, Executive Secretary Guernsey I-1616, reel no. 5783, series 3, AAR Archives.

58. See Carol Oja's chapter, "Picked Young Men," in this volume.

59. W. R. Spalding, "Music Composition," in *American Academy in Rome: Twenty-Fifth Anniversary*, ed. Christopher Grant LaFarge (New York: American Academy in Rome, 1920), 26.

60. Ibid.

61. Ibid.

62. Ibid.

63. Walter Raymond Spalding, *Music: An Art and a Language* (Boston: Arthur P. Schmidt, 1920), 329, singles out "Converse, Carpenter, Gilbert, Hadley, Hill, Mason, Atherton, Stanley Smith, Brockway, Blair Fairchild, Heilman, Shepherd, Clapp, John Powell, Margaret Ruthven Lang, Gena Branscombe and Mabel Daniels."

64. Richard Aldrich, "Aid for American Composers," *New York Times*, April 18, 1920, 3. Aldrich stated two items that did not come to pass—that the fellowships would be open to women and that one of the fellowships would honor Oscar Hammerstein.

65. Charles Henry Meltzer (1853–1936) was born in London and studied music at Oxford and in Paris. He served as music critic for a number of newspapers in the early 1900s. For more information on Meltzer, see the obituary notice in the *New York Times*, January 19, 1936. The *Weekly Review* ran a notice about the Rome Prize asking its readers to contribute funds, in which a million dollars is treated as "asking comparatively little." See "Brief Comment—At Home," *Weekly Review* 2, no. 52 (May 8, 1920): 475.

66. Charles Henry Meltzer, "The Proposed 'Prix de Rome' for Musicians," *Weekly Review* 3, no. 61 (July 14, 1920): 50–51.

67. Meltzer visited both the Academie française and the American Academy in 1921. He later wrote a more temperate article about this experience in "Two Homes of Art in Rome, the Academies of Old France and Young America," *Arts and Decorations* 16 (November 1921), 15–17.

68. Meltzer is described this way in an obituary tribute in the *New York Times*, January 19, 1936. His papers are in the Special Collections of the Robert Scott Small Library, College of Charleston.

69. Minutes of the Board of Trustees, 1921. S. B. P. Trowbridge is chair at this time. From the records of the American Academy in Rome, series 3: New York Office, reel no. 5783.

70. W. J. Henderson, "Favors Scheme of American Academy in Rome to Aid the Composer of Music," *New York Herald*, October 31, 1920, 7. All subsequent quotations are from this article.

71. Daniel Gregory Mason, "Music Fellowship at Rome," *The Arts* 2 (February–March 1921): 6–7.

72. Walter Damrosch, *My Musical Life* (New York: Charles Scribner's Sons, 1930), 302. Damrosch visited the Academy in 1922.

73. Yegül, *Gentlemen of Instinct and Breeding*, 3.

74. Pearcy, *Grammar of Civility*, 7.

75. La Farge, "Field of Art," 254.

Chapter Four

"Picked Young Men," Facilitating Women, and Emerging Composers

Establishing an American Prix de Rome

Carol J. Oja

> A week devoted to ultra-modern music gave us the power to distinguish styles and form judgments as to its value and merits. We returned to Rome more than ever impressed with the fact that classical composition must be the foundation on which we must build.
>
> —Felix Lamond, professor of music, American Academy in Rome, 1925

In 1921, the American Academy in Rome (AAR), which had been established amidst the affluence and philanthropy of the Gilded Age, entered the postwar era when it initiated a long-desired fellowship program for composers. The product of a major internationalizing impulse in the United States after World War I, the composer fellowships appeared in a very different moment from that when AAR had been conceived. The notion of the "Europeanized American" gave way to that of a transnationally recognized artist who frequently—even proudly—asserted an American identity through composition. This postwar period brought its own version of affluence, albeit with new money and a tendency toward an aesthetic eclecticism. It was a time of self-conscious modernization in the culture at large, and a whole new generation of American composers vied for the mantle of "American genius."[1] A select number eventually succeeded, most notably the Brooklyn-born composers Aaron Copland and George Gershwin, whose major new concert works were reaching New York stages by the middle of the 1920s.

Yet as it turned out, those vanguard impulses, which in hindsight appear as the most valorized musical products during the interwar years, were not the main goal of the Academy. Instead the institution adhered to its bedrock principle of advocating "classical" values, thereby extending to musical composition the goals it promoted for artistic expression as a whole. Patronage networks that had supported art and architecture at the Academy in the first two decades of the twentieth century were expanded to embrace music, and the role of women as patrons of the Academy's composers became particularly important. This new composers' prize, an American counterpart to the French Prix de Rome, culminated the celebration of AAR's twenty-fifth anniversary. The prize emerged at an historical moment when an unprecedented advocacy of composers took hold in the United States, yielding a growing infrastructure to support their work. Felix Lamond, the inaugural "Professor in Charge of Music" and a prime mover in the establishment of the Academy's composition program, described a prinicpal goal of the prize in one of his annual reports: "I am confident that their [i.e., American composers'] work will soon be recognized in the United States as it has been in Europe, and that it will turn the tide in favor of the development of a National American musical art."[2]

This chapter explores the early history of composer fellowships at the American Academy in Rome. I focus on the 1920s, with the 1930s entering the narrative occasionally, and there are four main sections. I begin by considering the deep stylistic conservatism generally advocated—in some respects even mandated—by the Academy. In the second section, I chronicle the enormous fund-raising initiative that launched the composer fellowships, exploring how philanthropy and high society were tightly connected to artistic recognition and achievement. I then examine the simultaneous exclusion of women as fellows and the dependency on them as major fund-raisers; I also consider the initial resistance to permitting the wives of fellows to live at the Academy. Finally, I explore the makeup of selection juries, which privileged certain composer networks, and the degree to which the Academy's fellows constituted a core constituency among one of the earliest waves of American composer-academics. The sources consulted include AAR's archive (annual reports, composer applications, administrative correspondence, clippings); correspondence between Leo Sowerby and Elizabeth Sprague Coolidge; and contemporaneous coverage in the *New York Times, Chicago Daily Tribune, Musical America, Musical Times,* and other periodicals.

Conservatism, Antimodernism, and American Composers

While the American Academy in Rome emerged as an important mechanism for transnational interaction after World War I, the degree to which its elders clung to the past—to the known and the comfortably established—was remarkable. In many ways, it was a nostalgic enterprise, and it embraced exclusivity by honoring "picked men," as AAR's own language repeatedly put it.[3] At the Academy's bucolic setting on the Janiculum Hill, the era of Henry James and Edith Wharton retained a gaslight glow, whereas in the greater artistic arena the switch had been flipped to the hard-edged modernism of T. S. Eliot and Djuna Barnes.

The founding precepts of the Academy that had been articulated by Charles McKim in the late nineteenth century—especially "devotion to tradition, continuity, and good taste"[4]—were reinscribed after World War I. In an era when the fundamental precepts of civilized behavior had been brutalized on the battlefield, the Academy's ideology of traditionalism carried a strong antimodernist bent. "The Director has succeeded in laying the foundation of a tradition," wrote Breck Trowbridge, a trustee who visited AAR in 1919. "He has created an atmosphere which inspires high ideals, which is conducive of creative effort . . . complete freedom of thought and action but in which there is no taint of that sordid Bohemianism which so often invades artistic communities."[5] An annual report from 1923–24 reasserted that philosophy, stating that the Academy's programs overall were "founded upon a settled belief" based on "the unquestionable acceptance of the supremacy of the arts of classical antiquity and the Italian Renaissance, to the exclusion of all other styles and periods."[6] And in 1926, Felix Lamond issued a statement about the perils of modernism—one that he reiterated at intervals over the years: "In view of the wave of ultra-modernism and noise that has been occupying the minds and ears of European musicians it is worthy of note that Germany, in my opinion at least, is turning to saner paths. We find that Mozart and Puccini are receiving more attention than the moderns in several of the cities of Germany."[7]

As a result, affirming allegiance to the glories of high art and conservatism took on the air of reciting the pledge at the start of a school day. Examples abound. During a fund-raising concert for AAR at Carnegie Hall in 1922, Walter Damrosch told the audience he was "sure" that AAR "would do much to preserve the feeling for beauty, now so much needed."[8] Randall Thompson (FAAR 1922–25) decried the cult of "personality": "Among our composers, the itch to be different amounts to a plague."[9] And Burnet Tuthill opened his profile of Sowerby in the *Musical Quarterly* by quoting Oscar Sonneck at "one of the early Berkshire Festivals of Chamber Music." When asked "Who are the three B's?" Sonneck delivered an ideology-defining quip: "Bach, Beethoven, and SowerB!"[10]

Ideological links between Rome's American and French academies, the latter of which had begun offering composer prizes in 1803, provide an interesting perspective on the aesthetic stance of AAR. The postwar period yielded a prime historical moment for Americans to establish a music prize to parallel an esteemed French award. A massive cultural realignment was then underway that shifted the affinity of American composers from Germany to France. Calling the American award a "Rome Prize" and echoing the French affirmed the connection, and the press of the day frequently did so. For example, in 1929, the Chicago-based *Musical Leader* drew a comparison between the two prizes in an article summarizing the opportunities that the Rome Prize provided American composers. The logic went like this. "During this century . . . every great French composer, save only one, was a Prix de Rome man"; thus Americans stood to gain the same cultural authority through a parallel prize.[11] Yet historians have chronicled the degree to which French composers made stylistic "concessions," as one scholar has put it, to win the Prix de Rome, forcing their individuality and innovativeness into the confines of the tradition-bound entrance requirements.[12] Berlioz won after five attempts. Ravel never got the big prize. AAR's roster of composer-winners during this early period similarly included figures who played by the rules, with no record of actively challenging established norms.

It is intriguing to contemplate how much the stylistic conservatism advocated by AAR found a compatible environment—perhaps even an energizing one—in Mussolini's Italy. The scholar Andrew Dell'Antonio has written of a "rhetoric of Italian predestination" in the early twentieth century, of "an unbroken tradition of Italian glory over the millennia."[13] Mussolini assumed power in 1922 within "this atmosphere of xenophobia," as Dell'Antonio puts it, and that sense of a continuous artistic vision, with the past ecstatically informing the present, bears comparison with the aesthetic tenets of AAR.

Mussolini visited AAR in February 1933, and Lamond extended a gracious welcome, giving a speech that connected the American music prize with Napoleon's establishment of the Grand Prix de Rome in 1803.[14] A number of American newspapers covered the story. One fellow, an American sculptor named William M. Simpson Jr., told a reporter that Mussolini's detectives were "swarming all over the place." The reporter continued: "The Italian Premier is very partial to modernism in art and modern architecture. . . . But he 'commented favorably' on two of Mr. Simpson's subjects which had been done in conventional form."[15] This link between Italian politics and AAR's aesthetic credo deserves further research, including an exploration of the politics of Roman composers within AAR's "Musical Circle." Ottorino Respighi, whose ties to fascism were complex, was among the signatories of a manifesto in December 1932, which "attacked the more adventurous musical trends of the time."[16] In March of that same year, he made a strong antimodernist statement to a reporter while visiting New York, using language that easily could have

Figure 4.1. Mussolini at AAR, 1933, accompanied by AAR Director James Monroe Hewlett. Photograph by Bruni Photograph Agency. Courtesy of the American Academy in Rome.

emanated from AAR: "Atonality is dead among us," he declared unequivocally. "Italian opera, after much experimentation, is turning again to its own genius of melodic and polyphonal clarity."[17] Respighi was an important figure at AAR during this period, working closely with resident composers.[18]

Back to the Beginning: Fund-Raising and Implementation of an American Prix de Rome

Since AAR's fellowships for composers were a product of a cultural boom in the years immediately following World War I, it is not surprising that key figures in the early years played prominent roles in war work, and my narrative now shifts back to the earliest years of the music program. During World War I, transatlantic musical exchanges had ground to a halt, which seriously derailed the unveiling of major new works and the interaction of composers. Immediately afterward, the cork exploded off a bottled-up scene, yielding an extraordinary burst of activity. This was fueled in part by an exceptional focus on international cooperation, spearheaded by the founding of the League of Nations in 1919–20.[19] This postwar energy inspired composers and performers to focus on building international alliances, as the victorious allies shifted their collaboration from the battlefield to cultural arenas. In 1921, the Conservatoire américain opened in Fontainebleau, France, launching an historic tie between American composers and the famed teacher Nadia Boulanger, and a string of modern music organizations started to spring up, all of which had international exchange at the core of their missions. American artists increasingly stood out as talented and capable, with the capacity to hold their own in a transnational market. Their strength, in part, came through collective action, especially in New York, where a group of internationally focused new music organizations took shape. First among them was the Franco-American Musical Society, later renamed the "Pro Musica Society," whose inaugural language duplicated that of the League of Nations, proclaiming "internationalization in music" as its "ideal." It was established in 1920 by E. Robert Schmitz, a French immigrant.[20] One year later the International Composers' Guild appeared, which also had transnational collaboration at its core; it too was founded by French immigrants, in this case Edgard Varèse and Carlos Salzedo. The Guild was followed in 1923 by the League of Composers, which worked especially hard to put the works of American composers alongside those of Europeans.[21] All of these American organizations modeled themselves on parallel European societies, including Arnold Schoenberg's Verein für musikalische Privataufführungen, founded in Vienna in 1918, and Alfredo Casella's Corporazione delle Nuove Musiche, established in Rome five years later.[22] Meanwhile, the International Society for Contemporary Music, which presented summer festivals in continually shifting European venues, took shape in 1922.

AAR joined the fray by sponsoring a concert of American music in Rome at the Augusteo in March 1919, four months after Armistice Day.[23] This event sent an early signal about the deep tie of music at AAR to the war, also about the alliances and geographic networks that constituted its core. Selected "by the Trustees of the American Academy in Rome," the concert included music by the American composers Henry Gilbert, Arthur Foote, and Horatio Parker, all of whom were then still alive (Parker died that December). Albert Spalding, the celebrated American violinist, performed the Mendelssohn Violin Concerto. He had served in Italy during World War I, which was highlighted in press coverage. "Mr. Spalding," reported the *New York Times*, "was already well known and liked here [in Rome] during his flying visits to the Eternal City when in the Aviation Corps. He had played several times for private entertainments, but this was his first professional appearance since he left the army. The musical authorities urgently asked him to be present today, to make the performance even more American."[24] A bit of postwar theater was woven into the event, as the *Times* further recounted: "Mr. Spalding succeeded in getting his discharge here instead of returning home."

At this incipient moment, then, a cast of characters started to be assembled for AAR's music program, and it gave hints of a budding network. Spalding, for example, had a long and close association with Walter Damrosch, conductor of the New York Symphony Society, and Damrosch, in turn, became a stalwart of the American Academy, soon having one of three composer fellowships named for him. Also, Horatio Parker, who was among the composers featured in this early concert, had another of the fellowships established in his honor. Felix Lamond, an English organist who had settled in New York in 1892 and become a US citizen, led the way in launching the music prizes. He taught at Columbia Teachers' College and was organist and choirmaster at Trinity Chapel in New York. Founded in 1697, Trinity Church was a famous Episcopalian landmark, reputed to be the wealthiest congregation in the country and located in the heart of the financial district of Wall Street.[25] Lamond also worked as a critic and had been an intermittent visitor at the Academy.

Lamond's success within the Academy built on his skills as a musician and administrator. By 1913, he had already been at Trinity Chapel for over fifteen years, overseeing its choir of boys and men.[26] There he acquired a reputation in church-music circles as both a fine organist and "an absolute perfectionist in style and taste"; he was considered "one of the outstanding teachers of his day."[27] In 1913 he became founding director of the Trinity School of Church Music, which proclaimed itself the "first school for the instruction of church organists" in the United States.[28] Lamond described the school's goal as training musicians in "the ancient methods of historic church services."[29] Lamond also served as associate editor of *The Churchman* from 1898 to 1916, an important journal of the Church of England.

The eventual choice of Lamond as AAR's first Professor in Charge of Music—the title for the chief administrative officer of the music program—illustrates other connections that could bring one to the Academy. This included a tie to Columbia University, where the Academy's roots lay in part, and work with the Red Cross. Gorham Phillips Stevens, director of the Academy before and after the war, also was part of the Red Cross, as was Mrs. Whitelaw Reid, who will enter the story soon as codirector of fund-raising for the composer fellowships.[30] Lamond was another of AAR's leaders in music who had risen to the challenge of war work. He had become a "Major" within the American Red Cross while he directed its distribution of aid to American soldiers returning from France, gaining credentials as an able administrator.[31] In January 1918, the American Red Cross established a Permanent Commission in Rome and commandeered Academy buildings for offices. All the while, as a Red Cross official later wrote, they rounded up a "motley company" of Americans to assist in the war effort, including Academy residents. His description illuminates the broad-based social and artistic world for which the Academy served as a focal point:

> The Commission set out to enlist the services of available Americans who were on the ground, artists, connoisseurs and dilettanti, and men and women of leisure who had made Italy their home, Americans married to Italians, travelers caught and held by the war,—here a professor of Logic from a Western University, there a chorus girl who had sung in a popular light opera, here a well known impresario, there a singer who as *Carmen* or *Aida* had delighted audiences at the Metropolitan, etc., etc., and large drafts were made on the students and teaching force of the American Academy at Rome.[32]

Thus, in the postwar period a geographic triangle quickly took shape among supporters of the music prizes, with vertices in New York (Lamond and Damrosch), Boston (Gilbert and Foote), and Chicago (Spalding's father ran A. G. Spalding & Bros., a well-known and extremely successful sporting goods company, in Chicago, which continues to thrive today).[33] And a core theme was also clear: AAR's music fellowships drew on a history of Americans from high society with ties to Italy, including women of wealth and cultural ambition. By moving into the realm of music, AAR produced a new coalition of funders, expanding beyond the patronage of architecture that had been underwritten by such financial titans as J. P. Morgan.

Felix Lamond adroitly managed the process of raising funds, doing so with dispatch over a period of approximately eighteen months. In an era before air travel and widespread use of the telephone, he implemented his plan in person and via post. In the spring of 1920, a "Visiting Committee" took trips to solicit donors, traveling to Philadelphia, Boston, Washington, Pittsburgh, Cincinnati, Cleveland, Detroit, Toledo, Chicago, Milwaukee, Minneapolis-St. Paul, St. Louis, and Louisville. This initiative began on February 9 and ended

April 10.[34] It appears that the "committee" did not travel as a group, but rather that individuals divided up to approach potential funders. The group included "Major" Lamond, Charles Moore, Mr. Mellon, Mr. [Ferruccio] Vitale, Mr. [S. Breck] Trowbridge, and Mr. Stevens.[35] But Lamond personally extended his hat time and again. In Philadelphia, he enlisted the aid of Leopold Stokowski, conductor of the Philadelphia Orchestra, to approach Mr. Edward William Bok (1863–1930), editor of *The Brooklyn Magazine* and eventually *The Ladies' Home Journal*, whose wife Mary Louise Curtis Bok (1876–1970) was to found the Curtis Institute of Music in 1924, and she became a major supporter of the avant-garde composer George Antheil.[36] Mr. Bok initially declined Stokowski's overture on behalf of AAR, but his wife chipped in.[37] Lamond also approached George Eastman of Rochester, New York, one of the founders of Eastman-Kodak, who endowed the Eastman Conservatory of Music in 1921.[38] While Eastman appears not to have emerged as an initial funder of AAR's music program, he eventually did get involved in the new enterprise, as Lamond revealed in his Annual Report nearly a decade later (1928): "The weekly rehearsals of the string quartet which is maintained by the Eastman Fund have been of immense value to the fellows."[39]

Correspondence related to this fund-raising tour in 1920 reveals the strategy undertaken, with wealthy women and industrial magnates as the main targets. Approaches to key figures in the Midwest exemplify this. In Detroit, the Junior League—an exclusive women's club—was contacted, and Rev. Dr. S. S. Marquis of the Ford Motor Company was asked to solicit Henry Ford as a possible donor.[40] In St. Paul, a letter requesting help from Mrs. George Theron Slade revealed that at this point AAR intended "to admit women to all the advantages of the Academy."[41] In Chicago, Cyrus McCormick was targeted, together with his son and daughter-in-law; this resulted in Cyrus Jr. contributing $1,000.[42] Lamond also spoke to AAR's "Chicago Committee" during a gathering at the home of Harold Fowler McCormick. According to an invitation to the event, this "committee" had nineteen members, including Mr. and Mrs. John Alden Carpenter—the former of whom played an important role in AAR's selection juries.[43] Fifteen of the committee's members were women.

Within AAR's fund-raising correspondence, a letter from February 1920 (presumably written by Lamond, although there is no signature) details the ambitions of the new enterprise with exceptional thoroughness.[44] At the same time, it gives a generalized sense of the kinds of philanthropists being sought. This particular document was addressed to William H. Murphy of Detroit, who was later described by the *New York Times* as a "patron of music and art, financier and capitalist; . . . one of the original backers of Henry Ford and a founder of the Cadillac Motor Car Company."[45] Murphy was a major supporter of the Detroit Symphony Orchestra as well as the Detroit Art Institute. He was a driving force behind construction of the Penobscot Building in downtown Detroit, which was completed in 1928. At forty-seven stories, it was then the eighth tallest building in the world and was constructed in an era of skyscrapers—before the Empire State Building.

The vision of the music program as communicated to Murphy was somewhat different from the ultimate result. Women composers were part of the scheme, and the model was the French Prix de Rome: "The Academy in Rome proposes a similar plan [to that of France] for promising young American composers. It intends to invite young men and women throughout the country to compete for the privilege of a three or four year's sojourn in Europe under the most favorable conditions."[46] Furthermore, an educational experience—one that would also bring young Americans to France—was in the mix at this early date: "The French government has invited our successful competitors to a free one or two years course at the Paris Conservatoire. After this period of study, the appointees will be sent to Rome to the Academy." While in Rome, composers were to enter a sort of League of Nations in music, interacting with "French, German, British, Spanish and Brazilian artists. (The governments of these countries having established music foundations in Rome)." In this early scheme, AAR's composers were to "be fully instructed in operatic stage-craft by being admitted to the work of preparation and production very frequent in Italy of operas at the theatres." There was also a goal to facilitate "personal contact with eminent European composers" by being given "ample opportunity of travel to musical centers such as Milan, Vienna, Munich, etc. at the expense of the Academy."

Rather than promoting an open-ended vision of concert-music composition, Lamond's goal at this early stage was very specific: to establish an "institution" that could produce "a great opera and symphonic composer." This would be achieved through a strikingly conservative educational opportunity—by coming "into touch with the beginning of operatic and symphonic composition through access to the Vatican and Santa Cecilia libraries."[47]

The letter to Murphy also disclosed financial information. "The Founders of the Academy each of whom has contributed $100,000.00 are H. C. Frick, Henry Walters, J. Pierpoint Morgan, W. K. Vanderbilt and Harvard University. These amounts have served to equip the present buildings in Rome."[48] A subsequent section, which was crossed out by hand at some point, states that the "members of the Music Department of Harvard are now engaged in a drive for $50,000.00 for the Music Foundation."[49] This was followed by another clause, which was left intact: "The present plan is for an Endowment Fund of $1,000,000 ($250,000 for the Music Foundation and $150,000.00 for the Department of Landscape Architecture)."[50]

The chairs of Lamond's fund-raising drive were identified in the letter to Murphy as "Mr. Elihu Root" and "Mrs. Whitelaw Reid, Chairman of the Woman's Committee," a revealing detail about the networks that built the music program at AAR.[51] A famed lawyer and career diplomat, Elihu Root (1845–1937) had a longstanding tie with AAR, having sat at the head table of architects, alongside President Theodore Roosevelt, at an AAR dinner in

1905.[52] He won the Nobel Peace Price in 1912 for an extended series of peacekeeping initiatives in Central and South America, also China and Japan. After World War I he became the first president of the Carnegie Endowment for International Peace.[53] A "Carnegie" thread runs through AAR's story, as does the notion of composer fellowships as tools of cultural diplomacy.

Meanwhile, Mrs. Whitelaw Reid (1858–1931) is especially intriguing. A noted philanthropist with strong European ties, Elizabeth Mills Reid was born into money (her father, Darius O. Mills, founded the Bank of California).[54] She also married a man of wealth and power—Whitelaw Reid (1837–1912), who served at various points as the American ambassador to England and to France.[55] As with Root, Elizabeth Reid represented transnational diplomacy. Her husband was also editor of the *New York Tribune*, and their son, Ogden Mills Reid, with his wife Helen Rogers Reid, oversaw the merger of the paper during the 1920s into the highly regarded *Herald Tribune*. Mrs. Whitelaw Reid and her husband lived at 451 Madison Avenue, "a three-story brownstone structure of the French Renaissance style. . . . It resembles very much the town houses seen in Mayfair, London."[56] When the Duke of Connaught, the "only surviving son of Queen Victoria and uncle of the King of England," visited the United States in 1912, Mrs. Reid had "the distinction of being the first New York hostess to entertain British royalty as house guests."[57] Her husband died the same year as that royal visit, and she shifted her focus to philanthropy.[58] At some point in the first decade of the twentieth century, she had purchased a property on the rue de Chevreuse in the Montparnasse section of Paris, which was the former site of the Helen Keller Institute. In response to an artists' club for American men that had been formed on the rue Paul Séjourné, she decided to establish an "American Girls Club" for women artists. In 1913, not long after her husband's death, she bought an additional neighboring property and constructed a group of seven artist studios with an adjoining grande salle.

Here, too, World War I emerges as a theme. During that conflict, Mrs. Reid turned her building on rue de Chevreuse into a clinic for wounded soldiers, and the site remained "in the hands of the American Red Cross until 1922."[59] Thus she was affiliated with the same organization as Gorham Stevens and Felix Lamond. Mrs. Reid continued to champion the artistic development of women after the war. A group calling themselves "The Ladies" entered into an agreement to turn her building on rue de Chevreuse into a Franco-American retreat for women students, artists, and professors. The structure was rechristened "Reid Hall," and Nadia Boulanger was among its guest lecturers. Included among "The Ladies" was a strong nexus of figures from the world of women's colleges: Mrs. Reid's daughter-in-law, Helen Rogers Reid (a Barnard alumna), Virginia C. Gildersleeve (Dean of Barnard College), and M. Carey Thomas (founder of Bryn Mawr College). The building was subsequently bequeathed to Columbia University and rechristened the "Columbia University Institute for Scholars at Reid Hall," which it remains today.

Given Reid's history of supporting women artists and her ties to women's colleges, it is reasonable to guess that she supported AAR's composer initiative because, as the letter to Murphy put it, "the Academy proposes to open all its departments to women." When those plans collapsed—and the details about how they did so remain unclear—Reid's commitment seems to have ended. Whatever the case, her name does not turn up in subsequent correspondence.

By the time the fund-raising drive for the music program drew to a close, it had been refocused to produce endowments of $50,000 for each of three composer fellowships. One of the first funds was named for Horatio Parker, the American composer whose music had appeared on the 1919 concert in Rome. Parker stood at the head of America's composer establishment at the time, small as it was. A professor at Yale, he was one of the earliest composer-academics in the United States, and today he is perhaps best known as a teacher of Charles Ives. Parker died in December 1919, and four months later, the *New York Times* announced that an AAR fellowship in honor of him had received "the approval of the Corporation of Yale University."[60] The article went on to state: "The money needed would be $50,000 and an honorary committee of fifty is being formed in New York City to take the matter in charge." A typescript list in the AAR archives details those "Invited to Serve on Honorary Committee of Horatio Parker Fund."[61] Among those included were the music publishers H. W. Gray, Charles H. Ditson, Gustav Schirmer, and Theodore Presser; the composers George W. Chadwick, Arthur Foote, Frederick S. Converse, Arthur Whiting, Daniel Gregory Mason, Henry Hadley, and David Stanley Smith; and the critics H. E. Krehbiel, Richard Aldrich, James Huneker, and Philip Hale. At this point, the Parker committee appeared to be largely male, with only a few women appearing on the list: Mrs. Frederick S. Coolidge, Miss Gertrude Watson, Mrs. George Montgomery Tuttle, and Mrs. Francis Osborne Kellogg. Yet when the fund-raising campaign ended, the demographics had shifted remarkably: of the sixty-one donors who contributed to the Parker Fellowship, thirty-six were women, and they gave amounts ranging from $2 to $8,000.[62] Thus the gender balance tipped toward women as funding for the music program progressed.

In addition to the Parker Fellowship, two awards were proposed in memory of Oscar Hammerstein I—not the famed Broadway lyricist but his grandfather, the impresario and founder of the Manhattan Opera Company, a competitor with Gatti-Casazza and the Metropolitan Opera. This initiative fit tidily with AAR's projected focus on opera. Like Parker, Hammerstein died in 1919. The day after the *New York Times* announced the fellowship in honor of Parker, it published an article about those for Hammerstein: "As soon as Major Felix Lamond had presented to me the musical aims of the Academy," Hammerstein's wife told the *Times,* "I knew immediately that to become a founder of the Academy would have been the sort of memorial my husband would like to have reared [*sic*] to him. . . . During his life, it was his pet dream to establish a national opera, truly American in every way."[63] Mrs. Hammerstein planned a series of benefit concerts and "entertainments" to raise $100,000. "The first of which has already been announced," she continued, "at the Hippodrome the evening of May 2, featuring Mme. Tetrazzini and as many of the members of the old Manhattan Opera Company as we can get together."[64] The AAR Archives includes a list titled "Hammerstein Memorial Concert," which cites possible benefactors.[65] Here, unlike the parallel document for the Parker Fellowship, the names do not focus initially on composers or on the music industry. Rather, from the start, they largely include women patrons and their husbands, with figures such as Mrs. F. S. Coolidge, Mr. and Mrs. Harry Harkness Flagler, and Mrs. Harry Payne Whitney.

Over the course of the next year, the Hammerstein plan fell through. In July 1921, when the *New York Times* announced the inception of the "three" composer fellowships, no such award appeared. Rather, one fellowship had been established "in the name of Frederick A. Juilliard, who recently pledged $50,000 to support it."[66] Frederick was the nephew of the famed arts philanthropist Augustus Juilliard.[67] Underwriting this fellowship (with money inherited from his uncle) appeared to be Frederick's way of establishing an identity in the world of music patronage that was separate from his uncle. The other two fellowships were not named in the *Times* article (not even the one for Parker), but the big donors received acknowledgment:

> The Carnegie Corporation, through its titular head, President J. R. Angell of Yale, has also provided a large fund. Mrs. Willard D. Straight and Mrs. E. H. Harkness, both of this city, and Mrs. Thomas H. Emery of Cincinnati contributed $10,000 each toward the fund for fellowships. Cyrus McCormick, Jr., Mrs. E. W. Bok, Mr. and Mrs. H. H. Flagler, Paul D. Cravath, former President William H. Taft, Henry Seligman and others were further contributors.[68]

Even as the fund-raising scheme for the new music fellowships was being realized, however, Lamond's candidacy as the head of the new program was still in question. Behind the scenes Daniel Chester French, the famed American sculptor who was an old friend of Lamond and had been involved with AAR from its inception, had been lobbying for Lamond's appointment, and he stepped in as a troubleshooter when Lamond's selection was being debated. On June 12, 1921, French wrote to William R. Mead (of the architectural firm of McKim, Mead and White), who was then president of the Academy, giving a clear sense of behind-the-scenes agitation. All trustees clearly were not supporting Lamond, and French's letter is remarkable enough to quote at length:

> As you inferred, the meeting the other day made me sick largely on Mr. Lamond's account, but also because there seemed to me no sufficient reason for deferring action upon the appointment of Lamond and the actual starting of the department of music. . . .

As you say, Mr. Lamond ought to have been given official recognition in the beginning so that he would not now be in the embarrassing position in which he is placed. I wish Mr. Norton had made the motion that he suggests in his note to you. I think something ought to be done even now so that he will know where he stands. I feel that he has been treated very shabbily.

Apparently, in spite of all that Trowbridge and I have said, Mr. Lamond is still considered as a man looking for a job and all his altruistic work in raising money is regarded as a means to this end. As I said the other day, from the first he saw a chance to do a great work for the development of music in this country and he espoused the cause with all the enthusiasm of a devotee. You know how he has worked, with the result that the large sum of money that was said to be required was raised and, instead of a note of thanks, he was treated as if he had done something reprehensible. Really the two hundred and fifty thousand dollars that he has found for us is almost as much of a gift as if he had taken it out of his own pocket and, if he had been a multimillionaire instead of an artist he would have been treated with proper respect.

I suppose it is not to be expected that the other members of the Executive Committee should appreciate Lamond's fitness for the position as I do, but I look on him as combining almost ideally the qualities that we should look for and I should consider it a calamity to lose him. He is not only an artist with a knowledge of all that pertains to music such as few men possess, but he is an organizer and practical man of affairs as was sufficiently proved by the way he ran the Red Cross section of the Distributory Hospital at Greenhut's store. He was at the head of it and conducted it so well that it was used as a model by the Government, although he had never done anything of the kind before the war. What other musicians think of him was indicated by the response that they made to his appeals for the Academy in the recent campaign. . . .

Pardon this splutter and pardon also the shabbiness of this type-writing. My machine has sprung a leak.[69]

The lobbying of Daniel Chester French must have made a difference, for qualms about Lamond were overruled, and he emerged as the first professor in charge of music at AAR, bringing his Anglican roots and skilled musicianship to a sunny hilltop in Rome.

Implementation of the awards moved forward. That June (1921), Lamond traveled to Rome to arrange housing for the fellows. "The Villa Chiaraviglio, opposite the Academy main building, was selected," Lamond reported, because it provided "a music hall, living quarters for the Professor and three studios for the Fellows."[70] The rooms were outfitted through the purchase of "suitable furniture, a library of musical works and orchestral scores, and pianos." At this point, the idea of a "women's building," which had been part of the plan presented in the letter to William Murphy, had clearly been abandoned.[71]

With the logistics organized and fund-raising under control, the launching process culminated on October 1, 1921, when Leo Sowerby of Chicago was "appointed" the first fellow.[72] He did not have a named fellowship, and his initial term was two years—not three, as was to become the norm. The selection committee consisted of Richard Aldrich (music critic for the *New York Times*), John Alden Carpenter (the Chicago composer involved in AAR fund-raising), Walter Damrosch (of the New York Symphony Orchestra), W. J. Henderson (music critic for the *New York Sun*), Walter Spalding (of the Harvard music faculty), and Owen Wister (a Harvard alum and novelist who published *The Virginian* in 1902).[73] When Sowerby applied for a third year, the funds "were available through the efforts of Mr. John Alden Carpenter, Mrs. F. S. Coolidge, Mrs. Walter Brewster, and Mrs. E. Burlingham [*sic*] Hill."[74] In other words, at that point the financing of the fellowships had not yet been fully systematized. An "open competition" for "American born" composer fellows was then launched, and at a meeting on November 1, 1921, Howard Hanson "of San Jose, Calif." was appointed the Frederick A. Juilliard Fellow.[75] "A second competition" then took place, and on May 1, 1922, Randall Thompson "of Harvard" was named the Walter Damrosch Fellow.[76] Thompson's appointment completed a full complement of fellows, and, as Lamond reported, "henceforth three men will be in residence."[77] The terms of the fellowships were as follows: "The annual stipend of the Professor [Felix Lamond] is $3,000 with $1,500 for travel. Each Fellow receives $1,000 per annum for maintenance, with lodging (food at cost), and $1,000 for travel."[78]

In between the appointments of Hanson and Thompson, more fund-raising took place—this time to endow the final fellowship, which was named for Walter Damrosch. Conductor of the New York Symphony Society from 1885 until its merger with the New York Philharmonic Society in 1928, Damrosch was among the most prominent musicians in New York and a galvanizing figure in establishing transnational ties for American musicians immediately after World War I. Much of what he represented, in terms of both his international reach and conservative aesthetic ideology, fused resoundingly with AAR's mission. For one thing, Damrosch had undertaken prominent war work, organizing a training school for bandmasters with the American Expeditionary Force in France. He also actively raised funds for French musicians.[79] After the war, he took the Symphony Society on a European tour—the first such junket by an American orchestra—and he spearheaded founding the Conservatoire américain at Fontainebleau, France. As a conductor, he championed conservative American composers such as John Alden Carpenter, Charles Martin Loeffler, and Deems Taylor—some of the same figures who played prominent roles, along with Damrosch, on AAR's selection committees. Yet another tie to AAR's world might have come through Damrosch's long association with Columbia University. Damrosch's father, the conductor Leopold Damrosch, received an honorary degree from Columbia in 1880, and Walter was given one in 1914.

Finally, Walter Damrosch also had links to old money in New York, having been involved in persuading Andrew Carnegie to build Carnegie Hall.[80] Carnegie money was certainly important to AAR, including the Carnegie Corporation, which made substantial early contributions to the composer fellowships.[81] Perhaps Damrosch's connection to large sums of cash enhanced the idea of naming the final fellowship for him. There is yet another institutional and financial link here: Damrosch's brother Frank had been a founder of the Institute of Musical Art in 1905, and he was its director in 1926, when it became the Juilliard School of Music.[82] In other words, the Damrosch family had ties to the Juilliard fortune as well.

Damrosch also brought high-flying visibility to AAR's music program. On February 27, 1922, he was fêted in New York with a gala concert featuring three orchestras (the New York Philharmonic, New York Symphony Orchestra, and the Philadelphia Orchestra) and five conductors (Joseph Stransky, Arthur Bodansky, Albert Coates, Willem Mengelberg, and Leopold Stokowski), which had been designed to endow an AAR fellowship in Damrosch's name. It was a showy event, and it also celebrated Damrosch's "fifty years' service to American music." He was presented with a bronze plaque, "designed and executed by Mrs. Harry Payne Whitney [Gertrude Vanderbilt Whitney]."[83] No American music appeared on the program; rather, it included a parade of European orchestral blockbusters, ranging from the opening preludes to Wagner's *Lohengrin* and *Die Meistersinger* to Berlioz's *Rákóczy March*. Here, too, women entered the scene. Not only did Gertrude Whitney make the plaque (she was an artist as well as the primary patron of the French American composer Edgard Varèse and his International Composers' Guild), but women also headed up the "Executive Committee" that shaped the event, which included some of the major patrons of the New York Philharmonic.[84] Led by Mrs. Henry Fairfield Osborn, the committee also included Mrs. Charles S. Guggenheimer ("Minnie," who was the force behind the summer concerts in New York's Lewisohn Stadium) and Mrs. Newbold LeRoy Edgar (also known as "Countess Mercati"; she was another Philharmonic patron).[85] The bottom line for the concert honoring Damrosch came with an announcement that it brought in $18,000—nearly half the total required to endow a single composer's fellowship.[86]

Thus, when the substantial job of underwriting AAR's composer prizes had been completed—and done with lickety-split efficiency—the dimensions of the program were tidily articulated in the *New York Times*: "There will be one prix de Rome winner in musical composition each year. The fellowship provides three years of residence and study in Rome or two years in Rome and one year in Paris for each fellow. After three years there will be three American composers constantly studying abroad with the aid of the musical department of the Academy."[87] Application requirements were also spelled out:

> Those in charge of the competition for a fellowship in musical composition to be awarded by the American Academy in Rome have announced that applicants for admission to the competition are required to file with the Secretary of the Academy, not later than March 1, 1922, an application, together with letters of reference as to character, education and artistic ability.

> They must also submit . . . two compositions, one for orchestra either alone or in combination with a solo instrument, and one for string quartet or for some ensemble combination such as a sonata for violin and piano, a trio for violin, 'cello and pianoforte, or possibly for some less usual combination of chamber instruments.
>
> The compositions submitted should show facility in handling the larger instrumental forms, such as the sonata form or free modifications of it. A sonata for pianoforte or a fugue of large dimensions will be accepted, but songs and short pianoforte pieces will not be considered.
>
> The award will be made only to a musician of exceptional promise already thoroughly trained in technique. Manuscripts should bear, not the name of the composer, but a pseudonym, and should be accompanied by a sealed envelope bearing on its face the pseudonym and containing within the name and address of the sender.[88]

The candidate pool was limited to "unmarried men who are citizens of the United States."[89] Thus the terms were clear: applicants were to be single males who had completed formal training as composers. Their work was to fit into traditional forms—symphonies, sonatas, fugues—and a mechanism for blind adjudication appeared to be in place.

As a matter of explicit principle, then, a select group of young men were handed the keys to an exclusive club. In fact, the homogeneity of the fellows was narrowly defined: there were no Jews, no African Americans, no women. The first two bans remained unstated, and the final one was a founding principle, repeatedly articulated over the years. The AAR fellows enjoyed its financial good fortune thanks to substantial American philanthropy, much of it facilitated by wealthy women. Rooted in old money, AAR's mission with composers continued to cling to other aspects of the "old," including the stylistic conservatism it held so dear.

Men, Women, and Gender at the American Academy in Rome

As has been chronicled here, when the American Academy in Rome set out to celebrate its silver anniversary, it planned "to admit women to all the advantages of the Academy"—that is, to the full sweep of its programs in classical studies—and "to put in a foundation for musical composition and landscape architecture."[90] The climate was certainly right, with the Nineteenth Amendment granting women the right to vote, ratified in August 1920. At some point, though, the door closed to women composers. It is not clear when that happened, but the key had been tossed out by the time the fellowships were launched in 1921.

One problem might have been the lack of separate housing, since plans for a "woman's building" had been abandoned at some point in the blitz of fund-raising.[91] Here, too, the French Academy in Rome served as a comfortable model, but even "Old France," as the title of one article of the day put it, was able to inch toward a degree of equity that "Young America" seemed incapable of delivering. According to a comparison of the two institutions from 1921, prizewinners at the French Academy enjoyed "the charm of Rome, . . . the companionship of men of their own kind, the beauty and repose of their environment."[92] At that point, there was "one woman" among the twenty-four fellows, and she happened to be a composer: Margarite Canal (1890–1978), who won the French Prix de Rome in 1920.[93] She had been preceded by "one other prix de Rome of the fair sex" and that was Lili Boulanger.[94] In other words, the practice of excluding women had a strong precedent, but the French had begun to make progress. American women did not receive even this limited access.

Yet women were part of the Academy's music program: as patrons and, eventually, as spouses of the fellows. In terms of patronage, a fundamental paradox was glaringly present: women composers might not have been welcome at AAR, but the many female patrons who helped launch the composer fellowships continued to sustain the institution. The degree to which women threw themselves into fund-raising for AAR's music fellowships has already been chronicled, as has the fusion of its networks with the women's clubs of high society.[95] Yet even though Mrs. Whitelaw Reid—cochair of the initial fund-raising committee and founder of a retreat for American women artists in Paris—might have dropped out of the picture once the fellowships headed in a male-only direction, I have found no canary in the coal mine—no figure like Lucy Stone, a leader in the women's suffrage movement of the nineteenth century, who rebelled against the degree to which her labor was benefiting men, as recounted by the historian Nancy Cott: "While she was sewing for an education society it occurred to her 'how absurd it was for her to be working to help educate a [male] student who could earn more money toward his own education in a week, by teaching, than she could earn in a month; and she left the shirt unfinished and hoped that no one would ever complete it.'"[96] The women behind AAR's composers left no such record of outrage. Elizabeth Sprague Coolidge, to name the most prominent example, deepened her connection to AAR during the 1920s, despite the ban on women composers. She seemed reconciled (or oblivious) to the inequities around her. The composers Amy Beach and Rebecca Clarke were among Coolidge's friends, so she certainly did not exclude women from her inner circle. But there is no record that she lobbied for change.[97] Rather, Coolidge supported concerts at AAR, and she became a primary benefactor of Gian Francesco Malipiero, including his edition of the works of Claudio Monteverdi. Coolidge loved Italy, and her patronage turned her visits there into professional junkets.

Yet in at least one notable instance, women patrons stretched AAR beyond its rigid constrictions. This took place not within the realm of gender equity but rather in that of challenging "tradition" and it unfolded within one of AAR's more unusual fund-raising events. In April 1924 a committee that included Mrs. Charles S. Guggenheimer (or Minnie Guggenheimer), Mrs. Christian R. Holmes, Mrs. Otto Kahn, and Mrs. Harry Harkness Flagler—all of whom were major patrons of the New York Philharmonic, some also of Edgard Varèse's International Composers' Guild—organized a benefit concert in New York featuring the famous dance-band leader Paul Whiteman. It took place two months after Whiteman had presented the infamous "Experiment in Modern Music" at Aeolian Hall with its premiere of the *Rhapsody in Blue* by George Gershwin. The novelty pianist Zez Confrey also appeared on AAR's program.[98] It was an aesthetic-stretching moment for an institution constricted to sonatas and symphonies. A week before the concert, the *New York Times* reported that "a bombardment of questions [had] been sustained by Mrs. Christian R. Holmes" about the match of Whiteman with AAR, and she deftly finessed a rationale that plugged into the Academy's pursuit of The Great American Composer. "From among the many Americans who are writing jazz music today," Holmes told the press, "there may emerge a genius who, under the stimulating influence of a fellowship in the academy, may have a far-reaching effect on the future development of American music."[99] This event again brought AAR to the society page, with an article stating "there will be a corps of débutantes to dispose of programs, headed by Miss Clara Oldfield Barclay."[100] Leo Sowerby, the Academy's first fellow, wrote two works for the Whiteman concert—*Monotony* and *Synconata*.[101] The second title is as revealing as Mrs. Holmes's statement to the press. *Synconata*—a fusion of "syncopation" with "sonata," of jazz with the classical tradition, of profane and sacred.

Was jazz being used here as a kind of fashionable exoticism, or was the aesthetic challenge serious? Whatever the case, this seemingly adventuresome foray for AAR in New York City was delivered as a high-society event.

Women entered the saga of the early years of composer residencies at AAR in yet another way: that is, as wives and lovers of the fellows. There, too, the story yielded exclusion, and administrative correspondence from the 1920s documents persistent problems. Guidelines stated that fellows needed to be "unmarried," and during most of that first decade the rules were unbending: fellows were "required to sleep in the Academy." If they decided to marry while at AAR, they "automatically cease[d] to become a Fellow."[102] The fellows challenged these limitations as the decade progressed, yielding slow but persistent change. Thus, the composer program at AAR was designed to follow a monastic model through which male composers would remove themselves from mainstream society for three years, devoting themselves entirely to professional pursuits. Creative productivity was linked to celibacy. When, for example, Herbert Elwell had "a mistress" during the winter of 1924, he was judged by the AAR administration as having "show[n] no signs of creative capacity."[103]

But AAR grew more flexible as the monastic model drew protests. By 1927, Alexander Steinert had a wife who lived elsewhere in Rome, while he "work[ed] at the Academy" and took "his lunches" there.[104] When Roger Sessions, who was married, inquired in 1928 about eligibility for a fellowship, he was told: "Under an amendment to our By-Laws, it is now possible to make exceptions to the rule in regard to marriage, and in exceptional cases an exceptional man may be appointed to a Fellowship. . . . Before a married man is appointed it is necessary that it be made clear that his wife must be taken care of independently of the Fellowship stipend."[105] Still, the issue of wives did not go away. With Werner Janssen's appointment as Juilliard Fellow in 1930, Roscoe Guernsey, director of AAR's New York office, wrote Janssen to clarify the terms:

> I note that you are married, but say "at present not living with wife." Our requirements are that competitors must be unmarried, but exceptions may be made in unusual cases. I shall have to present your case, with some others, to our Executive Committee at its meeting on March 11th. . . . Also please state whether there would be any possibility of your wife coming to live with you during the period of your Fellowship. Married men cannot live in the Academy, but have to find quarters elsewhere and this is a decided disadvantage.[106]

It turned out that Janssen not only had a wife but two children! His appointment required final approval, and at some point the administration of AAR learned that his marriage had broken up. Lamond then sent a telegram to the New York office stating, "Janssen desirable if without any encumbrance. Believe divorced."[107] He and his wife "became reconciled" after his appointment, and he wanted to bring the whole family to Rome.[108] A flurry of letters ensued. At first, the trustees rejected Janssen's appeal to have his wife join him.[109] This elicited an apology from Janssen, saying that he would resign if his wife was excluded.[110] Then a proposal was made for Janssen's family to settle in Florence while he lived at AAR; he agreed to this.[111]

The policy soon changed radically. In 1932, when Vittorio Giannini accepted a fellowship, he informed Guernsey that he had a wife. This time Giannini received a much more gracious response, and the agitation unfolded behind the scenes: "We certainly have no desire to separate you two," Guernsey wrote. "It will be fortunate if you will have also other sources for getting funds, as our stipend is scarcely large enough for supporting both of you completely. I regret that we have not in the Academy building accommodations for a married fellow. You and Mrs. Giannini will have to get rooms outside the Academy. Mr. Benton will help you to find quarters."[112]

Thus in its first decade, the music program of AAR had an unsettled and often vexed relationship with women. On the one hand, it thrived on the support of a select group of affluent females, while on the other it excluded women from competing for fellowships and only gradually accepted their presence in Rome as wives of the male composers being supported.

Style and Geography, Cronyism and Careers: The Selection Process for Rome Prize Composers

The American composers brought to Rome during these early years cannot all be characterized fairly as "academic" or "tradition focused" in their aesthetic orientation. Yet those descriptors certainly fit the first three prizewinners, as well as many others from the 1920s. After Sowerby, Hanson, and Thompson, winners of the prize during that decade included Wintter Watts, (George) Herbert Elwell, Walter Helfer, Robert Sanders, Alexander Steinert, Roger Sessions, and Normand Lockwood (see the appendix to this volume for a list of award winners with dates of residency).[113] With the sole exception of Sessions, all these men embraced traditional compositional idioms. Even more strikingly, Sessions was the only one whose music gained any sort of broadbased traction over the years. In the 1930s, Samuel Barber was the one composer fellow with a significant long-term impact.

But then the entrance requirements defined the applicant pool, and all the composers named as fellows could deliver the kinds of music stipulated. Applicants needed to submit two compositions, as stated in full earlier, which included "one either for orchestra alone or in combination with a solo instrument, and one for string quartet or for some ensemble combination. . . . The composition must show facility in handling large instrumental forms, as in the sonata form or free modifications of it."[114] This closed the door to someone like Henry Cowell, whose so-called ultramodern experiments of the early 1920s were largely concocted for unusual chamber ensembles or used extended piano techniques, without a fugue or sonata in sight. In fact, with the singular exception of Sessions, all the up-and-coming American modernists of the 1920s are missing from the list of Rome Prize recipients: no Aaron Copland or Roy Harris, no Ruth Crawford or George Antheil, no Virgil Thomson. Crawford obviously couldn't apply, and Copland apparently considered doing so but decided against it.[115] These fellowships were directed to an entirely different class of composer.

Another strong determinant of a consistent stylistic conservatism among AAR's fellows had to do with the strong networks that took shape immediately. They emanated out from the first three appointments and generated a scene that appears, in hindsight, to be fraught with insider trading, especially as the fellowship program moved into the 1930s. There were lineages from Harvard (Thompson, Helfer, Steinert, Sessions), Chicago (Sowerby, Sanders), the Juilliard School (Hanson, Watts, Giannini, Naginski), and the Eastman School of Music (Inch, Johnson, Kennan, Woltmann). Ernest Bloch's recommendation meant a great deal early on, with Thompson, Elwell, and Sessions among his former pupils, and for a time Nadia Boulanger's pupils also appeared prominently on the list (they included Elwell and Lockwood; she also wrote for Sessions). (The appendix to this volume includes a listing of where each composer studied.)

The juries changed little in these first two decades, and, moreover, jurors tended not only to favor hometown candidates but also to choose their own students. On the earliest panels, Harvard was represented by Richard Aldrich (1863–1937), music critic for the *New York Times* and graduate of the Harvard class of 1885. His ties to Harvard were strong enough that his son ultimately gave his father's library to Harvard.[116] Aldrich also had deep connections to Rome, where he moved permanently after his retirement. Other Harvard jurors included Walter Spalding (1865–1962) and E. B. Hill (1872–1960), both on the Harvard faculty; Owen Wister (1860–1938), a Harvard alumnus; and Chalmers Clifton (1889–1966), another Harvard graduate who replaced Carpenter on the jury in 1932.[117] With Chicago, the links came through John Alden Carpenter (1876–1951), who remained on the AAR selection committee from 1921 to 1931 (added to this, Carpenter was yet another Harvard alum), and Sowerby, who joined the selection committee in 1929.[118] The Eastman School of Music got its foot in the door through Howard Hanson, who became a dominant—even dominating—force in AAR politics as time passed. Hanson first appeared on the AAR jury in 1930; within the next decade, four of the ten fellows came from Eastman. The Juilliard School appeared in the person of Walter Damrosch, whose brother was its director; Damrosch served on the selection committee from 1921 to 1937. Former fellows were also enlisted to choose their successors, which reinforced the pattern of nepotism. Walter Spalding helped select Randall Thompson in 1922. Leo Sowerby helped engineer Robert Sanders's appointment in 1925 (although he was not a formal member of the jury).[119] Roger Sessions, who joined the jury in 1938, helped choose his student Charles Naginski that same year.

Nonetheless, the composers selected by AAR came from far-flung corners of the United States. This sort of transcontinental spread—or at least one that reached heavily into the Midwest—was clearly valued at the Academy. Most often these young men made their way to Rome by way of the "right" educational institutions.

In 1931, Felix Lamond seemed to smell the incest in the selection process, and he wrote a long letter to Charles A. Platt, who was then president of the Academy. Lamond's goal was to outline "some things which I thought would be of benefit to the Music Department," and his extensive memo is worth quoting at length.

> First: As to the Jury—I believe that it would be advantageous if this body were changed somewhat each year. Perhaps each member could be elected to serve for two or three years, on the same plan as the Trustees. This would tend to increase the number of competitors, as it would enlist the interest of many excellent musicians who are not at present identified with the work of the Department. For instance—I would name as prospective Jurymen: . . . [goes on to list] Carl Engel, Charles Martin Loeffler, Daniel Gregory Mason, . . . and it would be desirable to have at least one prominent

> Orchestral Conductor each year, such as: Frederick Stock, Chicago, Leopold Stokowski, Philadelphia, Arturo Toscanini, New York.
>
> Second: I strongly advise that no Juryman who is a teacher of (or recommends) any Competitor should be eligible as Judge.
>
> P.S. (Confidential) I suggest that Walter Damrosch, having served ten years as Chairman of the jury, might retire and be put on the Council of the Academy. I have good reason to believe that he is too much occupied with other matters to give attention to us.[120]

Hanson may have been the person who capitalized the most on his connection to AAR, adroitly leaping into its operations in multiple dimensions. Besides promoting Eastman students, he served as an active fund-raiser for AAR, especially in reaching out to Mr. [George] Eastman, who had been approached by the Academy during its initial fund-raising drive and contributed throughout the years. I have not pinpointed the full extent of Eastman's involvement, but he made a gift in 1928 to maintain a string quartet, and he appears to have done so again in 1931.[121] At the same time, Hanson's connectedness to AAR overlapped with his role as director of the Eastman School of Music (University of Rochester). There he became an early champion of the music of composers connected with the Academy, especially John Alden Carpenter. When fellowships started to be announced during radio broadcasts (in the 1930s), Hanson conducted, often showcasing his own music as well.[122]

Like Hanson, many of the Rome Prize winners went on to teach at American universities. From the outset, AAR became a central supplier of American academic composers, helping to establish a whole generation of composer-teachers. The influx of American composers into American higher education after World War II has received much attention, but the beginnings of this trend in the interwar period deserve further exploration. In 1931, an article in the *New York Times* listed previous Rome Prize winners and where they were teaching: Sowerby at the American Conservatory in Chicago, Hanson at the Eastman School of Music, Thompson at Wellesley College, Elwell at the Cleveland Institute of Music, and Helfer at Hunter College of CUNY. A list of the fellows' subsequent academic affiliations appears in the appendix.

AAR's fellows also played a prominent role in American church and choral music, especially in the early years with Sowerby and Thompson, who were both trained as organists. Sanders also had church jobs. This represents yet another arena in which the composer prizes thwarted change, as they sought to institutionalize genteel norms of the early twentieth century. When the Academy's stipends were first announced, they were billed as "giv[ing] a stimulus to musical composition throughout the country" and "ultimately giv[ing] to the world a great American 'symphonic, operatic or church-music composer.'"[123] Since Lamond had been a church musician and early summer tours involved stints at

British cathedrals and music festivals, this emphasis affected policy.[124] Also, this sacred-music strand reflects an era—meaning the nineteenth through early twentieth centuries—when writing for the church was a core activity for serious composers in the United States.[125] During the 1920s, church work receded in frequency and prestige, as modernist aesthetic impulses led to greater secularization. At the same time, a rising percentage of Jewish composers was gaining prominence and the established hierarchy between concert music and popular idioms was coming under challenge. In short, multiple cultural forces ultimately destabilized church music as a force in contemporary composition.

★ ★ ★

Thus, like the exclusive men's clubs that were a fixture of upper-class society in the early twentieth century, the inaugural era of the composers' program at the American Academy in Rome yielded major benefits for the "picked men" in its embrace, and as was the case in most American musical institutions of the day, it drew heavily on the resources of women. This white male preserve simultaneously had a populist aspect, however, making a richly textured European experience available to composers who earned the opportunity through talent and education but were not necessarily born to wealth.

AAR provided a substantial model of facilitating transatlantic interchange. In retrospect, its music program appears as an early stage in American cultural diplomacy, setting in place the notion of composer-as-ambassador that flourished after World War II. When Walter Damrosch took a European tour with the New York Symphony Society immediately after World War I, he set a precedent for the now-famous trips of Leonard Bernstein and the New York Philharmonic after World War II—especially to the Soviet Union in 1959. By then, the US government stepped in to fund such junkets, and the goal became more overtly political.[126] Even more strikingly, the composers sent abroad in the second half of the century were seasoned professionals—figures like Bernstein, Aaron Copland, John Cage, Gunther Schuller—who did not arrive in Europe to soak up a postgraduate experience but rather to transmit their art. They remained overwhelming white and male, at least within the realm of concert music, but they now included Jews, and they represented styles that were diverse and often revolutionary.

AAR also stood as an important early supplier of composers to the faculty of American conservatories and universities, and by safeguarding tradition, it helped sustain tonal composition through the aesthetic turbulences of the early twentieth century. Samuel Barber's internationally celebrated career constitutes a major chapter in that story.

Thus the early years for composers at the American Academy in Rome delivered a complex record—one that balanced the inequities of an elite institution with the aspirations and energy of a young country gaining strength on a global stage.

Figure 4.2. King's Visit, 1922 (King Victor Emmanuel III, *center*, with American Ambassador to Italy, Richard Washburn Child, and Mrs. Child to his left. Felix Lamond, professor in charge of music, is second from left end of photograph). Courtesy of the American Academy in Rome.

Notes

Epigraph. Felix Lamond, "Report of the Professor of Musical Composition: To the Trustees of the American Academy in Rome," "for the year ending September 30, 1925," in American Academy in Rome Annual Report, 51. Each year Lamond filed such a report. Throughout, I consistently refer to them as "AAR Annual Report." A full set of the annual reports is held in the Library of the American Academy in Rome (Rome).

1. For discussion of both the "Europeanized American" and "American genius," see Judith Tick, "The Classicist Origins of the Rome Prize in Musical Composition, 1890–1920" in this volume.

2. Felix Lamond, AAR Annual Report 1924, 55.

3. The phrase "picked men"—or "picked young men"—recurs in contemporaneous literature about the fellowships. Two such instances are: "Rome Fellowships in Music Announced," *New York Times*, July 9, 1921; and Karleton Hackett, "Rome Academy Gives Training to Americans," *Musical Leader* 57, no. 14 (October 3, 1929): 5.

4. Lucia Valentine and Alan Valentine, *The American Academy in Rome, 1894–1969* (Charlottesville: University Press of Virginia, 1973), 80, 6.

5. Ibid., 80–81.

6. Fikret K. Yegül, *Gentlemen of Instinct and Breeding: Architecture at the American Academy in Rome, 1894–1940* (New York: Oxford University Press, 1991), 80.

7. Lamond, AAR Annual Report 1926, 51.

8. Damrosch, as quoted in Richard Aldrich, "Three Orchestras in Gala Concert: Philharmonic, New York Symphony, and Philadelphia Play in Damrosch's Honor . . . Great Event Nets $18,000 for Fellowships in Rome," *New York Times*, February 28, 1922.

9. Randall Thompson, "The Contemporary Scene in American Music," *Musical Quarterly* 18, no. 1 (1932): 10.

10. Sonneck, as quoted in Burnet C. Tuthill, "Leo Sowerby," *Musical Quarterly* 24, no. 3 (1938): 249.

11. Hackett, "Rome Academy Gives Training to Americans," 5.

12. Ruth Berges, "That Elusive Prix de Rome," *Music Review* 55, no. 2 (1994): 146–52.

13. Andrew Dell'Antonio, "Il divino Claudio: Monteverdi and Lyric Nostalgia in Fascist Italy," *Cambridge Opera Journal* 8, no. 3 (1996): 275.

14. Text of the speech: "Comm. Felix Lamond's address to H. E. Benito Mussolini on the occasion of his visit to the American Academy," February 24, 1933, AAR Archive Microfilm, box 20, reel 5782.

15. "Swarm of Men Protects Mussolini, Says Sculptor," *New York Herald-Tribune*, May 5, 1933, AAR Archive Microfilm, box 29, reel 5794.

16. *Grove Music Online*, s.v. "Ottorino Respighi," by John C. G. Waterhouse, accessed March 29, 2014, http://www.oxfordmusiconline.com/.

17. "Return to Melody Hailed by Resphighi," *New York Times*, March 9, 1932.

18. For example, after Leo Sowerby returned to Chicago, he wrote to Elizabeth Sprague Coolidge: "I rejoice that such people as Respighi, Corti, Castelnuovo, etc. are my firm friends, and that they do not forget me, for I hear from them constantly" (Sowerby, letter to Coolidge, February 13, 1925).

19. The primary study of this period is Glenn Watkins, *Proof through the Night: Music and the Great War* (Berkeley: University of California Press, 2003).

20. All these composer organizations are discussed in chapter 11 of Oja, *Making Music Modern: New York in the 1920s* (New York: Oxford University Press, 2000), 177–200. Pro Musica's history has been chronicled in Ronald V. Wiecki, "A Chronicle of Pro Music in the United Sates (1920–1944): With a Biographical Sketch of Its Founder, E. Robert Schmitz" (PhD diss., University of Wisconsin, 1992).

21. See also David Metzer, "The League of Composers: The Initial Years," *American Music* 15, no. 1 (1997): 45–69.

22. See also R. Allen Lott, "'New Music for New Ears': The International Composers' Guild," *Journal of the American Musicological Society* 36, no. 2 (1983): 266–86.

23. The Augusteo was one of Rome's main concert halls. It opened in 1908 and was demolished in 1936. See Bianca Maria Antolini, "Rome, 1870 to the Present," in *Grove Music Online*, s.v. "Rome," by Günter Fleischhauer et al., accessed March 11, 2013, http://www.oxfordmusiconline.com/.

24. "American Concert in Rome," *New York Times*, March 18, 1919. The pieces performed were listed as an "overture" by Gilbert (probably the *Comedy Overture on Negro Themes* of ca. 1906), "four characteristic orchestral pieces" by Foote (i.e., *Four Character Pieces after the Rubáiyát of Omar Khayyám*; 1900), and "an organ concerto" by Parker (dating from 1902).

25. Robert Miraldi, *The Muckrakers: Evangelical Crusaders* (Westport, CT: Praeger, 2000), 53.

26. Lamond had been educated in the standards of the conservative Oxford Movement—or Tractarianism—of the High Church of England, which in its drive to emulate medieval liturgical rituals of the Roman Catholic Church limited its choirs to

boys and men. See *Grove Music Online*, s.v. "Anglican and Episcopalian Church Music," by Nicholas Temperley, accessed March 11, 2013, http://www.oxfordmusiconline.com/.

27. Leonard Ellinwood, *The History of American Church Music* (New York: Morehouse Gorham Company, 1953), 156.

28. "First School Here for Church Music: Trinity Back of It, with Organists and Choirmasters to Assist in the Work," *New York Times*, July 22, 1913.

29. Lamond, letter to the editor, *New York Times*, July 27, 1913, responding to an objection raised by another reader, who claimed the Guilmant Organ School had preceded that of Trinity Church. In his letter to the editor, Lamond differentiated Trinity's school from that at First Presbyterian by describing it as teaching "a musical tradition that belongs to the Anglican Church and Churches which in congregational worship pursue the ancient methods of historic church services that cannot obviously be used by other communions of Christians. This is the type of church music that the new school is intended to promote, and it is believed that it will do a work which has never been attempted before on this side of the Atlantic."

30. Stevens's work with the Red Cross is detailed in "American Academy in Rome Reopens," *New York Times*, January 25, 1920.

31. This biographical information comes from Lamond's obituary in the *New York Times*, March 17, 1940.

32. Charles Montague Bakewell, *The Story of the American Red Cross in Italy* (New York: Macmillan, 1920), 36–37.

33. Albert Spalding also had deep roots in Italy. According to his obituary, he studied at the Bologna Conservatory from ages seven to fourteen, and his debut took place in Paris in 1905. "Albert Spalding Dies in Home at 64," *New York Times*, May 27, 1953. Albert's father, A. G. Spalding, was a baseball hero—first for the Boston Red Stockings then the Chicago White Stockings. He began his sporting-goods business in 1876.

34. A draft of an "Itinerary of Visiting Committee" (typescript), dated April and May [1920], includes only some of these cities. But a more detailed version, also titled "ITINERARY OF VISITING COMMITTEE," gives a broader scope and details the dates of the visits (AAR Archive Microfilm, box 33, reel 5799).

35. These names come from the second itinerary cited in note 35. Ferruccio Vitale (1875–1933) was a landscape architect and S. Breck Trowbridge (1862–1925) was an architect as well as vice president and trustee of the American Academy.

36. "Edward Bok," in "Bok Tower Gardens," accessed March 26, 2014, http://boktowergardens.org/tower-gardens/our-history/edward-bok/.

37. "Rome Fellowships in Music Announced." Mrs. Bok was a major patron of the American composer George Antheil, a self-described "bad boy," whose aesthetic ran contrary to the vision of AAR. She also became a patron of Samuel Barber, who was a fellow at AAR in the 1930s.

38. Felix Lamond, telegram to Professor Theodore Miller, Rochester University, February 26, 1920, AAR Archive Microfilm, box 33, reel 5799.

39. Lamond, AAR Annual Report 1928, 43. Pressure continued to be placed on Eastman for funding. A letter to Howard Hanson from 1931—at a time when Lamond was trying to set up a composers' retreat in the south of France—acknowledges receipt of a "check for 190,000 lire" and adds: "I do not want you to relax your efforts to make Mr. Eastman do what I want him to do." Lamond, letter to Hanson, April 10, 1931, AAR Archive Microfilm, box 33, reel 5799. Another letter, written that same day to Mrs. Hutchison at the Eastman School of Music, states: "I feel that the idea of an Eastman unit is impossible now, but Dr. Hanson says he will make one last effort to get it from

Mr. Eastman." Lamond, letter to Mrs. Hutchison, April 10, 1931, same microfilm. On April 9, 1931, the *New York Times* had announced the gift of "a site on the French Riveria, including buildings and an endowment sufficient for maintenance," which had been made "to the Department of Musical Composition of the American Academy at Rome by Myron C. Taylor." "M. C. Taylor Gives Fund to Composers," *New York Times*, April 9, 1931. Lamond's approach to Eastman clearly was connected to this.

40. Elizabeth Miller, letter to Felix Lamond, March 17, 1920, letterhead for "The Junior League of Detroit, Inc.," and Lamond, carbon of letter to Rev. Dr. S. S. Marquis, March 29, 1920, AAR Archive Microfilm, box 33, reel 5799.

41. Lamond, carbon of letter to Mrs. George Theron Slade, March 26, 1920, AAR Archive Microfilm, box 33, reel 5799.

42. Lamond, carbon of letter to Mrs. Cyrus McCormick, Jr., March 29, 1920; Cyrus McCormick, Jr., letter to Lamond [no date]; Lamond, carbon of letter to Cyrus McCormick, April 26, 1920, AAR Archive Microfilm, box 33, reel 5799.

43. [Invitation to an event on April 19, 1920, in Chicago], AAR Archive Microfilm, box 33, reel 5799.

44. [Felix Lamond], letter to Mr. William H. Murphy [name crossed out], written from 101 Park Avenue, New York City, February 2, 1920, AAR Archives Microfilm, box 33, reel 5799.

45. "William Herbert Murphy: Detroit Capitalist and Patron of Music Dies Suddenly," *New York Times*, February 6, 1929.

46. [Lamond], letter to Murphy, February 2, 1920. All quotations in this paragraph come from this letter. Later that month, the intention to include women among the composition fellows was announced in the *New York Times*. "American Academy in Rome," *New York Times*, February 22, 1920.

47. [Lamond], letter to Murphy, February 2, 1920.

48. Ibid.

49. A model for this sort of endeavor was already in place at Harvard's Department of Music, which in 1912 had established a fund for student travel through the Paine Traveling Fellowships. They were begun by Mary Elizabeth Paine with a gift of $60,000 and established in honor of her husband, John Knowles Paine. Once again, a woman was the donor. See also Elliot Forbes, *A History of Music at Harvard to 1972* (Cambridge: Department of Music, Harvard University, 1988).

50. These sums do not add up, but the quotation is correct.

51. These two were also identified in the *New York Times*, although as part of an "Endowment Fund Committee," including also Thomas Nelson Page, Dr. Charles W. Eliot, and Mrs. Willard Straight. "American Academy in Rome," February 22, 1920.

52. See Tick, Classicist Origins, in this volume for a description of this event.

53. "Elihu Root," The Nobel Prize Foundation, accessed November 17, 2013 http://nobelprize.org/nobel_prizes/peace/laureates/1912/root-bio.html. Root's obituary, which appeared on the front page of the *New York Times*, states: "The greatness of his achievements were in the fields of world peace, international cooperation, the settlement of disputes between nations by diplomacy and arbitration instead of by war. It was such work—adjustment of difficulties between the United States and Japan, pacification of Cuba and the Philippines and his stand against discrimination in Panama canal tolls—that won him the Nobel Peace Prize in 1912." "Elihu Root, 92, Dies of Pneumonia Here; Worker for Peace," *New York Times*, February 7, 1937.

54. It appears that Elizabeth Reid's father was not involved with the founding of Mills College. Rather, he was for a time regent of the University of California; he also built

the Mills Building in San Francisco. See "Darius Ogden Mills," Virtualology's edited *Appletons' Encyclopedia*, http://famousamericans.net/dariusogdenmills/; and "Facts and Features," http://www.themillsbuilding.com/building/index.html (both sites accessed December 23, 2013).

55. "Reid Won Fame in Many Fields," *New York Times*, December 16, 1912. Most information about Reid and her husband included in this paragraph and the following one comes from "The Institute for Scholars at Reid Hall: Historical Background," Columbia University Institute for Scholars at Reid Hall, accessed December 23, 2013, http://www.columbia.edu/cu/reidhall/institut/history.html.

56. "Institute for Scholars at Reid Hall," http://www.columbia.edu/cu/reidhall/institut/history.html.

57. "Society at Home and Abroad: Visit of British Royalty to Make Brilliant and Busy Week: Mrs. Whitelaw Reid a Distinguished Hostess," *New York Times*, January 21, 1912.

58. Reid's obituary states that after her husband's death she "gave up her social life and embarked on a business and philanthropic career." "Whitelaw Reid's Widow Dies at 73," *New York Times*, April 30, 1931.

59. "Institute for Scholars at Reid Hall," http://www.columbia.edu/cu/reidhall/institut/history.html.

60. "Parker Memorial for Rome," *New York Times*, April 11, 1920. A second article in the *Times*, published one week later, reiterated much of the same information: Richard Aldrich, "Aid for American Composers," *New York Times*, April 18, 1920.

61. "Invited to Serve on Honorary Committee of Horatio Parker Fund," typescript list, AAR Archives Microfilm, box 33, reel 5799.

62. "Notes," *New Music Review*, AAR Archive Microfilm, box 33, reel 5799. The donors included Mrs. Edward S. Harkness, $8000; Mrs. Frederick [*sic*] S. Coolidge, $500; "The Misses Whitney," $8; Mrs. John Henry Hammond $25 (AAR Archive, box 33, reel 5799). Documents in the AAR archive records suggest opposition to the way plans for composer fellowships were being shaped. One exception occurred in a letter from Henry E. Krehbiel (1854–1923), the noted American critic and proponent of the German musical tradition, who lent his support to AAR yet questioned the goal of raising funds in Parker's memory: "If my name can be of any service to the Committee it is at your disposal. It is my conviction that more might be accomplished for music by a scholarship at the Yale School of Music than by a Fellowship at Rome; for in the field of music outside of opera Italy is worse than barren. . . . What is of direct concern is the memorial to Parker and with that in any form, dignified and worthy, I am in hearty accord." H. E. Krehbiel, letter to Lamond, April 22 [1920], AAR Archive Microfilm, box 33, reel 5799.

63. "Hammerstein Fund for Rome Academy," *New York Times*, April 12, 1920.

64. Quoted in "Hammerstein Fund." Luisa Tetrazzini was an Italian opera star brought to the United States in 1908 by Hammerstein to appear with his Manhattan Opera Company. An article by Richard Aldrich also announced plans for the Hammerstein Fund: "A series of benefit concerts and entertainments has been projected to help raise this amount [for the Hammerstein Fund], in which many artists formerly associated with Mr. Hammerstein will take part. Nothing more intelligent or of a greater artistic dignity could have been devised in Mr. Hammerstein's memory" ("Aid for American Composers").

65. "Hammerstein Memorial Concert," typescript list, AAR Archives Microfilm, box 33, reel 5799.

66. "Rome Fellowships in Music Announced." Juilliard's first name is variously spelled "Frederic" and "Frederick"; even the *New York Times* is inconsistent! The latter spelling seems to occur more often, so that is what I am using.

67. In her history of the Juilliard School, Andrea Olmstead calls Frederick Juilliard politically "conservative," saying that he was opposed to the covenant of the League of Nations and later campaigned vigorously against Franklin D. Roosevelt. With AAR, as Olmstead recounts it, Frederick "endowed a three-year composition fellowship . . . stipulating, as did the Academy, that only unmarried men (such as himself) might be awarded the grant." Andrea Olmstead, *Juilliard: A History* (Urbana: University of Illinois Press, 1999), 65.

68. "Rome Fellowships in Music Announced."

69. Daniel Chester French, letter to William R. Mead, June 12, 1921, French Family Papers, Library of Congress. Many thanks to Kitty and Dan Preston for bringing this letter to my attention.

70. The quotations in this paragraph come from Felix Lamond, letter to Dr. [Henry S.] Pritchett, June 24, 1922, AAR Archive Microfilm, box 33 reel 5799. Lamond's letter is couched as a report to a funding agency. The Carnegie Corporation had been founded by Andrew Carnegie in 1911 "to promote the advancement and diffusion of knowledge and understanding." "Carnegie Corporation of New York: Historical Note," Columbia University Rare Book and Manuscript Library, accessed June 5, 2007, http://www.columbia.edu/cu/lweb/indiv/rbml/collections/carnegie/CCNYhistory.html.

71. In that letter, the following phrase was crossed out: "It will erect a woman's building at a cost of $100,000.00." [Lamond], letter to Murphy, February 2, 1920.

72. Lamond, AAR Annual Report, 1922, 46. A distinction is made in the language of the report, where it is stated that a jury "unanimously appointed Leo Sowerby" and that an "open competition" resulted in a fellowship for Howard Hanson. Randall Thompson was subsequently "elected" Walter Damrosch Fellow. Press notices of Sowerby's award made this distinction clear. The *New York Times* stated: "His appointment, it was announced, will be the only one made by the committee, all later applicants for the scholarship being chosen by competitions" ("America's 'Prix de Rome,'" October 23, 1921). And the *Chicago Daily Tribune* stated: "Hereafter the successful candidate will be chosen by competitive examination. Mr. Sowerby, however, was selected because, although young, he is a composer of reputation and distinctive achievements" ("Chicago Composer Gets Appointment to the Prix de Rome," October 15, 1921).

73. Richard W. Etulain, *Owen Wister*, Boise State College Western Writers Series (Boise: Boise State College, 1973). Wister apparently once had plans to collaborate on an opera with the Boston composer Charles Martin Loeffler, suggesting his connection both to composers and to opera. See *Grove Music Online*, s.v. "Charles Martin Loeffler," by Ellen Knight, accessed March 11, 2013, http://www.oxfordmusiconline.com/. Regarding Spalding: It does not appear that Walter was related to Albert. Walter was from Northampton, Massachusetts, and son of a clergyman. See "Walter Spalding," in *Grove's Dictionary of Music and Musicians: American Supplement*, ed. Waldo Selden Pratt (New York: MacMillan, 1947), 367; hereafter *Grove's American Supplement*).

74. Lamond, AAR Annual Report 1923, 46. The last person listed was the wife of the Harvard composer Edward Burlingame Hill. Mrs. Walter Brewster was from Chicago; Lamond corresponded with her as he organized his fund-raising tour in the spring of 1920. Lamond, letter to Mrs. Walter S. Brewster, March 4, 1920, AAR Archive Microfilm, box 33, reel 5799.

75. Lamond, letter to Dr. [Pritchett], June 24, 1922. Hanson's appointment was announced in the *New York Times* on November 16, 1921: "Dean Hanson is Named."

76. "Wins Fellowship at Rome," *New York Times*, June 2, 1922.

77. Lamond, AAR Annual Report 1922, 46.

78. Lamond, letter to Dr. [Pritchett], June 24, 1921. Using the Consumer Price Index, this $2,000 stipend was worth around $22,525.14 in 2006.

79. *Grove Music Online*, s.v. "Walter Damrosch," by H. E. Krehbiel, Richard Aldrich, H. C. Colles, and R. Allen Lott, accessed March 11, 2013, http://www.oxfordmusiconline.com/.

80. Damrosch implies as much in his memoir, which includes a chapter about Andrew Carnegie. The two men met on a ship headed to Europe in the spring of 1887. Damrosch recounted that "Mr. Carnegie became more and more interested in the New York Symphony and Oratorio Societies and consented to become their president and chief financial supporter" and that "he built Carnegie Hall to give New York a proper home for its musical activities." In Walter Damrosch, *My Musical Life* (New York: Charles Scribner's Sons, 1930), 92, 94–95.

81. "Rome Fellowships in Music Announced." This last was in 1921. Another contribution to AAR from the Carnegie Corporation of $15,000 was given in 1925 ("Gives $360,500 Fund to Encourage Art: Carnegie Corporation to Divide Sum in Support of a National Program," *New York Times*, May 20, 1925). Richard Aldrich, Frederick Stock, and T. W. Surette were listed as members of the "corporation's advisers."

82. *Grove Music Online*, s.v. "Frank Damrosch," by H. E. Krehbiel, Richard Aldrich, H. C. Colles, and R. Allen Lott, accessed March 29, 2014, http://www.oxfordmusiconline.com/.

83. "Three Orchestras to Join: Damrosch Will be Honored at Fellowship Concert Tonight," *New York Times*, February 27, 1922.

84. I have previously written about Whitney and other women patrons of American composers in Carol J. Oja, "Women Patrons and Crusaders for Modernist Music: New York in the 1920s," *Cultivating Music in America: Women Patrons and Activists since 1860*, ed. Cyrilla Barr and Ralph Locke (Berkeley: University of California Press, 1997), 237–65. A different version of this article appeared as chapter 12 in Carol J. Oja, *Making Music Modern*, 201–30.

85. Aldrich, "Three Orchestras." Others among the patrons included Edward W. Bok of Philadelphia and Otto H. Kahn, a major benefactor of the Metropolitan Opera.

86. Ibid.

87. "Rome Fellowships in Music Announced."

88. "Give 'Prix de Rome' Terms," *New York Times*, February 12, 1922.

89. "Competition Opened by American Academy," *Musical America* 29, no. 21 (November 10, 1929). Although this announcement comes from late in the 1920s, the policy of entertaining applications from unmarried men had been in place since the beginning of the composer fellowships and remained so until World War II. The founding stage of this is chronicled in Valentine and Valentine, *American Academy in Rome*, 86–87. And announcements of the competition in 1939 and 1940 made the ongoing policy clear: "Rome Awards in Doubt," *New York Times*, December 11, 1939, and "June Bulletins," *New York Times*, June 9, 1940.

90. Lamond letter to Mrs. George Theron Slade of St. Paul, March 26, 1920, AAR Archive Microfilm, box 33, reel 5799. This same statement appears repeatedly in correspondence related to fund-raising for AAR in 1920. It also appeared in the press. For example: "This institution is to extend the field of its activities to include musical composition, opening its doors to women as well as to men" (Aldrich, "Aid for American Composers").

91. This refers to the letter from Lamond to Mr. William H. Murphy of Detroit (February 2, 1920), which has a line about a woman's building crossed out.

92. Charles Henry Meltzer, "Two Homes of Art in Rome: The Academies of Old France and Young America," *Arts & Decoration* (November 1921): 15.

93. *Grove Music Online*, s.v. "Marguerite Canal," by Caroline Potter, accessed March 29, 2014, http://www.oxfordmusiconline.com/.

94. Meltzer, "Two Homes of Art in Rome, the Academies of Old France and Young America," *Arts and Decoration* (November 1921): 15.

95. The role of women's clubs is discussed in chapter 5 of this volume, "Forging an International Alliance."

96. Nancy Cott, *The Bonds of Womanhood: 'Woman's Sphere' in New England, 1780–1835* (New Haven: Yale University Press, 1977), 155–56. The internal quotation in the Cott quotation comes from Alice Stone Blackwell, *Lucy Stone: Pioneer of Woman's Rights*, 2nd ed. (Boston: Little, Brown, 1930), 20, as quoted in Eleanor Flexner, *Century of Struggle* (New York: Antheneum, 1970), 34.

97. Coolidge's biographer calls her a "failure" at "encourag[ing] female composers with commissions"; Cyrilla Barr, *Elizabeth Sprague Coolidge: American Patron of Music* (New York: Schirmer Books, 1998), 244. Coolidge did, however, occasionally program music by women in concerts at AAR. A Trio by Clarke appeared on a concert in May of 1923 (Sowerby, letter to Coolidge, February 12, 1923).

98. "Jazz Music Concert for Rome Academy," *New York Times*, April 13, 1924.

99. Holmes, as quoted in "Links Concert and Jazz: Benefit by Paul Whiteman Orchestra is Explained," *New York Times*, April 13, 1924.

100. "Jazz Concert to Raise Money for American Academy in Rome," *New York Times*, April 20, 1924.

101. Tuthill, "Leo Sowerby," 262, dates *Synconata* as 1924 and *Monotony* as 1925; but both works apparently appeared on this concert in 1924. The scores remain in manuscript.

102. "Required to sleep" comes from a "confidential" letter from Gorham Stevens, director of AAR, to Thomas W. Surette, January 10, 1924, AAR Archives Microfilm, box 33, reel 5797; and "cease[d] to become a Fellow" is from Gorham Stevens to the American Consulate in Rome, October 30, 1922, AAR Archives Microfilm, box 33, reel 5797.

103. Stevens to Surette, January 10, 1924.

104. Steinert's case was presented as a model to C. D. Badgeley, a fellow outside of music, who wrote the trustees of AAR asking if he could marry at the beginning of his third year (Badgeley, letter to trustees, November 19, 1927). Gorham Stevens informed the trustees that he could do so if "he agrees to live as Musician Steinert has agreed to live." Stevens, letter to trustees, November 21, 1927; both letters are in AAR Archive Microfilm, box 33, reel 5797.

105. Roscoe Guernsey, letter to Roger Sessions, January 21, 1928, AAR Archive Microfilm, box 20, reel 5781. Another flexibility also crept in: "I would add also that it is possible to make exceptions to the rule which places the age limit at 30."

106. Roscoe Guernsey, letter to Werner Janssen, March 6, 1930, AAR Archive Microfilm, box 20, reel 5782. A segment of the text is not entirely readable, but it basically gives Janssen the same stipulations as Sessions: no cash from the stipend can go to support a wife or family.

107. Lamond, telegram to American Academy in Rome, New York (101 Park Ave), April 16, 1930, AAR Archive Microfilm, box 20, reel 5782.

108. Gorham Stevens, telegram to AAR office in New York, October 3, 1930, AAR Archive Microfilm, box 20, reel 5782.

109. [Charles A.] Platt, telegram to AAR office in New York, October 9, 1930, AAR Archive Microfilm, box 20, reel 5782: "Trustees will not consider now Janssen wife joining him."

110. Janssen, letter to Charles A. Platt, October 11, 1930, AAR Archive Microfilm, box 20, reel 5782. In it, he apologizes for notifying the trustees that he had reconciled with his wife but says he will resign if they do not allow his wife and children to join him.

111. Platt, telegram to Gorham Stevens, AAR in Rome, October 27, 1930, AAR Archive Microfilm, box 20, reel 5782: "It has been suggested that Janssen's family settle in Florence or some other Italian city and that he visit them occasionally by permission of the director if this can be done without detriment of his academic work. If his stay in Rome is conditional on his family joining him there his resignation must be accepted." Janssen subsequently accepted on the condition that his family would stay in "some Italian City not Rome." Stevens, telegram to Platt November 1, 1930, AAR Archive Microfilm, box 20, reel 5782.

112. Roscoe Guernsey, letter to Vittorio Giannini, June 1, 1932, AAR Archive Microfilm, box 20, reel 5782. This was preceded by a letter from Guernsey to Deems Taylor: "Upon inquiry . . . I learned that Mr. Giannini, to whom the jury voted to offer the fellowship, is now married and in Europe. So it is probably that he is unavailable for our purposes." April 23, 1932, AAR Archive Microfilm, box 20, reel 5782. Giannini then wrote Guernsey: "You remember I told you last year that I was going to be married and I did on June first—1931, therefore I took it for granted that there would not be any trouble on that account, and my wife and I can live together in Rome." May 19, 1932, AAR Archive Microfilm, box 20, reel 5782.

113. See Andrea Olmstead's essay in this volume, "The Rome Prize from Leo Sowerby through David Diamond," for a discussion of all the fellows in musical composition between the initial music fellowships and World War II. Watts's fellowship was cut short because of accusations of "his career of doing nothing" while a fellow at AAR (Sowerby, letter dated June 13, 1925, AAR Archive Microfilm, box 20, reel 5781). Robert Sanders filled Watts's final year, then he received his own fellowship—adding up to a total of four years. Meanwhile, Watts apparently stayed in Europe for a number of years, returning to New York in 1931. See "Wintter Watts Returns to New York after Long Residence Abroad," *Musical America* (December 10, 1931); clipping in AAR Archive Microfilm, box 29, reel 5794.

114. "Competition Opened by American Academy."

115. Copland wrote this in a letter to his friend and fellow composer Israel Citkowitz, May 29, 1930, Copland Collection, Music Division, Library of Congress.

116. *Grove Music Online*, s.v. "Richard Aldrich," by C. Colles and Malcolm Turner, accessed March 11, 2013, http://www.oxfordmusiconline.com/.

117. Information about Clifton's appointment as juror appears in "Herbert Inch Awarded Fellowship in Rome," *Musical America* 51, no. 9 (May 10, 1931): 4.

118. The first documentation for Sowerby's membership on a jury occurs in 1929, with the selection of Normand Lockwood: [Draft Press Release, 1929], AAR Archive Microfilm, box 20, reel 5781.

119. AAR administrative correspondence documents the influence of Sowerby and Carpenter on the appointment of Sanders, including a telegram from Carpenter to Roscoe Guernsey, head of AAR's New York office, stating succinctly: "Sowerby and I recommend appointment of Sanders." January 1, 1925, AAR Archive Microfilm, box 20, reel 5781.

120. Felix Lamond, letter to Charles A. Platt, September 28, 1931, AAR Archives Microfilm, box 33, reel 5799.

121. Initial solicitation of Eastman is documented in a telegram from Lamond to Theodore Miller, where he says he wants to see Mr. Eastman (February 26, 1920, box 33, reel 5799). Eastman's contributions to a string quartet are noted by Lamond in AAR Annual Report 1928, 43. And Eastman's 1931 gift is discussed in a letter of April 10, 1931, from Lamond to Hanson, AAR Archive Microfilm, box 33, reel 5799.

122. The broadcast in 1935 provides an example. Hanson conducted on the WEAF-WJZ networks on a Friday morning, and the concert featured "works of his own as well as of Leo Sowerby and Vittorio Giannini, the most recent winner" ("Behind the Scenes: Listeners to Hear the Opera Auditions in Series of Broadcasts," *New York Times*, December 22, 1935). The *Times* announced a similar arrangement in 1940 ("June Bulletins," *New York Times*, June 9, 1940).

123. "The American Composer," *New York Times*, February 27, 1922.

124. Lamond was organist and choirmaster at Trinity Chapel in New York from 1897 until he left for Rome in 1921 ("Felix Lamond Dies: Director of Music," *New York Times*, March 17, 1940).

125. Horatio Parker, one of the Rome Prize's namesakes, represented a prominent such case, with the oratorio *Hora Novissima* one of his best-known works. Charles Ives was an organist and also wrote choral music on religious texts. Amy Beach wrote a mass, as did John Knowles Paine. The list goes on and on.

126. For more about this topic, see: Amy C. Beal, *New Music, New Allies: American Experimental Music in West Germany from the Zero Hour to Reunification* (Berkeley: University of California Press, 2006). Another study looks at the role of the US government: Emily Abrams Ansari, "Masters of the President's Music: Cold War Composers and the United States Government" (PhD diss., Harvard University, 2009).

Part Three

Two Case Studies in Internationalism

Chapter Five

Forging an International Alliance

Leo Sowerby, Elizabeth Sprague Coolidge, and the Impact of a Rome Prize

Carol J. Oja

Educated in Chicago, the composer Leo Sowerby became the first composer fellow at the American Academy in Rome in 1921 at the age of twenty-six. His solid supporter as he traveled from the shores of Lake Michigan to the Janiculum Hill was the Chicago patron Elizabeth Sprague Coolidge. Zooming in on the professional relationship of this composer and patron reveals much about the networks of financial assistance, aesthetic affinity, and geographic origin that launched the music program at AAR, offering details about how that support affected one particular artistic career. Sowerby's story dominates, but Coolidge repeatedly enters the narrative, initially in Chicago, where both had ties to the Chicago Symphony and to the city's thriving culture of classical music. Before Sowerby headed to Rome, Coolidge programmed his music at her newly formed Berkshire Festival in Massachusetts, and after he had the prize in hand, she continued to connect with him in Italy. Coolidge's loyalty to Sowerby exemplifies how conservative aesthetics joined hands with American wealth and how high-powered transnational alliances could change individual lives. For Sowerby, the Rome fellowship broadened his world exponentially, giving him exposure to composers in Italy and providing an opportunity to travel throughout Europe. No son of privilege, he was well aware of the exceptional prospects that suddenly opened up for him. For Coolidge, supporting this rising musician meant she could champion a hometown boy. At the same time, doing so fit into her overarching mission to shape a meaningful role for herself in a burgeoning transatlantic cultural trade.

No full biography of Sowerby exists, nor does a comprehensive work list.[1] As a result, this case study draws on a variety of primary sources. Sowerby's letters to Coolidge have been preserved in the Music Division of the Library of Congress, providing a valuable account of his youthful impressions. He confessed his dreams to her, writing as if to a mentor more than to a financial underwriter. Yet the differences in their age and status were clear, with the letters consistently addressed to "Dear Mrs. Coolidge" and signed "Leo."[2] Sowerby's ascent as a composer is further revealed in the society and arts pages of the *Chicago Tribune*, and the annual reports of the Academy's music program chronicle his activities as a fellow.[3] Taken together, these sources illuminate the musical experiences that put Sowerby in a position to win the Rome prize. Overall, then, this chapter argues that Sowerby received the first Rome Prize in musical composition because the Chicago networks out of which he emerged intersected with those supporting AAR, and it poses Elizabeth Sprague Coolidge as a crucial force on both fronts. The young American composer who emerges here may have been perceived at times as writing music with a modernist edge, but in fact he was poised between the Gilded Age and the Roaring Twenties.

Introductions: Meet Leo Sowerby and Elizabeth Sprague Coolidge

Leo Sowerby (1895–1968) was born in Grand Rapids, Michigan, and moved to Chicago in 1909 to study piano and organ. Chicago remained his base until he traveled to Rome to accept the composer prize, which was offered to him on the basis of the reputation that his compositions had already achieved."[4] In the late 1910s and early 1920s, Sowerby appeared as one of the bright lights on the American compositional horizon. He was among a substantial cluster of American composers whom I have dubbed elsewhere as a "forgotten vanguard"—that is, figures who were eclipsed by the modernist movement.[5] This group also included Marion Bauer, Emerson Whithorne, Deems Taylor, Randall Thompson, and Howard Hanson. The last two, of course, joined Sowerby in the first class of composers at AAR. He (and they) wrote conservative, often tonal, music conforming to long-standing structures and values, and they did so at a time when exactly the opposite inclinations—newness, experimentation, even audacity—were privileged. In the early 1920s, the compositional scene was shifting at a dazzling pace, with no way of knowing which composers and aesthetic visions would get left in the historiographic dust.

Meanwhile, Elizabeth Sprague Coolidge (1864–1953) was a generation older than her young protégé. In the early twentieth century, she became one of the most prominent music patrons in the United States; she was also an accomplished pianist and had aspirations as a composer. Coolidge's father was Albert Sprague, a founder of Sprague Warner and Company, one of the

Figure 5.1 Painting of Leo Sowerby by Frank Fairbanks (FAAR 1912), 1924. Courtesy of the American Academy in Rome.

country's "most successful wholesale grocery houses," and a leader among Chicago's businessmen.[6] Through him she had strong ties to the Chicago Symphony Orchestra, and after her father's death, she memorialized him with a substantial gift to the CSO, which established pensions and medical benefits for the musicians.[7] Coolidge's husband, the Harvard-trained physician Frederic Shurtleff Coolidge, also died in 1915, and she turned to patronage as a means of finding a productive cultural role. In 1918, she founded the Berkshire Festival of Chamber Music in western Massachusetts, for which she commissioned new works. And in 1925 she established a trust at the Library of Congress, which issued commissions for a series of major compositions over the decades, including Aaron Copland's *Appalachian Spring* and George Crumb's *Ancient Voices of Children.* She also funded construction of the Coolidge Auditorium at the Library of Congress, which remains an active concert facility. Coolidge's ties to Italy were strong, with special support for the work of her close friend Gian Francesco Malipiero, most notably in subsidizing his edition of the music of Claudio Monteverdi.

Thus Sowerby and Coolidge both ended up establishing alliances well beyond the Midwest, but it was in the American heartland that they first discovered complementary transatlantic ambitions.

A Rising Composer in Chicago and Beyond: *Tribune*, October 15, 1921

As a teenager and young adult during the 1910s, Sowerby quickly became a force in the arts wing of Chicago's high society, which became a crucial launching pad for the Rome Prize. His professional story reaches back to November 18, 1913, when at age eighteen he made his debut as a composer with the Chicago Symphony Orchestra, conducted by Glenn Dillard Gunn (1874–1953), the longtime local music critic, conductor, and pianist.[8] The concert included pieces by three Chicagoans: Eric De Lamarter (1880–1953), George Colburn (1878–1921), and Sowerby.[9] Sowerby's contribution was a Concerto for Violin in G Minor, and it inspired heavy-duty praise: "The surprise of the evening," reported the *Chicago Daily Tribune,* "came in the composition of Mr. Sowerby, . . . whom Frederick Stock regards a genius. . . . [His Concerto is] wonderfully brilliant in its passages, broad in its treatment, ever original—a veritable musical prophecy."[10] Not bad press for a teenager on his first excursion with a major orchestra!

Sowerby's career as a composer began to take off not long before the United States entered World War I on April 6, 1917. He served as a soldier in the Eighty-Sixth Division at Camp Grant, Illinois, which opened in 1917 with a primary mandate of training infantry.[11] Soon he became bandmaster and rose to the rank of second lieutenant. "I am playing the clarinet in a band," Sowerby reported in the spring of 1918. "That is," he continued, "when they can't find something else for the band to do, such as hauling cinders, grooming horses, or digging ditches."[12] That summer, he sailed with his unit to France.[13]

The war gave a boost to this rising young midwestern composer. Like many American musical institutions, the Chicago Symphony Orchestra—Sowerby's hometown ensemble—rejected German musical traditions once the United States entered the conflict, even though, as was typical for American orchestras at the time, it had a German-born conductor—in this case Frederick Stock (1872–1942). Native talents benefited enormously. "American composers have their innings this year and for this the war is directly responsible," declared the *New York Times* in October 1917. "The Chicago orchestra will introduce an American work 'at every concert,' including compositions of Edward MacDowell, Edgar Stillman Kelly, Felix Borowski, Adolf Weidig, Eric De Lamarter, Howard Brockway, Henry Hadley, F. G. Converse, Leo Sowerby, John Alden Carpenter, Arne Oldberg and Theodore Otterstrom."[14] Sowerby's military service must also have been a valuable credential for the AAR's selection committee, since so many of the music program's founders had been active in war work.

During the late 1910s and early 1920s, Sowerby received regular premieres by the Chicago Symphony, fueled by consistent advocacy on the part of Stock: in 1915 for *Symphonic Sketch: The Sorrow of Mydath*; in 1918 for *A Set of Four: Suite of Ironics* (which was performed again in 1919); in 1920 for Concerto for Piano in F Major; on a separate concert that same year, for *Comes Autumn Time*; and in 1922 for Symphony no. 1 in E Minor.[15] Sowerby later recalled Stock as "a man from which [*sic*] I was to receive, not harsh criticism, but encouragement."[16] Stock had a history of supporting American composers, which stretched back before the hyperpatriotism of World War I. At the same time, Stock was described by Alfred Frankenstein, a Chicago native who became a progressive art and music critic for the *San Francisco Chronicle*, as "an old-fashioned and conservative conductor."[17] In other words, Stock backed homegrown composers, but he leaned toward those whose music was at the center of the compositional spectrum—or even, perhaps, a bit to the right.[18] That same combination of support for conservative musical values and local talent turned Stock into a steady champion of Sowerby. He programmed the young man's music repeatedly with the CSO, and he became a member of the earliest AAR preselection jury, laying the groundwork for Sowerby to be chosen for the first Rome Prize (see the appendix to this volume for a listing of AAR fellows from 1921 to 1940, with selection juries).[19]

Strikingly, when Sowerby made a statement acknowledging encouragement from Stock, as quoted several sentences ago, it appeared in a publication titled *Fashions of the Hour* and issued in 1929 by Marshall Field's, the well-known Chicago department store.[20] It points up a primary strain in Soweby's story: that is, the degree to which the women of high society in Chicago nurtured his emergence as a composer, thus putting him in a position to be considered for the Rome prize. "A list of distinguished patrons and patronesses will be present at the debut of Leo Sowerby, the Chicago pianist, which takes place this evening at Orchestra hall," reported "Here and There in the Society World," a column in the *Chicago Tribune* in January 1917.[21] The concert included Sowerby's Concerto for Cello and his Concerto for Piano, which apparently had a part for soprano.[22] An orchestra of sixty members drawn from the CSO performed under the direction of Eric DeLamarter, composer and "former *Tribune* musical critic," as the article identified him.[23] This was not a subscription concert of the orchestra but rather a special event, sponsored by a network of affluent and socially prominent individuals. A reviewer of the concert, again reporting on the society page, dubbed "Young Mr. Sowerby" as "clever [and] gifted." Yet the reviewer took exception to his compositional style as too radical, an admonition that was to recur in the Chicago press, where Sowerby was advised to "provide himself with a new set of friends, to take the place of those who tell him that he is a symbol of musical revolt: they will, if he pay[s] attention to them, lead him nowhere save out. The Greenwich Village idea is as futile in music as in any other form of art."[24] Given Sowerby's consistent use of tonality and traditional genres, it is fascinating that, at least in some quarters, he was perceived as a revolutionary.

One month later, in February 1917, Sowerby was again showcased within "Chicago society" and dubbed as "the youthful red headed [*sic*] musical anarchist" by the author "Mme X."[25] He had presented one of his works at "a musical program at a meeting of the Scribblers, an organization that includes many of the younger north side women who are not yet enrolled in the Fortnightly or the Friday Club." Mme X also went on to discuss a separate concert produced by the Friday Club and attended by three hundred, which was "one of its most successful functions." At that event, "one of its members, Mrs. Frederic Coolidge, now of New York but formerly of Chicago, presented her famous Berkshire quartet and a program of chamber music to the club."[26] This article offers yet another glimpse of how Sowerby and Coolidge moved within the same Chicago circles.

The action then shifted to the East Coast, where Sowerby made his New York debut on two programs in March 1918. In this instance, Coolidge played a direct role. One of the concerts featured the Berkshire Quartet, an ensemble that she had founded two years earlier.[27] They performed Sowerby's *Serenade*."[28] A second New York event, presented by the New York Symphony Society with Walter Damrosch conducting, included Sowerby's *Comes Autumn Time*, featuring the French flutist (and recent immigrant) George Barrère.[29] In September 1919, Sowerby's music was programmed at Coolidge's brand-new Berkshire Festival of Chamber Music, where his Trio for Flute, Viola, and Piano in E Minor was performed.[30]

This was the first year of Coolidge's festival, which took place in a newly designed auditorium, dubbed "the Temple," which she had built just outside of

Pittsfield, Massachusetts, at South Mountain.[31] There, historic ties to Chicago's elite ran deep, as the *Chicago Daily Tribune* reported in 1912:

> Every summer many Chicago society folk go to the ever lovely Berkshires in western Massachusetts. Some hie to Lenox; others to Stockbridge, but the larger number flock to Pittsfield, the same coterie returning there year after year. A majority of these are transients living in hotels or rented houses, but there are a half dozen who have roots in the ground, literally and figuratively, through having country places there of greater or lesser extent. . . . Other prominent Chicagoans living in Pittsfield are the Frederic Coolidges. . . . Mrs. Coolidge's parents, Mr. and Mrs. A. A. Sprague, always spend the summer near her.[32]

During these early Berkshire Festivals, Sowerby corresponded regularly with Coolidge, and, at the same time, the pace of his performances picked up substantially, with his music increasingly featured in both Chicago and New York.

One early letter to her discussed a performance of his First Piano Concerto by the Chicago Symphony Orchestra on March 5–6, 1920, conducted by Stock with Sowerby at the piano.[33] "A bomb was most certainly fired into the ranks of the 'old guard,'" Sowerby wrote to Coolidge, "I am so glad to have dedicated it to you."[34] Interestingly, no matter how conservative his idiom, Sowerby identified on some level with the claim to newness valued by his generation. He then aligned himself with the cultural nationalism so basic to American artistic expression right after World War I: "It pleased me to learn that so many musicians who heard the Concerto regarded it as a really American expression, for that is what I most wished to convey in it." He went on: "Mr. Stock urges me to prepare a couple of recital programs and go to [*sic*] concertizing next season, largely with the idea of making my own and other American compositions known. He also thinks I should appear in London playing my Concerto and perhaps something like the Delius Concerto, even before I attempt an appearance in New York."

From a subsequent letter to Coolidge, written several months later, Sowerby appears to have ignored Stock's advice to go abroad. There he announced: "Mr. E. Robert Schmitz has been engaged by Mr. Damrosch to play my concerto with the New York Symphony Orchestra Nov. 7 next."[35] This was the same work performed by Stock in Chicago two months earlier; the New York performance eventually took place in January 1921, in an event again conducted by Damrosch.[36] The pianist E. Robert Schmitz was the founder of the Pro Musica Society. Sowerby could not attend the performance, but he reported to Coolidge: "I have heard from friends who were at the concert that Mr. Schmitz played the solo part excellently, but that there was much to be desired from the orchestra."[37] Sowerby was clearly cruising at full throttle, as he revealed to Coolidge:

> Some friends of mine, I believe, are trying to engineer an engagement for me to play it [his Piano Concerto] later with Mr. Bodansky's Orchestra, but

> I do not know whether anything will come of this or not. Arrangements are pending for me to play it with the St. Louis Orchestra; Mr. Monteux has indicated a desire to have me play it in Boston, though no arrangements have been concluded; interest has also been shown by the conductors of the San Francisco and Los Angeles Symphony Orchestra in having me do the piece; an engagement with the Minneapolis Orchestra is under way; Mr. Gabrilowitsch is also interested, but prefers next season to do my Overture. That will be played several places next season including St. Louis, Detroit, Chicago, and quite possibly, New York.[38]

Soon after Sowerby's concerto emerged in New York, the "Visiting Committee" of the American Academy in Rome traveled to Chicago, staging a fund-raiser in April 1920 at the home of Harold McCormick. Notice of this gathering was reported by "Mme X" and appeared on the same society page that had been chronicling Sowerby's career. It placed women patrons at center stage:

> Chicago women are always involved in good works whose maintenance requires social activities of extensive and delightful nature. Nowhere do they sugar the pill better. They more than sugar it—they gild it. The American Academy at Rome is sending out a call for a million dollar endowment to reestablish it firmly in classic soil. Its agents, famous exponents of art and culture, are coming here to tell us of the aims and achievements of this institution.[39]

That same column included notice of a program of Sowerby's compositions "at the Arts Club last Wednesday evening," reaffirming that his support network was intertwined with the Academy's plans for a music program.[40]

Another Chicago figure linked with both Sowerby and AAR was Mrs. John Alden Carpenter (i.e., Rue Winterbotham Carpenter), wife of the Chicago composer who was on the AAR jury from its inception until 1931. Mrs. Carpenter was a major force in Chicago's artistic life and a member of AAR's fund-raising committee. In 1916, she helped found the very same Arts Club where Sowerby gave his performance, and, as an interior decorator, she designed its rooms. Her vision as a designer represented a fascinating fusion of high society, support for the arts, and exclusivity—the very trinity that constituted the allure of the American Academy in Rome. The Arts Club was "marked by clarity, elegance, and style. . . . . The lounge, open only to members, would be adaptable to lectures and concerts as well as teas, receptions, and parties."[41] That same spring (1920), rumors circulated in Chicago that Sowerby might be heading to Europe. In a society-page article titled "America Will Lose Its Greatest Composer If Sowerby Goes Abroad," the author rued: "It is understood some well meaning, well conditioned patroness of music in the east is contemplating making it possible for him [Sowerby] to start soon for Paris, there to 'continue' his musical studies."[42]

During this period, the relatively new Society for the Publication of American Music (SPAM) appeared in New York. Essentially a composers' collective, it was dedicated to releasing scores by Americans, and its "tentative winners" for 1921 included Sowerby's *Serenade for String Quartet*.[43] Sowerby already had published a number of scores through the Boston Music Company, but this new enterprise promised higher status and broader dissemination. SPAM grew out of the same nexus of patrons and composers as the Rome Prize, with a solid cluster of supporters in Chicago, and it shared an embrace of traditionalism. Its lifetime members included Cyrus McCormick and Elizabeth Coolidge. John Alden Carpenter was the organization's president from 1919 to 1929. And its on-the-ground energizer was Burnet Tuthill (1888–1982), whose father had been the architect of Carnegie Hall; Tuthill, too, had a tie to Coolidge.[44] Nearly two decades later, he authored a major article about Sowerby, which appeared in the *Musical Quarterly* and remains the best source available about him.[45]

Thus the appointment of Leo Sowerby as the first composer fellow at the American Academy in Rome in October 1921 did not appear out of nowhere. Rather, he had been nurtured within women's musical circles in Chicago and by the conductor of the Chicago Symphony Orchestra.[46] Once transported to New York City, he continued to be promoted heavily by Chicago's own Elizabeth Coolidge, at the same time as Walter Damrosch—one of the linchpins in AAR's music program—conducted his compositions. As though to underscore the importance of high society to both Sowerby and AAR, an announcement of his Rome fellowship appeared in *Vanity Fair*.[47]

The Impact of a Rome Prize

What effect did the Rome Prize have on the young Sowerby? During the final sprint to the big announcement on October 1, 1921, he enjoyed an exhilarating stretch, with notices of his music turning up frequently in the *Chicago Tribune* and the *New York Times*.[48] This brief intensification of activity showed how such an appointment could put a young composer in the news. It also demonstrated how Sowerby's field of activity had migrated to the east. In this geographic reorientation, Elizabeth Coolidge and her network of connections remained crucial.

At the same time, Sowerby's music was not universally acclaimed, and reservations about it emerged largely from one critic, Richard Aldrich of the *New York Times*. Since Aldrich was on AAR's selection committee, this turbulence is curious. Aldrich apparently endorsed the "classical" mission of AAR, yet he repeatedly found its first fellow to be lacking in an essential spark.

Concerts including Sowerby's music started off that fall with Coolidge's Berkshire Chamber Music Festival, where he had a wind quintet performed on September 30, and the critique by Aldrich began. A work in three movements, it was judged by Aldrich as showing "less mastery of his thought and of his material than . . . in the striking piano concerto that was played in New York last Winter."[49] The next day—the same one when announcement of the Rome prize took place—Sowerby's Suite for Violin and Piano appeared on Coolidge's program, and it took another hit from Aldrich, who described it as "belonging to his 'first period'" and "hardly worthy of a place in a chamber music festival."[50] Late that same month, the Society for Publication of American Music presented a program in New York of its recent publications, including Sowerby's *Serenade* for string quartet, and several days later, the violinist Ruth Ray performed his "new" Suite for violin and piano.[51] The former passed without remark, and the latter was judged as having "little to say."[52] A few days after that, an Italian pianist, Silvio Scionti, appeared at Town Hall in a program that seemed to honor the Italian American dialogue generated by the newly launched music program at AAR. It included works by Ferruccio Busoni, Alfredo Casella, and Sowerby, whose *Fisherman's Tune* triggered a rebuke from Aldrich. "Mr. Sowerby's piece seems to indicate that Percy Grainger has been visiting Chicago," Aldrich wrote. "It is a tune in the heartiest of folk song manner; a good tune well carried through, harmonized with a somewhat ostentatious avoidance of the obvious."[53] After SPAM announced publication of Sowerby's String Quartet on November 20, Sowerby's brief but intense whirl in the public eye wound down.[54]

One month after the Rome Prize became official, Sowerby wrote Coolidge about his aspirations, speaking with an endearing unpretentiousness. He envisioned a noble calling in his appointment, and he professed a strong sense of national identity. This was the lingering language of wartime, with its demand for absolute loyalty and its commitment to a common cause. The phrase "our art" seems almost poignant, and the feeling was palpable that this young artist felt the United States lacked crucial mechanisms for empowering him and his contemporaries:

> I truly hope that in going to Europe, I may find the intangible something that will be good and worth while [*sic*], not only for myself, but for our art. I am going to work hard to keep my head right where it belongs on my shoulders, and to remain a good and real American, in spirit, as in fact. But I know I shall get in Europe from its wealth of tradition, the very thing I never could get here.[55]

Sowerby set sail on November 3, which he did together with Felix Lamond.[56] Soon after arriving at the Academy, he again contacted Coolidge, confessing hopes for his residency:

> After a short stay of two weeks in Rome, I am convinced that this sojourn in Europe is going to do me a great world of good. . . . The principal thing . . . is

> that I shall come into contact with workers in other branches of art, and this cannot but have a favorable reaction on my thought and work. In America it seems to be difficult not to isolate oneself, so far as one's work is concerned.[57]

He was bursting with thoughts about the professional potential that suddenly lay before him, describing plans to go to "the big festivals" in Paris and England:

> I am expected to travel about six months of each year if I so desire, so that I can keep in touch with everything of importance going on in Europe. If I had simply been expected to come here to Rome, which after all, is not a great musical center, to work without being able to go about, I shouldn't have been interested at all in the idea, I am sure.

He had a small caveat: "The one thing I do not like here, and which I shall endeavor to free myself from, is the apparent importance ascribed to social affairs—teas and what not."

What did the next three years in Rome yield for Leo Sowerby? A sense of his experiences emerges through the annual reports filed by Felix Lamond and from intermittent coverage in the press. In a broad sense, it serves as a window on the activities of AAR's earliest fellows during their sojourn abroad.

Composition lay at the core of this residency, and Sowerby clearly had a strong work ethic. He wrote some fifteen pieces, including five for orchestra, a string quartet, and a violin sonata.[58] Surveying all this music is beyond the scope of this essay. But a sense of Sowerby's style from this period can be gained from a representative piece, his *Rhapsody for Chamber Orchestra*, composed in 1922.[59] The work shows Sowerby's deep commitment to European models of the late nineteenth and early twentieth century, affirming the allegiance to classical values and historic precedent that AAR promoted. The very notion of a "rhapsody" brought with it a historical grounding. The work is thoroughly tonal, with instruments of the orchestra employed according to traditional norms. Shaped in three contiguous parts, the *Rhapsody* has "unmistakable hints of American folk-music and (especially) jazz," as one writer has put it.[60] The composers Sowerby identified with—at least in terms of this piece—included César Franck and Vincent d'Indy, both turn-of-the-century French figures. Sowerby also seemed to connect with the British tradition of setting folk songs.[61] In fact, Burnet Tuthill believed that "from the beginning of his composing," Sowerby had "possessed . . . characteristic turns of melody."[62] Tuthill went on at some length about the musical traits of these melodies. He also perceived a strain of national authenticity:

> The tunes have a lilt and syncopation that make them akin to folk or popular music and have a quality that definitely marks them as American. . . . There is in these tunes a rhythmic crispness, a simplicity of tonality and a frankness and directness that belong to our native soil. . . . His melodies of contrasting

type have a wistful flow. . . . In some of these characteristics of melody there is, perhaps, a distant resemblance to Brahms in some of his extended and continuing phrases, and they are characteristics which postpone the ready apprehension and understanding of his music. One must exercise powers of concentration and memory to follow such melodies through the formal construction of Sowerby's music; not that there is any unusual complexity to the form, quite the contrary in fact, but that the melodies themselves are far from easy to commit to memory at a first hearing.[63]

Much of this description could also be applied to the *Rhapsody*. It revels in tunes, and it exhibits a sure sense of craft, showing a composer thoroughly on his feet. At the same time, it took no chances and hewed closely to the musical language Sowerby had inherited. In an era when neoclassicism was beginning to captivate composers and visual artists in both Europe and America, Sowerby avoided any hint of the "neo," sticking instead with a more Brahmsian, yet somehow American, version of "classicism."

While the *Rhapsody* did not get premiered until 1924 in Chicago, others among Sowerby's works were gaining an audience in Rome and elsewhere in Europe. This was possible because of mechanisms put in place at AAR by Lamond, who helped young composers make invaluable connections (see the appendix to this essay for a provisional list of Sowerby's performances abroad during his fellowship). Over the course of three years in Rome, Sowerby had works performed on nearly two-dozen concerts there, as well as in other parts of Europe.

This intense activity began at the start of Sowerby's residency. In his report "for the year ending September 30, 1922," Lamond proudly proclaimed Sowerby's progress and enumerated the ways in which he (Lamond) had cultivated a community of composers, reaching down from the Academy's Roman hill to embrace the artistic life of the city. All this added up to career facilitation for the young fellows:

Leo Sowerby completed in January, 1922, his first important work written after his arrival in Rome—a sonata for piano and violin. A recital was given at the Villa Chiaraviglio early in February, at which this sonata was played. A set of three piano pieces and a quintet for flute, oboe, clarinet, bassoon and horn (all composed by Mr. Sowerby) were also performed, the participants being Mario Corti, Leo Sowerby, Felix Lamond, and a quintet of wind instrument players from the Augusteo orchestra. A large number of Italian composers were present. The quintet was afterwards performed in Rome by the Società Filarmonica at the Sala Sgambati by the Quintetto di Santa Cecilia.[64]

This was the same Wind Quintet performed at the Berkshire Festival in the fall of 1921 and published by SPAM, and the "set of three piano pieces" was "Settings of Three Folk-Tunes from Somerset," a work dating from 1915.[65]

This first concert of Sowerby's music at AAR, which actually took place on January 23, 1922 (not in "early February," as Lamond stated), also marked the debut of the "Musical Circle," an innovation of which Lamond was particularly proud, calling it "a feature of Roman musical life."[66] Italian composers and performers consistently visited AAR to take part, and the events included "discussion by our Fellows and the composers who were present of the new works which have been performed."[67] A reporter for London's *Musical Times* noted that this first concert drew "about a hundred persons, including the principal musicians of Rome."[68] According to Lamond, the participants encompassed an impressive range of Italian composers: "[Italo] Montemezzi (1875–1952), [Renzo] Bossi (1883–1965), [Alfredo] Casella (1883–1947), [Vincenzo] Tommasini (1878–1950), [Francesco] Santoliquido (1883–1971), [Giacomo] Setaccioli (1868–1925), [Domenico] Alaleona (1881–1928), [Bernardino] Molinari (1880–1952), [Ottorino] Respighi (1879–1936), and Nina [*sic*] Boulanger (1887–1979)."[69]

Interestingly, these Italian musicians were not contemporaries of the American fellows at the Academy but rather their elders. They were potential advisers, not peers. And it is hard not to point out Lamond's error with the first name of Nadia Boulanger—the only female professional who appears to have entered the musical realm of AAR during this early period.

The "Roman Circle" continued an impulse that dated back at least to the "all-American" concert at the Augusteo in March 1919 and maintained a firm emphasis on the "classics." Late in the 1920s, Lamond affirmed: "The policy of devoting one-half of each program to classical compositions and one-half to works of the modern school has been continued with good results at the concerts at the Chiaraviglio."[70] Thus these performances yielded yet another means of keeping a focus on absorbing tradition as much as on supporting creativity, and this same bifurcation underpinned the scope of summer travels, as will soon be discussed.

Elizabeth Sprague Coolidge, with Sowerby at her side, played a key role in the development of the Academy's concert programs.[71] On May 2 and 5, 1923, "through the generosity of Mrs. F. S. Coolidge," two concerts of chamber music were presented at the American Academy, which transported works from the Berkshire Festival to the hills of Rome.[72] Sowerby's Trio for Piano, Flute, and Violin was on the program.[73] This was an ambitious undertaking, and once again, contemporary music mixed with social pleasures:

> These concerts attracted musicians from France, Belgium, England and Spain, and they aroused much interesting discussion on modern music which was of great value to our three Fellows [by then, Randall Thompson had joined the group]. The executants were Lionel Tertis, London; Gilberto Crepax, Bologna; Giuseppe Brugnoli, Parma; Corti, Casella and Sowerby of Rome, and the Quartetto pro Arts [*sic*], of Bruxelles, all of whom were engaged by Mrs. Coolidge. These concerts were followed by a Garden Party at the Villa Chiaraviglio in honor of Mrs. Coolidge and the visiting musicians.

Lamond singled out another concert on Sunday, May 3, which included new Italian chamber music, calling it "memorable": "Twenty-four eminent musicians were present, including Casella, Malipiero, Manuel di [*sic*] Falla and Kurt Schindler. The eager working out of theories of these modern composers was very instructive to our fellows; it was a lesson in what to imitate as well as what to avoid. This recital was complimentary to Mrs. Coolidge. Mr. Schindler described the meeting as the most interesting chamber music gathering he had ever attended."[74]

For Coolidge, this trip to Italy was only the second European junket she had taken since her honeymoon in 1892. The first of these journeys occurred the previous year (1922), and Coolidge's biographer Cyrilla Barr has observed that it signaled "almost an annual pilgrimage" up until World War II, marking "the beginning of her love affair with Italy."[75] Not previously recognized, however, is how Coolidge's Italian "affair" intertwined so closely with the inception of the music program at AAR; her close collaborations with Italian composers got a boost through contacts made within AAR's "Roman circle."

Coolidge's next major set of concerts in Rome appears to have occurred in May 1926, two years after Sowerby had returned to Chicago, when she subsidized two programs "with artists from the United States, Paris, and Venice," as Lamond reported.[76] Once again, the works "had obtained the prizes awarded at the Berkshire Festivals, and were most interesting to the large audiences that were present." The two American composers represented were Frederick Jacobi and David Stanley Smith. Neither was a fellow at AAR, but both represented a conservative aesthetic. Another such concert took place in 1931.[77]

Besides these concert opportunities in Rome, another major component of the fellowships for Sowerby and his colleagues came through funding to support travel across Europe. The result was an annual Grand Tour, which was designed for career enhancement, involving visits to international festivals and opportunities to make connections with European composers and publishers.

"The period of travel commenced in June," reported Lamond in 1922.[78] He undertook this journey together with Sowerby and Howard Hanson, AAR's second composer fellow, and they embarked on an elaborate itinerary. The trio started out in Venice, where they observed "the arrangement of classes and plan of study of the Accademia Marcello." For Hanson, as future director of the Eastman School of Music, this must have been especially valuable. Then they moved on to Vienna to conduct business: "Several conferences were held with the authorities of the great publishing house 'Universal Edition,' and as a result a large number of modern orchestral scores were added to our library. Discussions were also held regarding the publication of works of our Fellows." These "discussions" eventually yielded a small series of imprints by AAR fellows, starting with Sowerby's Sonata for Violin and Piano, which Universal issued in 1929.[79]

The next stop was Salzburg for an International Chamber Music Festival—the first such undertaking since World War I. Sowerby's Violin Sonata appeared on the program, and the only other American work came from the Swiss immigrant Ernest Bloch, yielding yet another sign of Sowerby's prestige at the time. This was the same piece that had been performed on Sowerby's first concert at AAR the previous February. Once again, the Italian violinist Mario Corti performed, with Sowerby at the piano. "This festival will certainly come to be regarded as historic," Lamond wrote in his report.

> For the first time since the war, several hundred composers, musicians, artists and critics of nearly every European country came together for the purpose of exchange of information and listening to new music. All found a common ground in their art at Salzburg. New compositions were played at seven concerts by composers of eleven countries, and it is gratifying to relate that America was represented by Leo Sowerby's new sonata for violin and piano.[80]

While Lamond recounted that Sowerby's piece was "most enthusiastically received," a different assessment appeared in the *Musical Times,* which described Sowerby's sonata as "well-written but not overwhelmingly original."[81] It was dubbed "the only hundred percent American work."

Sowerby, Lamond, and Hanson then spent two weeks at a "Mozart revival at the Mozarteum." Next they stopped in Munich for a festival of Wagner operas. They then took a trip down the Rhine to Cologne in pursuit of further career enhancement, seeking "valuable information as to the publication of musical works" by "the firm of Tischner and Jageberg." The next stop came in Bonn, where they made "a pilgrimage" to the birthplace of Beethoven, and "from thence . . . through Holland to London." The group then divided, with Lamond and Sowerby remaining in England, and Hanson traveling to Sweden.

In England, Lamond revealed his affinity for "modern English composers," which Sowerby clearly shared.[82] They attended a massive choral festival in Gloucester in early September, which reportedly sold some eighteen thousand tickets.[83] This was an event close to Lamond's core identity as a musician. He shaped his career within the English church-music tradition, and choral music not only turned up in visits to music festivals during subsequent years, but it also played a role in who was chosen for AAR composer fellowships. After the Gloucester Festival, Sowerby went to London "for the purpose of rehearsing his new sonata"—that is, the same one heard earlier that year in Rome and at the Salzburg Festival. It had a performance by the American violinist Amy Neill, with Sowerby at the piano, at Wigmore Hall on October 10, 1922.[84] He and Lamond also journeyed to the Leeds Festival, which placed contemporary British choral and orchestral music alongside the classics.[85]

For a young American composer in 1922, this trip added up to an extraordinary education, and Sowerby's first year at AAR as a whole must have brought a considerable sense of achievement. In addition to five performances in Rome since his arrival there, Sowerby had enjoyed renditions of his Violin Sonata in Salzburg and London.

In the summer of 1923, Sowerby, Hanson, and Lamond—together with that year's new arrival Randall Thompson—went again to the Salzburg Festival. Lamond's account of this event, which appeared to include no music by an American from the Academy, launched a recurrent ritual of decrying the evils of modernism:

> Musicians from all parts of the world, including many Americans, assembled to hear chamber music of the ultra-modern type. We learned that the idea of the Festival was that it should be "path-breaking," we found it "heart-breaking." Judging from the works given it seems to make little difference whether these paths seek out beauty or not. In our opinion much of the music was of the terrifying and unlovely Bolshevist type.[86]

That year the quartet moved on to Paris "with the object of examining the work of the American School at Fontainebleau." Then they split up: Hanson took off for Scotland, Thompson went to Exmoor in England, and Sowerby to the south of France. They reconvened in Worcester at the beginning of September for a festival at the Cathedral. With its focus on the beauties of the past, this event provided a balm after the agitations of Salzburg: "Here the chief point of interest was the opportunity to study the works of the old English writers, especially the fine unaccompanied music of Byrd."[87] Their journeys concluded in London, and Lamond wound up his report by enthusing about the value of travel, which he predicted to be "a continual source of inspiration in years to come."[88]

In 1924, the fellows traveled separately. In Sowerby's case, he made "a journey through Dalmatia, Germany, Belgium, France and England visiting the principal musical institutions in each country" before returning home to Chicago. Hanson spent time in London and Berlin before heading off to direct the Eastman School in Rochester. Meanwhile Thompson and the newest fellow, Wintter Watts, spent time in northern Italy before attending the Salzburg Festival.[89]

As Lamond shooed his first two birds out of the nest in 1924, he concluded his report with an endorsement of their experience under his stewardship: "The Fellows [i.e., Sowerby and Hanson] feel very strongly that their years in Rome have put them in a position to go forward freely and boldly, so that they can express themselves in their compositions in their own way."[90]

Sowerby, in turn, talked with local reporters in Chicago that same September, where he resumed his position teaching composition and theory at the American Conservatory. He confirmed that his experience at AAR "had been a marvelously stimulating one from every point of view" and that he had "come into close personal contact with the best-known composers, not only in Italy, but all over the continent and in England."[91] Upon his arrival in Rome, he had "found an amazing ignorance, even in musical circles" about American music, but felt that his larger works "were received with acclaim which, in many centers, had never before been granted to American compositions." Not long after arriving home Sowerby planned "to make a flying trip to Pittsfield, Mass., to perform his sonata for violoncello and piano with Hans Kindler, cellist, September 18 at the Berkshire Chamber Music Festival, organized by Mrs. F. S. Coolidge"—thus continuing a key alliance.[92]

A letter from Sowerby to Coolidge, written just five months after he returned home, affirmed that he had internalized Lamond's hopes for the fellows and that his professional network from Rome remained intact. "I am very much looking forward to the festivals in Washington, and am sure that we shall all enjoy them just as much as we have those in Pittsfield," he wrote. He referred to an extension of the Berkshire Music Festivals at the Library of Congress, where his and Coolidge's connections with Italian composers would be reaffirmed and furthered:

> I am particularly looking forward to this years' festival on account of Pizzetti's new Trio, and on account of his coming. Corti writes me lots about it, and I know that they are all looking to his coming here to help Americans realize that a serious school of symphonic composition exists in the land of Puccini and Mascagni. Corti looks forward to Pizzetti's having the opportunity to go about giving lectures.

In concluding his letter, Sowerby elaborated on Coolidge's continuing ties to the American Academy, and in the process he reflected on the pleasures of his own stint in Rome:

> How much you will look forward to your return to Rome this spring! I so often think of Italy, or Rome, and of the Academy, and particularly of the dear Lamonds, and wish it were not so difficult to drop back there for a month or so; I am very busy here, and very happy in my work, which I have arranged so that I have plenty of liberty, and considerable free time for composition, but I must admit to having a big feeling of "nostalgia" whenever I think of my three years in the land of blue skies and warm hearts, which were so full of joy and of work accomplished. I rejoice that such people as Respighi, Corti, Castelnuovo, etc. are my firm friends, and that they do not forget me, for I hear from them constantly.[93]

⋆ ⋆ ⋆

Sowerby and others among the forgotten vanguard retained a reasonable degree of visibility until the end of World War II. Most notably, when the first Pulitzer Prizes in Music were awarded, Sowerby and Howard Hanson—AAR's first composer fellows—won two of the first four awards. The Pulitzer in composition was first granted in 1943. William Schuman—a composer of a younger generation—won that year. Hanson did so in 1944 for his Symphony no. 4,

Aaron Copland in 1945 for *Appalachian Spring*, and Sowerby in 1946 for *The Canticle of the Sun*, a cantata with orchestra.

With the passage of time, the conservative artistic values and patronage network that sustained Sowerby in the early 1920s have been dispelled by shifting artistic and institutional winds. Since World War II, Sowerby's reputation as a composer has come to rest largely with his organ and choral compositions, which have become a mainstay of the Middle American Protestant church repertory, and he counts at least one major American composer—Ned Rorem—among his students.[94] His orchestral and chamber music, which in the early 1920s stood at the core of his output, has since fallen almost completely out of view.

Appendix

Leo Sowerby: Performances in Europe, 1921–24 (Provisional List)

The following gives a sense of the dissemination of Sowerby's music in Europe during his fellowship at AAR. It is a work in progress. Specific performance dates are not always known, nor are first names of performers. Unconfirmed performance details are indicated with the designation [?]. Unless otherwise stated, all performance information comes from Lamond's annual reports, newspaper reviews sometimes supplement his narrative, and dates of composition come from Tuthill.

January 23, 1922: AAR (Villa Chiaraviglio)
First Concert of AAR's "Musical Circle"

Works included:	Sonata for Violin and Piano (1922)[95] *Settings of Three Folk Tunes from Somerset* (1915) Quintet for flute, oboe, clarinet, bassoon, and horn (1916)
Performers:	Mario Corti (violin), Leo Sowerby (piano), Felix Lamond (piano), and a quintet of wind instrument players from the Augusteo Orchestra.

February[?] 1922: Sala Sgambati (Rome) by Società Filarmonica

Work included:	Quintet for flute, oboe, clarinet, bassoon, and horn (1916)
Performers:	Quintetto di Santa Cecilia

April 24, 1922: AAR

Works included:	"Musicale" of compositions by Sowerby and Hanson; no titles given

Performers: Sowerby (piano) and Howard Hanson (piano?); Signor Bozza (instrument?); Madame Lenart (voice)

May 1922: AAR
Works included: *Six Songs*
Gigue and Gavotte for Violin and Piano[96]
Performers: none listed

May 31, 1922: AAR
Concert in connection with a visit by King Victor Emmanuel III
Works included: *Gigue* for Violin and Piano[97]
Performers: Mario Corti (violin); Sowerby (piano)

August 10, 1922: Salzburg International Chamber Music Festival
Work included: Sonata for Violin and Piano (1922)
Performers: Mario Corti (violin); Sowerby (piano)

October 10, 1922: Wigmore Hall (London)[98]
Work included: Sonata for Violin and Piano (1922)
Performers: Amy Neill (violin); Sowerby (piano)

November 1922: AAR (Villa Chiaraviglio)
Works included: Sonata for Violin and Piano (1922)
Performers: Mario Corti (violin); Signora Corti (piano)

January 1923: Sala Sgambati (Rome)
Works included: Sonata for Violin and Piano (1922)[99]
Amy Neill (violin); other performers unknown

March 8, 1923: AAR, Villa Aurelia (Rome)
Work included: Suite (*From the Northland*) (1923)
Performer: Sowerby (piano)

April 8, 1923: Augusteo (Rome)
Work included: *Ballata* for two pianos and orchestra (1922)[100]
Performers: Sowerby (piano), Carlo Zecchi (piano), Augusteo Orchestra (100 players); Albert Coates (conductor)

May 2 or 5, 1923: AAR
Berkshire Festival Concerts, sponsored by Elizabeth Sprague Coolidge
Work included: Trio for Piano, Flute, and Violin[101]
Performers: Members of Pro Arte Quartet, possibly also Alfredo Casella or Lionel Tertis

May 17, 1923: AAR

Work included:	*Ballata* for two pianos and orchestra (1922)
Performers:	Sowerby (piano), Carlo Zecchi (piano); Augusteo Orchestra (65 players); Howard Hanson, conductor

September 27, 1923: Singakademie, Berlin

Work included:	Concerto for Piano and Orchestra (1919)
Performers:	Sowerby (piano); Berlin Philharmonic; Theodor Spiering (conductor)

March 1924: Concert with the Spanish Academy in Rome

Work included:	Sonata for Piano and Violoncello (1920)
Performers:	Gaspar Cassadó (cello); Sowerby (piano)

March 27, 1924: AAR

Work included:	String Quartet in D Minor (1923–24)
Performers:	Pro Arte Quartet

April 1924: Florence

Work included:	No titles given [Sonata for Violin and Piano?]
Performers:	Mario Corti (violin); Sowerby (piano)
	Concert presented by Maestro Castelnuovo-Tedesco

April 1924: Paris, Societé musicale independente[102]

Work included:	Quintet for flute, oboe, clarinet, bassoon, and horn (1916)
Performers:	unknown

May 1924: Rome, Italian Chamber Music Festival

Organized by Alfredo Casella

Work included:	Quintet for flute, oboe, clarinet, bassoon, and horn (1916)
Performers:	unknown

May 27, 1924: AAR[103]

Work included:	Suite for Orchestra (*From the Northland*) (1923)
Performers:	Rome Symphony Orchestra (75 players); Howard Hanson (conductor)

Notes

1. Most dates given here for Sowerby's works are drawn from a profile by Burnet C. Tuthill, which remains the main source of information for Sowerby's early years: "Leo Sowerby," *Musical Quarterly* 24, no. 3 (1938): 249–64. Tuthill's article appears to be the source for later work lists, including the one in *Grove Music Online*, s.v. "Leo Sowerby," by

Ronald Stalford and Michael Meckna, accessed February 11, 2012, http://www.oxfordmusiconline.com/.

2. The correspondence of Sowerby and Coolidge is contained within box 92 of the Coolidge Collection, Music Division, Library of Congress. Since all the Sowerby-Coolidge letters cited in this essay come from that same box, I will not repeat the location in subsequent footnotes. As of this writing, the financial details of Coolidge's support of Sowerby remain unknown. In a letter dated August 8, 1920 (that is, before receiving the Rome Prize), he wrote to her: "Please allow me to thank you most sincerely for your letter of July twenty-second, with your renewed offer of assistance in the furtherance of my compositional activities. I do not need to say to you again how very much I appreciate your interest, nor how much your offer serves to stimulate my work by relieving me of concern over petty financial troubles." Another letter from March 28, 1921, states: "May I venture to ask you whether you would be willing to send me at this time the other half of the second year's amount of the money you so generously offered me. I make bold to ask for it in this way, as you wished me to be free to let you know whenever it would be of value to me. I wish to use it mainly in helping along with my Symphony—parts etc. and leisure time to complete it."

3. Digitized access to the *Chicago Tribune* has provided a key resource for this case study.

4. Tutill, "Leo Sowerby," 250–51. Tuthill provides information about Sowerby's musical education, writing that he studied piano in Chicago with Calvin Lampert and composition and theory with Arthur Olaf Andersen, "who remained his only other teacher of musical theory."

5. See Carol J. Oja, "A Forgotten Vanguard: The Legacy of Marion Bauer, Frederick Jacobi, Emerson Whithorne, and Louis Gruenberg," in Oja, *Making Music Modern: New York in the 1920s* (New York: Oxford University Press, 2000), 155–76.

6. Cyrilla Barr, *Elizabeth Sprague Coolidge: American Patron of Music* (New York: Schirmer Books, 1998), 110.

7. Not long before his death, Albert Sprague had established a pension plan for employees of Sprague Warner, so Elizabeth paid tribute with a parallel gesture to the CSO (ibid., 110–11).

8. Gunn wrote a preview article about the concert: "Chicago Leads in Supporting the Native Composer," *Chicago Daily Tribune*, November 2, 1913. A very brief biography of Gunn appears in the guide for the "Glenn Dillard Gunn Collection," Music Division, Library of Congress, 2005, http://memory.loc.gov/service/music/eadxmlmusic/eadpdfmusic/2002/mu002001.pdf, p. 3: "Glenn Dillard Gunn, 1874–1963, music critic and pianist; music critic of Chicago tribune, Chicago herald examiner, and Washington times-herald."

9. "George Colburn" and "Eric DeLamarter" in Theodore Baker, *Baker's Biographical Dictionary*, 7th ed., rev. Nicolas Slonimsky (New York: Schirmer Books, 1984), 482. In the appendix to this volume, note that DeLamarter served on the AAR jury in 1938, during a year when he might have stood in as a temporary replacement for Sowerby.

10. E. B. K., "Gunn Conducts Concert of American Music," *Chicago Daily Tribune*, November 19, 1913. Tuthill, "Leo Sowerby," 261, dates this concerto as having been composed in 1913, with a revision in 1924, and he lists it as being in manuscript. Also, Sowerby's Violin Concerto is listed in "World Premieres," Chicago Symphony Orchestra, accessed February 13, 2012 http://cso.org/uploadedFiles/8_about/History_-_Rosenthal_archives/world_premieres.pdf.

11. Tuthill, "Leo Sowerby," 250; also "Orchestra Season in Closing Weeks . . . Music by Leo Sowerby," *New York Timees*, March 3, 1918. Information about Camp Grant

is available at "Gjenvick-Gjønvik Archives: Social and Cultural History," accessed February 11, 2012, http://www.gjenvick.com/Military/ArmyArchives/TrainingCenters/CampGrant/APictorialHistory/1918/index.html.

12. Sowerby, as quoted in "Orchestra Season in Closing Weeks."

13. Tuthill, "Leo Sowerby," 250.

14. "News and Notes: A New Season for the Orchestras," *New York Times*, October 14, 1917. Times were tough overall for German musicians in the United States immediately after World War I. Stock faced issues because his application for US citizenship had lapsed, a situation that forced him to step down as conductor of the Chicago Symphony on August 17, 1918, returning to the podium six months later. He became a citizen in May 1919. During Stock's forced absence, Eric DeLamarter replaced him as conductor of the CSO. Dena J. Epstein, "Frederick Stock and American Music," *American Music* 10, no. 1 (1992): 26.

In a parallel but far more dramatic situation, Karl Muck, who had been conductor of the Boston Symphony Orchestra since 1912, was arrested in March 1918 under the Alien Enemies Act and eventually deported. Muck "was accused of refusing a request to play 'The Star Spangled Banner'" during a BSO concert in Providence in 1917. "While claiming to be a citizen of the Swiss Republic," the *New York Times* reported, Muck "was born in Bavaria in 1859, before the foundation of the German Empire. And under the interpretation of the President's proclamation . . . any man born in Germany before the empire was established is amenable to the regulations under that document." "Arrest Karl Muck as an Enemy Alien," *New York Times*, March 26, 1918. This article recounted the shock of Muck's wife when her husband was arrested. Apparently he was taken completely by surprise, late at night. The *New York Times* reported that "Mrs. Muck spoke with a marked German accent."

15. This list of performances is synthesized from various sources, especially coverage of Sowerby in the *Chicago Daily Tribune*; a list of CSO performances of his music in Epstein, "Frederick Stock," 44; and Chicago Symphony Orchestra, "World Premieres." Tuthill, "Leo Sowerby," 261, dates the works listed here as follows: *Comes Autumn Time* (1916; published by Boston Music Corporation, 1927); Concerto for Piano no. 1 in F (1919; in manuscript); *A Set of Four* (1917; published by the Eastman School of Music, 1931); Symphony no. 1 in E Minor (1920–21; in manuscript).

16. Leo Sowerby, "Frederick Stock, an Appreciation," Marshall Field & Co., *Fashions of the Hour* (autumn 1929): 23 (cited in Epstein, "Frederick Stock," 22).

17. As quoted in Rita H. Mead, "A Conversation with Alfred Frankenstein about Henry Cowell's *New Music*," in *A Celebration of American Music: Words and Music in Honor of H. Wiley Hitchcock*, ed. Richard Crawford, R. Allen Lott, and Carol J. Oja (Ann Arbor: University of Michigan Press, 1990), 319. Also cited in Epstein, "Frederick Stock," 21.

18. Regarding Stock's conservatism, Epstein chronicles how his tastes became more liberal as the 1920s unfolded. She quotes him as declaring in 1930: "For the first time in history, Americans are writing better symphonic music than Europeans. I refer to such composers as Carpenter and Sowerby of Chicago, and to Copland, Sessions, Ruggles, and the League of Composers group in New York." Stock, as quoted in Alfred V. Frankenstein, "Twenty-Five Years a Conductor," *Review of Reviews* 81 (January 1930): 96 (cited in Epstein, "Frederick Stock," 28). As Epstein notes, these were "hardly the conservatives Stock was credited with favoring."

19. [Felix Lamond], draft letter to Mr. William H. Murphy, February 2, 1920, AAR Archive Microfilm, box 33 reel 5799. It should be noted, however, that Stock seems to have taken part in a preselection jury and appears not to have been part of the group that actually appointed Sowerby.

20. Ibid.

21. "Here and There in the Society World," *Chicago Daily Tribune*, January 18, 1917.

22. Tuthill, "Leo Sowerby," 262, does not list an early cello concerto by Sowerby, but he does include one dated 1929–34 and in manuscript. In Stalford and Meckna, "Leo Sowerby," however, a Cello Concerto is dated 1914–16.

23. "Here and There in the Society World." Like Sowerby, DeLamarter was trained as an organist. During 1918–19, he took over the CSO during Stock's absence. See "Eric DeLamarter," in *Grove's Dictionary of Music and Musicians: American Supplement*, ed. Waldo Selden Pratt (New York: Macmillan, 1947), 187. DeLamarter was also "Sowerby's boss at Fourth Presbyterian Church [in Chicago]," according to Francis J. Crociata, "Leo Sowerby: The 100th Anniversary Celebration of an American Original," *The American Organist* 29, no. 5 (1995): 50.

24. F. D., "Leo Sowerby's Program: Opera-News," *Chicago Daily Tribune*, January 19, 1917.

25. Mme X, "News of Chicago Society," *Chicago Daily Tribune*, February 25, 1917.

26. Ibid.

27. Both performances are announced in "Hofmann Cheered Playing Our Anthem," *New York Times*, March 11, 1918. The Berkshire Quartet existed from 1916 to 1920.

28. "Orchestra Season in Closing Weeks . . . Music by Leo Sowerby," *New York Times*, March 3, 1918. Tuthill, "Leo Sowerby," 262, dates the composition of this *Serenade* as 1916. In a letter of November 16, 1920, Sowerby told Coolidge, "I wrote [the Serenade] for you."

29. The *New York Times* dubbed *Comes Autumn Time* "more congenial and even more conventional than the recent 'Serenade.'" "Hofmann Cheered Playing Our Anthem," *New York Times*, March 11, 1918.

30. Richard Aldrich, "American Works in Music Festival," *New York Times*, September 27, 1918. Tuthill, "Leo Sowerby," 262, dates Sowerby's Trio as 1919 (in manuscript).

31. Barr, *Elizabeth Sprague Coolidge*, 134–52, chronicles the beginning of the Berkshire Festivals.

32. Mme X, "News of the Society World," *Chicago Daily Tribune*, September 22, 1912.

33. The performance does not appear to have been reviewed in the *Chicago Daily Tribune*, but it was listed in the paper's "The Music Calendar," February 29, 1920, with Sowerby identified as the soloist. This was the same concerto conducted in Chicago by DeLamarter in January 1917.

34. Sowerby, letter to Coolidge, March 16, 1920. All quotations in this paragraph come from this same letter.

35. Sowerby, letter to Coolidge, May 7, 1920.

36. Richard Aldrich, "Music," *New York Times*, January 24, 1921.

37. Sowerby, letter to Coolidge, March 28, 1921.

38. Sowerby, letter to Coolidge, May 7, 1920. The "overture" must have been *Comes Autumn Time* of 1916.

39. Mme X, "News of Chicago Society," *Chicago Daily Tribune*, April 11, 1920. This section of the column is titled "Hear Plea for American Academy."

40. Ibid.

41. James M. Wells, *Portrait of an Era: Rue Winterbotham Carpenter and the Arts Club of Chicago, 1916–1931* (Chicago: Arts Club of Chicago, 1986), n.p.; as quoted in Howard Pollack, *Skyscraper Lullaby: The Life and Music of John Alden Carpenter* (Washington: Smithsonian Institution Press, 1995), 36.

42. W. L. Hubbard, "American Will Lose Its Greatest Composer If Sowerby Goes Abroad," *Chicago Daily Tribune*, March 6, 1920.

43. "Honor Huss and Sowerby," *New York Times,* March 20, 1921. "Huss" was Henry Holden Huss. Sowerby's Serenade in G Major: Quartet for Strings was "Published for the Society for the Publication of American Music by G. Schirmer [NY]" in 1921. SPAM had been organized in 1919, and its composer members paid dues of one dollar a year. See William Merkel Holman, "A Comprehensive Performance Project in Clarinet Literature with a History of the Society for the Publication of American Music, 1919–1969" (DMA essay, University of Iowa, 1977). As already chronicled, the *Serenade* had been performed by Coolidge's Berkshire Quartet in New York City in March 1918.

44. Barr, *Elizabeth Sprague Coolidge,* 119.

45. Tuthill, "Leo Sowerby."

46. The Chicago network was clearly tight. As one striking example: when Elizabeth Coolidge planned a concert to dedicate the concert hall that she donated to the Library of Congress—the "Coolidge Auditorium"—she invited Stock to bring the Chicago Symphony. The event took place on November 24, 1925 (Epstein, "Frederick Stock," 27).

47. "A Group of the Younger American Composers," *Vanity Fair,* September 1923, 49. This was a photo spread, which included also Frederick Jacobi, Emerson Whithorne, Deems Taylor, A. Walter Kramer, Edward Royce, Louis Gruenberg, and Leo Ornstein.

48. "Chicago Composer Gets Appointment to the Prix de Rome," *Chicago Daily Tribune,* October 15, 1921.

49. Richard Aldrich, "Play Prize Work of H. Waldo Warner," *New York Times,* October 1, 1921. Leo Sowerby, *Quintet for Flute, Oboe, Clarinet, Horn, and Bassoon* (New York: G. Schirmer and the Society for the Publication of American Music, 1931). Tuthill, "Leo Sowerby," 262, dates this piece as being composed in 1916.

50. Richard Aldrich, "Composers Play Their Own Works," *New York Times,* October 2, 1921. Tuthill, "Leo Sowerby," 262, also dates the *Suite* as 1916; it had been published by the Boston Music Company in 1918.

51. "Music Publishing Society Meets," *New York Times,* October 29, 1921; and "Ruth Ray Plays New Suite: Violinist Heard in Leo Sowerby's Work Dedicated to Her," *New York Times,* November 4, 1921. The word "new" in the second review's headline raises questions. Tuthill, "Leo Sowerby," 262, lists one "Suite" for violin and piano, which would make this the same work (from 1916) performed a few days before on the Berkshire Chamber Music Festival. However, "two suites for violin and piano" are cited in "Sowerby," *Grove's Dictionary of Music and Musicians: American Supplement,* 366.

52. "Sowerby," *Grove's Dictionary of Music and Musicians: American Supplement,* 366. No byline appears with this review, but Aldrich presumably wrote it.

53. Richard Aldrich, "Music," *New York Times,* November 8, 1921. Tuthill, "Leo Sowerby," 263, lists "Fisherman's Tune" as a composition from 1919, which was in manuscript. It was subsequently published (Chapel Hill, NC: Hinshaw Music, 1975).

54. Richard Aldrich, "Music: New Musical Publications," *New York Times,* November 20, 1921. Sowerby's quartet was dedicated to Mrs. Coolidge. No performances of music by Sowerby occurred in New York in December 1921, and the next event was a recital by the composer-pianist Harold Morris on January 11, 1922, which included Sowerby's *Irish Washerwoman* on a program with music by John Powell, Albert Stoessel, and Marion Bauer—a core representation from the "forgotten vanguard" ("Harold Morris's Recital," *New York Times,* January 12, 1922). Tuthill, "Leo Sowerby," 262, dates Sowerby's *The Irish Washerwoman: Country Dance Tune* as 1916; it had been published by Boston Music Company in 1920.

55. Sowerby, letter to Coolidge, November 2, [1921].

56. In the same letter to Coolidge (November 2, [1921]), Sowerby says "I sail tomorrow." The fact that he traveled with Lamond is reported in a notice of Howard Hanson's appointment at AAR: "Dean Hanson Is Named: Appointed a Fellow in Musical Composition by Rome Academy," *New York Times*, November 16, 1921.

57. Sowerby to Coolidge, December 2, 1921, written from "American Academy, Porta San Pancrazio." Other quotes in this paragraph come from the same letter.

58. Until a complete work list is assembled for Sowerby, it is impossible to know exactly how much music he composed in Rome. He certainly was prolific. The number "fifteen" comes from: Francis Crociata, based in part on notes and essays by the late Ronald M. Huntington, Notes to "Music of Leo Sowerby from the Monadnock Music Festival," James Bolle, conductor, Gasparo Records, 1996.

59. Crociata, "Leo Sowerby" (no page), dates the *Rhapsody* as 1922; Tuthill, "Leo Sowerby," 262, states 1923. The work was included in James Bolle's recording, and it does not appear to have been published.

60. Crociata, "Leo Sowerby."

61. Besides showing an affinity for folksong in his compositions, Sowerby also arranged them, including twenty-three tunes for Carl Sandburg's *American Songbag* (New York: Harcourt, Brace & Co., 1927), a project that involved a cluster of Chicago composers (including also Eric DeLamarter and Ruth Crawford).

62. Tuthill, "Leo Sowerby," 254.

63. Ibid., 252–54.

64. Lamond, AAR Annual Report 1922, 47.

65. Tuthill, "Leo Sowerby," 262, lists the *Settings of Three Folk-Tunes from Somerset* as being published by Boston Music Company, but I cannot find any documentation of that score. He also dates the Sonata for Violin and Piano as 1922.

66. Lamond, AAR Annual Report 1922, 50. A specific date for the concert appears in Leonard Peyton, "Musical Notes from Abroad . . . Rome," *Musical Times*, April 1, 1922, 280–81.

67. Lamond, AAR Annual Report 1924, 51.

68. Peyton, "Musical Notes from Abroad," April 1, 1922, 281.

69. Lamond, AAR Annual Report 1922, 50. Lamond also described the "Musical Circle" in a letter to Dr. [Henry S.] Pritchett, June 24, 1922, AAR Archive Microfilm, box 33, reel 5799; in listing the figures involved, he added [Francesco] Bajardi (a pianist) and deleted Bossi.

70. Lamond, AAR Annual Report 1927, 43.

71. In a letter to Coolidge (December 28, 1922), Sowerby wrote: "Thank you for your letter telling me about your plans for the chamber music programs to be given in Rome in May." He then sketched out a series of practical options for these events, including possible venues and performers. He continued to be involved in planning the concerts and sent a proposed program in a subsequent letter to Coolidge (February 12, 1923).

72. Lamond, AAR Annual Report 1923, 47. Subsequent quotations about these particular concerts come from the same source.

73. Although Lamond did not list the program for this concert, it is included in "Music Overseas . . . Italy," *New York Times*, May 27, 1923.

74. Schindler (1882–1935) was a German American conductor and composer who in the 1920s also worked as an editor for G. Schirmer. See *Grove Music Online*, s.v. "Kurt Schindler," by Israel J. Katz, accessed March 11, 2013, http://www.oxfordmusiconline.com/. Lamond probably included him as part of his impulse to promote the work of composer fellows.

75. Barr, *Elizabeth Sprague Coolidge*, 195, 50.

76. Lamond, AAR Annual Report 1926, 48.

77. "On November 12th, on invitation of the Academy, Mrs. Elizabeth Coolidge gave a Concert of Contemporary Music at the Villa Aurelia. Two string quartets played works by Castelnuovo-Tedeso, Pilati, Casella and Malipiero. . . . On the following evening at the Royal Academy of Santa Cecilia a revival of the works of Monteverdi and Lully was given with the aid of a fine chorus and a group of artists from the Paris Opera and Opera Comique" (Lamond, AAR Annual Report 1932, 41–42).

78. Lamond, AAR Annual Report 1922, 48. Other quotations in this paragraph come from the same source. In a letter, Lamond gives the starting date for travel as June 26 (letter to Pritchett, June 24, 1922).

79. This was the sonata composed by Sowerby during his first year at AAR. In his annual report for 1927–28, Lamond stated that "Leo Sowerby's Sonata for piano and violin has been selected as the first of the publications of works by the Fellows of the Music Department. It has been undertaken by the 'Universal Edition' of Vienna, the largest and most important publishing house in the world. This firm has agreed to publish and circulate the publications of the Music Department and will issue next year the full score of Hanson's 'Nordic Symphony'" (Lamond, AAR Annual Report 1928, 44.) The next year Lamond recorded Sowerby's sonata as having been published "in July" (Lamond, AAR Annual Report 1929, 44.) Hanson's Symphony, meanwhile, was not issued by Universal but rather by the Eastman School. Other works by AAR fellows were published by Universal-Edition, including: Alexander Steinert, Trio for Violin, Cello, and Piano (1931); Walter Helfer, Appassionata for Violin and Piano (1932) and Elegiac Sonata for Piano (1935); and Vittorio Giannini, Requiem for Soloists, Chorus, and Orchestra (1937).

80. Lamond, AAR Annual Report 1922, 48.

81. Lamond, AAR Annual Report 1922, 49; Edwin Evans, "The Salzburg Festival," *Musical Times* 63, no. 955 (September 1, 1922): 628. The concert with Sowerby's Sonata took place on August 10, 1922.

82. Evans, "Salzburg Festival," 628.

83. Herbert Thompson, "The Gloucester Music Festival," *Musical Times* 63, no. 956 (October 1, 1922): 705–9.

84. Lamond's annual report for 1922 states that Sowerby's performance took place in Aeolian Hall (50). But the next year, when he returns to recount this event, he gives the location as Wigmore Hall (AAR Annual Report 1923, 50). The concert was also mentioned in "Current Music Notes of Interest and Events in Foreign Lands," *New York Times*, October 29, 1922; and Leonard Peyton, "Musical Notes from Abroad . . . Rome," *Musical Times*, March 1, 1923, 207.

85. Lamond, AAR Annual Report 1923, 49. This is recounted in the report for 1923, which includes a recapitulation of the following year's travels, dated "Leeds, October 7, 1922." Herbert Thompson, "The Leeds Musical Festival," *Musical Times* 63, no. 957 (1922): 796–98.

86. Lamond, AAR Annual Report 1923, 50. Works performed at the Salzburg Festival included Alban Berg's String Quartet, Arnold Schoenberg's *Das Buch der hängenden Gärten*, and Ernst Krenek's String Quartet no. 3 ("Some 'Moderns' at Salzburg," *New York Times*, September 2, 1923). The only American composer on the Salzburg Festival of 1923 was Emerson Whithorne with *New York Days and Nights*. Edwin Evans, "Donaueschingen and Salzburg Festivals," *Musical Times* 64, no. 967 (1923): 633.

87. Lamond, AAR Annual Report 1923, 51.

88. Ibid., 52.

89. Lamond, AAR Annual Report 1924, 53–54.

90. Lamond, AAR Annual Report 1925, 55.

91. "Leo Sowerby Returns to Chicago after a Three Years' Stay in Rome, Italy," *Music News*, September 19, 1924. The remaining quotations in this paragraph come from the same article.

92. Ibid. This concert was also covered in the *New York Times*: "The Berkshire Chamber Music Festival of South Mountain at Pittsfield," August 31, 1924; and Richard Aldrich, "Morning of Bach at Music Festival: . . . Audience Is Treated to an Afternoon of American Compositions," September 19, 1924. According to Tuthill, "Leo Sowerby," 262, Sowerby's cello sonata was composed in 1920 and remained in manuscript.

93. Sowerby, letter to Coolidge, February 13, 1925, written on stationery for the Fourth Presbyterian Church, Chicago.

94. Born in Chicago in 1923, Rorem studied composition with Margaret Bonds and music theory with Sowerby. See *Grove Music Online*, s.v. "Ned Rorem," by Anthony Tommasini, accessed February 11, 2012, http://www.oxfordmusiconline.com/.

95. In his annual report for 1922, Lamond stated that this concert took place "early in February" (47). But the date of "January 23" is given in Leonard Peyton, "Musical Notes from Abroad . . . Rome," *Musical Times*, April 1, 1922, 280–81.

96. I wonder if these could be movements from the Sonata for Violin and Piano. The titles do not appear to match, however. Those for the Sonata are: Very Slowly—Blithely and Merrily; Slowly and Moodily; With Furious Energy, Very Fast.

97. Same possibility as above.

98. Lamond's annual report for 1922 states that Sowerby's performance took place in Aeolian Hall (50). The next year, when he returns to recount this event, he gives the location as Wigmore Hall (1923 annual report, 50). Meanwhile, a brief notice of the concert appeared in the *New York Times*, listing Amy Neill as the violinist ("Current Music Notes of Interest and Events in Foreign Lands," October 29, 1922).

99. For this concert, Lamond states that "In January Miss Amy Neill played at the Sala Sgambati compositions by Sowerby and Hanson." A review in *Musical Times* reveals: "An American lady violinist, Amy Neill, has also given a concert at the Philharmonic, in which, besides compositions of Lalo, Tartini, Mozart, and Sinigaglia, she played the new Sonata in three movements of Leo Sowerby and the Sospiro of Howard Hanson" (Peyton, "Musical Notes from Abroad," March 1, 1923, 207).

100. Tuthill, "Leo Sowerby," 262, lists this as *Ballad of King Estmere*, for two pianos and orchestra. A brief review appeared in the *New York Times*: "Events of Music Overseas: . . . Italy," May 6, 1923. Also in "Musical Notes from Abroad," *Musical Times*, June 1, 1923, 433.

101. Additional information in: "Music Overseas . . . Italy," *New York Times*, May 27, 1923.

102. Additional information in: "Changing Leaders in England—Recent Events Here and Abroad . . . France and Fontainebleau," *New York Times*, March 16, 1924.

103. Additional information in: "Music Notes," *Chicago Tribune*, June 22, 1924.

Chapter Six

Class of '54

Friendship and Ideology at the American Academy in Rome

Martin Brody

Introduction: To Meet This Urgent Need

The story of music composition at the American Academy in Rome might be told as a series of *Bildungsromane* with each Rome Prize winner taking a turn as protagonist. This, in effect, was the method prescribed by the elders. The narrative was already intact when William Rutherford Mead, second president of the Academy, announced the new prize for composers. His statement was covered by the *New York Times* on July 9, 1921, two weeks to the day after the *Times* had reported on the opening ceremonies of a new "French-American" music school at Fontainebleau. Mead drew a sharp distinction: "The American Academy in Rome was not established to give instruction to budding artists," he declared. Rather, like its august French counterpart at the Villa Medici, the American Prize of Rome would promote a more ineffable exchange. "It was established," Mead elaborated, "in order that picked young men who had proved in competition here their capacity for their professions might gain in Rome the refinement and inspiration flowing from the monuments of the past."[1] In the development of mature, American composers, pedagogy and professionalism would go only so far. Budding talent would have to be plucked early and replanted in enriched soil, to gestate aesthetically and spiritually in the undying light and heat of the ancient world's ever-radiant monuments.

Mead's statement echoed a fervent appeal from a Harvard music professor, Walter Spalding, whose comments had appeared a year earlier, in the Academy's twenty-fifth anniversary book. Despite his illustrious career as a teacher, Spalding focused on the insufficiencies of American compositional pedagogy as he argued for the merits of the Roman sojourn. "Our Democracy has taken up music more vigorously and sympathetically than any of the other Fine Arts," he declared. "But although there are many schools and academies which turn out performers of the first rank, they never have, and in the very nature of things they cannot produce composers."[2] By excluding composers from a transitive scheme of cultural production (a democratic society, a flourishing musical education system, a proliferation of "performers of the first rank"), Spalding gave voice to an unsettling anxiety: that the unruly democratic vistas and mores of the United States might be fundamentally incompatible with the nourishment of refined musical creators.[3] A remedy would be found in the Eternal City. There, our composers, like their illustrious French Prix de Rome predecessors, would encounter "the inspiration and artistic nourishment that the first Napoleon believed that they would derive from Italy." Through the marriage of American talent and European aestheticism, a new artistic species would be born. "It is to meet this urgent need for bringing to its full fruition the wonderful musical talent of America that the Academy in Rome proposes to found its musical establishment."[4]

However remote it may seem now, the idealized Rome envisaged by the Academy's elders—a pristine place of transhistorical values and epiphanic encounters with the timeless art of the past—is hard to relinquish. We don't have to resonate with the metaphysical overtones in Mead's solemn language to think of the Academy as a space apart, or to acknowledge what Spalding, among many others, prophesied: the power of an American Prix de Rome in validating New World artists and composers. Many have flourished in the Academy's sequestered space and have made their mark on American music. In the following, however, I want to consider the *Bildungsroman* narrative as a subplot in a different kind of story, organized around a complementary premise—that the Rome Academy, while geographically fixed at an enduring cultural crossroads, came to be an ideologically volatile node in a rapidly morphing rhizome of cultural workers and organizations: a laboratory for recalibrating the relationship between the Old and the New World, conjuring the ancient past with an eye to shaping the immediate present, and promoting national agendas while simultaneously fashioning individual apotheoses. *This* American Academy in Rome was (and is) a site of intense cultural negotiation and reinvention: a hothouse for the cultivation of individual artists, but also laboratory for spawning ideologies, professional alliances, and patronage networks.

This multifaceted mission took on a distinctive guise during the early phases of the Cold War, when the Academy entered into an economy of cultural exchange that could not have been anticipated by its founding wise men. During the decade after Henry Luce announced the American Century, the national Academy of the United States in Rome surpassed its French counterpart as an essential rendezvous for an emerging cohort of cultural operatives and political agents: the swelling ranks of an international diplomatic corps stationed in postwar Rome, as well as a peripatetic cadre of top-tier arts and foundation administrators and an assortment of Allied government and NGO bureaucrats, all intensely interested in the precarious politics of the Eternal City. This rising generation of movers and shakers had been seasoned by intense wartime cultural battles that were being waged on various fronts. Its leading figures brought a finely honed repertory of skills and attitudes to the Cold War struggle, as it would come to be conducted in the sphere of arts and letters. They developed into highly effective agents of what Richard Taruskin has suggestively called an "infrastructure of prestige" to promote Western cultural causes in the US/USSR competition for global domination.[5]

The post–World War II Academy had a strong interest in stoking the ideological machinery of this infrastructure, as well as populating its interpersonal and institutional networks and burnishing its international prestige. AAR had a strong role to play as well. The Academy, I will argue, became a bastion of liberal anticommunist cultural politics in the decade after World War II. In the era of the Marshall Plan, a constellation of Cold War liberal ideas about the dynamics of American political power, artistic modernism, and international cultural exchange coupled productively, if improbably, with the institution's founding neohumanist premise: that a patrician coterie of American scholars and artists would in each generation flourish under the spell of Rome and return to the United States transformed. The Academy's aestheticism could both burnish and soften the image of postwar American hegemonic ambitions, even as those ambitions echoed imperial Rome. At the same time, a new strain of antitotalitarian cultural theory appearing on the domestic front might link, if not reconcile, Old World humanist aesthetics and American modernism. As the literary critic Will Norman has suggested, the often-dualistic terms of analysis proposed by New York intellectuals as early as 1939 (Clement Greenberg's "avant-garde" and "kitsch," or Philip Rahv's "experiential" vs. "ideological" art, or Dwight Macdonald's "high" culture vs. "midcult") articulated a stratified rather than evolutionary or dialectical model of culture.[6] Thus, canonic/Western art, "advanced" modernism, and pluralistic democratic culture might meet uneasily under the banner of the "liberal imagination," serving as a corrective to (Soviet) ideological rigidity as much as a paradigm of transhistorical aesthetic refinement. As Lionel Trilling declared, to restore the "first essential imagination of liberalism" was a crucial project of midcentury American scholarship and art—to produce "the fullest and most precise account of variousness, possibility, complexity and difficulty [and a] lively sense of contingency and possibility . . . those exceptions to the rule which may be the beginning of the end of the rule."[7]

Moreover, the nation's anticommunist intellectual elite spoke with broad authority in defining a liberal agenda that, in various guises, conflated culture and politics. As George Packer has suggested in describing one of the era's exemplary intellectuals, the historian Arthur Schlesinger Jr., "he spoke in the name of 'the liberals' with all the confidence and weight of that definite article, a group with political pull at the highest levels—the commanding brain of the country's ruling coalition."[8] With the support of such "commanding brains" as Schlesinger, George Kennan, and Nelson Rockefeller, the schemes of international cultural exchange promoted under the banner of liberalism could be transformed into *Realpolitik*. Cultural liberalism thus provided an explicit alternative to the more coercive forms of anticommunist persuasion implemented by the American government on the European continent. As I will argue, it also helped to light a new path in American music, one that Elliott Carter would come to powerfully exemplify: an alternative both to radical avant-gardes taking hold in Europe after World War II and the intense structuralism emanating from academe on the home front—and also to the adaptation of American regional idioms, which had come to seem redolent of "midcult" and the contrivances of the Popular Front.[9]

In the following, I will consider one chapter in a longer narrative about the Academy's role in promoting liberal anticommunist cultural exchange and bolstering an international "infrastructure of prestige" for American high art during the Cold War. Unraveling a few threads in this story—sorting out the players and describing the diverse and often incongruous strategies in play—in sum, envisioning Taruskin's infrastructure—will involve a far ranging dramatis personae. I will consider the chemistry of the personal relationships and ambitions involved in relation to bigger picture questions about power dynamics, aesthetic/ideological alliances, and geopolitical agendas. In defining and pursuing its postwar mission, the Academy's director, Laurance Roberts, found a strong partner with another Cold War cultural liberal, the composer Nicolas Nabokov, the secretary general of the Congress for Cultural Freedom. Nabokov organized an ambitious, international festival of contemporary music in Rome in 1953–54, while also serving as resident in musical composition at the Academy. His residency at AAR allowed him not only to expand his burgeoning network of anticommunist operatives, but also to weave a tight-knit international coterie of composers within the larger network of cultural workers. This group collaborated efficiently in reshaping the values and institutions of international musical modernism. Elliott Carter, a fellow of the Academy in 1953–54, was close to its center. In the following, I will consider Carter and Nabokov's involvement in this tight-knit group; but first, I will describe some of the historical and ideological contexts of Taruskin's Cold War infrastructure of prestige in its Roman guise.

Part One: Infrastructure

Monuments Men

At the end of World War II, the dawn of a new era in the twentieth century's Pax Americana, the leaders of the American Academy in Rome brought an impressive array of cultural diplomacy skills and credentials to the task of

Figure 6.1. GIs' leave courses at AAR, 1945. GIs pictured with Colonel Peter Van Daehn, AAR acting librarian during World War II. Courtesy of the American Academy in Rome.

redefining the institution. The soldier-scholars who shaped the Academy post-war mission had earned their stripes in various contexts. War had become the continuation of cultural affairs by other means, and numerous American aesthetes lost their innocence abroad in the struggle to preserve the Italian national high art patrimony. The American military's "monuments men," a cadre of fine-arts specialists, classicists, historians, and archeologists, including several who would become prominent AAR figures, were called on not merely to absorb and reflect the refinement and inspiration radiating from the luminous monuments of the past but also to join the fight to secure these artifacts from Nazi looting and, by extension, to safeguard the Italian nation's cultural identity in toto. To meet this kind of urgent need would require an unusual mix of talents and virtues: historical erudition and keen artistic sensibilities as well as shrewd diplomatic skills and bravery in the line of fire. AAR's picked men, young and old, had been uniquely well prepared to take up the cause. The senior art historian Charles Rufus Morey, a specialist in medieval iconography and a fellow of the Academy in 1903, exemplified the new breed and its *Bildungsroman.* A scholar turned cultural activist and government servant, the septuagenarian Morey relinquished his position as chair of the Princeton art and architecture department at the war's end in order to serve simultaneously as AAR's acting director and cultural attaché of the newly revived American Embassy to Italy. His activities in Rome, as described in a biographical sketch written for the *Princeton Companion,* were a model of American savvy, sophistication, and resolve.

> During his tour of duty in Rome, he was credited with healing more war wounds than would have been possible for a professional diplomat. Using army trucks and naval vessels, he reopened the flow of journals, books, and photographs between Italy and America before the usual postal channels were operating. Aided by former students, some still in uniform, he located and restored to Italy paintings, sculptures, even whole libraries that the Nazis had removed. He drew Roman archaeological and historical institutions into a union that helped their depleted staffs become effective once again. In spite of great difficulties, he even met the Metropolitan Museum's request for a loan of two statues (one a Michelangelo) for its diamond jubilee. Finding Lloyd's premiums exorbitant, Morey resolutely shipped the precious packages uninsured, commandeering a fleet of MPs on motorcycles and the battleship *Missouri* for their transportation.[10]

A younger elite scholar-cum-war hero, Mason Hammond led the Academy's School of Classical Studies from 1937 to 1939 and twice thereafter during the 1950s. A Harvard professor specializing in Roman constitutional law, Hammond began his war service as an Air Force captain and became the first American military officer to enter the Monuments, Fine Arts, and Archives Program of the Civil Affairs and Military Government Sections of the Allied Armies. He joined US troops as they prepared to invade Sicily in 1943 and supervised the preservation of Italy's national art treasures as the military fought its way north. Close to the war's end, he collaborated closely with one of the highest-placed Americans on the international arts and cultural diplomacy scene: Francis Henry Taylor, director of the Metropolitan Museum and AAR trustee (1941–51), who was serving a crucial role as the head of the US government's Committee on Axis-Appropriated Property. Taylor and Hammond worked shoulder to shoulder to secure Italy's artistic legacy.[11]

Even before the advent of the Marshall Plan, the critical missions of the US government's monuments men thus forged new links in a network of American cultural activists in Europe that included a mixed bag of scholars, arts administrators, diplomats, and military officials. During World War II, another AAR elder, Myron Taylor (not to be confused with Francis Henry) was tightening a different strand in the US/European diplomacy network, one that would eventually connect the Academy to the American government's Cold War strategies at the highest level. An AAR trustee and steward of its properties during the war, Myron Taylor had been recruited to the board of US Steel by the most powerful of Academy cofounders, J. P. Morgan. He ascended to the chairmanship of US Steel during the Depression and then served in the Roosevelt and Truman administration as personal envoy to Pope Pius XII in the 1940s. In the latter capacity, he negotiated to limit the wartime Allied bombing of Rome and established American relief funds for Italy, all the while watching over the Academy's magnificent properties at the top of the Janiculum. After the war, while steering the Academy's transition into the postwar era, Myron Taylor maintained his official relationship with the Vatican as US envoy. By the time AAR reopened after World War II, the Holy See had become a high-functioning, if somewhat sub-rosa, partner to the US State Department in combating communism throughout the continent.[12]

Thus, by the time the Academy appointed Laurance Roberts as its first long-term postwar director in 1947, it was already variously embroiled in a burgeoning American military-industrial-*cultural* complex that was resolutely testing soft power initiatives in Rome and beyond. Wartime service had schooled Roberts in a different aspect of American cultural diplomacy from those practiced by other prominent Academy elders. Mason Hammond and Charles Rufus Morey exemplified a newfound link between studying the radiant monuments of the past and pursuing American cultural authority and political interests in the present. Myron Taylor personified AAR's access to the upper echelons of government, both in the homeland and abroad. Roberts added another dimension: he represented a strain of cultural cold warriors keenly attuned to the uses of high art in general, and contemporary American art in particular, as an instrument of foreign policy. Moreover, unlike many of the AAR's other principals who returned to academic life shortly after the war, he made the Academy's retooled mission, especially in linking the cultivation of artistic refinement to cultural diplomacy, his sole calling for over a decade.

A specialist in East Asian art who became director of the Brooklyn Museum in 1938, Roberts had served in army intelligence as a crypto-analytic officer from 1942 to 1946. He had been a Princeton classmate ('25) and friend of John D. Rockefeller. He and his wife Isabel remained close to the Rockefeller family throughout their lives. Roberts also rendered "loyal and valued services . . . during the war years while serving as a member of the official staff" in Nelson Rockefeller's Office of the Coordinator of Inter-American Affairs (OCIAA).[13] Serving on OCIAA's distinguished Fine Arts Committee, he joined a small group of powerful arts administrators that included Francis Henry Taylor, the AAR trustee at the center of the US government's monuments preservation programs in Europe, and Alfred Barr, director of the Museum of Modern Art (MOMA). Working in OCIAA, they created an import/export system for contemporary art that would become a blueprint for promoting American geopolitical interests through international cultural exchange.[14] Whether or not it was his OCIAA work with Francis Henry Taylor that first brought Roberts into the Academy fold, his experience working in Rockefeller's office provided crucial alliances for his ensuing Academy service. OCIAA principles of cultural diplomacy strongly informed Laurance Roberts's stewardship of the American

Academy in Rome, as well as the agendas of various other of the Academy's European and American organizational partners.

Something Unique Even for Washington

The Office of the Coordinator of Inter-American Affairs was created by President Franklin D. Roosevelt in 1940 to forge alliances and push back against Axis and (after the war) Soviet Fifth Column propaganda efforts in Latin America. OCIAA was the brainchild of Nelson Rockefeller, who had substantial business interests in Central and South American to protect; he pitched the idea of OCIAA to Roosevelt's secretary of commerce, Harry Hopkins, and, over misgivings in the Department of State, Roosevelt sanctioned the new office and appointed Rockefeller as its head. Artistic/cultural exchange was at the heart of the OCIAA program to promote an inter-American coalition. In announcing the launch of the organization's first international exhibition tour, Rockefeller clearly spelled out a principle that would be sustained throughout the Cold War and applied on a global scale. "An important foundation for our schema of hemispheric defense must be a social order in which there is balance and perspective. In no better way can this be aided than by encouragement and free interchange of the art of each American republic."[15]

As described in a 1941 *New York Times* article by James Reston, the OCIAA was "something unique even for Washington," a new kind of agency with a hybrid mission: "It's not really a government office," Reston elaborated, "but a combination international bank, trade bureau, art gallery and propaganda office."[16] Even in its own charter, when aiming to clarify a modus operandi to encourage free interchange of the art of the Americas, the OCIAA deliberately blurred the boundaries between government and private initiatives, the affairs of state and the affairs of art:

> Local organizations, such as cultural institutes, committees of American citizens, or other groups aided by the Coordinator or the Department for special work, will be utilized or established as fully independent agencies, not administratively connected with the United States Government. In each appropriate capital or other center, the Coordinator's Office and the Department will select an American citizen or citizens, not officials of the United States government, who, under the guidance and supervision of the chief of mission, will assist in coordinating and supervising the activities of the American colony and advise on the use of the Coordinator's funds in his community.[17]

While invoking a principle of interagency independence, the OCIAA's mission statement clouded the issue of state and local organizational relations in American "colonies." The OCIAA's modus operandi for interweaving government and private agency in foreign "missions" also portended an asymmetrical relationship between the United States, clearly first among equals, and its inter-American allies. OCIAA-style "free artistic exchange" would occur in the context of a bipolar (and Manichean) struggle dominated by the United States and guided by overarching "universal" (Western) values that would subsume the cultural diversity of the Americas to a common cause.[18]

As Eva Cockcroft has argued in the influential article "Abstract Expressionism: Weapon of the Cold War," one universal value in particular rallied liberal, anticommunist cultural elites in and out of government both to the cause of modern art and to the hybrid approach to cultural exportation promoted by OCIAA: freedom of speech. In the early phases of the Cold War, proponents of contemporary art found themselves battling domestic foes to free speech as well as foreign threats to Western values in toto. As Cockcroft suggests, federal agencies, such as the United States Information Agency, had been "handcuffed by the noisy and virulent speeches of right-wing Congressmen like Representative George A. Dondero (Michigan) who regularly denounced from the House floor abstract art and 'brainwashed artists in the uniform of the Red art brigade.'" By contrast, "freed from the kinds of pressure of unsubtle red-baiting and super-jingoism applied to official governmental agencies like the United States Information Agency (USIA), CIAA and MOMA cultural projects could provide the well-funded and more persuasive arguments and exhibitions needed to sell the rest of the world on the benefits of life and art under capitalism."[19]

Serving on OCIAA's Fine Arts Committee while sustaining a close friendship with its leader, Nelson Rockefeller, Laurance Roberts had ample opportunity to join the fight and refine the arguments for life and art under capitalism. Along the way, he could also compile an unusually fat and highly functional rolodex of contacts.[20] During his time at OCIAA, the organization collaborated closely with MOMA (and de facto with the CIA, which provided secret funding for numerous projects launched after the war). Nineteen exhibitions were developed for international distribution throughout South America. These projects were spearheaded by a variety of culture leaders-cum-US government hot (and later cold) warriors: the museum's board chairman, John Hay Whitney, who worked during the war for the OSS; Porter McCray, who served both as director of CIA international programs and OCIAA staff member; and Thomas W. Braden, who had been MOMA's executive secretary before joining the CIA.[21]

Ambassador De Facto If Not De Jure

Regardless of Roberts's diverse credentials and contacts, reviving the American Academy in Rome after the war would prove a formidable challenge, both in theory and practice. As he found immediately upon arrival in Rome, supplies were short in the ravaged Italian capital. In many cases, the Academy was forced to refurbish its facilities with an assortment of *objets trouvés* from the city's central flea market at the Porta Portese.[22] Rome was also a difficult test for the OCIAA approach to artistic and cultural exchange that Roberts had practiced during the war. When he arrived in Rome, the Academy's most eminent advocate on the ground, Myron Taylor, was spearheading a massive relief aid effort for the impoverished country and collaborating with the Holy See to create an alliance of anticommunist religious and political movements across Europe. Meanwhile, the newly formed Central Intelligence Agency—implementing a playbook that had been written by the now infamous spymaster and CIA founding father, James J. Angleton—was promoting diverse schemes of expensive (and illegal) covert operations throughout the Italian peninsula aimed at swinging local elections away from the Communist Party and toward the pro-US Christian Democrats. The historian Robin Winks has succinctly summarized this blunter side of US anticommunist deployment of soft power:

> According to the revelations of the 1970s, when a combination of a series of leaks, exposés in the press, congressional investigations, and unprecedented candor by the then-director of Central Intelligence, William Colby, had made public a number of the agency's "family jewels," the CIA was putting nearly $10 million a year into Italy [during the 1950s] to influence elections at the local level, for campaigning expenses, the financing of splinter groups that might divide the Communists, straightforward bribes, and anti-Communist propaganda. In 1974, one of the "whistle blowers," Victor Marchetti, set the figure even higher, at $30 million a year, or maybe more.[23]

Entering into this rough and tumble political economy, Roberts found another road to Rome by developing an ingenious if idiosyncratic program to burnish the image of American prestige and affirm the cult of art. Notwithstanding his wartime government service, the Academy's new director came to the Eternal City with no obvious political agenda and no State Department or CIA handlers. Under his leadership, the American Academy in Rome neither partnered in Angleton's hard-edged, covert CIA initiatives nor established a colonial outpost of the US government, at least in the strict sense prescribed by the OCIAA. Nonetheless, if the international cultural networks he advanced were less taut than those envisioned by and for the OCIAA, they produced an apposite effect. As Francis Henry Taylor suggested, under Roberts,

> the American Academy has risen steadily in [the Italian intelligentsia's] estimation. The reason for this they quite candidly admit is that due to the discretion, tact and often calculated diffidence of the Director, the Academy has been content to take its legitimate place in a rather circumscribed and highly critical intellectual society. . . . Not only do they find this refreshing politically, but they are aware that there still exists in the United States a hard core of people who value art and learning for their own sakes and who have no ulterior motive in their exploitation.[24]

Far from Washington but close to its ambassadorial delegates, and still hard-wired into its networks, Laurance Roberts (and his wife, Isabel, a virtual codirector at the Academy) produced a counterbalance to the grittier political business being negotiated down the hill, in the center of the city. At Rome's summit, they gradually created a site of sociability that also served as a diplomatic safe haven and a testing site for alchemical reactions mixing aestheticism and Realpolitik in varying doses. As Isabel Roberts's journals document, the Robertses were unstinting hosts, inviting an endless stream of high-power guests to their Roman home, the Academy's Villa Aurelia.[25]

Writing to the couple shortly before Laurance Roberts retired from AAR in 1959, their dear comrade in arms, Sir Harold Acton, warmly summarized the ways that the Academy had come to transform the OCIAA model of cultural exchange: "You have been Ambassadors de facto if not de jure, and all the Roman world of art, literature and music will miss you and lament your absence, including this old pal in Florence."[26] Indeed, during their years in Rome, Laurance and Isabel Roberts nudged their Rome-based "world of art, literature and music" into the narrow space between de facto and de jure political service, blurring the boundaries between autonomous art and affairs of the state. In this new community of international patronage and ambiguous public/private enterprise, they cultivated myriad, effective relationships between artists, arts institutions, nongovernmental organizations, cultural impresarios, and state officials. In the following section, I will discuss the emergence of one such set of relationships and its implications for American new music in general and the career of Elliott Carter in particular.

Part Two: Prestige

No Mere Festival

Laurance and Isabel Roberts staged one of their many lavish entertainments at the Villa Aurelia in early April 1954: a party celebrating La Musica nel XX^{0} Secolo, a grand festival of modern and contemporary music concurrently being held in Rome. Two of the principals on the scene were Elliott Carter and Yehudi Wyner, the Academy's picked composers for 1953–54; another was Nicolas Nabokov, AAR's composer in residence. Wyner, Carter, and Nabokov, along with continuing fellows, Frank Wigglesworth and Robert Moevs, comprised what I will loosely call the Class of '54. As Wyner has recalled:

> I don't know whether Nicolas organized the party, but a lot of his famous friends were there. I was just a kid, and I was dazzled. I especially remember seeing Poulenc, slouched in a low chair with his head in his hands, looking like a recently destroyed butterfly. I assumed that he was ashamed to be in the presence of Stravinsky. I wasn't going to miss my chance, so I got up my

> nerve to introduce myself to the great maestro. I walked up to him and said something inane about what an honor it was to meet him. Meanwhile I put my hands on both of Stravinsky's arms, and he literally flexed his muscles to show me how strong he was. Then I was introduced to Salvador Dali. His mustache was waxed hard and the points at the end were about a centimeter from the pupils of his eyes. I thought that he would have blinded himself if he had broken out in a grin.
>
> As for the Italian literati, I didn't know those people; that was Elliott's crowd. I don't know if Silone was there, but he was a close friend of Elliott.
>
> Sam Barber and Lenny and Aaron and some others had come to Rome, but I don't remember if they were at the party. I met Barber while he was staying at the Academy, and I played through my piano sonata for him.[27]

Wyner casts himself as the kid in the candy store in this account, and it's not difficult to see why. The occasion of this celebrity gathering was, like the gathering itself, spectacular. La Musica nel XX° Secolo was an object lesson in OCIAA-style staging of American prestige and power abroad. In addition to the luminaries that Wyner would have recognized, there were surely many other illustrious guests, delegates of the festival's many sponsors that had bankrolled its array of splashy, high-profile events. The official list of backers was in itself dazzling: an alliance of state, foundation, and corporate sponsors including the Congress for Cultural Freedom, the European Centre of Culture of Geneva, the Italian nation radio and television network (RAI), the Rockefeller Foundation, and the state bureaucracies of various NATO countries.[28] "This was no mere 'festival,'" the British critic Reginald Smith Brindle gushed in his "Notes from Abroad" column in the *Musical Times*, "but a bringing together of some of the greatest musicians of today, to discuss and listen to this century's music in large quantities and in its most extreme forms. . . . Some two hundred musicians assembled in Rome for a ten-day programme of six discussions, thirteen concerts, and two operas."[29] In addition, the festival promoted a composition competition with three awards under the grandiose title "Twentieth-Century Masterpiece Festival Prizes." The US government flew in Samuel Barber, Aaron Copland, Leonard Bernstein, and Virgil Thomson for the festivities; the American delegation stayed at the Academy.[30]

La Musica nel XX° Secolo was organized by Nicolas Nabokov, operating in the dual capacity of AAR composer in residence for 1953–54 and also secretary general of the Congress for Cultural Freedom (CCF).[31] Nabokov had first encountered the Academy in the summer of 1951 on a brief stay as a guest of the director, an arrangement brokered by Aaron Copland.[32] As he described it in a letter to his friend Arthur Schlesinger, the newly appointed secretary general of the CCF came to the Academy during a summer that he had spent "travelling like a Fuller Brush Man all over Europe, trying to sell to reluctant customers the idea of collaborating with the Congress for Cultural Freedom. I have been in Germany, England, Belgium, Italy and in various provincial cities of France." At the conclusion of this forced march, as Nabokov informed Schlesinger, "I feel myself steeped in a kind of curious vaseline. It may be good for the skin, but it certainly is not good for one's nerves."[33] However hard on the nerves his proselytizing on behalf of the CCF may have been, it provided an opportunity to begin a close and enduring relationship with Isabel and Laurance Roberts during his Roman sojourn.

In realizing a mutual ambition to promote American culture abroad, Nabokov and the Congress for Cultural Freedom were ideal partners for the Robertses and the American Academy in Rome. Invited to become the Academy's resident in musical composition in 1953, Nabokov found an artistic raison d'être to be in Rome. Disguised, as he wrote a bit too poetically in a letter to Isabel Roberts, in "sheep's closing [*sic*]," he might adopt a semblance of artistic purity to soften the image of his ambitious cultural and political agenda.[34] The association with Nabokov and the CCF, an organization that had quickly become an unparalleled engine of American prestige and anticommunist cultural warfare throughout the world, yielded numerous advantages for the Academy and its fellows as well. In the following, I will discuss the impact of this network on the career of Elliott Carter and, more broadly, on the development of postwar international musical modernism. First, however, we will need to sketch out some of the backstory of Nabokov's ascendancy as cultural impresario and consider the diverse assets he brought to the CCF cause.

To Hold Our World Together

The itinerate Nabokov had taken a circuitous road to Rome, passing through Paris, Berlin, Washington, and New York along the way. He had made many key connections and acquired a good deal of heavy political baggage during his long migrations.[35] Exiled from Russia, he made his way into the Diaghilev circle in Paris in the mid-1920s, befriended Stravinsky, and in 1927 composed a ballet-oratorio, *Ode*, on a Diaghilev commission. Nabokov immigrated to the United States in 1933 and shortly thereafter began work on another ballet, *Union Pacific*, on a scenario by Archibald MacLeish and with a commission from the Ballets Russes de Monte Carlo. His connections in the Russian émigré ballet world put him into contact not only with the impresario of the Ballet Caravan, Lincoln Kirstein, but also with the company's music director, Elliott Carter, and its patron, Nelson Rockefeller. Carter and Nabokov became fast friends. During the war years, Nelson Rockefeller brought Kirstein into the sphere of the OCIAA, which funded a major Latin American tour of the company.[36]

Between 1936 and 1945, Nabokov held several academic positions, at Wells College, the Peabody Conservatory, and St. John's College, where he taught with Carter in a position that Carter had helped him to land.[37] At the war's end, he decamped for Germany, serving as an officer of the newly formed "Music Control Branch of the Information Control Division" of the Berlin Office for the American Military Government (OMGUS). Hence, his career in cultural politics began in earnest. "Music Control," by order of a 1946 Joint Chief of Staff directive, was directed to "encourage German initiative and responsible participation in this work of cultural reconstruction and [to] expedite the establishment of those international cultural relations which will overcome the spiritual isolation imposed by National Socialism on Germany and further the assimilation of the German people in the world community of nations."[38] Thus, by military decree the valence of a century of cultural exchange between the United States and Germany would be reversed. American musical emissaries, including the Russian émigré Nabokov, could cast themselves as the cultural redeemers of a materially depleted and spiritually isolated Germany.

In 1947 Nabokov left the German Music Control Branch and settled in New York. Although he had flourished in the military government in Germany, his path to further government service during the early days of the Cold War was quickly blocked. As he reported in one of his two autobiographical memoirs, *Bagazh*, "after two years of service with our Occupation Government in Berlin and six months of helping Charlie Thayer to shape the Voice of America to Russia . . . I had quit government service, vowing never to return."[39] Charles Thayer had been a foreign-service officer since 1937 and had headed up the OSS operation in Austria after the war. Most likely, Thayer met Nabokov through Thayer's brother-in-law, the eminent diplomat Charles Bohlen, a long-time Washington operative who had already had a decisive impact on Soviet American relations when he began a close friendship with Nabokov in 1941. While running the Voice of America, the "delightful" Thayer, as Nabokov called him, crossed swords with J. Edgar Hoover. Thayer became a target of Hoover's and Joseph McCarthy's attentions; Nabokov was collateral damage. As Andrea Pitzer describes it in *The Secret History of Vladimir Nabokov*, both Vladimir and Nicolas Nabokov had been candidates for the directorship of Russian broadcasts of Voice of America. Nicolas was chosen over his cousin, but he quickly found himself under intense scrutiny:

> In the 1948 review of his application, Nicholas's [*sic*] life was dissected to a . . . disconcerting degree. . . . His psychiatric hospitalizations, his diagnosis as a manic-depressive, his divorces, his enmity with several former friends and co-workers, and his involvement with female students at multiple U.S. colleges were all investigated and appear to have been confirmed. Rumors of drug addition, venereal disease, admiration for Stalin, membership in the French Communist Party, and efforts to move back to the Soviet Union were unsubstantiated.
>
> In the cavalcade of real or imagined offenses, only one matter seems to have truly troubled the FBI: they wanted to know if Nicholas Nabokov was homosexual.[40]

By the summer of 1948, as George Kennan informed him in a frank assessment, Nabokov's hopes for government service were doomed:

> I have now had a chance to look into the matter which was troubling you. My answer is this: I think you should tell Charlie [Thayer] or Allen [Dulles], or whoever it is who in your case represents the Government, that you have given up any intention of working for the U.S. Government at this time, and that you are withdrawing any formal application which you may have on record in this respect.
>
> I am giving you this advice (which causes me considerable sadness and a very real concern) only because I have not been able to clarify this matter to my own satisfaction, and cannot assure you a freedom of further unpleasantness if you go ahead with the plan of working again with the Government.[41]

Meanwhile, Joseph McCarthy, J. Edgar Hoover, and various FBI investigators and congressional surrogates continued to investigate Thayer for political and sexual deviance. McCarthy's persecution of Thayer reached a head in 1953 during confirmation hearings of his brother-in-law, Charles Bohlen, for appointment as American ambassador to the Soviet Union. Thayer was forced to resign from a consular position in Germany. And, as the historian Robert D. Dean summarized, "the bohemian Nabokov, who had formerly been with the Voice of America met with the senator's censure too. 'I would throw him out in a minute,' [Senator Robert A.] Taft opined."[42]

Although he had effectively been exiled from government, Nabokov's service as a cultural politician was only beginning, and he would operate at the borderline between state and private agencies for the ensuing decade and a half. In New York liberal-elite circles from Rockefeller's OCIAA/MOMA milieu to the *Partisan Review* crowd, his persecution at the hands of Joseph McCarthy and Co. must have been seen as a kind of Red Badge of Courage, burnishing his reputation as a heroic public intellectual. He sustained a close, mutual loyalty with Bohlen's Russian circle, above all the iconic anti-Soviet intellectual, Isaiah Berlin, throughout his years with the Congress for Cultural Freedom.

Nabokov's first star turn as a Cold War cultural diplomat and public intellectual famously occurred at a Soviet-backed conference at the Waldorf-Astoria in March 1949. The Waldorf conference put him (and modern music) front and center in the cultural argument between the United States and the Soviet Union, and it dramatically demonstrated that American as well as European hearts and minds were at stake in the debate. In a showdown of luminaries, the Soviet emissary Shostakovich lined up with such hopeful proponents of social democracy as Paul Eluard, Clifford Odets, Aaron Copland, and Lillian Hellman. They were opposed by a formidable cadre of lapsed Trotskyites, liberal anticommunists, and born again neocons: Sidney Hook, Dwight Macdonald, Mary McCarthy, and Nabokov, among others. In a moment of high political theater, Shostakovich excoriated Stravinsky, who was absent from the scene, for his "moral barenness" and "openly nihilistic writings." Nabokov responded by challenging Shostakovich to take a stand on *Pravda*'s denunciation of three "lackeys of imperialism," the émigré composers Hindemith, Schoenberg, and Stravinsky. Taunted by Nabokov, Shostakovich declared that such decadent Western (or Westernized) modernists should be barred from the Soviet Union and their music banned in the homeland. The exchange was widely reported in the American and European press. It bolstered the rationale for a rapidly coalescing anticommunist intellectual cohort whose watchword would be freedom of political and artistic expression.[43]

A year later at the Congress for Cultural Freedom's founding conference in Berlin, Arthur Koestler inscribed the argument against state censorship of the arts and letters into a manifesto for the new anti-Soviet organization: "We hold it to be self-evident," the document began, "that intellectual freedom is one of the inalienable rights of man."[44] Nabokov attended, with Arthur Schlesinger at his side. "Nicolas Nabokov and I took advantage of our Berlin stay to talk with some Russian escapees," Schlesinger wrote to Averell Harriman, who was then in Paris supervising the Marshall Plan. "We had hoped to have a talk with you and Chip [Bohlen] about it. . . ." The matter at hand was a scheme to counter Soviet propaganda about American imperialism.[45] Within a year, Nabokov was appointed as the CCF's secretary general. And in less than a decade the Congress grew into an impressive global system of cultural production and distribution. As Peter Coleman has described it,

> [The CCF] sponsored a network of magazines including *Encounter, Survey, Preuves, Tempo Presente,* and *Cuadernos* and helped others ranging from *Quest* in Bombay to *Quadrant* in Sidney. It conducted large and small international seminars. . . . It orchestrated international protests against oppression of intellectuals. . . . It organized festivals and helped refugee writers. 'I can think of no group of people,' George F. Kennan wrote to Nicolas Nabokov . . . 'who have done more to hold our world together in these last years than you and your colleague.'"[46]

Crimes in the Name of Dodecaphony

Improbably, Nabokov had convinced his colleagues and their many backers—including, it was later revealed, the CIA—that a clash of values represented by two Russian composers, the émigré Stravinsky and his Soviet counterpart, Shostakovich, was a signal battle in the Cold War; and by extension, that the production of grandiose displays of Western cultural supremacy was essential to the cause of freedom. The Rome Music Festival of 1954 was the fourth expensive and splashy international conference that ensued, and its second enormous European music festival in two years. Prior conferences had been staged in Berlin and Bombay in 1950 and 1951, and the first music festival held in Paris in 1952.[47]

Even at the flashpoints of the Cold War, however, Nabokov's schemes to promote the cause of freedom by producing grandiose arts events were widely greeted with skepticism. For many in the CCF rank and file, the role of high-profile music festivals in the decisive ideological struggle of the epoch often seemed dubious. As John Roche, a member of the Congress, put it, "Nicolas Nabokov, one of the CCF's guiding spirits, suggested that the Congress organize cultural fetes to convince the European masses that Western culture was superior to Stalinist and thereby wean them away from the then huge French and Italian Communist parties. This struck me as hilarious, on a par with Sir Robert Peel's 1832 support for the National Gallery on the ground that it would ease class friction."[48]

However hilarious his festivals may have seemed to many of Nabokov's fellow travelers, the impresario's virtuoso skills in mingling sober political agendas with lofty artistic ambitions, warm friendships, and raucous parties were unparalleled. By the time he returned to the Academy in the fall of 1953, Nabokov had planted himself firmly in a rapidly ramifying network of artists, intellectuals, military and government officials, institutional and foundation elites, and nongovernmental organization leaders. He had already played an instrumental role in laying the ideological and organizational groundwork for a new pan-European cultural cold war. His networking skills must have impressed even his most skeptical colleagues, who generally admired the form of his enterprise if not its contents.

Only a few years before, however, when Nabokov was wandering in the wilderness (that is, after his abrupt departure from the Voice of America and before the advent of the Congress for Cultural Freedom), the new music scene in Europe was changing in ways that would challenge the ascendant cultural impresario. Two young American composers, John Evarts and Everett Helm, had assumed prominent roles in the Music Branch of Information Control in Germany shortly after the war. They implemented their military orders in ways that Nabokov, the patrician neoclassicist, would likely not have imagined and surely not endorsed. Championing the newly formed courses for contemporary music at Darmstadt, a veritable breeding ground of the postwar and predominantly leftist avant-garde, they complicated the senior impresario's schemes considerably. The young European composers who came to be aided by the US military's support of the Darmstadt program famously included Boulez, Stockhausen, Maderna, and Nono: ambivalent participants in a Manichean conflict of world powers perhaps, but determined agents of a new European cultural order. The effect of the Darmstadt initiative was decisive. Elliott Carter summarized it in a 1959 report to the *Musical Quarterly*: "A US Army Music and Theater officer in Wiesbaden, [Everett Helm] helped to establish the Darmstadt School after the war and at various times since has saved it from being overwhelmed. [He has] earned the gratitude of a whole generation of young European musicians."[49]

As the musicologist Mark Carroll has shown, the postwar generation of European composers that had been aided by Evarts and Helms had grown into a force to contend with, and a thorn in Nabokov's side, by the time he had come to the Academy as its resident composer in 1953. Ironically, Nabokov, the delegate of Western cultural freedom, had been accused of obstructing free speech when he produced the first of his grand international modern music fetes in Paris, two years before the Rome Festival. In the Paris Festival, Nabokov favored the stars of international prewar modernism, especially his revered friend Stravinsky, in favor of the emerging generation. Having been excoriated for suppressing the music of the postwar avant-garde in Paris, he tested a new strategy in Rome: to unleash the avant-garde in the name of free speech. And thus, an East-West competition of cosmopolitan Western modernists versus Soviet socialist realists gave way, at least in part, to a demonstration of aesthetic pluralism as a sign of cultural freedom. Henze, Nono, Petrassi, Maderna, and Carter displaced Debussy, Mahler, Berg, Ravel, Milhaud, Hindemith, Schoenberg, and Britten as featured composers in the celebration of the freedoms of the West.[50]

For our reviewer at the *Musical Times*, Reginald Smith Brindle, the results were catastrophic. His description of the major American chamber works performed at the festival went from bad to worse, as it followed a path from atonality to dodecaphony to noise: "The atonal string quartet of Elliott Carter (U.S.A.) showed exceptionally virile writing, but a fantasy so uncontrolled that it abandoned musical coherence. Copland's piano quartet, an attempt at dodecaphonic methods, was received with evident disapproval, and should make him blush. The 'Octandre' for wind instruments of the French-American Varèse revealed a genius for making noises but not music."[51] Smith Brindle was no chauvinist: the atonal and twelve-tone works of British and continental composers fared no better in his review, and the international competition for festival prizes was singled out for special censure: The nominated works "ranged from the naïve to the violently offensive," he scoffed, and he summarized the festival tersely: "many crimes were committed in the name of dodecaphony. . . . If this selection of music is typical of Western civilization . . . one must conclude that there is a universal orientation towards atonality."[52]

The critic, it seems, was looking for signs of (capital C) "Civilization," but what he got instead was (small c) "culture" in its messiest, most pluralistic, and conceptually unresolved forms. In an especially emblematic moment, Stravinsky was refused admittance to the performance of Henze's in-your-face, antibourgeois adaptation of *Manon Lescaut,* the ninety-minute montage *Boulevard Solitude,* because the éminence grise of modernism wasn't wearing a tuxedo. Reporting on the performance for the *New York Times* on April 8, Michael Steinberg wrote, "Last night, the Rome Opera House was a turbulent place, inside and out. There were minutes at a time when the conductor's movements and the singers' open mouths gave the only clue that the opera still was being performed."[53] For the patrician Nabokov, to produce, let alone sit through, an expensive opera by the young communist, Henze—or to support a performance of Luigi Nono's *Epitaph for Garcia Lorca no. 2*, conducted by Hermann Scherchen, known as the "Red dictator" by his players, or to engage in shrill debates with the critics of the communist newspaper, *l'Unitá*, or to lock horns with the young and perennially skeptical Boulez, a fervid member of the disgruntled chattering class ubiquitously on the scene—was a giant leap of faith in the principle that free artistic expression must be encouraged, whatever the cost. Thanks to this decisive step, however, the 1954 Rome Festival was, for all the American musicians living at the Academy, an opportunity like no other: a cross between a glamorous gala, an opportunity to hobnob with the celebrities of modernism (and an international array of diplomatic and foundation types), and a crash course in postwar aesthetics at a musical ground zero. It briefly yielded a nexus of protagonists and ideas that was, however challenging for Nabokov, highly apposite for Carter.

The Most Qualified of European Listeners

For Carter, the timing was impeccable, and his friendship with the newly empowered Nabokov yielded a range of professional rewards. Nabokov had served on the committee that selected Carter for the Rome Prize. The impresario also insured that Carter's fiendishly difficult First String Quartet would be performed during the 1954 Rome Festival, over and above the objections of its eventual champions, the Parrenin Quartet.[54] This crucial performance occurred at a time when Carter's music had moved close to the edge of viability vis-à-vis contemporary music performance practice. During the previous half decade, his work had decisively emerged from its neoclassical sources and now incorporated a level of rhythmic and contrapuntal complexity and intricacy of pitch procedures that would rival the most hardcore of European late serialists. Just as he was taking up residency in Rome, he learned that his First Quartet won the Concours International for string quartets in Liège.[55]

Yehudi Wyner recalls the Rome performance of Carter's First Quartet as an epiphany. And, unlike the ambivalent Smith Brindle, an American critic who was writing again for the *New York Times*, Michael Steinberg, was ecstatic. "Elliott Carter may be the least known of the three composers," he suggested in reviewing Carter's quartet alongside works by Copland and Stravinsky, "but this recent String Quartet of his stands head and shoulders over every other work yet played at this conference."[56] The piece also stirred an intensely enthusiastic response from an eminent Italian audience that Enzo Restagno would later dub "the most qualified of European listeners," in particular Goffredo Petrassi and Roman Vlad, who became close friends of Carter.[57] Within a year, Petrassi would be elected international president of the ISCM and Carter and

Vlad would become its vice presidents.[58] Carter's career in Europe, by his own reckoning, was thus launched. Within a decade he could write, in a report from Europe submitted for the first volume of *Perspectives of New Music*, that "the proliferation of European festivals and conferences focusing on contemporary music is becoming so great that if any of the group of musicians regularly invited were to accept all of his invitations, he would be kept busy almost all year simply in traveling from one country to another."[59] This was the authoritative voice of experience, and virtually all of his American readers might have been green with envy. Only a very select few of Carter's fellow Americans would join him in that eminent, invited group. Three decades later, William Schuman would summarize the situation in a note to Carter: "There is no doubt in my mind that of all American composers you are the one who has most impressed Europeans. It is a source of great satisfaction for me to see one of my colleagues so recognized. The success that you have had on the continent is enormously important for all those who have a deep concern for the position of the American composer."[60]

Carter's experience in Rome contrasts dramatically with that of other emerging American atonalists and dodecaphonists operating primarily on the domestic front. Back at home, many in his cohort of emerging composers were still grappling with the significance of the diaspora of émigré European musicians who suffered the war in exile. Meanwhile, Carter and his fellow Americans at the 1954 Rome Festival were partying with Italian composers of the older and younger generations alike, those who had struggled with shifting political and cultural allegiances through the war years, as well as those who invigorated the Darmstadt new music course. Speaking about the New York scene, Milton Babbitt described his encounters with the revered German émigré musicians as an ongoing source of Oedipal anxiety. "I remained in the eyes (and probably ears) of those older and surely educationally differently oriented European musicians," Babbitt recalled, "a young American, perhaps 'clever' and 'knowledgeable,' but forever doomed by the absence of that *Geist und Seele* which was not acquirable, yet was the necessary attribute of a 'real' composer."[61] This perceived gap between revered German elders and their forever younger American counterparts would never be entirely filled, but, as Babbitt went on to suggest, the wish to close it fueled his desire to recast the ideas of Schoenberg and Schenker in the language of logical positivism, and thus to erase the impenetrable metaphysical halo of "*Geist und Seele*" surrounding their work. This impulse produced an extremely productive but deeply academic project—involving a close interweaving of music theory, composition, set theory, and philosophy of science. This was an entirely different stripe of structuralism from that developed by Boulez, Nono, Maderna, or the other Darmstadt alums and Italian avant-gardists that Carter might have encountered in Rome in the spring of 1954. Boulez had already made it perfectly clear a couple of years earlier, in an infamous polemic, that Schoenberg, still a key figure for Babbitt, was not only dead, but never to be resurrected. Similarly, Babbitt's dedication to the project of *Aufbau*—a reconstruction and formalization of tonal theory, modeled on the work of the politically retrograde Heinrich Schenker, who called himself a monarchist to his dying day in 1935—would surely have seemed perverse to the young firebrand Henze, author of *Boulevard Sunset*, who viewed the evocation of tonality in contemporary music as a way to represent the alienated ethos of bourgeois capitalism.

This disjunction of Babbitt's brand of structuralism and those of the European postwar avant-garde seems to confirm an idée fixe of sorts of American postwar music historiography: that the American serialists dominated academic musical culture in the United States, while Cage and the downtown experimental cohort were almost alone in establishing a tenuous foothold in the slippery ideological terrain of postwar European avant-garde music, primarily in Germany, and especially in Darmstadt.[62] However, in this scenario, an important episode in postwar internationalism, the story of Carter (and Nabokov) in Rome in 1953–54, is elided. Carter, who was not a serialist and only an intermittent and generally reluctant academic, was more likely to acknowledge an eclectic and non-Germanic lineage (e.g., Ives, Varèse, and Cocteau) rather than Schenker and Schoenberg, in constructing his modernist pantheon. As a delegate of American music at the Rome Festival, he presented a new register in the aesthetic spectrum and a new kind of musical persona: a composer who exemplified the operations of Trilling's liberal imagination, adapting high culture to the polyphonic pluralism of democratic cultures. In its abstention from "midcult" in its myriad forms, the liberal brand of cultivation Carter instantiated favored subjective complexity and far-ranging erudition over closed structural systems and epistemic clarity. In sum, it exemplified a rehabilitated form of liberal humanism as a Cold War American subject position. Moreover, Carter's newest work was immediately attractive to the older generation of Italian posttonalists, such as Dallapiccola and Petrassi, who were then eager to distance themselves both from the Mussolini legacy and the rise of the Italian Communist Party. Carter would also quickly come to the attention of at least one dominant figure of the younger avant-garde, Pierre Boulez.[63]

Carter might well have made the crucial connections with Petrassi, Roman Vlad, and Dallapiccola, among others, without Nabokov's intercession, but Nabokov was in an ideal position to nurture the relationships.[64] They remained in close contact with each other and with the American Academy in Rome throughout Laurance Roberts's tenure as director: Petrassi was composer-in-residence at the Academy in 1955–56. Carter returned regularly to the Academy and would become its resident composer three times after Roberts's term concluded, in 1963, 1969, and 1980. Carter, Petrassi, and Nabokov all corresponded regularly with Mario Labroca, the composer who directed the music program for the Italian national radio (RAI) during the

1950s and facilitated a prestigious performance series of AAR fellows at the Academy by the RAI orchestra. Labroca remained an essential contact for all three when he became the organizer of the Venice Music Festival and president of the UNESCO International Music Council in 1959.[65]

Infrastructures of Prestige

The full story of these relationships calls for a more extensive documentary study, but for now I want to reconsider Richard Taruskin's phrase "infrastructure of prestige" and offer a brief historiographical homily. Taruskin suggests that the Congress for Cultural Freedom's 1954 Rome Festival can be understood as a key episode in the development of a Cold War music patronage system. He proposes that the CCF, by mandate, "showcased the arts and sciences of the 'free world,' especially undertakings of a modernist, individualist variety that totalitarian powers rejected and harassed."[66] This project went hand in hand with the building of an "unprecedented infrastructure of prestige to support and encourage advanced art and its creators." Furthermore, as Taruskin has argued, the CCF's campaigns to underwrite its expensive, high-profile events established a "pattern of patronage . . . that . . . spread to corporate and institutional America throughout the decade of the 1950s, at first primarily through the Ford and Rockefeller foundations (both of which had been strong financial backers of the Congress for Cultural Freedom)." Singling out the Rome Festival and indicating its importance for Elliott Carter in particular, he suggested that "institutional critical, and corporate support made it possible for such artists [i.e., creators of 'advanced art'] (especially those blessed like Carter with independent sources of income) to have outstandingly successful public careers in the virtual absence of an audience: a unique and perhaps never to be repeated phenomenon."[67]

Like Taruskin, I read the story of the Rome Festival as a parable of Cold War arts patronage; but I want to redirect his quizzical closing salvo and propose a different kind of peroration. As I have demonstrated, we need to picture the Cold War infrastructure of prestige for musical modernism both as a dynamic network of personal relationships and aspirations as well as a (rickety) scaffolding of unstable institutions and values—a construction site rather than a solid edifice. To be sure, this arrangement could be highly effective. Even a small push from within the military-industrial-cultural complex might go a long way in changing the dynamics of postwar new music. But the networks of agency woven through the Cold War military-industrial-cultural complex are difficult to trace. They were intricate, far ranging, and diffuse, and the interests of the participants often incongruous, enigmatic, and undocumented. The patterns of causality at work are hard to reconstruct. They were made so, at least in part, by intent.

Moreover, to the degree that it functioned efficiently, the Cold War prestige machine for advanced art hardly churned out a uniform product. While Taruskin doesn't suggest that it did, he seems eager to find a stable set of meanings and values at work in the production of the 1954 Rome Festival. The purpose of the festival, he suggests, "was to nominate, through showcase concerts and a series of prize competitions, a corps of standard-bearers for the Congress's highly politicized notion of cultural freedom, which in reality boiled down to sponsorship of the avant-garde, the type of art most obviously uncongenial to totalitarian taste." Citing a comment of France Stonor Saunders (that Stravinsky's presence at the festival "signaled a major moment in the convergence of modernist tributaries in the 'serialist orthodoxy'"), Taruskin insinuates an ideological kinship and stable bond linking cultural freedom, the avant-garde, and serialism. In turn, he suggests that Carter ("not a serialist but often taken for one") came to benefit, both in Rome and thereafter, by association of his music with serialism and its cultural meaning.[68]

The facts on the ground, I would propose, were messier. For one thing, Stravinsky's conversion to serialism was hardly a done deal in the spring of 1954, and his twelve-tone works (only later) came to be a rallying cry for an emerging American academic cohort—but not for the Darmstadt crowd and the Italian avant-garde intentionally highlighted in Rome. To the degree that Stravinsky had dabbled with ordered pitch class sets in his new *Septet* (the new work of the master performed in concert at the Rome Festival alongside the Carter First String Quartet), it was, at least structurally, a one-off affair that seemed precisely aimed to show that "serial" and "twelve-tone" were not identical terms and that the former could be as congenial with "neoclassicism" as it was with "avant-gardism." Moreover, the younger generation featured at the festival (which included, for example, such disparate figures as Lou Harrison, Luigi Nono, and Hans Werner Henze, to mention just a few) hardly spoke with a single voice. And for Nabokov, the master impresario, there were diverse relationships to cultivate and an older generation to keep in play. Performances of Britten, Prokofiev, and Poulenc, as well as Milhaud conducting the Satie *Socrate,* occurred alongside the disparate artifacts of the postwar generation. The Rome Festival, I would argue, was thus an etude in the display of democratic dissensus and the exigencies of coalition building rather than a signal moment of converging aesthetic streams. The festival's foremost propaganda message crystallized at a high level of abstraction: diversity of expression as a manifestation of free speech *tout court* rather than a fixed set of meanings associated with serialism.

Furthermore, however potent the symbolism of recondite modernism as a marker of Western freedoms and subjectivity may have been, the principles that animated the American music export system at work in the Rome Festival and the American Academy in Rome's cultural diplomatic efforts were not fixed ciphers in a static parable. While toiling under the capacious canopy of the Pax Americana, the builders of Taruskin's prestige/patronage framework grappled with a wide variety of ideological dualisms and incongruities—propaganda versus aestheticism, autonomy versus political engagement, elitism versus pluralism. However impossible these were to resolve, such tense oppositions signaled the possibility of a new cultural order. It is not hard to imagine an advanced guard of composers striving to form an elite subculture (roughly the size, say, of the readership of the *Partisan Review* or *Encounter*) while claiming to represent national culture to a far larger audience as exemplars of the liberal imagination.[69] Or, spurred by anti-Soviet sentiments, to seek a reconciliation of democratic pluralism and the mandates of Old World cultural refinement. American society in its diversity thus might be seen as a conducive milieu for the production of urbane individualists (and masters of complex modes of artistic expression) who were uniquely primed to resolve the contradictions of pluralistic and high culture and to reframe the *Bildungsroman* as an American fable.

From this perspective, Cold War patronage for modern music can be seen as a unique harbinger of a pervasive condition. If a Manichean, bipolar geopolitical conflict temporarily stabilized a symbiotic relationship between the aspirations of cultural elites and the objectives of North Atlantic hegemony, the situation would prove ephemeral. The cultural topographies imagined by liberalism's commanding brains would not entirely survive the détente of the 1970s or the fall of Saigon (let alone of the Wall). Mark Slobin has deftly summarized the ensuing state of cultural affairs: "Nowhere is it safe to draw conclusions about what belongs to whom."[70] Thus, the Cold War turn in American musical modernism can be understood an episode in a longer trajectory, poignant in the ways it reconciled democratic pluralism as a cultural value with patrician (and nostalgic) ideas about cultivation and prestige. Milton Babbitt notoriously resolved this tension by positing compositional specialization as both an index of cultural pluralism and an antidote to midcult.[71] If Babbitt's "composer as specialist" adumbrated a dissolution of ideological claims of "general culture," the exigencies of Cold War cultural diplomacy (especially as it was practiced at the American Academy in Rome, with its Janus-like gaze looking simultaneously forward and back) portended a different possibility—a reconciliation of American pluralism with a mythos of universal Western values: a poetics of hegemony that could be pressed into the service of a marginal elite. The triumph of the West might yet be figured in the emergence of an American "master" composer, a man who had ventured into the American desert to conjure a consummately personal musical idiom and to write a consummately complex string quartet that would come to be lauded in the Eternal City.

After Babbitt, however, we are likely to hear the rhetoric of Cold War artistic genius as a swan song and posit a deconstruction rather than reconstitution of myths of *Gemeinschaft* as the enduring legacy of the period. Viewed from this angle, the Congress for Cultural Freedom succeeded in demonstrating the operations of Western freedoms most effectively just when it most spectacularly failed in its ostensible mission of building consensus around cultural and artistic values, winning hearts and minds, and even expanding the audience for American contemporary music. I would argue further that the post–World War II American Academy in Rome fulfilled its mission most effectively by opening its doors to a restless, unruly, and ambitious community of artistic and diplomatic elites competing to fulfill their disparate agendas. As Walter Spalding had anticipated, the messiness of "Our Democracy's" cultural pluralism would remain difficult to square with the aspiration to produce a coherent and sophisticated national high culture. But fractiousness, while hardly an exclusive American franchise during the Cold War, was surely one of the nation's most virulent cultural exports—and since has become a defining condition of our planetary cultural ecosystems.

Coda: To Have Those Live Together

In closing, I would like to return to the youngster of the Class of '54, the twenty-four-year-old Yehudi Wyner, an innocent abroad during the cultural moment of the 1954 Rome Festival. Two decades junior to Carter and Nabokov, fresh out of a master's program at Harvard, Wyner came to Rome without the kind of bond that already sustained his elder colleagues and with little awareness of the political undercurrents of Nabokov's festival. Nonetheless—and however star struck the young composer might have been—he surely must have felt himself to be swept along in a sea change of American prestige and authority on the international front.

The impact of the encounter with his elders, especially Carter, was great. After their meeting in Rome, he sustained a lifetime friendship with Carter—principally, he has told me, through the good graces of the elder composer's wife, Helen, who Wyner described as the "catalyst of their friendship, the decision maker, someone who could otherwise be marvelously, decisively contemptuous."[72] Even before coming to Rome, when informed that Carter would be his "classmate" at the Academy, Wyner sought out a relationship with Carter's music. As he told Vivian Perlis in an interview for the Oral History of American Music archive, he began to study some of Elliott Carter's music as soon as he learned that they had both been chosen for the Rome Prize: "I really had had no experience with it whatsoever. . . . I began to look into his music. Oh what an impact it had!"[73] The mark that this impact left on Wyner's music can be palpably felt in the great achievement of his Rome fellowship years, the *Concert Duo* for violin and piano.

We can imagine Wyner a virtuoso pianist, studying Carter's scores, especially the Sonata for Cello and Piano (1948), and later recalling the tactile feel and sonority of many of its small details as he composed his own grand duo at the piano. Wyner explicitly adapted Carter's now famous rendering of contrasting,

Figure 6.2. Yehudi Wyner accompanying the soprano Anna Moffo—a recipient of a Fulbright Fellowship to Italy—in AAR Salone, 1955. Courtesy of the American Academy in Rome.

simultaneous time frames—the string instrument's brooding "psychological" time versus the piano's insistently chronometric ticking. But if Carter's cello sonata evokes the sense of two simultaneously unfolding aspects of modern experience, Wyner's *Duo* dramatizes a more mercurial, nervous, internal, and idiosyncratic sensibility. There may be no "school of Carter" in American music, but the personal bond between Carter and Wyner formed at the Academy, by Wyner's own account, emboldened the younger composer to assimilate some of the elder's compositional procedures and to move forward in a new direction.[74]

This brings me to a final point. As Wyner told Vivian Perlis, he was deeply affected by the experience of Rome:

> The Italian experience—which in the beginning lasted three years—I would say was among the profoundest and most long-lasting influences on my life in terms of an approach to life: a view of other cultures, and a kind of influence on a profound level of my artistic thinking; a connection with the past, the chain of generations; a tolerance and an acceptance of many other ways of life, of culture; the possibility for integrating, even in an informal way, ideas from all over the world and ideas from all over one's internal landscape, finding things that would be normally regarded as disparate, disorganized or as

> simply messy; finding that there were ways to have those live together, to be integrated, to result in a new synthesis.[75]

This (Cold War) Rome, a site of majestic and provisionally integrated but ever-disparate elements, is a far cry from William Rutherford Mead's image of refinement and inspiration flowing from the monuments of the past. Indeed, Wyner's description of Rome, the last few phrases especially, might aptly describe the way he experienced Elliott Carter's First String Quartet when he heard it for the first time in the Eternal City in April 1954. I would go further to suggest that Wyner's epiphanic experience of the interrupted continuities and formal innovations of Carter's Quartet might well have helped him to appreciate Rome. As he told Perlis, it took him a while to *get* Rome. His relationship with Carter and the elder composer's music developed earlier and more easily. Thus, I want to propose that with Yehudi Wyner, Mead's founding premise for the arts at the American Academy in Rome was turned on its head: An inspiring experience of contemporary American music may have come to shape a young composer's appreciation of the radiant monuments of the European past. Furthermore, noting this inversion is one way to mark American music's belated self-confidence in its coming of age.

Notes

Thanks to Elena Aronova, Brigid Cohen, Stephen Dembski, Felix Meyer, Carol Oja, Katharine Park, and Anne Shreffler for their critical readings and comments on this essay. Excerpts from the Laurance P. and Isabel S. Roberts Papers, 1910–2005, located in the Biblioteca Berenson, Villa I Tatti, the Harvard University Center for Italian Renaissance Studies, are reproduced courtesy of the President and Fellows of Harvard College.

1. "Rome Fellowships in Music Announced," *New York Times*, July 9, 1921.

2. W. R. Spalding, "Music Composition," in *American Academy in Rome: Twenty-Fifth Anniversary*, ed. Christopher Grant LaFarge (New York: American Academy in Rome, 1920), 26. See Judith Tick's essay in this volume, "The Classicist Origins of the Rome Prize in Musical Composition, 1890–1920," for an extended reading of this passage.

3. Spalding's tendentious turn of phrase, "Our Democracy" (ironically?) conjures Waldo Frank's *Our America*, which had appeared to great acclaim less than two years before the Academy initiated its fellowship in music composition. In his lyrical reflection on the friction between America's highly developed materialism and its inchoate artistic achievement, Frank pointed to Walt Whitman as a talismanic figure prefiguring the nation's uncertain artistic apotheosis. Spalding was presumably less inspired than Frank by the Bard of Brooklyn, but similarly interested in divining the nation's artistic character and destiny.

4. Spalding, "Music Composition," 26.

5. See Richard Taruskin, "Standoff (II)," *The Oxford History of Western Music*, vol. 5 (New York: Oxford University Press, 2005), 293. Taruskin's analysis of the Cold War system of musical production is discussed in part two, section five of this essay.

6. A portion of Will Norman's work on the New York intellectuals and their relation to émigré cultural theorists was presented in "Émigré Culture Critique in the

Early Cold War," a research presentation given at the Newhouse Humanities Center, Wellesley College, November 22, 2013. See Clement Greenberg, "Avant-Garde and Kitsch," *Partisan Review* 6, no. 5 (1939): 34–45; and Philip Rahv, "Proletarian Literature: A Political Autopsy," *Southern Review* 4, no. 3 (1939): 615–29.

7. Lionel Trilling, *The Liberal Imagination* (New York: New York Review of Books Classics, 2008), 12.

8. George Packer, "A Historian in Camelot," *New York Times Book Review*, December 22, 2014, 9.

9. My argument about Cold War liberalism and postwar music touches on a broad range of issues that will require further elaboration. Richard Taruskin's consideration of Carter in the *Oxford History of Western Music* also raises a range of historiographical questions, some of which are teased out in an exchange between Taruskin and Charles Rosen—in Taruskin's "Nicht Blutbefleckt," *Journal of Musicology* 26, no. 2 (2009): 274–84; and Rosen's "Music and the Cold War," *New York Review of Books*, April 7, 2011, http://www.nybooks.com/articles/archives/2011/apr/07/music-and-cold-war/. For an extended discussion of Taruskin's historiography, see Michael Gallope, "Why Was This Music Desirable? On a Critical Explanation of the Avant-Garde," *Journal of Musicology* 31, no. 2 (forthcoming). The shifting relationship between Elliott Carter and Aaron Copland also warrants further consideration. Copland was deeply involved in US cultural diplomacy and participated actively in the work of Nelson Rockefeller's Office for the Coordination of Inter-American Affairs, discussed in this article. As Emily Ansari suggests, Copland "rebranded" himself during the Cold War, in a shift toward the "vital center" of American liberalism. See Emily Abrams Ansari, "Aaron Copland and the Politics of Cultural Diplomacy," *Journal of the Society of American Music* 5, no. 3 (2011): 335–64. As I will suggest in the following, Nabokov and Carter were able to occupy another ideological space on the liberal high ground—one from which they could practice their own brand of internationalism.

10. Martha Lou Stohlman, "Morey, Charles Rufus," in *A Princeton Companion*, by Alexander Leitch (Princeton: Princeton University Press, 1978).

11. Hammond's war service is summarized in "The Heroes," Monuments Men Foundation, accessed August 27, 2012, http://www.monumentsmenfoundation.org/bio.php?id=123. Robert M. Edsel's *The Monuments Men: Allied Heroes, Nazi Thieves, and the Greatest Treasure Hunt in History* (New York: Center Street, 2009); and Lynn H. Nicholas's *Rape of Europa: The Fate of Europe's Treasures in the Third Reich and the Second World War* (New York: Vintage, 1995) discuss Hammond's war work in its broader context.

12. See, for example, Taylor's "Introduction" to *Wartime Correspondence between President Roosevelt and Pope Pius XII* (New York: Macmillan, 1947), 1–11; and W. David Curtis and C. Evan Stewart, "President Franklin D. Roosevelt's 'Ambassador Extraordinary,'" in http://www.lawschool.cornell.edu/library/WhoWeAre/Mission/upload/CLS2007MyronTaylor.pdf for a summary and vivid visual documentation of Taylor's mission in Rome.

13. "Office of the Coordination of Inter-American Affairs War Service Certificate," Laurance P. and Isabel S. Roberts Papers, 1910–2005.

14. See Clarissa J. Ceglio, "The Wartime Work of U.S. Museums," 2010, a report on research conducted at the Rockefeller Foundation Archives, http://www.rockarch.org/publications/resrep/ceglio.pdf.

15. Press release from the Office for Coordination of Commercial and Cultural Relations between the American Republics, April 10, 1941, quoted in Ceglio, "Wartime Work of U.S. Museums," 6. National Archive records describe the founding of the

OCIAA, which existed under several names, as follows: "The Office of Inter-American Affairs was established by an Executive order of July 30, 1941, in the Office for Emergency Management, as the successor to the Office for Coordination of Commercial and Cultural Relations between the American Republics. Until March 1945 the agency was named the Office of the Coordinator of Inter-American Affairs (OCIAA). Its purpose, as stated in the Executive order was to 'provide for the development of commercial and cultural relations between the American Republics' and thereby to increase the solidarity of the Western Hemisphere and further 'the spirit of cooperations [*sic*] between the Americas in the interest of Hemisphere defense.'" "Records of the Office of Inter-American Affairs (RG 229)," Holocaust-Era Assets, National Archives, accessed January 7, 2013, http://www.archives.gov/research/holocaust/finding-aid/civilian/rg-229.html. See also Catha Paquette, "Soft Power: The Art of Diplomacy in US-Mexican Relations, 1940–46," in *Américas Unidas! Nelson A. Rockfeller's Office of Inter-American Affairs*, ed. Gisela Cramer and Ursual Prutsch (Madrid and Frankfurt: Iberoamericana), 2012.

16. James Reston, "Our Second Line of Defense," *New York Times*, June 29, 1941.

17. *History of the Office of the Coordinator of Inter-American Affairs*, Donald W. Rowland, US Bureau of the Budget, Historical Reports on War Administration, US Government Printing Office, Washington, DC, 1947, 247–48.

18. By focusing on the OCIAA's approach to cultural diversity, inter-American unity of purpose, and the power asymmetry in its exchange scheme, I want to flag a point that will surface explicitly in the second part of this essay: that OCIAA-style Cold War cultural diplomacy provided a model for proponents of "difficult" American modern music to reconcile the specialized subcultures of modernism with claims about the universality of Western artistic values and expression.

19. Eva Cockcroft, "Abstract Expressionism: Weapon of the Cold War," *Artforum* 15, no. 10 (1974): 39–41.

20. Hobnobbing with the Rockefeller family and gaining informal access to its philanthropic operations and diplomatic networks was surely an exceptional perquisite for the new director of AAR. The correspondence in the Isabel and Laurance Roberts Archive includes numerous warm notes between Mr. and Mrs. Roberts and various Rockefeller family members, including Nelson. Writing to Isabel in 1952 about a range of topics from foreign affairs to a new car that she had helped him choose, Nelson Rockefeller offered a rave review of the Robertses' early years in Rome: "You and Laurance are doing the outstanding job of all Americans in Europe for our country." In a breezy thank-you note after a visit that occurred a few years later, Blanchette Rockefeller gushed about a visit to the Academy. "It's been very hard to come down out of the clouds and face the fact that we really are at home again. . . . You don't know how we miss you and Laurence [*sic*] and the Villa Aurelia! I just can't tell you what a marvelous glamorous, restful, fattening, and in all respects perfect time we had with you. Tod [Nelson Rockefeller's first wife] says—'once you've gone sight-seeing with Isabel you might as well stay home, for nobody else seems like any fun by comparison.'" Laurance P. and Isabel S. Roberts Papers, 1910–2005.

21. Eve Cockcroft, "Abstract Expressionism, Weapon of the Cold War," *Artform* 15, no. 19 (1974): 39–41.

22. See Elliott Carter, "For the Academy," in this volume.

23. Robin Winks, *Clock and Gown: Scholars in the Secret War, 1939–1961* (New Haven: Yale University Press, 1987), 384.

24. Card dated May 28, 1957, attached to a letter from Francis Taylor to the American Academy's Board of Trustees, Laurance P. and Isabel S. Roberts Papers, 1910–2005.

Also quoted in Martin Brody, "Cold War Genius: Music and Cultural Diplomacy at the American Academy in Rome," in *Crosscurrents: American and European Music in Interaction, 1900–2000,* ed. Felix Meyer, Carol J. Oja, Wolfgang Rathert, and Anne Shreffler (Woodbridge, UK: Boydell & Brewer, 2014), 382.

25. The villa, built in the middle of the seventeenth century for Cardinal Giralomo Farnese, was an ideal site for testing the premises of the American century in a foreign outpost. It had served as Garibaldi's headquarters during the 1849 French siege of the city. A Philadelphia heiress, Clara Jessup Heyland, purchased the estate in 1885 and bequeathed it to AAR in 1909. The AAR elder, J. P. Morgan, quickly acquired the contiguous land at the top of the hill on behalf of the Academy. A century after Garibaldi's last stand on the Janiculum, Isabel and Laurance Roberts restored the rundown estate, turning it into an unparalleled staging ground for lavish entertainments and political/artistic networking on the Roman front. A small part of the story of the Robertses' strategic entertaining is included in a companion piece to this essay: Brody, "Cold War Genius." Isabel Roberts intermittently recorded the official guest lists of the Academy—an extraordinary catalogue of international luminaries in the arts, foreign academy and ambassadorial representatives, US government officials, and AAR's own fellows and residents—in her journals, held in Laurance P. and Isabel S. Roberts Papers, 1910–2005.

See also Richard Trythall's "A Brief History of the Rome Prize in Composition: 1947–2006" in this volume for a discussion of the importance of the Robertses' role as host to an international coterie of artists and diplomats.

26. Handwritten letter to Laurance and Isabel Roberts, December 11, 1959, Laurance P. and Isabel S. Roberts Papers, 1910–2005.

27. Yehudi Wyner interview with Martin Brody, conducted on July 27, 2007.

28. Frances Stonor Saunders, *Who Paid the Piper? The CIA and the Cultural Cold War* (London: Granta, 1999), 143.

29. Reginald Smith Brindle, "Notes from Abroad: The Rome International Conference of Contemporary Music" *Musical Times* 95, no. 1336 (1954): 328–29.

30. Stonor Saunders, *Who Paid the Piper?*, 145.

31. Founded in 1950, the Congress for Cultural Freedom was created through the combined efforts of various figures in and out of the US government, from such virulent anticommunist public intellectuals as Sidney Hook and James Burnham to burgeoning CIA/Office of Policy Coordination leaders as Frank Wisner and the anticommunist trade unionist Irving Brown. In addition to the kinds of CCF activities discussed in this article, it maintained a broad range of influential cultural journals and nurtured a vast network of anticommunist intellectual/cultural operatives. See especially Stonor Saunders, *Who Paid the Piper?*; and Peter Coleman, *The Liberal Conspiracy: The Congress for Cultural Freedom and the Struggle for the Mind of Postwar Europe* (New York: Free Press, 1989).

32. Nabokov wrote to Copland on 5 July 1951, thanking him for establishing his relationship with the Academy. "I stayed at your lovely apartment in Rome and I think it is due to you that I was offered it by the Robertsons [*sic*] (who by the way are real angels). Thank you so much, dear Aron. I am thinking of you all the time and of the immense burden the school must be for you without our wonderful friend Sergej Alexandrowicz." Copland was then presiding over the Tanglewood composition program. Letter from Nabokov to Copland, courtesy of the Nicolas Nabokov Archive, Harry Ransom Center, University of Texas, Austin.

33. Nicolas Nabokov to Arthur Schlesinger, July 19, 1951, Nicolas Nabokov Archive.

34. For the context of Nabokov's "sheep's closing" quip, see Brody, "Cold War Genius," 383.

35. The Congress for Cultural Freedom plays a curiously small but compelling role in Nabokov's autobiographical reflection (a "story-maker's" book, as he puts it), *Bagazh: Memoirs of a Russian Cosmopolitan* (New York: Atheneum 1975), vii. His account of the rise and fall of the CCF in *Bagazh* displays the master's inimitable mix of unbridled ambition, patrician hauteur, mischievous charm, and a parodic naïveté that strains credulity. In introducing the topic of the CCF, he forthrightly declares: "No one before had tried to mobilize intellectuals and artists on a worldwide scale in order to fight an ideological war against oppressors of the mind, or to defend what one called by the hackneyed term 'our cultural heritage'" (242). And then, only a page later: "Not in my wildest dreams could I have expected that my 'dream festival' would be supported by America's spying establishment, nor did I know that the fare for my delightful first-class flight to Paris was being paid by the CIA via the [American] labor union's European representative, the cheerful Mr. [Irving] Brown" (243). Nabokov's political attitudes and Washington networks are succinctly summarized in Ian Wellens, *Music on the Frontline: Nicolas Nabokov's Struggle against Communism and Middlebrow Culture* (Burlington, VT: Ashgate Press, 2002).

36. As Lynn Garafola notes in "Lincoln Kirstein, Modern Dance, and the Left: The Genesis of an American Ballet," in *Journal of the Society for Dance Research* 23, no. 1 (2005): 18–35: "In 1941 the company, now united with Balanchine's defunct American Ballet and rebaptized American Ballet Caravan, toured Latin America under the semi-official auspices of the US Department of State. . . . More than $140,000 in government funds flowed into the company's coffers" (29). See also Martin Duberman, *The Worlds of Lincoln Kirstein* (Random House: New York, 2009) for a discussion of the ongoing Kirstein-Rockefeller connection.

37. See Brody, "Cold War Genius," 384–85.

38. Department of State Bulletin (July 27, 1947), quoted in Amy Beal, "Negotiating Cultural Networks: American Music in Darmstadt, 1946–56," *Journal of the American Musicological Society* 53, no. 1 (2000): 112. As Beal notes, the directive was given to General Lucius Clay, head of the military government, on July 11, 1947.

39. Nicolas Nabokov, *Bagazh*, 172.

40. Andrea Pitzer, *The Secret History of Vladimir Nabokov* (New York: Pegasus Books, 2012), chapter 9.

41. Letter from George Kennan to Nicolas Nabokov, July 14, 1948, Nicolas Nabokov Archive.

42. Quoted in Robert D. Dean, *Imperial Brotherhood: Gender and the Making of Cold War Foreign Policy* (Amherst: University of Massachusetts Press, 2001), 137.

43. The story of the Waldorf Conference has become a touchstone for the study of postwar Euro-American music and politics. See, for example, Alex Ross, *The Rest Is Noise: Listening to the Twentieth Century* (New York: Farrar, Straus and Giroux, 2007), 373–8, and Stonor Saunders, *Who Paid the Piper?*, 101–3.

44. The Manifesto is reprinted in Coleman, *Liberal Conspiracy*, 249–50.

45. "Arthur Schlesinger to Averell Harriman, July 19, 1950," in *The Letters of Arthur Schlessinger* (New York: Random House, 2013), 33.

46. In Coleman, *Liberal Conspiracy*, 9.

47. The international music festivals sponsored by the Congress for Cultural Freedom are discussed in Stonor Saunders, *Who Paid the Piper?* and Mark Carroll, *Music and Ideology in Cold War Europe* (Cambridge: Cambridge University Press, 2003).

48. John Roche, "On the Intellectual Barricades," *New Leader* 72, no. 17 (November 13, 1989): 18.

49. See Beal, "Negotiating Cultural Networks," 112. There are many twists and turns in this story. Evarts, for example, joined the army after a stint as a faculty member at

Black Mountain College, where he had worked closely with the set designer Xanti Schawinsky, a student of Kurt Schwitters and one of the wilder Bauhaus alums to immigrate to and teach in the United States. The young Evarts was thus a crucial link between the pre- and postwar German avant-gardes. See Martin Brody, "The Scheme of the Whole: Black Mountain and the Course of American Music," in *Black Mountain College: Experiment in Art*, ed. Vincent Katz (Cambridge: MIT Press, 2002), 240–44.

50. See Carroll, *Music and Ideology*, for an extended discussion of the ideological context of the 1952 Paris Festival and its implications for Nabokov's 1954 Rome Festival.

51. Smith Brindle, "Notes from Abroad," 329.

52. Ibid.

53. Michael Steinberg, "Rome Music Fete Upset By Turmoil," *New York Times*, April 9, 1954.

54. See James Wierzbicki, *Elliott Carter* (Champagne: University of Illinois Press, 2011), 51. Wierzbicki notes that Nabokov, as well as Aaron Copland and Walter Piston, Carter's composition teacher at Harvard, were all on the Rome Prize selection committee that year. "This is not to suggest that Carter's success had anything to do with pulling strings by him [Nabokov] or anyone else," Wierzbicki proposes. Whether or not this was the case, the documentary evidence suggests that the performance of Carter's First String Quartet in the 1954 Rome Festival did require Nabokov to pull strings. The correspondence between Nabokov, Fred Goldbeck (an administrator for the CCF), and the Parrenin Quartet indicates that Carter's Quartet would not have been performed in Rome without Nabokov's intervention. "*Carter Trop difficile*" was the curt remark in a telegram from the Parennin sent to the CCF office in the fall before the Rome performance. A Henze piece was proposed as an alternative, but the Carter prevailed. See Brody, "Cold War Genius."

55. A portion of the story of the Liège Prize and its relation to the performance of the First Quartet in Rome is told in Daniel Guberman, "Composing Freedom: Elliott Carter's 'Self-Reinvention' and the Early Cold War" (PhD diss., University of North Carolina), 151–58.

56. Michael Steinberg, "Rome Fete Hears Three Chamber Works," *New York Times*, April 12, 1954.

57. Enzo Restagno, *Elliott Carter in Conversation with Enzo Restagno for Settembre Musica 1989*, ISAM Monograph, 52. Taruskin, "Standoff (II)," *Oxford History*, also notes the importance for Carter of his burgeoning connections with the elite composers of postwar Italy.

58. Brody, "Cold War Genius," discusses the negotiations in spring 1954 to shift the ISCM international headquarters from New York to Rome, in which Carter and Roger Sessions, the current ISCM president in New York, played the key roles.

59. Elliott Carter, "Letter From Europe," *Perspectives of New Music* 1, no. 2 (1963): 195.

60. Letter from William Schuman to Elliott Carter, March 2, 1982, congratulating Carter on receiving the Ernst von Siemens Music Prize.

61. Milton Babbitt, "My Vienna Triangle," in *The Collected Essays of Milton Babbitt*, ed. Stephen Peles (Princeton: Princeton University Press, 2003), 480.

62. Amy Beal, *New Music New Allies: American Experimental Music in West Germany from the Zero Hour to Reunification* (Berkeley: University of California Press, 2006), tells the crucial story of Cage's reception in Germany during the early Cold War. And, of course, the literature positing and rebuking claims about postwar American serial hegemony is extensive. Joseph Straus, "The Myth of Serial 'Tyranny' in the 1950s and 1960s," *Musical Quarterly* 83, no. 3 (1999): 301–43, is a touchstone. My comments on Carter's singular position in the postwar international scene are intended to pry loose whatever remains

of reified dichotomies: uptown/downtown, American academic serialism/European zero-hour avant-garde. Not every European composer of the Cold War era found the earth beneath them quaking or history resetting at the zero hour; Cage was hardly the only American connected with emerging European new music communities. The cultural map of uptown and downtown postwar American composers and their pathways to Europe still need a good deal of filling in.

63. See Elliott Carter, "For the Academy," in this volume for a brief comment on the beginning of Carter's and Boulez's friendship in Baden-Baden in 1954. Without a significant textual equivalent to the Boulez-Cage correspondence, the well-known connection between Carter and Boulez is difficult to weave into the historiography of postwar avant-gardes and musical modernism.

64. This was also true of another of Carter's important friendships during the 1953–54 year, with the novelist Ignazio Silone—an imposing figure in Italian letters memorably described by William Weaver as "a haunted man, full of sorrows." See "The Mystery of Ignazio Silone," *New York Review of Books*, March 14, 2002, 35. Carter tells us in the brief memoir of his time in Rome that appears in this volume that he met Silone at Edmund Wilson's apartment in New York, and that their friendship resumed and deepened during Carter's year as a Rome Prize fellow. The not entirely invisible hand of the incomparably cosmopolitan Nabokov may be felt here as well. Silone was a charter member of the CCF, worked closely with Nabokov and corresponded regularly with him about the strategic planning of Congress activities in Italy.

65. These relationships and their impact on Carter, Petrassi, and Nabokov are documented in the extensive correspondence between them, now held in several archives. A few of the pertinent sources are the Carter archive at the Sacher Foundation in Basel, the American Congress for Cultural Freedom archive at the University of Chicago, the Nicolas Nabokov archive, and the Laurance and Isabel Roberts Papers.

66. Taruskin, "Standoff (II)," *Oxford History*, 293.

67. Ibid., 295.

68. Ibid., 294–95.

69. There are many threads in this story. For example, the development of the long-playing vinyl record, as much as the appearance of the electronic medium for "advanced" musical composition, portended the possibility of a new role for modern music in the public sphere. Here the story touches another strand in the New York cultural prestige network: the cohort around Goddard Lieberson at Columbia Records that briefly generated pathbreaking recordings of canonical European modern music and a "Modern American Music" series. Under Leiberson's leadership, Columbia Records and CBS offered unprecedented promise for the distribution of difficult modern music.

70. Here is a bit of the context: "Nowhere is it safe to draw conclusions about what belongs to whom, because it isn't how the music *sounds*, but how it can be *thought* that counts: outsiders—even if certified by doctorates in music—all have tin ears." Mark Slobin, *Subcultural Sounds: Micromusics of the West* (Hanover: Wesleyan University Press, 1993), xiii.

71. Babbitt's 1958 "The Composer as Specialist" (alternatively titled "Who Cares If You Listen?"), in Milton Babbitt, *Collected Essays of Milton Babbitt*, 48–54, is the locus classicus.

72. Wyner/Brody interview.

73. Vivian Perlis, interview with Yehudi Wyner, Oral History of American Music, Yale University Library, New Haven, Connecticut. Quoted with permission.

74. Ibid.

75. Ibid.

Part Four

Primary Sources

Chapter Seven

What They Said

American Composers on Rome

Vivian Perlis

Introduction

I arrived at the American Academy in Rome for a stay of several weeks during the summer of 2003. The city was in the midst of an extreme heat wave. Romans were leaving early for the customary August vacations at the seashore or mountains, while those who reluctantly stayed in Rome tended to move and speak as if in slow motion. At the Academy, fans and ice were the most valued possessions, and both were in short supply. Residents gradually replaced professional attire with shorts and T-shirts that became barer and shorter as the heat wave continued. Meals were taken at the long tables in the courtyard, with the desperate hope of catching an occasional breeze.

On my first evening at the Academy, I chose a table and introduced myself. When I asked the person seated next to me about her field of study, she replied simply, "I am a classicist." Following a second and third similar rejoinder, I was asked to describe my own work, and I said (partly in jest), "I am a modernist." "Well, what is a modernist?" I floundered over a description and then tried, "Americanist," which drew even more puzzled reactions. I soon realized we were not speaking the same language: classical art and architecture had nothing to do with what musicians think of as "classical" music. Furthermore, for classicists, modernism was thought to have begun somewhere around the time of Bernini. I found myself in an unusual (and humbling) situation—no one knew who I was or about my work. Studies in contemporary arts and recent history were rare, and with few exceptions, American composers were unfamiliar names.

When Aaron Copland had been in residence at the Academy in 1950, he commented in a letter to his young friend Leonard Bernstein that the only

American composer known in Italy was George Gershwin. More than half a century later, but for the addition of Copland himself, and perhaps a few pieces by Leonard Bernstein, Charles Ives, and John Cage, the situation had not changed remarkably.

Like others who had come to the Academy in Rome through the years, I found that my anonymity had advantages—it was a reminder of other worlds and other people, with widely varying values and pursuits, in which the insular world of contemporary music played only a small part, if any. To communicate with scholars and researchers at the Academy, I needed to consider anew the contradictions and inadequacies of our musical terminology and to develop definitions and explanations beyond those currently in use in music history and musicology.

An advantage of the terrible heat wave of 2003 was that it provided a language and a communal topic of conversation: how could a newcomer swipe an extra fan from a sleeping colleague? Where were the air-conditioned movies? Which churches had the coolest underground grottos? The weather, in its extremes, became the dominant challenge for everyone, whether classicist or modernist.

I soon met the two Rome Prize fellows in composition. With great relief (at least for me as the newcomer), we found shared interests and mutual acquaintanceships in the closely connected smaller world of contemporary American music. The Academy had a long history of influence on American composers, and I was eager to discuss its impact on these two most recent arrivals. Both agreed to be included in the Yale project called Oral History of American Music, referred to for convenience as OHAM. We arranged for recorded interviews, agreeing to dispense with the whirring fans—a major concession—for the sake of the recorded sound quality. In these interviews, the composers spoke freely about their experiences before and during the past year as they were thrust into lives that differed dramatically from their American roots. I hoped to collect and preserve their impressions of Rome and of the unique atmosphere and quality of life at the American Academy. Most important would be the effects of these unique experiences on their creative work.

What They Said

What they said and what other composition fellows of the Academy said in the past can be read from interview transcripts or heard in full at OHAM in the Yale Library, where the material is preserved. The historian George Kennan once said that history is not what happened in the past, but what it felt like to be there when it happened. OHAM's interviews, directly in the voices of the composers, aim to reveal what it felt like to be at the Academy at a particular time in a life history. For some, the effect was on specific pieces; for others, especially the Rome Prize fellows (in contrast to senior composers who came as "RAAR"s—residents, who were more advanced in their careers), the experience was crucial, almost invariably occurring at a pivotal time in a career.

The interviews conducted in the summer of 2003 at the Academy were with David Sanford and Mark Kilstofte, both in their midtwenties. They had completed their formal training and were at the start of teaching careers and into productive and energetic periods of creativity. These two composers, from very different personal and family backgrounds and divergent musical influences, described similar feelings and impressions upon their arrivals in Rome. They were overwhelmed at the wide range of scholarship at the Academy and were astonished at the physical presence of Rome and its baroque architecture. Their personal tastes and educational influences had been toward modern art and stylistic simplicity; their past experiences had been largely with modernism in art and architecture, literature, and music. Despite the initial sense of displacement and strangeness, David Sanford and Mark Kilstofte agreed that the Rome experience was extraordinarily positive and powerful.

David Sanford's music is characterized by jazz rhythms and big band sounds. Accustomed to working with experienced jazz players in New York and New England, to his surprise he eventually found excellent professional performers in Rome, and he drew on their abilities in presenting his own compositions at the Academy. Mark Kilstofte came to Rome from a college teaching position in the American South where he was becoming well known as a talented instrumental and choral composer. Mark was aware of the importance of the timing of his fellowship. He said, "Initially back in March of 2002, when I got word that I was going to Rome, I was pinching myself. It was pretty hard to take in. I had been writing a symphony for a very long time and reached the point at which I would either finish it soon or never get it done. And that's one reason this year was so important. I don't think I could have completed it unless I had this kind of time to work" (OHAM, August 2003).

The histories of many composers as we look back from these two Rome Prize fellows of 2003 reveal thoughts and feelings about their experiences at the Academy.

Here is a segment from an interview with Aaron Jay Kernis:

> I was about sixteen when I felt an outcast, heavily involved in musical activities in school, and I began not to care about very much else, which is actually the reason I went into conservatories. As the time neared to go to college I was afraid of going to a university—my time would be divided so much that I would not be able to develop the way I wanted to, and now looking back, particularly with some of my more recent experiences—such as the AA Rome with more scholarly people—I began to have an intense awareness of a lot of other things in the world. [Previously,] I [had] felt somewhat cheated because I don't have a good knowledge of art history or world history or insights into literature, especially poetry. In a way, I'm sorry I didn't take a more liberal

> approach to my education—a more varied approach. In September of '84 I went to the Academy with the other fellow, Paul Moravec—gee, it was difficult at first to make the adjustment. It was my first European anything. I had been commissioned to write a small orchestra piece for the Youth Symphony of New York, and I was in total state of confusion. The piece turned out to be what I was feeling at the time. (OHAM, November 1986)

Kernis returned to Rome in 1986 from Amsterdam to visit with friends at the Academy. He said, "I found it a very necessary place, having come from Amsterdam where I didn't feel the same kind of emotional warmth."

Paul Moravec, also at the Academy during 1984–85, spoke in an OHAM interview in 2006 about absolute music and programmatic pieces and his dependence on the particular conditions or on the commission. "Pieces come to me in all varieties, all different ways. It's serendipity, really. . . . I wrote a piece called *Atmosfera a Villa Aurelia,* which is about the villa on the campus of the American Academy in Rome. That title was given to me by the violinist Bobby [Robert] McDuffie, who premiered it with his friends in the summer of 2005. That was part of the commission. It also gave me the catalyst for how to make the piece."

Copland at the Academy

The OHAM archive also provides a sense of what Rome felt like for those who came as resident composers, usually older and more experienced artists. Reading interview transcripts today with composers who had been residents in the past, it becomes clear that the Academy produced a strong and continuing relationship with European music and the European scene on American composers. In this regard, Aaron Copland is a prime example. Copland has often been referred to as the "dean of American composers," the "president of American music," or as Virgil Thomson called him, the "Mother of Us All," but Copland himself believed (as did some of his colleagues such as Arthur Berger and Elliott Carter) that the "Americana" aspect of his work was overemphasized. Copland's early musical education was European, through Rubin Goldmark, who taught traditional forms. In fact, Goldmark would not allow his student to leave for France until the sonata form was properly mastered. Later, through Nadia Boulanger and Copland's years in France, the setting, the *solfège,* and the milieu all were European. Asked to name primary musical influences, it was invariably Bach first, followed by Fauré and Stravinsky (through Boulanger), Liszt, Berlioz, and Mahler. While Copland admired Ives, he did not turn to him or other American composers. When faced with a commission for a work, Copland would carefully study pieces of the European masters in the particular genre.

During the thirties Copland discovered Mexican music and the Mexican people through Chávez, and there followed a twelve-year hiatus in his travels to Europe. After the war, he wrote in one of his travel diaries: "Europe is coming alive again in the world of the arts."[1] Copland planned a trip abroad for May and June of 1949. He was then living with Erik Johns, a dancer (later his librettist for the opera *The Tender Land*). Johns traveled with Copland to Europe, where they visited Britten and Tippett in London. Copland enjoyed a nostalgic reunion with Nadia Boulanger in Paris. She introduced him to "the new Boulangerie" and to Boulez, who "was the topic of conversation wherever music people got together."[2] Copland found performances of his own music in Europe disappointing and a lack of published pieces everywhere, including Rome, where he paid his first visit to the Academy. "Upon our arrival we were met by composer Alexei Haieff, who showed us around. There were the usual receptions and sightseeing. I was interviewed on the radio and somehow managed to reply in Italian after some heavy coaching. We left Rome for Florence, which seemed nice and small-townish. . . . I spent some time with Luigi Dallapiccola [and] Newell Jenkins, who told me that the Italians don't really care a fig about knowing American music and are completely unaware of it, except for Gershwin."[3]

But Copland's urge to be in Europe had returned. He applied for a Fulbright scholarship for 1951. "I was offered two million lira, and for two exciting minutes I thought I was a millionaire! Then I rushed for a pencil, and it turned into $3,250! But the crossing was paid for, and I would be staying at the American Academy in Rome beginning in Jan."[4] (In an OHAM interview, the composer Jack Beeson explained the relationship between the Fulbright program and the Academy that allowed composers on Fulbright Fellowships to support and extend their residency periods at the Academy.) Copland sailed on the Queen Elizabeth on December 23, 1950, again traveling with Erik Johns. He had sublet his house in Westchester to the pianists Arthur Gold and Robert Fizdale. Copland's income had returned to what he called a "more normal low" after the Hollywood years.

In one of his travel diaries, the composer wrote: "After landing at Cherbourg, we went on to Paris, and on New Year's Eve, I took the train to Rome. A rep from the American Academy met me at the station. I was given an apartment overlooking all of Rome. It came with a cook and a good Bechstein grand piano." Copland's only complaint was about the (lack of) heat: "I was condemned to cold feet for several months!" he wrote. Harold "Sonny" Shapero and Lukas Foss were at the Academy when Copland arrived, and Leo Smit was also in Rome. Copland wrote, "They all helped me get acquainted with things Roman."[5] (Lukas Foss described the same period of time in an OHAM interview.)

Copland's hope was to get started on a piano concerto for the Louisville Symphony and William Kapell, but this plan did not develop further, and he continued to compose piano music with no plan for its final form. He wrote to Arthur and Esther Berger, "Life is almost too soft," and to Claire Reis, "It's a heavenly town! But there's not much music going on by American standards."[6] Copland took what he called a "big plunge" by buying a car—a green Morris-Minor. As he wrote in a letter to his sister Laurine in February 1951: "Dear La, today I get the tiny car I bought for a thousand dollars—it's said to get thirty miles on a gallon—and since gas is 80 cents a gallon here, everyone buys small cars for economy sake. Also, many streets are so narrow that a Buick wouldn't fit!"[7] He went on to describe his days: composing mornings and exploring afternoons in the car with Smit and other friends. Copland commented in his diary, "Wherever I go, everybody in Rome kept telling me that the Pope and I look alike!"[8]

Copland had accepted duties for the State Department that included lectures on American music in various cities, including Naples, Genoa, and Bologna. He tried to speak as much as possible in Italian. He wrote in a diary, "It was a small musical world in Italy. When Leo gave a recital at the Academy, there were too many Americans present and not enough Italians. The same situation held when I gave my first lecture on music, with Leo playing the examples."[9]

While in Rome, Copland received letters from friends, among them Bernstein, who wrote (March 15, 1951): "*Sul Gianicolo,* it's as though you should always have been enthroned on this mighty hill being the real Dean (I don't mean this nastily but truly), and exuding your charm and Vishnu-like balance over the young. How wonderful June is there! Write me about it and about Israel." That spring, from Rome, Copland made his first visit to Israel. When he returned, he conducted David Diamond's "Rounds," Copland's first conducting of a work other than his own. The concert (May 1, 1951) featured Copland's Clarinet Concerto. The Rome radio also invited him to conduct an all-Copland concert, and he found the orchestra surprisingly good. Leo Smit said in an interview, "We decided to program Aaron's [1920] Piano Concerto, and the outcome was that we recorded it for the Concert Hall label." Smit added, "Aaron didn't talk much about composers, but when we played four-hands from my Bach chorale preludes, I heard him mutter, 'He's the best.'"[10]

Copland looked back at his time in Rome as an oasis of serenity. There were major changes in his life at that time, both personal and professional—not the least being the sudden deaths of Copland's mentor, Serge Koussevitzky, and his publisher, Ralph Hawkes. News of both deaths came while Copland was in Rome. Another serious change was the marriage of Victor Kraft, his longtime personal partner. The Morris-Minor from Rome was given as a special wedding gift.

One day, Copland was surprised to fine a letter in his mailbox from Harvard University: he had been chosen to deliver the Charles Eliot Norton lectures during the 1951–52 academic year! It was yet another first for Copland: Stravinsky and Hindemith had the honor earlier, but Copland was the first American-born composer chosen for the poetry chair. Copland wrote, "I immediately began to worry about what I could possible say! I spent most of my remaining time in Rome at the Academy's excellent library reading on aesthetics, hoping to stimulate my thoughts."[11] Copland's European-ness is nowhere more evident than the music he chose for the concerts that followed his Norton lectures: Stravinsky, Berlioz, and Bizet; Mozart, Couperin, de Falla, Schubert, Ravel, and Webern; Tippett, Chávez, and Villa-Lobos. Finally, several jazz artists and a few pieces by Americans—Ives, Thomson, and Copland himself. Whereas most composers credit the Academy as a place that nurtured the composition of particular pieces of music, for Copland, it was his book, *Music and Imagination,* based on the Norton lectures, that had its genesis in the library of the American Academy in Rome. As with his pieces considered most "American," about the Norton lectures, Copland said, "I seemed to find America while abroad."[12]

Others at the Academy

Jack Beeson was a Rome Prize Fellow from 1948 to 1950. Here is an excerpt from a 1999 interview with him:

> I started teaching in '45—theory, which I didn't like doing, and humanities, which I did like doing. I got married in '47, and had the idea to take a year off to go somewhere and compose. I applied for a Guggenheim and the Rome Prize. Douglas [Moore] called me into his office. He was apparently on both juries. And he said, "you're being offered both and you can't have both. It's not allowed. So I would suggest that you take the Rome Prize because that's given to younger people, and Guggenheims can be got any time. Well, it was a little unnerving to be offered both at once. I took his advice, and we went to Rome.

Lukas Foss was at the American Academy in Rome in 1951. He was not quite thirty. German-born, Foss emigrated to the United States as a teenager, and he soon came to be considered one of the most talented of young American composers. As with Copland, Foss was identified with a few pieces reflecting the American experience, one such was "The Prairie." And as with Copland, the essentially European quality of much of his music tends to be underestimated:

> The Rome Prize and the Fulbright were combined, so I had about two years at the Academy. I got married in Rome. And I wrote my Piano Concerto no. 2 and the *Parable of Death* while at the Academy. Both pieces are highly neoclassic—the Piano Concerto very Beethovenian and the *Parable* modeled after Bach's Passions with the story being told in a narrative, but interrupted by little poems from Rilke. And that is an idea I got from Bach, because he interrupts the story of the death of Christ with poetry of his day. So I did the same, except I chose one poet. I translated an entire book of Rilke's while in Rome

and decided to set the one story, "The Parable of Death." I set it in German and actually had to enlist the help of [the poet] Anthony Hecht, who was also at the Academy, to help with the English translation so it would be metrically the same as the German. Another piece I wrote in Rome was the Saxophone Quartet, commissioned by the Amherst Quartet in Buffalo. Overlooking the ancient buildings of Rome, I wrote, of all things, a saxophone quartet that was not jazzy.

Going to Rome, to Italy, was like nothing I had known, and I fell in love with it totally and utterly. It's still my favorite country. And those Rome days were wonderful. To have a studio at the Academy, not to worry about anything, to have meals with other artists. . . . I had experienced that first at the MacDowell Colony, where I wrote *The Prairie.* That was a little similar—freedom, no money concerns, just the chance to compose. (OHAM 1988)

Andrew Imbrie's time in Rome goes back a few years earlier, to the reopening of the Academy after the War:

The American Academy in Rome had closed during World War II, and this was the first two years they were reopening. They didn't have a competition—I was just invited. I think it was that people recommended me. The other composer was Alexei Haieff. He stayed on in Rome. He just became a Roman. I wrote several pieces and I got to know some Italian composers, like Dallapiccola and Petrassi. It was a wonderful opportunity to be independent and to work and meet people in the other arts, and to travel, to speak Italian, and to get a feel for what Europe is really like. It was an experience I do think important for any American to have. In fact, I think it would be important for Europeans to come to America for the same reason. I don't think they've ever been very curious about us. They typecast us as much as they can. It was true right after World War II, and it's still true today. They think of America as being represented by Copland on the one hand and Cage on the other, and perhaps Ives—and that's it. But in fact some of our music was performed in Rome. It began to be customary for the Rome radio orchestra to play works by students at the Academy, although we didn't call ourselves students. We were very proud of being professionals.

I wrote my Whitman piece in Rome, *On the Beach at Fontana,* a choral piece for chorus and strings. I remember hearing pieces in Rome for chorus with a lot of brass. Big pieces by Italian composers, and I decided, wouldn't it be nice if you had just strings with chorus. So that was a reaction to all the very brassy choral pieces. We also put on concerts in town in conjunction with Italian composers, and they were courteous and even encouraging. But one had the feeling it was all just part of the game—there was sort of a superficial polite interest in what we were doing. (OHAM 1983)

The composer Betsy Jolas, who holds dual citizenship in France and the United States, said: "Rome came at just the right time. It was the millennium, and I was writing a piece for Bill Christie—a big piece for orchestra, chorus, and soloists, with a text by Lucretius. It's called *Motet III.* I was at the Villa Aurelia, and it was such a perfect place to do this. Picked lemons and grapefuits and had three pianos in my *capella,* one built for Liszt" (OHAM 2001).

Conclusion

Many other composers describe meaningful experiences at the Academy in OHAM interviews. Among them: Yehudi Wyner, Ellen Zwilich, Ezra Laderman, Tania León, Ned Rorem, George Rochberg, Scott Lindroth, Stephen Jaffe, Chris Theofinidis, Jacob Druckman, David del Tredici, and John Harbison. These oral history testimonies make up, at least in part, for the lack of traditional correspondence due to the ubiquitous use of telephone and e-mail. The American Academy in Rome has had a powerful and continuous impact on generations of American composers. It is urgent that scholars collect and preserve this material, while still possible, from the primary sources. The voices of those who make our musical history hold an authenticity and spontaneity that cannot be duplicated elsewhere. The dialogue between American composers and the American Academy in Rome runs throughout the narrative of the arts of our times. It deserves to be made permanently available to historians now and in the future.

Notes

1. Aaron Copland and Vivian Perlis, *Copland: Since 1943* (New York: St. Martin's Press, 1989), 145.
2. Ibid., 146.
3. Ibid., 147–48.
4. Ibid., 147.
5. Ibid., 170.
6. Ibid.
7. Ibid., 171.
8. Ibid.
9. Ibid.
10. From a 1987 interview with Smit for ibid.
11. Ibid., 175.
12. See, for example, this passage from Aaron Copland, "The Composer in Industrial America," in *Music and Imagination* (Cambridge: Harvard University Press, 1952), 99–100: "My years in Europe from the age of twenty to twenty-three made me acutely conscious of the origins of the music I loved. Most of the time I spent in France, where the characteristics of French culture are evident at every turn. The relation of French music to the life around me became increasingly manifest. Gradually, the idea that my personal expression in music ought somehow to be related to my own back-home environment took hold of me. The conviction grew inside me that the two things that seemed always to have been so separate in American—music and the life about

me—must be made to touch. This desire to make the music I wanted to write come out of the life I had lived in America became a preoccupation of mine in the twenties. It was not so very different from the experience of other young American artists, in other fields, who had gone abroad to study in that period; in greater or lesser degree, all of us discovered America in Europe."

Chapter Eight

The New Music Scene in Rome and the American Presence since World War II

Excerpts from a Roundtable, Moderated by Richard Trythall

Edited by Martin Brody

Mauro Bortolotti, Composer, Cofounder of Nuova Consonanza

Rebirth after the War

For those of us who were students then, the postwar years meant a rediscovery of freedom, the departure of a regime that had kept cultural frontiers closed for a long time. The censorship had been severe: no poetry, no music from abroad. In 1950 we were still students, although we were pretty advanced, and we craved to know what was going on in Europe and America. To this end, a group of young composers studying at the Santa Cecilia Conservatory, myself included, decided to do something to create systematic opportunites to increase our awareness, beyond what our individual contacts would allow. Although it didn't become official until a few years later, we created an association of new music performers and composers in the late fifties, Nuova Consonanza. The founders were Domenico Guaccero, Franco Evangelisti, the often-forgotten Mario Bertoncini, and Daniele Paris, who was to become Nuova Consonanza's favorite conductor (a fate that almost ended his composition career). Egisto

Macchi came in later. All but Evangelisti were students of Petrassi. The name, Nuova Consonanza, bore a slight hint of criticism for the current contemporary music dogmas, such as serialism. At that point, there was no aleatoric music and no improvisation—and electronic music was in its infancy.

It soon became clear that the only way we could break into the academic Italian music world was by making a new initiative. We couldn't afford to produce our programs at the major musical institutions. The costs of putting something on at Santa Cecilia would have sent us into bankruptcy. So we chose to ask the foreign academies in Rome if we could count on their help—especially to use their rooms as concert halls. The American Academy, the Goethe Institute, and the Japan Cultural Institute in Rome agreed first. They were eager to make their facilities available—though we usually had to bring our own chairs! But this allowed us, even required us, to hear new music from abroad, since each concert hosted by an academy had to include music by both Italian composers and the composers of the hosting institution's nation.

Michele Dall'Ongaro, Composer, Founder of Spettro Sonoro (A Broadcast of Contemporary Music by RAI)

Visitors from the United States

After World War II, there was a huge difference between Rome and Milan. Milan was really the capital of musical modernism in Italy. There were the big publishers, the most advanced teachers, La Scala. And of course Central Europe is just around the corner. Rome, on the other hand, had the most reactionary conservatory in the country—though that fact was partly counterbalanced by a few big assets: Goffredo Petrassi, Nuova Consonanza, and the academies of various foreign countries. And, of course, an agreeably warm climate. For some reason, the flux of immigrating American composers focused on Rome rather than Milan. Perhaps it was because of climate, but perhaps it was because of the cultural climate—more liberal, less tied to the dogmas of the avant-garde. People like me, who attended the Conservatory around 1970, could make exciting encounters. Here are a few snippets from my personal memories.

1. A night at Beat 72, a venue far from the mainstream: The audience had come there to listen to a pianist—I omit his name because he didn't show up. But Alvin Curran, a musician we much admired, was there, and he spontaneously sat at the piano and started improvising. Soon after, some of us joined at the organ, percussion, and so on. The music making continued until 11 pm. It was a great alternative to our dreary conservatory routine.

2. In 1976 the students occupied the Conservatory. It may have been the first time something like this had happened since the age of Palestrina! Everybody was making music everywhere—stairs, corridors, and so on. Enter Frederic Rzewski, who started to play his piano variations on "*El pueblo unido jamás será vencido*"—This was possibly a premiere. The police stepped in—but they waited for the end of the piece.
3. A few years after, I was playing piano in the RAI (Italian Radio) Symphony Orchestra. A heroic Lukas Foss was conducting. The program included Foss's own Variations on a Scarlatti sonata and Ives's Fourth Symphony. The orchestra stalwartly refused to play the Ives. But Foss, with incredible serenity, managed to come to an agreement with them. The program would include Foss's own piece, then the Respighi, and only the last movement from Ives's symphony. It was a great success!
4. Back to my youth. Some students, myself included, founded an ensemble, Spettro Sonoro, entirely devoted to contemporary music. As I remember, the first things we studied, apart from Franco Evangelisti and Aldo Clementi, were pieces by Cage (First Variation), Earle Brown, Morton Feldman, and Christian Wolff.

Paolo Coteni, Artistic Director, Silenzio

Walking through Rome with American Composers

The late sixties and early seventies were a golden age, a cultural utopia in Italy. Every kind of art circulated freely. I represent what Michelangelo Zurletti has called the "underground area," and our connection to the American Academy was peculiar. We lived "on the street" and our relationship to music and arts was more direct and informal. I consider myself lucky for having had the opportunity to found Beat 72, Rome's original underground venue. In the period of Beat 72 there was a huge colony of American composers in Rome, people like Philip Glass, Terry Riley, LaMonte Young. I virtually lived with them for a long stretch of time and I was in close contact with all of them—we often exchanged ideas. Of course, all this activity was going on outside of the musical institutions. Alvin Curran, too (please forgive me, Alvin), was a noninstitutional artist, but not by his own will: he really wanted to be inside the institutions!

The composer Alvin Lucier and his friend the late English pianist-composer Cornelius Cardew lived in Trastevere, on Vicolo Moroni, near the Cinema Trastevere. I often visited them. Each time I stepped into Lucier's house I felt like I was entering a huge, resonant soundboard. Every kind of instrument hung from the ceiling. Many dancers also came by, among them Trisha Brown. And the singer Joan LaBarbara was often there. All this was due in part to the American Academy—it was a kind of umbilical cord. The Academy is up on the Janiculum hill, and from such heaven you could walk down to Trastevere, a downtown inferno, where every kind of creativity was mixed together.

Alvin Curran, Cofounder, Musica Elettronica Viva

A Bunch of Mavericks Out There

The American Academy was a place of cultural magnetism when I arrived here in 1964. It was a place of exchange and contact. Lately I have been divorced not from the Academy so much as Rome itself, since my work often takes place elsewhere. But I come back with fond memories. Around the time when I first came to Rome, there was a sudden rush in the air around the word "electronic," and I got a bug in my head to make a tape piece, but I had no equipment to make it with. It must have been John Eaton or Bill Smith [composition fellows at AAR] who said, "Oh, don't worry about it, just come to our studio here and use our Ampex tape recorder." This was a marvelous dream at this time, to use these professional monophonic (!) tape recorders. And so I busied myself with a project that brings another important and interesting place to mind—the American Church in Rome on via Nazionale, which was directed then by a pastor named Wortham, who was an amateur musician and a Jungian psychologist—anyway he was just a nut, but he understood that by giving these spaces to young, promising artists, something like the American Center in Paris might spring up in Rome. I made a sound installation for a show of paintings at the American Church by the painter Edith Schloss, an artist who had long been in Rome. I created a piece quite naturally using the sounds around me, I just went around with a cheap tape recorder in the streets and recorded anything involving the sound of water. And you know there's a lot of water here in Rome. This piece was called *Water Colormusic*, and it was produced right here.

All the communities of musicians that were eagerly coming into being during the mid-sixties always looked forward to every concert that occurred at the American Academy in Rome—or to the performances by any of the Americans that were working in this city. Not that we were particularly harbingers of the new, but we just had that we-don't-know-what American style that was and is a very necessary and attractive component of a cultural exchange that I hope will never cease between the European and American mind. On the other hand, as we know there are also big barriers and areas where you run up against walls. A lot of what I think and do in my own practice reminds me constantly of my own sense of being . . . I don't know what to call it, I want to avoid using the word "expatriate." But after forty years of living abroad and living particularly here, you go through different periods of assimilation and of separation.

Without really knowing it, my coming to Europe was part of the Congress of Cultural Freedom story that we heard about earlier (Martin Brody, "Class of

'54," in this volume). After graduating from Yale, where I studied with Elliott Carter, I turned down a Fulbright grant to study with Berio, in order to continue on with Carter and go to Berlin, where at the last minute this Ford Foundation program had emerged. This was 1963, and there was a program that invited major artists from around the world, a very international program—not only was Elliott Carter in Berlin, but also Iannis Xenakis, Luciano Berio, and Roger Sessions. I met Nicolas Nabokov, I met Stravinsky, as a scraggly kid I met these illustrious people. It was years later when I began to understood the context of what this Ford Foundation program was and why it was: the remarkable plan that set American politics on a course of cultural aggression, as it were, against a Soviet threat, in this case using culture as the weapon instead of bombs and missiles. It's a remarkable moment in twentieth-century history.

The Ford Foundation program was given over to the German government, the Bundes government, and was transformed into an exchange program that is known as the DAAD, which is now a continuing major grant for individual artists. It was originally set up so that one major artist could bring two assistants or students with him. I was there with Joel Chadabe, and later Frederic Rzewski came under the same program. Berlin at that time was a dreary place but also a terrifying place—the Wall had just gone up. But we were given a stipend just to be brilliant and do our work and go on to be great artists. That ended in December 1964, and I hopped into Joel Chadabe's Volkswagen bug and went to Rome, not knowing what I was going to do but knowing that it was a cheap place to live, less than one dollar a day. I got an apartment in the Piazza Navona and started to play in piano bars on the via Veneto to make a little living. In no time, a group of other musicians, for example Richard Teitelbaum, who was on a Fulbright to Rome, and Frederic Rzewski, who had lived in Rome, and other Americans, namely, Carol Plantamura, Jon Phetteplace, and Allan Bryant—I wouldn't call them drifters, but other Americans in Rome spending the year in a cheap, warm, wonderful place, hoping to further their music careers. We all got together and formed a group called Musica Elettronica Viva, which was posited on a kind of utopian premise—to create a music without any score, without any conductor, without any beginning, without any end, and with no form of authority whatsoever.

This was 1966, right in the heart of the Vietnam War, of the great rock 'n' roll revolution, right before the beginnings of the student revolution, which was going to burst on the world in 1968. And in the middle of this period of heavy political and social change, I would say an explosion, the music of our group, which was essentially a spontaneously made music on found, amplified pieces of junk, plus the grace of one Moog synthesizer, the first synthesizer to appear in Europe (which Richard Teitelbaum had gotten hold of), we became an overnight success. And so before I knew it, I wasn't playing at piano bars anymore but making experimental music of the most ferocious kind to audiences of needy people, that is in front of mobs of students who were ready to occupy a university, or occupy a theater in Venice, or denounce somebody, or charge somebody. So I found myself in this fantastic situation, which I didn't understand very clearly at the time. I felt personally very divorced from the political aspects of what was going on, which I didn't understand completely. But the energies behind everything were automatic, you didn't need commands, you didn't need to think, you didn't even have to smoke dope, it was just happening, there was this flow of amazing energy. That also coincided with extraordinary collaborations between musicians and small avant-garde theaters—projects on the streets of Rome itself and projects at Beat 72, a single avant-garde space that saw the birth of just about a whole generation of avant-garde artists in this city.

That said, I'm going to mention just one of many special occurrences in this city that affected my musical life. A bunch of students occupied the Academy of Theater Arts, and they called me to come down and just do some act of solidarity with them, because I was sort of a well-known figure here in the mid-seventies—I had produced a set of records with a group closely connected with Giacinto Scelsi, called Ananda Records. And when the occupation ended, I was asked to join the faculty at the Academy, which I did for five years, until they noticed that I had been hired illegally. What I did while I was there was to create a whole body of improvised vocal music, especially for actors, performers who only use their voice and their bodies. While working at this theater academy, I began to focus on this—making music for nonmusicians who used only their voices and bodies. It became a very important basis for a whole new direction for me, involving the creation of music theater on the streets, on lakes, on rivers, on monumental steps, using all kinds of architectural spaces. This was very much à la mode at the time, because with the political focus in Rome, in fact all over Italy, where the local governments were almost inevitably in the hands of the Communist Party in the middle 1970s, the ideas of renewal and youthful and creative use of public spaces was very high on the agenda of the politicians. Similarly, the idea to bring the contemporary arts to the public via the media was the heritage of Socialist and Communist Party intellectuals who were in charge of the public radio. These kinds of social and political perspectives are very important to the story of music in the latter part of the twentieth century.

There has always been a phenomenally tight relationship between the city of Rome and the Academy. At times, we have seen protesters outside the gates hurling stones at the Academy. We are now living in a time where the foreign policies of the United States are provoking a great deal of difficulty for Americans and American culture in Europe. These things go in cycles, and we will continue to live through them. I can't prophesize the future, but I can say that the bonds between between individuals have been real, and the important institutions, for example the RAI radio and orchestra, has sometimes greatly favored American ideas and trends. And they are always aware that there are a bunch of mavericks out there.

Marcello Piras, Musicologist, Specialist on Jazz and African American Music

Jazz and the Context of Postwar Music in Rome

I want to fill in a little of the historical context of this discussion—about the relation of church and state in Rome, and also a little about jazz, my own research area. What I want to say is relevant to the composition milieu as well.

Of course, Rome is well known for its ancient history, but the contemporary scene is quite another story. With regard to music, there was a long hiatus between the early eighteenth century (when Alessandro Scarlatti and the young Handel were here) and 1870, the year the French left the city after their defeat at Sédan. The French had provided the pope with military protection, and under papal control, the reins on new ideas were held tight. During this period, Rome was hardly a cosmopolitan musical center. As an abbot in Tivoli, Franz Liszt had gathered an international group of musicians around him, comprising a kind of personal court. But this oasis was an exception to the rule. After the French defeat, however, Rome was left unguarded. The Italian army was able to chase the French away, and Rome was able to join the new kingdom of Italy.

The Eternal City thus underwent a slow rebirth during the fin de siècle period. In particular, culture flourished in the early twentieth century under mayor Ernesto Nathan, the most overtly secular mayor Rome ever had and, incidentally, a Jew. Vatican City did not yet exist, and Rome was bubbling with new ideas and new art. Puccini, D'Annunzio, and the Futurists—who had started staging many of their scandalous events in town by 1910—helped restore the city's status as an international culture capital. In Milan, where the war front was not far away, many cultural activities and most live entertainment came to a stop in 1915, when Italy entered World War I. But Rome only underwent a moderate decrease of activity. It remained a lively scene that did not immediately change, even with the rise of fascism. In chapter 1 of this volume, Andrea Olmstead sketched a fascinating picture of the American Academy fellows' relationship with Respighi and the Augusteo in the twenties. It would be valuable to know whether fellows of the Academy also interacted with Italian and American musicians in the Roman jazz and hot-dance music scene that was emerging contemporaneously. I note, for example, that the jazz master Sidney Bechet played in Rome in 1927, during the same decade that composers began to arrive as fellows at the American Academy. (Bechet's Rome appearance later became famous, unfortunately, for its grim finale: One of the musicians in the Bennie Peyton band, which was performing with Bechet, apparently threw away a lit cigar, setting the venue on fire. Four people were killed.)

What I want to emphasize is that a performance by Bechet was still possible in 1927 when Rome was open to new art and culture. The worst cultural repression had yet to come, and it did come in 1929, when the concordato between the pope and Mussolini established the foundation of the Vatican as an independent state. In no uncertain terms, the decree endorsed by Mussolini and Cardinal Gasparri declared Rome's status as a holy city. This changed the scene dramatically. "Appropriate" measures were taken to assure the propriety of the holy city: night clubs opening onto a public way were no longer allowed, and so the only jazz activity that took place in Rome between 1929 and 1944 occurred in hotels and embassies. Rome's best jazz orchestra, led by the clarinetist Sesto Carlini, played exclusively in hotels or at command performances for royal family parties.

After World War II, however, Rome tasted freedom yet again. In fact, a sense of newly achieved freedom pervaded the city and its art and entertainment scene. An outburst of creativity ensued. Many things were happening then—the American Academy was just a pixel in the picture. Modern music was being composed and performed, modern art produced by young talents, and jazz seemed to burst out everywhere. At last, it seemed that anything could be done. And it was done, with a vengeance, in reaction to the oppression that had long come from either the church or the state. Art and music took on a radical quality. In my opinion this is a basic difference between Rome and Milan. In Rome, artists were radicalized in reaction to previously repressive conditions, and they had a penchant for scandal. Rome had Franco Evangelisti, whose stance was extreme to the point that he declared the death of music with the certitude of a mathematical theorem. And Rome had Domenico Guaccero, who endlessly broke taboos and wrote some of the most exciting music of Italian modernism. There is a sort of continuity with the Futurist experiences here, a deep impulse just to go beyond. Although I believe that the experimental impulse had largely dissipated by 1980, when it was still intense, Rome was also a haven for some of the most radical of American composers. I'm not sure whether they could have been equally at ease in Milan or Turin.

A final point. After the war, there were strong connections between the musicians hosted at the American Academy and the Roman jazz world. Bill [William O.] Smith was at the center of it all—he was literally everywhere, promoting premieres of contemporary music or jamming in jazz clubs. I also especially want to call attention to the Italian musician Ivan Vandor. He was originally a jazzman, playing soprano and then tenor saxophone in Rome's first and foremost Dixieland amateur outfit, the Roman New Orleans Jazz Band. By the late fifties, after studying composition with Petrassi, he began to incorporate his new compositional skills into his jazz activities—as an arranger, for instance. However, even in the period when he devoted all of his creative energies to "legitimate" composition, you can still hear jazz elements in his music, like a fading echo of an uninhibited era when such things could happen. I don't want to conclude without mentioning the activity of a great American jazz improviser in Rome: Steve Lacy. There is an important, though now virtually unobtainable, double LP that Lacy recorded with Musica Elettronica Viva for the short-lived Horo label, where he performs with Alvin Curran, Richard Teitelbaum, and Frederic Rzewski.

As a rule, however, the period of bold musical experimentation in Rome that we have been discussing is severely underdocumented on sound recordings. The city has long suffered from a weak recording industry, since the bulk of Italian companies have been located in Milan. However, although Rome lacked record companies, Cinecittà was here, and I expect that a lot of interesting stuff is waiting to be discovered in television documentaries and film soundtracks still buried in the Roman film industry's archives.

Notes

The roundtable discussion from which these excerpts were culled also included Guido Baggiani, professor of music composition, Santa Cecilia Conservatory, Rome; James Dashow, cofounder, Centro di Sonologia Computazionale at the University of Padova; Nicola Sani, composer and artistic director of project "Sonora," CEMAT Foundation for the promotion of contemporary music; and Daniela Tortora, musicologist, University of Rome, "La Sapienza"; as well as the participants represented by the extended comments that appear here. The panel was conducted largely in Italian with simultaneous translations and paraphrases by Richard Trythall. Further translations were made by Marcello Piras, and the comments presented here were edited by Martin Brody.

Chapter Nine

For the Academy

Elliott Carter

Great gratitude to the American Academy—without its generosity I would not have been able to complete many of my larger compositions, and without it I could not have grown to know so much of Italy and made so many Italian friends.

Over the years I was also able to visit a vast number of important sites so meaningful to me: Greece, Crete, Sicily—Siracusa, Agrigento, Segesta, Florence, Siena, Perugia, and many others.

In 1953 my wife, young son, and I arrived in Italy on a steamship bringing us from New York to Naples. I myself had come to Rome with my mother in the early twenties, and again in the thirties during an Anno Santo. And then again during an Easter when my teacher, Nadia Boulanger, was there—for my interest in Italy sometimes overpowered my antifascist leanings. When the three of us arrived in Naples in 1953, we were picked up by, I think, Nicolo, a driver from the Academy, and driven to Rome. At once I learned from the secretary of the director, Laurance Roberts—the Principessa Rospigliosi—that we could not stay as a family there but had to find an apartment for ourselves. After meeting the other musical fellows, Frank Wigglesworth and Yehudi Wyner, who were already friends, we were driven into the city and put up in the Hotel Inghelterra, a fleabag then, but very grand now. After a month of real estate wonderings, we found a nice apartment near the Piazza Fiume—via Trebbia 3, the rental of which was more than the allowance the Academy gave me and was an hour's ride on bus 75 to my ground floor studio in the Academy's Casa Rustica. The studio came with a piano and a leaky roof.

At the time the Academy was still recovering from World War II, during which it was closed and many beds, etc., were stolen. Roberts had replaced these with beds bought at the Porta Portese flea market. The help at the time lived in small accommodations in the basement of the Academy building. A few years later they were unionized, which nearly bankrupted the Academy, since they had to be paid increases in their salary from the time of the war; but this allowed the staff to find their own living quarters in the city.

My son went to the American school just north of Rome near the Tomba di Nerone. To keep things going, we had to rent out a room in our apartment at via Trebbia to Mrs. Stringfellow Barr, the wife of the president of St. John's College, where I had taught. The director of the Academy, Laurance Roberts, led a rather grand life. He had the walls of the dining room of the Villa Aurelia, where he lived, frescoed by Eugene Berman, a painter much admired at the time for his stage designs for the Ballet Russes de Monte Carlo. Roberts gave receptions for Roman society and fellows. It was at one of them that I renewed my friendship with Darina Silone, who Helen and I met at Edmund Wilson's a year before. We then often went out with Darina and Ignazio, a writer I always greatly admired.

In the Casa Rustica studio I was working very slowly on my *Variations for Orchestra,* commissioned by the Louisville Orchestra, which because of many interruptions I could not complete during my stay. For it was the year that my friend, Nicolas Nabokov, with his fourth wife, Marie-Claire, was living in the Academy's Apartment A by the side of the Villa Aurelia. He was the composer-in-residence, and during this time he organized a large festival of contemporary music, financed by his Congress for Cultural Freedom. It was in that year that he founded the magazine *Tempo Presente,* edited by Silone, and did many other surprising things. During that festival he had the French Parrenin Quartet come and play my First String Quartet, which was so much liked that Goffredo Petrassi and Luigi Dallapiccola and Roman Vlad became fast friends.

Although Mr. Roberts asked me to stay another year, I felt that the long trips on the no. 75 bus, the bothersome school for my son, and the financial agreement made me want to return to the United States, as much as we loved Italy. Later when I was back in the United States, a few delegates from the Academy came to offer me the directorship of the Academy. I refused—I am not good at working in offices and dealing with the many problems such a job would entail.

However, I returned three times as composer-in-residence. We were then given Apartment A. Each time I rented a tiny piano, which I put in a small room where I composed my Piano Concerto and Concerto for Orchestra. And then later when the capella next to the Villa Aurelia was renovated, I wrote my *Night Fantasies* there.

In between residencies, we went to Italy often. Once for the biennale of my music in Venice and once to serve on a jury in Parma and also for various commemorations of my birthdays at San Felice Circeo, with concerts at Sermoneta and Priverno, organized by Raffaele Pozzi and Riccardo Cerocchi. I have always been in close contact with the French Academy, the Villa Medici, and was a friend of Jacques Ibert and later Balthus, with whom we organized a concert of music by French, German, and American academicians at the Palazzo Farnese.

In 1954 Petrassi was made president of the ISCM, and they asked Roman Vlad and myself to be vice presidents. The festival that year was in Baden-Baden, with the first performance of Boulez's *Le marteau sans maître.* And then Boulez and I became friends.

Chapter Ten

Two Visits in 1981

John Harbison

In the spring of 1981 I served as resident in music at the American Academy in Rome. As with so many others who have been fortunate enough to spend some time there, the experience was indelible. As the following brief reminiscences suggest, the association with the Academy opened some doors, and made possible some connections otherwise unlikely. But the thing that is most difficult to convey is the impact of the city. Once it is absorbed, even superficially, it never departs. For generations American scholars and artists have walked down the Gianicolo from the Academy, found themselves in places unlike anywhere else, and returned changed.

Visit to Montale

When Rose Mary Harbison and I arrived in Rome in January 1981, it was cold. Our rooms in the smaller of the servants' quarters at the Villa Aurelia really never shook off their chill until April. We brought baggage from the states: One week before the first performance of my *Violin Concerto*, in January, my sister Helen, a cellist, died of cancer. Her despair and anger—she had not gone gently—seemed to follow us to Rome. The piece, which I had meant to be a predictive metaphor for its first performer, Rose Mary Harbison, traveling from storm to sunlight, seemed born in uncertainty and doubt.

The invitation to be a resident in music at the American Academy in Rome, welcome as it was, triggered an episode of the imposter syndrome, that old American character role. It was five years since my last commission. I was forty-two years old and wondering if I would write "volunteer" pieces the rest of my life. *Full Moon in March*, an opera, *Samuel Chapter*, a cantata, concertos for violin and piano, and an hour-long song cycle, *Mottetti di Montale*, all had to go looking for their first performances, and while I believed in them, I was hardly competent to *represent* them.

A nervous stray cat moved in the second week, deciding to live with us. He remained strange and unpredictable.

The weather was strange and unpredictable.

One of the first people I met at dinner was the resident in literature, Joseph Brodsky. He was strange, unpredictable, charming, and boorish. He quickly discovered I loved Stravinsky. "How could Vera [Mme. Stravinsky], who had known the embraces of Mandelstam and Sudeykin, waste herself on that little Mountebank?" How was he enjoying the Academy? "Far too little sexual tension!" Did he know the Italian poet laureate, Montale? (Here I had a purpose, described below.) "I know him, he is not well, I will see him next week, what about it?"

I explained I had written, on impulse, a very large piece, a setting of all twenty motets from Montale's second book, *Le Occasioni,* and I was belatedly seeking permission to use the poems, first from Montale's publisher, Mondadori, who directed me—pessimistically—to the poet himself.

"Not a chance," said Brodsky, a twinkle in his eye. "Can you stay a minute? I'll bring you something to read."

A few minutes later he appeared with copies of Montalian essays, among them "Words and Music" (1949). Brodsky was positively mischievous. I read with a sinking feeling the opening line: "Words set to music, words that are sung, are not pleasing to the most refined connoisseurs of the art of sound." In other essays it got worse: Schubert and Schumann were taken to task for the inadequacy of their settings of Goethe. Montale seemed to feel that settings of lyric poetry are *at best* unnecessary. The only texts he reluctantly approved for setting were some of the libretti for nineteenth-century melodrama, Verdi and Bellini, words to which we attend only vaguely. (Montale trained as an operatic baritone and reviewed music, especially opera, for the *Corriere della Sera.*)

"Well," I asked Brodsky, "is there any reason to try to persuade Montale?"

"It's hopeless, but I'll give you his number. You speak Italian?"

"Under duress, yes."

Before I called I did some research. I was truly in trouble. I learned that Montale was indeed very serious in his dislike of settings of his own (and other poets') work. It appeared that permission was out of the question. I had naively guessed that with his strong musical background and interest he would be especially receptive—now it appeared the reverse was true!

"I will ask you to speak directly with Signor Montale," said the voice at the other end of the line, a voice I knew to be that of Gina Tiossi, his housekeeper. I had learned as much as I could about the poet from his biographies, annotators, even from his appearances in *Gente* (the Italian parallel of *People* magazine), strolling the streets of Milano with a woman identified as Gina Tiossi.

"So Mr. Arbisone, I can only say, if you are so reckless as to have written this piece, let me see the score." Thus I heard, for the only time, the rich bass-baritone of Montale, not encouraging, not entirely discouraging.

Rose Mary Harbison and I made immediate plans to go to Milano; it somehow seemed that hand delivery was appropriate. It is not simply melodramatic to state that on both my appearances at via Bigli a chill winter rain was falling and my inappropriate cloth overcoat was soaked, on that first occasion by procrastination. As I handed the handwritten but bound, complete fifty-five minute unperformed score to Signora Tiossi, having called ahead, I heard the operatic resonance, distantly: "Tell him I will look right away, he is to call in three days."

So we stayed and paced around the city a little longer than expected, finally finding ourselves back in the hallway of the poet's apartment, awaiting the smiling courier, who said simply, "He has approved, he will call Mondadori. He sends his compliments but is unwell today."

When I called the publisher the next day they were indeed informed. I had slipped through the net and felt lucky, not just in this instance. Seven months later the poet was dead, his heart (which he once described as "a mistuned instrument") having given out, and for some time an embargo persisted on setting his texts.

It is still impossible to describe the intensity of this nonencounter with a man who was, for me, so much more than a reluctant collaborator; his presence had influenced so much of my inner life. When we embrace the companionship of great artists they know nothing of it. We admit them to an intimacy that asks nothing more of them, but a great deal of us.

As I stood outside of Montale's apartment at via Bigli I thought of the strange ways an artist's personality comes to inhabit another soul. I had read his poems, many of the essays, knew a lot about the poet's friendships, his geography, his influences. (Eventually I even visited many of his haunts in Liguria.) But the depth of the connection was through the inspired imprecision of the words themselves, their mystery, the vast inexplicit and unexplained provinces they visited that answered my own loneliness, confusion, aspiration, and skepticism. That they resided in the haze of my imperfect Italian may even have increased their ambiguous power.

Did the well-qualified score-reader making that decision, so incidental to him that afternoon, sense in what he was reading any of this indebtedness and celebration?

Visit to Petrassi

As spring arrived, haltingly, in Rome early in 1981, I developed a dual program for the waning months of my time as resident at the American Academy in

Rome. First, I resolved to devote part of each day to discovering something about Rome. This slowed progress on the two pieces I was writing, a piano quintet and a first symphony, but nourished them in the end. Second, I resolved to try to make as much contact with musicians in Rome, visiting them or inviting them to the Academy when it seemed appropriate.

The first part of the program bore various fruits, such as finally gaining entrance to San Ivo on the fifth try (a little attention to the portiere in the form of a few "Bellinis" helped) and trying Rome's most illustrious coffee (I was awake for three days). The second was trickier, but eventually brought Henze to the Academy for a fellows' concert, and Rzewski for a pair of lunches, and very strange encounters with two Donatonis, the classroom autocrat and the coffee bar wildman.

As an admirer of many pieces by Petrassi, I was interested in meeting him, but was told he was old, over eighty, near blind, and isolated. (Since he lived twenty more years, and continued for a long time various contacts with the world, he must have somehow confronted these difficulties.) I phoned for an appointment with him, and was encouraged by the patient, clear quality of his Italian. He was evidently accustomed to speaking with foreigners, including a long and illustrious string of British students.

On the appointed day, however, when I was due at one, there was—not surprisingly—a total bus strike. I called Petrassi, innocently expecting to negotiate a rain check.

"Of course you will just have to walk then," he said.

"Of course," I replied, as if it was the expected solution.

It was, in fact, a terrific walk of just over an hour through crowded, relatively quiet streets from the Gianicolo to his apartment high above the Piazza del Popolo, where we proceeded to engage in a wide-ranging conversation, still by far the longest I ever attempted in Italian, that ended as dark fell five hours later.

What I actually said, with my limited vocabulary and odd grammatical circumlocutions necessary to avoid total embarrassment, I have little idea. Occasionally a tactful smile passed across his face at inadvertently comic moments. But what he said is well remembered, since it returned so often to the crux of his aesthetic thought, and was stated and restated so resourcefully.

I had sent ahead some of my music, a score and tape of the *Violin Concerto* and a score of the large song cycle *Mottetti di Montale*. As I recall, no music was played, but many pages were turned. He began by thanking me for the visit and for the scores in the most courtly way. He then went on very directly to discuss the *Violin Concerto*. He began by saying he found the piece very disturbing, very puzzling. How was it possible that a composer with such a good concept of musical issues, such confident details and sense of movement, should produce a piece lacking in what he considered the most important attribute.

Pained and of course eager to know, I asked, "And what is that?"

"Aggiornamento," he said (keeping up-to-date), introducing a theme to which he would frequently return. The piece to him lacked a sense of the year in which it was written, in fact it lacked the sense of being written at *any* time, it was not historical, it was simply not now.

I tried to describe the way in which some of my earlier music had been concerned with *now* in ways I judged to be predominantly unproductive. He was impatient with this idea. His assertion was that the *sense of now* is always good, always productive, and that "aggiornamento" was one of the "duties" of the composer.

Here I attempted another tack, saying that the nowness of a piece, like its place of origin, its nationality, is inherent and need not be self-consciously underlined. I was thinking about the career of such composers as Krenek, Foss, and Petrassi himself, where constant adjustment to the present seemed often a little late and anxious.

Petrassi then picked up the score (and how did he find his way, barely able to see?). He went to some specific moments, saying, "This is classicism, in the '50s we knew it was a dead end." Here I too boldly injected my enthusiasm for his orchestral concerti of the fifties, examples of a fertile classicism that seemed to me to look forward. He was not pleased. "From there I had to move on, we all had to move on."

This seemed like a good time to ask him about Peter Maxwell Davies, his former student, who was just at that time embarked on his giant symphonies, which he declared direct descendants of Mahler and Sibelius. Petrassi first insisted on his devotion to Davies and his music, then suggested he was "alarmed" by the *First Symphony*, a "step back."

Somewhat ill at ease now, I mentioned my involvement with Dallapicola's music, as an adherent and performer. Petrassi visibly stiffened, and I realized that all the warm birthday greetings exchanged, the kind mutual words for publication, may have been masking a Britten-Tippett-like relationship of official camaraderie that disguised a private distance and distaste. As I savored this bit of body language, I remembered an all-smiling photo of Montale, Ungaretti, and Machado, the smiles formal at best, and nervously mentioned it. Petrassi said, "No meeting of the minds there," and seemed relieved.

The name of Montale magically lifted the conversation out of its trail of obstacles.

Petrassi took out the score of his only opera, *Il Cordovano*, with a libretto based on Cervantes by Montale. I was embarrassed to learn at that moment of the existence of this piece, but fascinated to hear Petrassi discuss the collaboration, Montale's method of shaping a text for opera (based on his impressive knowledge of the Italian operatic literature), and Petrassi's testimony that Montale's vaunted distaste for the whole idea of words set to music had *never* entered their discussions. Interestingly, Montale's enthusiastic review of the revival at La Scala of a revised *Il Cordovano* never mentions his own participation in the piece.

The last part of our conversation was carried on essentially as coenthusiasts for Montale, with no direct mention of the songs I had sent him, only a general remark, "Our language can't be set by foreigners," (pause, smile) "except Mozart." It was by then getting dark in his already dark apartment, and only his face was visible, lit by a corner window. I remember thinking back to the times I had been fortunate enough to spend in brief conversation with other important composers—Stravinsky, Varése, Dallapicola, Copland, and many of more recent generations. How little we get, appropriately, of their temperament and passion. Here was Petrassi, the composer of the most sublime of all setting of texts by St. John of the Cross. In his fine black suit he looked tough, crafty, worldly, like a sharp Italian businessman, youthful and alert, and above all, up-to-date.

Chapter Eleven

Music Resources at the American Academy in Rome

Christina Huemer

Several articles in this volume have shed light on the early history of the music program at the Academy. How much of that history is documented at the Academy itself? What can a new fellow in musical composition learn about the work of his illustrious predecessors? How can we ensure that his or her own work here is preserved for the future? As librarian, I have taken a special interest in our music resources since my arrival. These are a well-kept secret, unfortunately: we have some treasures, but on the whole I would characterize our resources as incomplete, dispersed, not fully cataloged, in need of preservation, and underutilized. We have made some progress in documenting our own history, but much more remains to be done. I would like to summarize what is here, what isn't, and what needs to be done.

The music collection originated in 1918 with a gift of over two hundred scores from Kate Freeman Carter, the wife of the Academy director Jesse Benedict Carter. These, and a handful of books on music, were originally kept in the Villa Chiaraviglio, the first home of the new music department of the School of Fine Arts. The music program was presided over by Felix Lamond. The music collection was transferred to the main library in 1932, and promptly relegated to the basement. In 1937–38, several rare music titles came to the library as part of a gift of books from the Rev. Harry de Nancrède, canon of the English Church in Rome. The music collection became a significant scholarly resource, however, only in the late 1970s and early 1980s with the donation of the personal musicological library of Professor W. Oliver Strunk (1901–80, author of *Source Readings in Music History* and an expert on Byzantine music). After that almost no purchases were made for about a decade, then purchasing resumed on a small scale, using the Randall Thompson Endowment Fund.

In 2002 Professor Thomas Forrest Kelly, FAAR 1986, RAAR 2002, a musicologist from Harvard University, helped us update our collection, using special funds from the Department of Education. The purpose of this grant was to build core collections in various "postclassical" subjects. (The library is strongest in classical antiquities, so we have lots of books on ancient Greek music, but hardly anything on Bach or Schoenberg or jazz.) We are now trying to maintain this core collection, but for in-depth research, our fellows need to make use of other music collections, such as the German Historical Institute and the Accademia di Santa Cecilia in Rome and the Morrill Music Library at the Villa I Tatti, Florence. Our collection of books and periodicals in music is only about two thousand titles and still fits into the little room at the top of the library stairs. (I should have said that at some point the collection moved from the basement to the attic, so to speak, but it is still not in the public eye.)

In addition to books and periodicals, the music collection includes musical scores, of which an estimated 3,500 are by twentieth-century American composers. These are found in three different locations:

1. Approximately four hundred older scores, including the original Carter gift, are cataloged and shelved with library books. They range from Monteverdi to Elliott Carter, but very few of them are represented in our online catalog. When we did our online conversion project back in the early 1990s, there was no format available yet for musical scores and recordings. Now there is, but we need new funds to automate the catalog records. So to find these you have to use the old card catalog.
2. The second group is approximately three thousand published scores of twentieth-century American composers, assembled by the United States Information Service (USIS) circa 1963 "for the use of all interested and qualified persons throughout Italy" and supplemented with new material in 1964 and 1968. The collection was donated by USIS to the American Academy in Rome in 1977. It has a little card catalog of its own.
3. And finally there is an uncataloged backlog of about a hundred more recent scores, received as gifts from fellows and residents after 1980. Some of these are photocopies or Ozalid copies (on thin paper) of manuscript scores rather than formal publications; thus they represent a kind of "gray literature" between original manuscript and formal publication, and present both cataloging and preservation problems.

Scores by American Academy fellows and residents can be found in all three categories above: they total around 650 to 700. We still to integrate these collections and get them all into our online catalog.

Then there are the musical recordings. In 2003, with the help of the Delmas Foundation, we digitized our most important collection, the101 unique reel-to-reel tapes of Academy concerts and RAI concerts from 1955 on. These are a priceless heritage, as they feature the world premieres of compositions by Academy fellows written during their fellowship years. We made digital copies in two different formats, and CD copies are now available for listening in the library. We also cataloged the recordings in our online catalog, URBS, and made some musical excerpts available on the Academy website. This project was realized by Richard Trythall, music liaison at the Academy.

The Academy also holds a collection of published LPs and CDs, including approximately 250 recordings of twentieth-century American music, not unique but probably unparalleled in Italy. This collection was formed from gifts and from modest purchases over the years, supplemented by a major gift from the Alice Ditson Fund of Columbia University in 1957–58. The majority of the American recordings are by Academy composers, including a series of recordings (LPs) of Rome Prize winners sponsored by the American Academy of Arts and Letters. It would be a good idea to convert this group to CDs. In many cases the Academy holds both recording and score for the same composition, although they are not currently shelved together. Unfortunately, all of these collections are virtually unknown outside of the American Academy community.

Finally, I would like to mention other archival resources that scholars should be aware of. The early institutional archives of the American Academy in Rome are not here, but are located in the Archives of American Art in Washington, DC. These have been microfilmed, so they can be consulted in New York and at other regional centers, and there is an excellent finding aid online: http://archivesofamericanart.si.edu/findaids/ameracar/ameracar.htm. The Academy archives include the files of Felix Lamond, the first and only professor of music, and of the music department from 1920 to 1940. As far as I know, no one has systematically studied these files yet. In our Rare Book Room here in Rome, we have some manuscript letters of early fellows to Lamond (written after they returned to the United States). The library also holds a complete run of annual reports of the Academy, which include Professor Lamond's annual report of the music department.

Other archival materials here in Rome include the portraits of music fellows from the bar (these originally hung in the billiard room). Black-and-white photographs of these are kept in our photographic archive. The photo archive includes some photographs of concerts, part of our "events" collection. In the library, we have a collection of early concert programs from 1922 to 1932. Most of these concerts took place at the Academy, but some took place at the Augusteum or Augusteo, the Italian state concert hall located on the top of the Mausoleum of Augustus. The Augusteum was destroyed in 1936 by Mussolini, as part of his massive program of urban renewal. Information about the Augusteum concerts can be found in *Gli anni dell'Augusteo* (1990).

The Academy's annual reports are often the best source of information for the music program after World War II. We also have some photocopies of concert programs, which accompany our digital concert archive, thanks to Richard Trythall, who saved them systematically for years. And there is the occasional photo in our archives of the New York office.

To summarize the situation today: The music collection is still out of sight, but it is continuing to grow. We have a decent, if not comprehensive, collection of books on music and are trying to improve it. We have online access to the *Grove* dictionaries from our public catalog stations. The library currently aims to collect all published works of its fellows and residents, especially works that they wrote or performed during their time here. Thus donations of scores and recordings are welcome.

Appendix

Composers at the American Academy in Rome, 1921–40

Compiled by Carol J. Oja

Following is a list of Rome Prize winners from 1921 to 1940, together with the dates of their fellowships, place of birth, education, and employment after AAR. Also included are the names of jury members, with jury committee chairs listed first. Jury lists are compiled from Annual Reports, which are part of the Academy's files in New York, and from other sources, as footnoted.[1] The fellowship years traditionally began on October 1. Dates of the appointments are extracted from the annual reports prepared by Felix Lamond. Since a number of these figures are obscure, tracking down biographical information can be difficult.[2]

Fellowship dates	Name of fellow	Hometown	Where educated	Fellowship committee	Positions held after Rome Prize
[1920–21] Period of fund-raising for fellowships				"American national jury" during a time of fellowship formation: Walter Spalding Owen Wister John Alden Carpenter Frederick Stock "one other composer"[3]	
1921–24[4]	Leo Sowerby (1895–1968)	Born in Grand Rapids, Michigan; moved to Chicago in 1909	American Conservatory in Chicago; also Bush Conservatory	Walter Spalding[5] Walter Damrosch John Alden Carpenter W. J. Henderson Richard Aldrich Owen Wister	American Conservatory Organist at Episcopal Cathedral of St. James, Chicago
1921–24	Howard Hanson (1896–1981) (Frederick A. Juilliard Fellow)	Wahoo, Nebraska	Luther College, Wahoo; Institute of Musical Art (Juilliard School); Northwestern University	Walter Spalding[6] Walter Damrosch John Alden Carpenter W. J. Henderson Richard Aldrich Owen Wister	Director, Eastman School of Music

1922–25	Randall Thompson (1899–1984) (Walter Damrosch Fellow)	New York, New York	Harvard (studied with Spalding and E. B. Hill); studied privately with Ernest Bloch	Walter Spalding Walter Damrosch John Alden Carpenter W. J. Henderson Robert Aldrich Owen Wister	Wellesley College UC–Berkeley Curtis Institute University of Virginia Princeton Harvard
1923–25	Wintter Watts (1884–1962) (Horatio Parker Fellow)	Cincinnati, Ohio	Institute of Musical Art (Juilliard School)	Walter R. Spalding Walter Damrosch John A. Carpenter Leo Sowerby Richard Aldrich	Watts lived in Europe until 1931; it is unclear what he did after returning to New York
1924–27	(George) Herbert Elwell (1898–1974) (Juilliard Fellow)	Minneapolis, Minnesota	University of Minnesota; studied with Ernest Bloch and Nadia Boulanger	Walter R. Spalding Walter Damrosch John A. Carpenter Leo Sowerby Richard Aldrich	Cleveland Institute of Music; music critic for *Cleveland Plain Dealer*; Oberlin Conservatory; Eastman Summer School
1925–28	Walter Helfer (1896–1959) (Damrosch Fellow)	Lawrence, Massachusetts	Harvard	Walter R. Spalding Walter Damrosch John A. Carpenter Leo Sowerby Richard Aldrich	Hunter College (CUNY)

(continued)

Fellowship dates	Name of fellow	Hometown	Where educated	Fellowship committee	Positions held after Rome Prize
1925–29	Robert Sanders[7] (1906–1974) (Parker Fellow)	Chicago, Illinois	Bush Conservatory (student of Sowerby)	Walter R. Spalding Walter Damrosch John A. Carpenter Leo Sowerby Richard Aldrich	Conductor, Chicago Civic Symphony; Organist, First Unitarian Church, Chicago; American Conservatory; Dean, School of Music, Indiana University
1927–30	Alexander Steinert (1900–1982) (Juilliard Fellow)	Boston, Massachusetts	Harvard; Paris Conservatoire[8]; also studied privately with Charles Martin Loeffler, Charles Koechlin, and Vincent d'Indy	Walter R. Spalding Walter Damrosch John A. Carpenter Leo Sowerby Richard Aldrich	Active as conductor and arranger in Hollywood; also worked as pianist for Boston Symphony Orchestra
1928–31	Roger Sessions (1896–1985) (Damrosch Fellow)	Brooklyn, New York	Harvard; Yale (studied with Horatio Parker); studied with Ernest Bloch	Richard Aldrich John A. Carpenter Edward B. Hill Leo Sowerby	Smith College Cleveland Institute Princeton UC–Berkeley Juilliard

1929–32	Normand Lockwood (1906–2002) (Parker Fellow)	New York, New York Raised in Ann Arbor, Michigan	University of Michigan; studied with Respighi and Boulanger (both before Rome Prize)	Walter Damrosch[9] John Alden Carpenter Richard Aldrich Edward B. Hill Leo Sowerby	Oberlin Conservatory; Union Theological Seminary; Columbia University; Trinity University (San Antonio); University of Hawaii, Manoa; University of Oregon; University of Denver
1930–33	Werner Janssen (1899–1990) (Juilliard Fellow)	New York, New York	Dartmouth College; New England Conservatory	Walter Damrosch[10] John Alden Carpenter Edward B. Hill Howard Hanson Leo Sowerby	Conductor of a series of American orchestras, beginning with the Baltimore Symphony and Janssen Symphony in Hollywood
1931–34	Herbert Inch (1904–1988) (Damrosch Fellow)	Missoula, Montana	State University of Montana; Eastman School of Music	Walter Damrosch[11] Chalmers Clifton Edward B. Hill Howard Hanson Leo Sowerby	Eastman School of Music; Hunter College (CUNY)
1932–36	Vittorio Giannini[12] (1903–1966) (Parker Fellow)	Philadelphia, Pennsylvania	Milan Conservatory; Juilliard (with Rubin Goldmark)	Walter Damrosch Carl Engel Howard Hanson Leo Sowerby Deems Taylor	Juilliard School; Manhattan School of Music; Curtis Institute; North Carolina School of the Arts

(continued)

Fellowship dates	Name of fellow	Hometown	Where educated	Fellowship committee	Positions held after Rome Prize
1933–35	Hunter Johnson (1906–1998)[13] (Juilliard Fellow)	Benson, North Carolina	University of North Carolina; Eastman School of Music (studied with Bernard Rogers)	Walter Damrosch Leo Sowerby Howard Hanson Deems Taylor (Carl Engel did not attend the selection meeting)	University of Michigan University of Manitoba Cornell University University of Illinois University of Texas
1935–37	Samuel Barber (1910–1981) (Parker Fellow)[14]	West Chester, Pennsylvania	Curtis Institute (studied with Rosario Scalero)	Walter Damrosch Leo Sowerby Deems Taylor Carl Engel (Howard Hanson did not attend the meeting, nor did he review scores beforehand)	Curtis Institute Professional composer
1936–39	Kent Kennan (1913–2003) (Juilliard Fellow)	Milwaukee, Wisconsin	University of Michigan (studied with Hunter Johnson); Eastman School of Music	Walter Damrosch Carl Engel Howard Hanson Leo Sowerby Deems Taylor	Kent State University University of Texas Ohio State University

1937–39	Frederick Woltmann (1908–1965) (Damrosch Fellow)	New York, New York	Eastman School of Music	Walter Damrosch[15] Carl Engel Howard Hanson Leo Sowerby Deems Taylor	Professional Composer; lived in Europe, then Hollywood
1938–40	Charles Naginski (1909–1940) (Damrosch Fellow)	Cairo, Egypt	Juilliard (studied with Rubin Goldmark); also studied with Roger Sessions	Deems Taylor[16] Aaron Copland Eric DeLamarter Roger Sessions Philip James	Died shortly after completion of RP fellowship (drowned, August 6, 1940, at Lenox, MA).
1939–41	William D. Denny (1910–1980) (Parker Fellow)	Seattle, Washington	University of California at Berkeley (studied with Randall Thompson)	Leo Sowerby Eric DeLamarter Philip James Albert Stoessel Roger Sessions	UC–Berkeley Harvard Vassar
1940–42	Arthur Kreutz[17] (1906–1991) (Juilliard Fellow)	La Crosse, Wisconsin	Columbia University; Royal Conservatory in Ghent	Leo Sowerby[18] Philip James Roger Sessions Albert Stoessel Randall Thompson (This list is confirmed by AAR New York office records.)	University of Mississippi

(continued)

Fellowship dates	Name of fellow	Hometown	Where educated	Fellowship committee	Positions held after Rome Prize
				AAR Annual Report lists the jurors as follows: Leo Sowerby, Aaron Copland, Rudolph Ganz, Walter Piston, Randall Thompson	
1941–43	Harold Shapero (1920–2013)	Lynn, Massachusetts	Harvard University (studied with Walter Piston); Malkin Conservatory Longy School in Cambridge (with Nadia Boulanger)	Annual Report lists: Leo Sowerby, Aaron Copland, Rudolf Ganz, Howard Hanson, Walter Piston, Randall Thompson; AAR New York files list: Leo Sowerby, Howard Barlow, Howard Hanson, Walter Piston, Albert Stoessel	Brandeis University

1942–44	David Diamond (1915–2005)	Rochester, New York	Eastman School of Music (studied with Bernard Rogers); American School at Fontaineblau (studied with Nadia Boulanger); studied with Roger Sessions, New York City	Leo Sowerby Aaron Copland Rudolph Ganz Walter Piston Randall Thompson	The Juilliard School

Notes

1. Thanks to Sylvia Kollar, AAR archivist, and Shawn Miller, AAR program director, for their assistance in compiling the jury lists.

2. Unless otherwise stated, a composite of the following sources was used:
American Academy in Rome Annual Reports and Archives
Theodore Baker, ed., *Baker's Biographical Dictionary*, 7th ed., revised by Nicolas Slonimsky (New York: Schirmer Books, 1984).
Grove's Dictionary of Music and Musicians: American Supplement, ed. Waldo Selden Pratt (New York: MacMillan, 1947).
Grove Music Online, ed. Deane Root, http://www.oxfordmusiconline.com/
H. Wiley Hitchcock, and Stanley Sadie, *The New Grove Dictionary of American Music* (London: Macmillan, 1983).

3. [Felix Lamond], letter to Mr. William H. Murphy [name crossed out], written from 101 Park Avenue, New York City, February 2, 1920, AAR Archives Microfilm, box 33, reel 5799.

4. Sowerby's initial appointment was for two years. In 1923, it was extended for a third year (Lamond, AAR Annual Report 1923, 46). He did not receive one of the named fellowships, probably because of the special nature of his appointment.

5. This committee is listed in numerous sources, including: Lamond, letter to Dr. [Henry S.] Pritchett, Acting President, Carnegie Corporation, June 24, 1922, AAR Archives Microfilm, box 33, reel 5799. The same committee appointed Hanson and Thompson (Lamond, AAR Annual Report 1922, 46).

6. "Dean Hanson Is Named," *New York Times*, November 16, 1921.

7. Sanders finished Watts's residency (Lamond, AAR Annual Report 1925, 47). Then he was elected to his own two-year term (Lamond, AAR Annual Report 1926, 48). He is still listed in the report for 1929, however, where it states he is returning "to Chicago" (AAR Annual Report 1929, 41).

8. The Paris Conservatoire is listed in "Wins Juilliard Award," *New York Times*, May 25, 1927.

9. [Draft Press Release, 1929], AAR Archive Microfilm, box 20, reel 5781.

10. "Werner Janssen Wins Fellowship in Rome," *Musical America* 50, no. 9 (May 10, 1930): 4. The AAR Annual Report list does not include Carpenter.

11. "Herbert Inch Awarded Fellowship in Rome," *Musical America* 51, no. 9 (May 10, 1931): 4.

12. Giannini might have been able to stay for a fourth year, since Hunter Johnson's appointment ended in 1935.

13. Only two fellows were in residence in the year beginning October 1, 1934 (Lamond, AAR Annual Report 1935, 28). Hunter Johnson is one of the central figures in Drew Massey's *John Kirkpatrick, American Music, and the Printed Page*, Eastman Studies in Music (Rochester: University of Rochester Press, 2013).

14. In the Annual Report for 1936, Barber is listed as holding the Damrosch Fellowship (34); in that for 1937, he is cited as the Parker Fellow (35).

15. "Frederick Woltmann Wins Juilliard Fellowship Award," *Musical America* 57, no. 8 (April 25, 1937).

16. Members of the jury are listed in a press release: "Musical Composition," April 14, 1938, on stationery for "American Academy in Rome," AAR Archive Microfilm, box 33, reel 5781.

17. "Arthur R. Kreutz, 84, Composer and Teacher," *New York Times*, March 13, 1991.

18. Members of the jury are listed in: "Music Prize Is Won by Arthur Kreutz: Wisconsin Composer Gets Award of American Academy in Rome," *New York Times*, June 27, 1940. The article expressed concern about the effects of World War II on the Rome prize: "If European conditions prevent Mr. Kreutz from going to Italy, he will have the option of deferring his fellowship or fulfilling it in America. He has indicated that he will study in New York, if he cannot go abroad."

Selected Bibliography

Archival Sources

American Academy in Rome Archives. New York, NY.

American Academy in Rome records. Archives of American Art, Smithsonian Museum. Washington, DC.

Personal archives of Richard Trythall. Rome, Italy.

Assorted Concert Programs, American Academy in Rome, 1952–2006.

"Music Composition and Performance Activity, 1948–1994," original manuscript and related source materials.

"American Academy in Rome: Concert Recordings Archive," 2003, ninety-three-page document listing contents of the Recordings Archive; arranged in chronological order by concert date and subdivided in three sections: Spring Concerts, AAR/RAI orchestra concerts, and miscellaneous concerts; master index for the collection of CDs and DVDs containing recordings of Academy concerts from 1955 to 2002 (analog-to-digital recording project supervised by Richard Trythall); original manuscript and related source materials are in the author's personal archive.

"Music Liaison Correspondence with Fellows and Residents of the American Academy in Rome," 1976–2006, collection of questionnaires and letters returned to music liaison by Academy composers in October 1976 and June 1991 in preparation for the "Music Composition and Performance Activity" brochure issued in 1977 and updated in 1994; letter and e-mail correspondence from the fall of 2006 regarding preparation of the present history; original manuscript and related source materials.

Published Sources

Ansari, Emily Abrams. "'Masters of the President's Music': Cold War Composers and the United States Government." PhD diss., Harvard University, 2009.

Apthorp, William F. "Two Modern Classicists, Part One." *Atlantic Monthly*, October 1893, 488.

Babbitt, Milton. *The Collected Essays of Milton Babbitt.* Edited by Stephen Peles. Princeton: Princeton University Press, 2003.

———. "The Composer as Specialist." In *Collected Essays of Milton Babbitt*, 48–54.

———. "My Vienna Triangle." In *Collected Essays of Milton Babbitt*, 466–87.

Bakewell, Charles Montague. *The Story of the American Red Cross in Italy.* New York: Macmillan, 1920.

Banner, Leslie. *A Passionate Preference: The Story of the North Carolina School of the Arts—A History.* Winston-Salem: North Carolina School of the Arts Foundation, 1987.

Barr, Cyrilla. *Elizabeth Sprague Coolidge: American Patron of Music.* New York: Schirmer Books, 1998.

Barr, Cyrilla, and Ralph Locke, eds. *Cultivating Music in America: Women Patrons and Activists since 1860.* Berkeley: University of California Press, 1997.

Beal, Amy C. "Negotiating Cultural Networks: American Music in Darmstadt, 1946–56." *Journal of the American Musicological Society* 53, no. 1 (2000): 105–39.

———. *New Music, New Allies: American Experimental Music in West Germany from the Zero Hour to Reunification.* Berkeley: University of California Press, 2006.

Berges, Ruth. "That Elusive Prix de Rome." *Music Review* 55, no. 2 (1994): 146–52.

Blackwell, Alice Stone. *Lucy Stone: Pioneer of Woman's Rights.* 2nd ed. Boston: Little, Brown, 1930.

Blair, Karen J. *The Torchbearers: Women and Their Amateur Arts Associations in America, 1890–1930.* Bloomington: Indiana University Press, 1994.

Bomberger, E. Douglas. *A Tidal Wave of Encouragement: American Composers' Concerts in the Gilded Age.* Westport, CT: Praeger, 2002.

Brody, Martin. "Cold War Genius: Music and Cultural Diplomacy at the American Academy in Rome." In *Crosscurrents: American and European Music in Interaction, 1900–2000,* edited by Felix Meyer, Carol J. Oja, Wolfgang Rathert, and Anne Shreffler, 375–87. Woodbridge, England: Boydell & Brewer, 2014.

———. "The Scheme of the Whole: Black Mountain and the Course of American Music." In *Black Mountain College: Experiment in Art,* edited by Vincent Katz, 237–68. Cambridge: MIT Press, 2002.

Carroll, Mark. *Music and Ideology in Cold War Europe.* Cambridge: Cambridge University Press, 2003.

Carter, Elliott. "Letter from Europe." *Perspectives of New Music* 1, no. 2 (1963): 195–205.

Ceglio, Clarissa J. "The Wartime Work of U.S. Museums." Rockefeller Foundation Archives. 2010. http://www.rockarch.org/publications/resrep/ceglio.pdf.

Chanler, Margaret. *Memory Makes Music.* New York: Stephen-Paul, 1948.

Chanler, Mrs. Winthrop [Margaret]. *Roman Spring: Memoirs.* Boston: Little, Brown, 1934.

Cockcroft, Eva. "Abstract Expressionism: Weapon of the Cold War," *Artforum* 15, no. 10 (1974): 39–41.

Coleman, Peter. *The Liberal Conspiracy: The Congress for Cultural Freedom and the Struggle for the Mind of Postwar Europe.* New York: Free Press, 1989.

Copland, Aaron. "Contemporaries at Oxford, 1931." *Modern Music* 9 (November 1931): 17–23.

Cott, Nancy F. *The Bonds of Womanhood: Woman's Sphere in New England, 1780–1835.* New Haven: Yale University Press, 1977.

Crawford, Richard. "Edward MacDowell: Musical Nationalism and an American Tone Poet." *Journal of the American Musicological Society* 49, no. 3 (1996): 528–60.

Crawford, Richard, R. Allen Lott, and Carol J. Oja, eds. *A Celebration of American Music: Words and Music in Honor of H. Wiley Hitchcock.* Ann Arbor: University of Michigan Press, 1990.

Crociata, Francis J. "Leo Sowerby: The 100th Anniversary Celebration of an American Original." *The American Organist* 29, no. 5 (1995): 50–53.

Damrosch, Walter. *My Musical Life.* New York: Charles Scribner's Sons, 1930.

Dean, Robert D. *Imperial Brotherhood: Gender and the Making of Cold War Foreign Policy.* Amherst: University of Massachusetts Press, 2001.

Dell'Antonio, Andrew. "Il divino Claudio: Monteverdi and Lyric Nostalgia in Fascist Italy." *Cambridge Opera Journal* 8, no. 3 (1996): 271–84.

Dizikes, John. *Opera in America: A Cultural History.* New Haven: Yale University Press, 1993.

Duberman, Martin. *The Worlds of Lincoln Kirstein.* Random House: New York, 2009.

Edsel. Robert M. *The Monuments Men: Allied Heroes, Nazi Thieves, and the Greatest Treasure Hunt in History.* New York: Center Street, 2009.

Ellinwood, Leonard. *The History of American Church Music.* New York: Morehouse Gorham Company, 1953.

Epstein, Dena J. "Frederick Stock and American Music." *American Music* 10, no. 1 (1992): 20–52.

Ewans, Michael, Rosalind Halton, and John A. Phillips, eds. *Music Research: New Directions for a New Century.* Cambridge: Cambridge Scholars Press, 2004.

Falconer-Salkeld, Bridget. *The MacDowell Colony: A Musical History of America's Premier Artists' Community.* Lanham, MD: The Scarecrow Press, 2005.

La Farge. John. "The American Academy at Rome, The Field of Art." *Scribner's Magazine,* August 1900, 253–58.

Finck, Henry Theophilus. *Anton Seidl: A Memorial by His Friends.* New York: C. Scribner, 1899.

Flexner, Eleanor. *Century of Struggle.* New York: Antheneum, 1970.

Forbes, Elliot. *A History of Music at Harvard to 1972.* Cambridge: Department of Music, Harvard University, 1988.

Gallope, Michael. "Why Was This Music Desirable? On A Critical Explanation of the Avant-Garde," *Journal of Musicology* 31, no. 2 (forthcoming).

Garafola, Lynn. "Lincoln Kirstein, Modern Dance, and the Left: The Genesis of an American Ballet." *Journal of the Society for Dance Research* 23, no. 1 (2005): 18–35.

Gilman, Lawrence. *Edward MacDowell: A Study.* New York: John Lane, 1908.

Granger, Alfred Hoyt. *Charles Follen McKim: A Study of His Life and Work.* Boston: Houghton Mifflin, 1913.

Greenberg, Clement. "Avant-Garde and Kitsch," *Partisan Review* 6, no. 5 (1939): 34–49.

"A Group of the Younger American Composers." *Vanity Fair,* September 1923, 49.

Guberman, Daniel. "Composing Freedom: Elliott Carter's 'Self-Reinvention' and the Early Cold War." PhD diss., University of North Carolina, 2012.

Heyman, Barbara. *Samuel Barber: The Composer and His Music.* New York: Oxford University Press, 1992.

History of the Office of the Coordinator of Inter-American Affairs. US Bureau of the Budget. Historical Reports on War Administration, 1947.

Horowitz, Joseph. *Classical Music in America: A History of Its Rise and Fall.* New York: W. W. Norton, 2005.

Johnson, Alva. "American Maestro." Pts. 1 and 2. *New Yorker,* October 20, 1938, 22–26; October 27, 1938, 23–26.

Kohl, Benjamin G., Wayne A. Linker, and Buff Suzanne Kavelman, eds. *The Centennial Directory of the American Academy in Rome.* New York and Rome: American Academy in Rome, 1995.

Kostof, Spiro, and Dan Cuff. *The Architect: Chapters in the History of the Profession.* Reprint, Berkeley: University of California Press, 2000.

Leitch, Alexander. *A Princeton Companion.* Princeton: Princeton University Press, 1978.

Levy, Alan Howard. *Edward MacDowell: An American Master.* Lanham, MD: The Scarecrow Press, 1998.

———. "The Search for Identity in American Music, 1890–1920." American Music 2, no. 2 (1984): 70–81.

Lewis, R. W. B. "1898–1907: The Founders' Story." In *A Century of Arts & Letters: The History of the of Arts and Letters and the American Academy of Arts and Letters as Told, Decade by Decade, by Eleven Members.* New York: Columbia University Press, 1998.

Logan, George. *The Indiana University School of Music: A History.* Bloomington: Indiana University Press, 2000.

Lott, R. Allen. "'New Music for New Ears': The International Composers' Guild." *Journal of the American Musicological Society* 36, no. 2 (1983): 266–86.

Lowens, Marjorie. "The New York Years of Edward MacDowell." PhD diss., the University of Michigan, 1971.

MacDowell, Marian. "MacDowell's 'Peterborough Idea.'" *Musical Quarterly* 18, no. 1 (1932): 33–38.

Martin, George. *The Damrosch Dynasty: America's First Family of Music.* Boston: Houghton Mifflin, 1983.

Meltzer, Charles Henry. "The Proposed 'Prix de Rome' for Musicians." *Weekly Review* 3, no. 61 (July 14, 1920): 50–51.

———. "Two Homes of Art in Rome: The Academies of Old France and Young America." *Arts and Decoration* (November 1921): 14–17.

Metzer, David. "The League of Composers: The Initial Years." *American Music* 15, no. 1 (1997): 45–69.

Miller, Kiri. "Americanism Musically: Nation, Evolution, and Public Education at the Columbia Exposition, 1893." *Nineteenth-Century Music* 27, no. 2 (2003): 1137–55.

Miraldi, Robert. *The Muckrakers: Evangelical Crusaders.* Westport, CT: Praeger, 2000.

Moore, Charles. *Daniel Burnham: Architect: Planner of Cities.* Vol. 2. Boston: Houghton Mifflin, 1921.

———. *The Life and Times of Charles Follen McKim.* Boston: Houghton Mifflin, 1929.

———. *The Promise of American Architecture: Addresses at the Annual Dinner of the American Institute of Architects, 1905.* New York: American Institute of Architects, 1905.

Morris, Edmond. *The Rise of Theodore Roosevelt.* Rev. ed. New York: Random House, 2000.

———. *Theodore Rex.* New York: Random House, 2001.

Nabokov, Nicolas. *Bagazh: Memoirs of a Russian Cosmopolitan.* New York: Atheneum, 1975.

Nicholas, Lynn H. *Rape of Europa: The Fate of Europe's Treasures in the Third Reich and the Second World War.* New York: Vintage, 1995.

Norton, Kay. *Normand Lockwood: His Life and Music.* Metuchen, NJ: Scarecrow Press, 1993.

Oja, Carol J. *Making Music Modern: New York in the 1920s.* New York: Oxford University Press, 2000.

Olmstead, Andrea. "The American Academy in Rome." In *Grove Dictionary of American Music.* Edited by Charles Hiroshi Garrett. 8 vols. Oxford: Oxford University Press, 2013.

———. *Conversations with Roger Sessions.* Boston: Northeastern University Press, 1987.

———. *The Correspondence of Roger Sessions.* Boston: Northeastern University Press, 1992.

———. *Juilliard: A History.* Urbana: University of Illinois Press, 1999.

———. *Roger Sessions: A Biography.* New York: Routledge, 2008.

———. *Roger Sessions and His Music.* Ann Arbor, MI: UMI Research Press, 1985.

———. *Who Was F. Scott Fitzgerald's Daisy?* Los Gatos, CA: Smashwords, 2012.

Pearcy, Lee T. *The Grammar of Our Civility: Classical Education in America.* Waco, TX: Baylor University Press, 2005.

Peyton, Leonard. "Musical Notes from Abroad . . . Rome." *Musical Times,* March 1, 1923, 207–8.

Pitzer, Andrea. *The Secret History of Vladimir Nabokov.* New York: Pegasus Books, 2012.

Pollack, Howard. *Harvard Composers.* Metuchen, NJ: Scarecrow Press, 1992.

———. *Skyscraper Lullaby: The Life and Music of John Alden Carpenter.* Washington: Smithsonian Institution Press, 1995.

Porter, Susan L., and John Graziano, eds. *Vistas of American Music: Essays and Compositions in Honor of William K. Kearns.* Warren, MI: Harmonie Park Press, 1999.

Respighi, Elsa. *Ottorino Respighi: Dati biografici ordinati da Elsa Respighi.* Milan: Ricordi, 1954. Translated by Gwyn Morris as *Ottorino Respighi: His Life-Story* (London: Ricordi, 1962.)

Restagno, Enzo. "Elliott Carter in Conversation with Enzo Restagno for Settembre Musica." ISAM Monograph, 1989.

Roche, John. "On the Intellectual Barricades." *New Leader* 72, no. 17 (November 13, 1989): 18.

Roosevelt, Theodore. "True Americanism." *The Forum Magazine,* April 1894.

Rosen, Charles. "Music and the Cold War." *New York Review of Books,* April 7, 2011. http://www.nybooks.com/articles/archives/2011/apr/07/music-and-cold-war/.

Ross, Alex. *The Rest Is Noise: Listening to the Twentieth Century.* New York: Farrar, Straus and Giroux, 2007.

Schlessinger, Andrew, and Stephen C. Schlelsinger, eds. *The Letters of Arthur Schlessinger.* New York: Random House, 2013.

Schwab, T. "Edward MacDowell's Mysterious Malady." *Musical Quarterly* 89, no. 1 (2006): 136–51.

Slobin, Mark. *Subcultural Sounds: Micromusics of the West.* Hanover: Wesleyan University Press, 1993.

Smith Brindle, Reginald. "Notes from Abroad: The Rome International Conference of Contemporary Music." *Musical Times* 95, no. 1336 (1954): 328–29.

Spalding, Walter Raymond. *Music: An Art and a Language.* Boston: Arthur P. Schmidt, 1920.

Stonor Saunders, Frances. *Who Paid the Piper?: The CIA and the Cultural Cold War.* London: Granta, 1999.

Straus, Joseph. "The Myth of Serial 'Tyranny' in the 1950s and 1960s." *Musical Quarterly* 83, no. 3 (1999): 301–43.

Taruskin, Richard. "Nicht Blutbefleckt." *Journal of Musicology* 26, no. 2 (2009): 274–84.

———, ed. *The Oxford History of Western Music.* Vol. 5. New York: Oxford University Press, 2005.

Thompson, Randall. "The Contemporary Scene in American Music." *Musical Quarterly* 18, no. 1 (1932): 9–17.

Trilling, Lionel. *The Liberal Imagination.* New York: New York Review of Books Classics, 2008.

Tuthill, Burnet C. "Leo Sowerby." *Musical Quarterly* 24, no. 3 (1938): 249–64.

Valentine, Lucia, and Alan Valentine. *The American Academy in Rome, 1894–1969.* Charlottesville: University Press of Virginia, 1973.

Vance, William. *America's Rome.* New Haven: Yale University Press, 1989.

Watkins, Glenn. *Proof through the Night: Music and the Great War.* Berkeley: University of California Press, 2003.

Watson Gilder, Richard. *A Book of Music.* New York: Century, 1906.

Wellens, Ian. *Music on the Frontline: Nicolas Nabokov's Struggle against Communism and Middlebrow Culture.* Burlington, VT: Ashgate Press, 2002.

Wells, James M. *Portrait of an Era: Rue Winterbotham Carpenter and the Arts Club of Chicago, 1916–1931.* Chicago: Arts Club of Chicago, 1986.

Wiecki, Ronald V. "A Chronicle of Pro Music in the United Sates (1920–1944): With a Biographical Sketch of Its Founder, E. Robert Schmitz." PhD diss., University of Wisconsin, 1992.

Wierzbicki, James. *Elliott Carter.* Champagne: University of Illinois Press, 2011.

Winks, Robin. *Clock and Gown: Scholars in the Secret War, 1939–1961.* New Haven: Yale University Press, 1987.

Woodberry, George Edward. "Mr. Gilder's Public Activities." *Century Magazine* (1910): 626.

Yegül, Fikret K. *Gentlemen of Instinct and Breeding: Architecture at the American Academy in Rome, 1894–1940.* New York: Oxford University Press, 1991.

Contributors

Martin Brody is Catherine Mills Davis Professor of Music at Wellesley College, where he has served on the faculty since 1980. Brody was Fromm Composer in Residence at the American Academy in Rome in 2001 and served as the Academy's Andrew Heiskell Arts Director, 2007–10. He has received numerous awards as a composer, among them a Guggenheim Fellowship and the Academy-Institute Award from the American Academy of Arts and Letters. He has written extensively about modern and contemporary American music and is president of the Stefan Wolpe Society.

Elliott Carter, recipient of two Pulitzer Prizes, the United States National Medal of Arts, Germany's Ernst Von Siemens Music Prize, and the French "Commandeur dans l'Ordre des Arts et des Lettres," among many other honors, is an iconic figure in American music. His music—over 150 compositions—has been championed by many distinguished performers, among them Pierre-Laurent Aimard, Daniel Barenboim, Pierre Boulez, Paul Jacobs, Heinz Holliger, James Levine, Ursula Oppens, and Charles Rosen. Carter was a Fellow of the American Academy in Rome (1953) and Resident Composer in 1963, 1969, and 1980.

John Harbison has received numerous awards and distinctions, including the prestigious MacArthur Foundation's "genius" award, the Pulitzer Prize, and the Heinz Award in the Arts and Humanities. Harbison has composed music for most of this country's premier musical institutions, including the Metropolitan Opera (for whom he wrote *The Great Gatsby*), the Chicago Lyric Opera, the New York Philharmonic, the Chicago Symphony, the Boston Symphony, the Los Angeles Philharmonic, The Chamber Music Society of Lincoln Center, and the Santa Fe and Aspen festivals. His works include five string quartets, six symphonies, a ballet, three operas, and numerous chamber and choral works. He has served both as Composer in Residence at the American Academy in Rome and as a Trustee of the Academy.

Christina Huemer (1947–2010) was educated at Mount Holyoke College and held a MLS from Columbia and a MA in art history from Cornell University. Before leading the Library of the American Academy in Rome (1993–2008), she held positions at Cornell (1970–75), the Art Index (1975–76), Oberlin College (1975–76), the Avery Architectural and Fine Arts Library of Columbia University (1980–85), and in Rome as assistant librarian at the International Centre for the Study of the Preservation and Restoration of Cultural Property. From 1988 to 1992 she was the editor, Italian office, of the Bibliography of the History of Art, a pioneering research database then based at the Clark Art Institute and now centered at the Getty Research Institute in Los Angeles. Huemer edited *Spellbound by Rome: The Anglo-American Community in Rome, 1890–1914*; the *Founding of the Keats-Shelley House*; and (with Pierluigi Petrobelli) *Remembering Oliver Strunk, Teacher and Scholar.*

CAROL J. OJA is William Powell Mason Professor of Music at Harvard University. She is also on the faculty of Harvard's graduate program in the History of American Civilization. Oja's *Making Music Modern: New York in the 1920s* won the Lowens Book Award from the Society for American Music and an ASCAP-Deems Taylor Award. Other books include *Aaron Copland and His World* (coedited with Judith Tick); *Colin McPhee: Composer in Two Worlds; A Celebration of American Music: Words and Music in Honor of H. Wiley Hitchcock;* and *American Music Recordings: A Discography of 20th-Century U.S. Composers.* Her newest book, *Bernstein Meets Broadway: Collaborative Art, Race, and Progressive Politics in a Time of War,* is to be published by Oxford University Press. Oja has held fellowships from the Newhouse Center for the Humanities at Wellesley College, the National Humanities Center, the National Endowment for the Humanities, and the Mellon Faculty Fellows Program at Harvard. She is past president of the Society for American Music.

ANDREA OLMSTEAD is the author numerous articles, reviews, and liner notes, as well as of six books, including a history of the Juilliard School, four books on the composer Roger Sessions, and the e-book *Who Was F. Scott Fitzgerald's Daisy?* She has held four writing fellowships from the Virginia Center for the Creative Arts, nine visiting scholar residencies at the American Academy in Rome, and three fellowships from the National Endowment for the Humanities. She was the Christopher Hogwood Research Fellow at the Handel & Haydn Society from 2005 to 2007. Olmstead has taught music history at the Juilliard School, the New England Conservatory of Music, the University of Massachusetts-Amherst, and is currently a professor at the Berklee College of Music. Married to the Rome Prize composer Larry Thomas Bell, she is also a librettist (www.HolyGhoststheopera.org) and CD producer.

VIVIAN PERLIS is the founding director of Oral History, American Music. Her book publications include *Charles Ives Remembered: An Oral History* (New Haven: Yale University Press, 1974), for which she was awarded the Kinkeldey Prize of the American Musicological Society, and *An Ives Celebration* (Urbana: University of Illinois Press, 1976). With the composer Aaron Copland, Perlis is coauthor of *Copland: 1900 through 1942* (New York: St. Martin's Press/Marek, 1984), which received a Deems Taylor/ASCAP award, and *Copland: Since 1943* (New York. St. Martin's Press, 1989). Her honors and awards are: The Charles Ives Award from the National Institute of Arts and Letters (1972); a Grammy nomination for *Charles Ives 100th Anniversary* (1974); the Harvey Kantor Award for excellence in the field of oral history (1984); a Guggenheim Fellowship (1987); and the Irving Lowens Award for distinguished scholarship in American Music from The Sonneck Society (1991).

JUDITH TICK, Matthews Distinguished University Professor Emerita of Music at Northeastern University, is a leading authority on American music in general and the history of women in music in particular. She is coeditor with Jane Bowers of the anthology *Women Making Music: The Western Art Tradition, 1150–1950* (1986), a pioneering work in its field, and the author of *American Women Composers before 1870* (1983) and the biography *Ruth Crawford Seeger: A Composer's Search for American Music* (1997), which won an ASCAP Deems Taylor Award. In collaboration with the art historian Gail Levin, Tick also published *Aaron Copland's America: A Cultural Perspective* (2000). In 2000 she received a Distinguished Alumna Medal from Smith College. In 2004 she was elected to the American Academy of Arts and Sciences as an "innovator in the field of musical biography." Her book, *Music in the U.S.A.: A Documentary Companion*, was published by Oxford University Press in 2008.

RICHARD TRYTHALL has been associated with the American Academy in Rome since receiving the Rome Prize in Music Composition in 1964. As a composer he has also received a Guggenheim Fellowship, the Naumburg Recording Award, a Fulbright Fellowship, and composition commissions from, among others, the Fromm Music Foundation–Berkshire Music Center, the Dorian Woodwind Quintet, and the Gruppo Percussione Ricerca (Venice, Italy). He has been on the faculty of New York University (Florence), St. Mary's College (Rome), and the University of California (in Rome and in Davis), and was a creative associate at SUNY Buffalo's Center for the Creative and Performing Arts (1970–72). Also active as a concert pianist, he won the Kranichsteiner Competition for Interpreters of Contemporary Piano Music (Darmstadt, Germany, 1969), has performed as soloist at every major Italian contemporary music festival, and has recorded extensively for RAI Radio. His repertoire includes the music of Charles Ives, Aaron Copland, Elliott Carter, George Gershwin, Chick Corea, Keith Jarrett, and Jelly Roll Morton (whose work he has transcribed and recorded), as well as his own compositions. He has written for numerous Italian publications and for *Keyboard* magazine and is a well-known spokesman for American music in Italy.

Index

Page numbers in italics indicate photographs.